TAIL-END CHARLIES

TAIL-END CHARLIES

The Last Battles of the Bomber War, 1944–45

John Nichol and Tony Rennell

THOMAS DUNNE BOOKS

ST. MARTIN'S PRESS NEW YORK

THOMAS DUNNE BOOKS.
An imprint of St. Martin's Press.

www.stmartins.com

Design by Phil Mazzone

Library of Congress Cataloging-in-Publication Data

Nichol, John, 1963–
    Tail-end Charlies : the last battles of the bomber war, 1944–1945 / John Nichol and Tony Rennell.—1st U.S. ed.
        p. cm
    Originally published: London; New York : Viking, 2004.
    Includes bibliographical references and index.
    ISBN 0-312-34987-4
    EAN 978-0-312-34987-5
    1. Great Britain. Royal Air Force. Bomber Command. 2. World War, 1939–1945—Aerial operations, British. 3. United States. Army Air Forces. Air Force, 8th. 4. World War, 1939–1945—Aerial operations, American. 5. World War, 1939–1945—Campaigns—Germany. 6. Bombing, Aerial—Germany—History—20th century. I. Rennell, Tony. II. Title.

D786.N53 2006
940.54'4941—dc22

                                                                      2006040350

First published in the United Kingdom by the Penguin Group

First U.S. Edition: May 2006

10   9   8   7   6   5   4   3   2   1

To all the men of the United States Eighth Army Air Force and Royal Air Force Bomber Command. They were willing to make the ultimate sacrifice for us.

CONTENTS

LIST OF ILLUSTRATIONS

Picture Credits

1, 23: copyright 388th Bomber Group Association

2, 16, 17, 18: copyright David Hastings

3, 7: copyright John Nicol

4, 5: copyright Chris Pierson

6, 12, 22: Crown copyright, RAF Museum. Crown copyright material is reproduced with the permission of the controller of Her Majesty's Stationery Office.

8: copyright *Evening Standard*

9: courtesy of the Sächsische Landesbibliothek, Deutsche Fotothek

10, 11: courtesy of the USAAF

13, 14: by permission of the Imperial War Museum, London (CH10675 and CH13020)

15: copyright the Salvation Army International Heritage Centre

19: copyright Fran Waugh and the 306th Bomb Group Association

20: copyright Finn Buch, Denmark

21: courtesy of Ditto Publishing

Every effort has been made to trace the copyright holders and we apologize in advance for any unintentional omission. We would be pleased to insert the appropriate acknowledgment in any subsequent editions.

TAIL-END CHARLIES

PREFACE

SHOULDER TO SHOULDER

IT WAS A LATE SPRING DAY IN THE LUSH GREEN ENGLISH COUNTRYSIDE, the sun trying to peep through and cast a glow on the slowly ripening grain in the fields, glimpses of blue sky above through fast-moving clouds, whipped along by an unseasonable wind. In the bus, the talk among the American visitors was all of war. It was May 2003. The Middle East was a cauldron. Baghdad had fallen to American forces but the dictator Saddam Hussein was still at large, and attempts to impose authority and stability on the liberated country were faltering. Daily, American soldiers were dying on the city streets as open warfare turned to vicious guerrilla fighting. American boys losing their lives on a foreign battlefield—for those on the bus, traveling from the ancient university city of Cambridge, where they had spent the night, to the bases from which they had once fought *their* war, the historical parallel did not go unnoticed. On board were American airmen, Second World War veterans of the 388th Bomb Group, and their families. They were coming back to the scene of their youth.

Sixty years had gone by since they crossed the ocean as young men on a mission. When, in December 1941, the United States joined the conflict, Britain had been at war for more than two years—half of that time entirely alone as the Belgians, Dutch, and French fell one by one to the invaders from Nazi Germany. Isolated on their island, threatened with invasion, and bombed mercilessly in their homes, the "boys in blue" of the Royal Air Force had been bravely taking the fight to the Germans at a time when no one else would or could. Night after night they had flown their bombers across occupied Europe to drop bombs on the enemy. In return for Hitler's Luftwaffe raining destruction on London and other British cities from Liverpool to Southampton, Germany got a taste of her own medicine. The defiance alone was worth the risks for the British people—boosting their morale at the darkest of hours. The German people were stunned. The overweight and vainglorious Luftwaffe chief, Reich Marshal Herman Goering, had once jested boastfully that if an enemy bomb ever fell on the capital, Berlin, then "my name is Mueller." "Herr Mueller," as many Germans now called him (behind his ample back, of course), had had to eat his words. It was the first indication that the Nazi juggernaut that had rolled through Europe crushing all before it might actually be stopped.

And there was every chance that it could not just be stopped but rolled back and destroyed. With the arrival of the Americans to join the fight, the British at last had a determined and active ally in the fight against tyranny. The RAF's Bomber Command and the Eighth Air Force—the "boys in blue" and the "boys in brown"—were side by side when the world was in crisis. Sixty years later they still were, and for the elderly veterans on that bus it did not go unnoticed that it was American and British troops shoulder to shoulder in Iraq—teaming up to fight a dictator while others sat on the sidelines, just as it had been for them all those decades ago.

America's youth had flooded across the Atlantic in their hundreds of thousands, bringing with them their fleets of Fortresses and Liberators, all with pet names like *Jolly Roger, Honey Bucket*, and *GI Jane* painted garishly on their sides alongside cartoon figures (often nude women) and insignia. The staid British gawped. Who were these brash, bright newcomers from the New World, flashing their smiles, their dollar bills, their crazy music, their jitterbug dances? They gawped—and then they welcomed the gum-chewing Yanks as brothers in arms. Great swathes of eastern England became Little Americas as the United States fed its military might and its manhood into a total war against the Nazi Third Reich.

That spring day in 2003, some of those young men—older now, less sprightly, fuller in face and physique, chewing on prescription pills and vitamin supplements rather than gum—had come back to find the past that still haunted them, that was still a part of their present. They had grown up in England, turned from boys into men; they had learned the harsh realities

of life and death here. They had lost friends they could never forget in circumstances they would have preferred not to remember but which still
reeled through their minds in nightmare memories of the past. Our destination was a stand of tall chestnut trees on a remote crossroads surrounded
by high hedges and succulent fields. Here, on the site of what had once been
the entrance to the United States Army Air Forces base at Knettishall, a service was being held to rededicate a stone memorial to the men of the 388th
who died on bombing missions. Dozens of local people with fond memories of the American presence in their neighborhood and their lives all those
years ago had gathered to add their good wishes and prayers. An old khaki-
colored United States Air Force jeep was drawn up on the grass verge alongside a truck named *Lindy Lou* with bench seats in the back on which the
aviators had once sat as it chugged around the perimeter roads of their base
to the cookhouse, the bunkhouse, and the PX, and to and from their parked
aircraft as they went off to war. The vehicles had been dumped in the rush
to depart in 1945. Local enthusiasts had rescued and restored them, the
past revived to inform the present.

Old men stood to attention, hands held to hearts, as the strains of
"The Star-Spangled Banner" soared out and the flag itself was saluted by
an honor guard of young American airmen from the nearby U.S. base at
Lakenheath. *"Age shall not weary them, nor the years condemn."*[1] As
these noble words in remembrance of those who died in battle rang out
through the silence, beneath the tall trees on that country lane, tears
trickled down cheeks and feet held firmly to attention shuffled with the
emotion of the moment. *"At the going down of the sun and in the morning, we will remember them."* Five hundred and twenty-four American
airmen from this station alone had died between the summers of 1943
and 1945. Eight hundred more had become prisoners-of-war. Close on
two hundred bombers had taken off from Knettishall's three miles of
concrete runways—now overgrown, returned to the fields of crops it had
been carved from—and never come back. A black marble slab recorded
the simple, stark statistics. But the minds of those present were putting
flesh and bone on those cold figures, bringing back the faces and names of
real men who had done their duty and died for it—friends long lost but
never, ever forgotten. Augustus Bolino, a navigator in the 562nd Squadron
sixty years ago and one of the many men whose stories we will tell in the
pages of this book, summed up the feeling of his fellow veterans when he
said he hoped that "when people see the memorial in the years ahead, after

we are all gone, they will remember what we did and say that we were gallant warriors."

The weather was unreliable that day—appropriately, because it was the uncertainty of the English weather that so imprinted itself on the minds of that 1940s generation of visitors from America. The rain, the fog, the cold—some never got used to the conditions or the unpredictability. It made the flying harder, the dying more likely. They cursed England for the weather in their letters home and in their reminiscences. By the time we got to our next stop—a still functioning airstrip where local flying clubs had turned out to offer rides in their light aircraft to the veterans—there was sleet and hail to contend with. It was just like 1944—when General Dwight Eisenhower gambled on the weather to launch the D-Day invasion—all over again. In the sunny breaks and in defiance of the strong wind, just as they did sixty years ago, the veterans flew, their years and infirmities no bar to this relived adventure. One was lifted from a wheelchair into a three-seater plane and headed out across the flat countryside he and his comrades had known so well to the Wash and the North Sea. Once a thousand and more heavy bombers of the Eighth Air Force would have assembled in the skies there in the early morning before streaming eastward into the danger zones of Nazi-occupied Europe. Many would never come back. Now, though, there was a guaranteed return to base and pints of beer—warm and weak, as ever to American palates—in the Sun, a local pub decked out with the red, white, and blue of the Stars and Stripes and the Union Jack. Old, brown-faded photographs of the base in its heyday lined the walls. The landlady was wearing the shapely blue uniform of a 1940s member of the WAAFs, the Women's Auxiliary Air Force, complete with black seamed stockings. Over a loudspeaker, the music of Glenn Miller was heard again six decades after he and his orchestra played in person at Knettishall and American airmen showed English girls how to boogie and jive to the best band in the land.

But it was not just nostalgia that had drawn the Americans. They came, as one of them told us, as a pilgrimage. Twenty-five thousand of America's finest young men had died in the air battles over Germany. Unlike the British, their land had not been bombed; they were not under threat of invasion. They had come to a strange country far away from home and from their loved ones to fight an enemy who threatened freedom. They had died in that cause and they deserved to be honored by those who survived while they still could.

But it had been a war fought by *two* nations—as the linking of the flags of the United States and of the United Kingdom on that reunion day made clear. There were vast differences between them—in background, in wealth, in culture, in the military strategies adopted by their commanders. But they had a common cause—and it is the fight for that common cause that is the subject of this book, told through the voices of the men of the United States Eighth Air Force and Royal Air Force Bomber Command who together, shoulder to shoulder, took the war to the heart of Germany.

Why "Tail-End Charlies"? Here was a term common to both air forces, though—as with so much in the shared language of Britain and the United States—they meant different things. To the men of the Eighth Air Force, it referred to aircraft—to the vulnerable last ones in any of the giant formations that formed in the skies over England and headed eastward toward the well-defended shores of Nazi-occupied Europe. To be at the end was to be without the protection of other planes. To be at the end was to be the last one over the target when the enemy gunners manning the antiaircraft artillery on the ground were sure of their range. To be at the end was to be last home, if you got home at all.

Colonel William B. David of the 388th had been in the position as he flew *Big Red,* his B-17 Flying Fortress, back to England after bombing a German airfield. He had started out the mission in pole position, leading from the front, as was only right and proper for the commander of an Eighth Air Force Heavy Bombardment Group. Sitting in the copilot's seat, he had guided formation after formation in to drop its bombs, circling above the target, waiting until the operation was complete before heading home, covering his men's tail from the back. Suddenly, out over the sea, a pack of German fighters caught up with *Big Red.* Twenty-millimeter cannon shells slammed into the right wing, igniting the fuel in the tanks. At the same time, a head-on attack sent bullets slashing into the cockpit, wounding the pilot and holing the hydraulics and the oxygen tank.[2]

The cockpit was on fire as David grabbed the conn from his injured pilot. *Big Red* was yawing and heaving wildly. As he fought furiously to bring the huge aircraft back under control, he was engulfed in flames that burned his hair, face, and hands and shriveled his leather flying jacket. He decided bailing out at 21,000 feet was too risky and that his only option was to put her into a dive. His gamble paid off. As they screamed downward through

the air . . . 17,000 feet . . . 15,000 . . . 13,000 . . . 11,000, the fire blew itself out. At 10,000 feet, he pulled back hard on the conn, bracing himself,
hanging on with all his strength, and managed to level the plane out.
Amazed that the wings had stayed on and the leaking fuel tank had not exploded, he headed *Big Red* and her crew home.

But enemy fighters were still on her tail. They had followed the stricken
B-17 down and were now pouring tracer bullets into the stream of leaking
fuel pouring from the wing to try and finish her off. David corkscrewed and
zigzagged to try and throw them off while, from the mid and rear turrets, his
gunners fired furiously at their attackers. In that twenty-minute battle out
over the Atlantic Ocean, they brought down four enemy fighters and managed to drive off the rest. As the surviving Germans fled the scene, David
steered the plane the five hundred miles home to Knettishall. As she eased
onto the runway, he was one of nine on board with injuries that needed treating. Here, then, were the dangers of being a Tail-End Charlie. No wonder the
other term for that position in the formation was "Purple Heart Corner."

To the British, a Tail-End Charlie was not an aircraft but an individual in
the crew of a bomber. The name was given to the gunner in the rear seat of
a Lancaster or a Halifax bomber as it dodged flak and fighters over Germany. It was a lonely and very dangerous position. "It takes guts to be a
gunner," began a piece of doggerel written by a Canadian airman named
George Harding, who fought with the RAF in the Second World War, "To
sit out on the tail, When the Messerschmitts are coming and the slugs begin
to wail."[3] The man in the back—and this applied as much to the rear gunner of a B-17 or a B-24 as it did to a Lancaster—was uniquely exposed,
staring out into nothingness, just a thin layer of Perspex between him and
twenty thousand feet of thin air. He was the original man in a glass house
waiting for stones to be thrown at him. Except that, for stones, we have to
read bullets and shrapnel. He sat there with his guns at the ready—on guard
for hours on end, covering the backs of the rest of the crew. He was given
huge respect for what he did. As Harding's verse went on to say:

> The pilot's just a chauffeur
> It's his job to fly the plane;
> But it's we who do the fighting.
> Though we may not get the fame.

Bob Pierson was just such a man. The authors met him on a winter's day in 2003, an old man, tall, white-haired, with a kindly face, limping into the hut on the edge of a disused airfield in the flat fen land of eastern England. He stopped and leaned on his stick. The long legs were a problem these days, had been since the war, but they were getting worse. It was increasingly difficult to tend the flowers in the garden at his bungalow on the outskirts of the nearby cathedral town of Lincoln. For support, too, he had his son, the youngest of his three children, a father himself and in his early forties. We shook hands—a firm grip for such a frail frame. He was thrilled to have been invited. He would love to talk about the old days. He remembered it all, the men, the machines, the emotions, especially being here, back on an old Lancaster bomber base in Lincolnshire. The gray, cold waters of the North Sea were just ten miles away. He remembered them too. Ditching had been one of his greatest fears. The Lancaster was a great aircraft, but she was a bitch to escape from if she came down in water, especially those fast-flowing waters. A man's stamina, his life, could be measured in minutes out there.

We were at East Kirkby, home of 57 Squadron and 630 Squadron of Bomber Command for the latter part of the Second World War. A surprising amount of it remained more than sixty years on. Part of the area was given over to a chicken farm, but the old runway was still there, its concrete surface pitted and lined but still in use. So, too, was the square block of the control tower jutting out onto the apron, its high glass windows giving a 360-degree view of the airfield and those vast East Anglican skies above it. There were long, low half-moon-shaped buildings with corrugated iron roofs that were dormitories or mess halls or workshops *back then*.

Back then, these quiet agricultural acres buzzed with the life and purpose of an RAF station at war, busy with people with vital jobs to do, always on the alert, rarely still, their work punctuated by the shattering roar of powerful aircraft engines as bombers took off or returned. Two hundred or more aircrew, the heart of the operation, young men in blue uniforms, strode purposefully to briefings or exhausted to bed after yet another flight through enemy flak and fighters to Germany. As many ground crew and support staff in oily overalls were on hand at all hours to keep damaged planes in a fit state to fly, or to load up the bombs and the bullets. WAAFs[4] in brown coats packed parachutes; others in neat blue blouses, calf-length skirts, and sensible black shoes, manned the radio receivers, sending the boys off, seeing them safely back home. Hundreds of others—office staff and storemen, padres and policemen, cooks and medics—went about their business. Here was an entire community living its own secret life behind the miles of barbed wire perimeter, in readiness twenty-four hours a day and seven days a week and all dedicated to the one task of dropping tons of bombs on an enemy who was trying to conquer the world and had to be stopped.

It was quieter now. Visitors were looking round what is now a heritage center, a place of homage to the aircrews of sixty years ago. We had come here to meet Pierson, who in his day had flown not from this particular station but from one very similar twenty-five miles away. What drew us all here was a rare treasure hidden away in a hangar. For the first time since he left the RAF at the end of the war, Pierson was going to be close up to a Lancaster bomber of the type he trained in, fought in, and nearly died in back in 1944 and 1945.

We drank hot sweet tea just as the crews of the Second World War would have done before setting out, and then we shuffled outside and across to the hangar. Bob limped behind in the rear. The sight of *Just Jane* stopped us in awe. She was a mighty machine, a long, thin tube of a fuselage split by wings that from tip to tip were half the width of a soccer field. The cockpit towered twenty feet in the air. Each of the four engines was the size of a compact car. In her wartime green-and-brown camouflage, she would fly us back in time.

Pierson had now forged excitedly ahead of us, studying every facet of her, pointing out the gun turrets at the front and in the middle, the bubble where the bombardier lay to direct the fusillade of high explosives and incendiaries on some benighted German city, the astrodome behind the cockpit where you could look out and see the stars—or the bursting flak from antiaircraft guns on the ground. Most of all, he wanted to be inside and back in *his* spot—the Tail-End Charlie's rear turret, the place where he had fought his war. He ignored his anxious son's plea to slow down, not to get carried away. The walking stick was tossed aside as he scrambled up the ladder just forward of the rear wheel. Then he was inside and gone. A man in his eightieth year, he scrambled on his hands and knees like a boy over the high wall of the bulkhead housing the tail spar. Then he slipped with unforgotten ease down into the narrow turret, his fingers quickly curled around the two twin-triggers of the four .303 machine guns. The years rolled away. This was where he had sat night after night—not on the ground under the shelter of a hangar but at twenty thousand feet in the air, roaring along at two hundred miles an hour and swaying up and down and from side to side as the winds buffeted the Lancaster's tail. And not under the friendly gaze of family and friends but sought out by guns and searchlights that would identify him as a hostile, an intruder, and try to destroy him.

We, a fraction of his age, picked our way gingerly through the narrow fuselage, past the waist gunner's port and the wireless operator's cubbyhole, to sit in the pilot's seat, grip the wheel, stare at the complex array of dials and handles and buttons. And wonder how she must have shaken and rattled as she thundered down the runway to take off, weighed down with several tons of bombs and full tanks of fuel, the roar of her four Rolls-Royce engines filling the cabin and the night. She seemed so small and fragile inside. For those who find the open spaces of a modern airliner confining and uncomfortable enough, here was a real cause for claustrophobia. The ceiling was so low you stooped to move, the walls so narrow it was impossible not to bang your knee, snag your coat. And we were safely on the ground and stationary. The imagination took over, posing a hundred and one questions. How would I have moved in this tight space when wearing three thick layers of clothing (to keep out the chill), jerkin, life jacket, and parachute? And at night, in pitch darkness, with the plane heaving and yawing in the wind and the turbulence or diving to escape a Messerschmitt fighter? Or spinning out of control, on fire, smoke and flames pouring from a ruptured engine . . . Could I have done that? Would I have had the guts?

Night after night, young men of Bob Pierson's generation from both sides of the Atlantic steeled their nerves and willed themselves to climb into what can be truly described as hellholes. Then they flew off to battle in the certain knowledge that their chances of returning alive or unharmed were small, that someone would die that night, and it could just as well be them. Why did they do it? What were their feelings? How did they conquer their fear? To find out, one only has to listen and learn as the old men tell their tales.

Many factors link the men whose stories of battle we are about to tell. The most important is that they were all comparative latecomers to the war. This book concentrates on the tail end of the war, the period from the start of 1944 until the German surrender in May 1945. In that sense, everyone who flew and fought in that final phase of the bomber war—whether as pilot, engineer, navigator, wireless operator, bombardier, or gunner—was a Tail-End Charlie. Hence another reason for our title.

But the period in which they did their fighting is one that has become mired in bitter controversy. Thousands of airmen died to bring Germany to the point of defeat, flying endless missions night and day to batter the followers of Hitler into submission. But modern historians and commentator have often tended to skip over this victory—achieved at great cost—and remember only the terrible destruction the Lancasters, the Fortresses, and the Liberators carried to German cities and civilians. However, the criticisms are less directed at the Americans. The men of the Eighth Air Force went home satisfied with a job well done and to a nation that had few qualms about what they had had to do to win the war. It was not so for the British airmen. Here the experiences of the two air forces diverged sharply.

Historians of the air war are quick to laud the heroics of the Battle of the Britain and the earlier bomber offensives against Germany when Britain was alone with her back to the wall. But the period after that—the period covered by this book—is too often portrayed as a sideshow to the main thrust of the war, a misdirected, mismanaged waste of effort and lives, all culminating in bitter recrimination and controversy. The terrible firestorms caused at Hamburg and Dresden laid a pall not only over those cities but over the men who flew the aircraft that bombed them. Their heroic efforts in those difficult and dangerous years have gone unsung, silenced by moral questions and ethical uncertainties. Though the flying and the dying ended in 1945, these Tail-End Charlies have never ceased coming under fire. Sixty years on, they still face the flak. They have been made to feel shame about what they did, treated as pariahs, their great achievements and conspicuous bravery lost in clouds of controversy, just as tens of thousands of their comrades were lost in the skies over Germany.

For the men of the RAF's Bomber Command who died during this period there was no glory and for those who survived no honor. After the war, they were criticized and abused for what they had done. Once they had completed it, the job they did was denounced as shameful, unnecessary, criminal even. In 1945, with the war over, they came home to the same sort of reception that American soldiers would receive thirty years later at the end of the Vietnam conflict. The nation on whose behalf they had risked their lives, seen their comrades die in their tens of thousands, turned its back on them. The bitterness that Vietnam veterans felt on their return home—and many still feel—was a rerun of the experience of the British bomber crews in 1945. There was an important difference. Vietnam was a defeat, and in defeat a disappointed nation unfairly sought scapegoats. But the British airmen were the victors. Why, then, were they so shabbily treated?

Nor has time dulled either the argument or the pain. On that country crossroads in England, there were no protesters to question the honor of the dead. The American memorial was carefully tended, looked after with pride, by those who respected what the men it honored had achieved. Sixty miles away in the center of London stands a public statue to honor Air Marshal Sir Arthur Harris, the commander in chief of Bomber Command during the Second World War. It was not erected until 1992, an indication in itself of precisely how long the row over him and his men had gone on. And when it was finally put on display, pacifist demonstrators defaced it with blood-red paint and hurled abuse at the Queen Mother, who came to unveil it. The argument goes on. In 2002, in a best-selling book in Germany, historian Jörg Friedrich denounced the bombing of his country as a war crime.[5] It was followed by more calls from his fellow countrymen for Britain to apologize, calls that increased in volume and vehemence with the sixtieth anniversary of the bombing of Dresden, followed by the celebrations to mark the end of the war itself, in 2005. This belief in the RAF's culpability surfaces at an individual level, too. One former bomber pilot told us, with tears in his eyes, how his grandchildren had come home from school one day after a history lesson, and accused him of being a murderer. Another recalled being invited by a film unit to take part in a documentary. He refused. "I was suspicious of their motives. It seemed to me all too likely that the RAF crews would be depicted as butchers. It was trial by modern liberal conscience, with no right for the defense to call its witnesses."[6]

Here in this book is that defense. This is their side of the story—the voices of men an ungrateful British nation tried to forget. It is told as they lived it and as often as possible in their own words, as recorded in letters, diaries, memoirs, and face-to-face interviews. It is essentially the tale of very ordinary men. Here you will find a homage to what Sir Arthur Harris perceptively called "the courage of the small hours."[7] Night after night men—boys really, they were all so young—fought their fears, and conquered them. Kids from Kansas and Kent, New York and old York, forced themselves through a mental pain barrier and made themselves do what every instinct in their body shrieked against doing. They are now mainly in their eighties, and their voices will soon be stilled. The survivors, down to the very last one, will sooner or later follow the 55,000 British airmen and 25,000 American airmen who died in combat over Europe sixty years ago. But not before they are given their proper place in history. And not before the true worth of that Anglo-American cooperative effort, shoulder to shoulder and wing tip to wing tip, to defeat the Nazi tyranny is recognized.

1

IN THE FIRING LINE

"The coldest, loneliest, most dangerous job of all."
—RICHARD HOLMES, MILITARY HISTORIAN

SITTING IN THE COPILOT'S SEAT OF A B-17 FLYING FORTRESS NICKNAMED *La-Dee-Doo*, twenty-year-old Jim O'Connor from Chicago had plenty of time to contemplate his fate. It was not so very long since he had been at a desk in high school sweating for his English Lit exams. He still carried in his pack a relic of those days—a book called *A Treasury of Great Poems*—and he would seek solace in the inspirational words he found there before setting out on every mission. It seemed a lifetime ago now, but just a couple of months earlier, back in the United States, he had flung off his uniform, with its newly acquired pilot's wings and second lieutenant's bars, and reveled in a day of exceptional loveliness in a lush Oklahoma valley. A warm sun shone in a cloudless sky. "It was a rare moment of peace and beauty in our uprooted, uncertain and somewhat chaotic young lives," he later recalled. He swam in a lake and then soaked his head under a spectacular waterfall. Now he was on his way to a baptism of fire over Germany.

As a member of the 388th Bomb Group based at Knettishall in eastern England, he was waiting to take up the "Tail-End Charlie" position, so often assigned to rookie crews like his, in a huge bomber formation. He knew that bringing up the rear of 700, 800, maybe 1,000 aircraft would leave him exposed to enemy fighters in search of an easy kill or to antiaircraft gunners on the ground who had finally got their range. The experience that

day would be imprinted on O'Connor's mind for the rest of his life. It had
begun, as it always did, with a midnight awakening.

The duty sergeant, a big pleasant former gunner from North Carolina,
quietly entered the barracks and shone a flashlight on a roster in his hand.
He spoke softly as he aimed the flashlight beam into the face of each crew
member scheduled to fly that day. "Lootenant, wake up. You all are flying
today." He slowly worked his way the length of the hut, skipping a relieved crew here and there who were getting the day off. He finally arrived at our corner, and we were up, into our long underwear, woolen
uniforms, flight suits, and A-2 leather jackets in a couple of minutes. After breakfast we loaded into GI trucks which raced through the darkness
and disgorged us in front of the briefing room. Thirty-six crews—360
airmen plus a few intelligence, weather, and auxiliary officers—looked up
at a stage containing a covered wall-size map of England and northern
Europe. Our target that day was a deep-penetration one—a heavily defended factory at Schweinfurt producing most of the ball bearings for the
entire German military. A groan went up when it was announced.

The briefing would end with the synchronizing of watches at around
3:00 A.M. Each crew member then had a particular duty to perform. As
the copilot, mine was to pick up the crew's parachutes and escape kits
from stores. Meanwhile, the Catholics in our ranks went off to a
makeshift chapel on the flight line where the chaplain administered the
sacraments and gave a farewell blessing. The Protestant and Jewish fliers
had similar arrangements. After the tasks were all completed and the ship
checked over, there was usually a wait of a half hour or more before takeoff time. The crew gathered around the stove in the ground-crew tent and
either dozed off on the cots or had a last smoke. Everyone was alone with
his own thoughts.[1]

At 4:00 A.M., as the first streaks of dawn began to appear in the eastern sky,
a green flare shot up from the control tower giving the signal to start engines. A tremendous roar shattered the peace of the night as 134 powerful
1,200 horsepower engines sprang into life. Then a second flare shot sky-
ward and the aircraft began the taxi out toward the runway. In *La-Dee-
Doo,* O'Connor and his crew followed the other heavily laden ships

waddling up to takeoff position. After the magnetos were checked and tail wheel locked, the skipper offered a final comforting glance to his crew as the engineer rammed the throttles full forward. The skipper gave the final nod and the brakes were released.

We roared down the runway. The excitement of that moment of takeoff never diminished. It took some two hours for the entire force to form over England. We would fly in a big lazy climbing circle until the last ship, squadron, group, and wing were in position in the bomber stream. That day we were in the last wing (100-plus ships), the last group (36), the last squadron (12) and the last element (3), flying in so-called Purple Heart Corner, the most vulnerable position in the formation. Out of the hundreds of bombers hitting Schweinfurt, we would be the very last one over the target. We headed out over the North Sea toward the continent and climbed to altitude. The gunners practiced firing their guns. At 10,000 feet we went on oxygen and put on steel flak helmets. Every ten minutes or so we had an oxygen check, with each crew member reporting in to the copilot.

Over the target, the sky was black with flak, the worst we had ever seen. And being at the tail end of the bomber stream, the German gunners by then had the exact range. Bursts of flak were exploding right below and around our ship, bouncing it up and down and sending jagged pieces of shrapnel through the fuselage. Our usually unexcitable tail gunner got on the intercom and yelled out, "Lieutenant, de flak is right on us. Let's get de hell out of heah!" The flak was so devastating that immediately after bombs away, the group leader made an abrupt forty-five-degree right diving turn off the target to get out of the range of gunfire. Being the last ship on the outside of the formation, the speed and angle of turn was greatly exaggerated for us.

The plane was practically standing on its wing at a ninety-degree angle to the ground as the air speed rapidly increased. The skipper could not see anything from his seat, so I had to take over control and fly the plane myself on my own. By now there was both a gray undercast and a gray overcast, absolutely nothing visible by which I could gauge our flight attitude. Vertigo gripped me. I lost all balance and perspective. All I had to hang on to was the aircraft alongside—which meant that if she was heading for the ground then so were we. Eventually the group stabilized, and we rejoined the mainstream for the long haul home. The crew started breathing again and assessed the battle damage. The flak had taken out rudder and trim cables, and put more than twenty large holes in the side. The tail gunner and radio operator had near misses and the navigator was grazed by a piece of flak that tore his flight jacket and pierced his equipment bag.

Just before 1:00 P.M. we landed back at base. As the wheels touched down, we were about to let out a collective sigh of relief, when the ship began to vibrate and bounce. A tire had been shot out. The skipper yelled at me to unlock the tail wheel. He then gunned the engines, pulling the ship off the runway into the muddy infield, thus keeping the landing strip clear for the other incoming aircraft, many with battle damage or wounded on board. That day only thirty-two out of the thirty-six aircraft that had taken off for battle from our base returned. As the skipper cut the engines, we sat there for some moments completely whacked out until a truck came out to pick us up. At debriefing, we felt we had earned the shot of bourbon which was waiting for us.

O'Connor and his crew had survived their first experience as Tail-End Charlies and their first encounters on Purple Heart Corner, but four bombers from his group, along with forty of his comrades, had not. It had been every bit as bad as they feared, and they hoped to be spared a second experience. But a few weeks later they were rostered in the same position for a thousand-bomber raid on "the Big B," Berlin. "When the target was announced, a spontaneous groan erupted from the assembled bomber crews. I looked round the room and knew several crews would probably not make it back." He felt sure his would be one of them. Not only were they Tail-End Charlies again, they had also been assigned an older, patched-up B-17 for the trip, one that creaked and groaned as they rose into the morning sun. O'Connor felt like a medieval knight heading into battle, "knowing that the ultimate gamble was at hand, the throw of the dice that would determine life or death." That day death came very close. From his cockpit, O'Connor watched the Fortress next to his in the formation explode, its oxygen tanks hit by the same flak that had put a handful of harmless holes in his own aircraft. He and his men made it home. The other crew went on the list of 250 men missing that day. "How sweet it was to be alive!" O'Connor later wrote in his diary.

Life for others in the Tail-End Charlie position was not so sweet and many could not escape disaster. On a deep-penetration haul to the Leuna oil refinery, a B-17 named *Knockout* was in the last group of the thousand-plane formation, with navigator Dean Whitaker, lying in the nose cone, straining his eyes to catch sight of the full might of the Eighth Air Force ahead as it went in for the kill. What he saw was a huge black cloud—the flak from hundreds of 88mm guns, so many he thought the Germans must have moved every gun they had to protect their valuable oil supplies. He could see B-17s spiraling out of that cloud, some on fire, others missing a wing or tail. "Knowing it would soon be our turn to run the gauntlet made my blood pressure rise." If that was happening to the vanguard, what chance did those in the rear have?

They slowed to one hundred and fifty miles an hour for the bomb run, and to Whitaker it felt as if they had come almost to a stop. "Flak was to the right, left, overhead, ahead, sometimes so close you could hear the dull thud of it exploding. I smelt burning metal and knew we had been hit. A shell exploding directly in front of us sent bits of steel through the nose." Bombs gone, and they wheeled away, out of the black cloud and into clear blue sky. The relief was momentary. "Bandits" came a cry over the intercom, and they were being chased by enemy fighters. "All hell broke loose. Our tail must have been shot off because the plane was going every way but straight." The rear gunner was dead. The aircraft began to nosedive, the stick and wheel useless in the pilot's hands. All that was left to do was lower the landing gear, a sign of surrender to the Germans, and jump.

More than half the crew of *Knockout* parachuted straight into enemy hands. Surrounded by German troops the moment they landed, evasion was never an option. A dozen other planes had been hit, too, on that mission and altogether fifty bedraggled American airmen held up their hands in surrender that day and went into captivity. They at least were safe. Four others from the crew of *Knockout* were not, the pilot Herb Newman among them. Winds had swept them in a different direction and they drifted down near a small village, whose police chief enlisted the help of other Nazi thugs to slaughter them on the spot.[2]

While "Tail-End Charlie" in the American Eighth Air Force referred to the last aircraft in a formation, it had a different meaning to the men of Bomber Command, where it was RAF speak for the rear gunners. And British Tail-End Charlies were considered just as vulnerable as their American namesakes. Isolated and alone in the rear of his aircraft, nineteen-year-old RAF Sergeant Bob Pierson could testify to that.

Unlike the Americans, who bombed in daylight hours, the British raids were launched at night, and so the red beacon shining in the darkening sky behind him was always his last sight of home. He sat with his back to the four engines of the Lancaster bomber, tucked into a space the size of a dustbin, and wondered, as he did every time, if he would ever see its glow again. Just ninety seconds earlier, as the Lancaster had turned on the taxiway and stood on full throttle, building up power before the pilot let off the brakes, Pierson, the rear gunner, had strained to see through the gloom of early evening. Yes, they were there—the adjutant, the ground crew, too, and lots of WAAFs, the RAF girls whose voices he would hope to hear from the control tower guiding them home to land in, what, eight and a half, nine hours' time. They were huddled round a small trailer, mugs of tea in one hand, all waving. Goodbye! Good luck! Charging down the runway, the Lancaster's rear wheel was first off the ground, and just before the front wheels lifted into flight the plane gave an involuntary "wag" of its tail. Pierson always felt it was as if the aircraft was waving goodbye to the well-wishers.

The bomber, with seven tons of explosives in its belly for a night-time raid on Germany, rose slowly, turned left, and climbed in circles to join the formation assembling in the sky over the Lincolnshire countryside. Pierson, gazing back from the coffinlike rear turret at the now-receding red light on a farm cottage at the end of the runway, reflected on how important it was to get a proper send-off, that people should be there to see them go. "It gave me a sense of hope and of support," he recalled sixty years later. If the padre was there, it was an extra blessing. "I took quite a lot of comfort from him before each op. You could talk to him about your feelings, about being scared. He would help you put aside the fear of dying."[3]

Once the war machine began to roll, that fear was unspoken, though it was a fellow traveler for all but the most devil-may-care airmen or the rawest recruits. Pierson remembered his very first operation over enemy territory, when he was overwhelmed by sheer excitement. "I felt just like a racing driver—not scared at all." Now experience had taught him what to expect and his mood was somber.

The strict preoperation routine helped to calm the nerves. He had written his last letters to his loved ones before the lorry—"the blood wagon," they called it, with typically ghoulish RAF humor—had come to pick up him and his crew from their hut to take them to their plane. The letters would be found in his locker if he didn't come back, one for his parents in north London, the other for Joyce, the girl he wished was his wife. Thoughts of her went through his mind as he stood on the edge of the airfield, waiting for the jeep to come racing along the perimeter track with the order to board the bomber. This was anxious time to kill. Some of the seven-man crews went through elaborate good-luck rituals. There would be banter and even songs. One navigator always crooned his way through "As Time Goes By" from *Casablanca*, the gritty Humphrey Bogart film they had all seen and loved on its recent release.[4] "A fight for love or glory, a case of do or die . . ." seemed appropriate for what lay ahead. Others would line up to urinate ceremonially against one of the Lancaster's huge front wheels, for good fortune or simply to empty their bladders before the long confinement. But Pierson's crew was a less boisterous bunch. "We tended to retreat into our own corners," he recalled. "The others were usually quiet, just sitting and thinking, but I liked to talk, probably because I was going to be on my own for the whole of the flight ahead."

Once tucked up in his turret at the rear of the plane, he would not move for the entire trip. He would be alone, almost in his own private war. The others—pilot, flight engineer, navigator, radio operator, bombardier, and middle-turret gunner—could edge their way around the cramped, narrow fuselage, though movement was never that easy in bulky flying suit, Mae West life preserver, and parachute. If necessary, they could struggle the twenty yards to the disgusting Elsan lavatory near the back or stand up, head sticking into the astrodome bubble behind the pilot's seat, and stare at the night sky and the hundreds of other bombers in the stream around them. They could also see and hear each other, feel their presence. But the Tail-End Charlie did his job in isolation.

So, in those moments before takeoff, he sought company. "I would lean on the fence and natter to the farmer whose cottage was at the end of the runway, the one with the red light on the roof. He came out each evening with his daughter—a lovely girl, I remember—and we'd have a cigarette and talk about the weather, the harvest, normal things, normal life— anything but the war, anything but where I was going with my crew that night. In some ways that was the hardest part. One minute we were leading an ordinary life. Then we were off for eight hours of hell, risking our lives to drop bombs on Berlin or the Ruhr valley in the middle of the night, and knowing we might never come back. Every evening the farmer wished the crews good luck, and there must have been many times when he chatted to men he never saw again. But he never asked what happened to them, never mentioned it." No one did.

The order to go interrupted Pierson's conversation. The others in the crew clambered up the ladder, dragging their parachutes and flight bags with them through the narrow hatch by the rear wheel, and turned right toward the front of the Lancaster. Squeezing themselves down the passageway and climbing over the aircraft's main spar, they made their way toward their positions. On the way hands reached out to check that the roof escape hatch was secured and that the "ready to destruct" switch was in the right position. Somebody always forgot to duck and cracked his head on the cylinder of nitrogen which would be used to douse the flames if fire broke out in the fuel tanks. The six of them crammed into a space no bigger than a small van—the pilot perched up in the cockpit with the flight engineer, while the navigator and the radio operator tucked into small corners below him and the bombardier lay flat on his stomach in front and the mid-upper gunner slid into his dome behind. They were cosy to the point of claustrophobia, but companionable.

Meanwhile rear gunner Pierson had gone left at the door—the only one to do so. He crouched down, then hauled himself along the narrowing fuselage, over the tail spar and the rear-wheel housing, before sliding down feetfirst into his seat and pulling the doors of his revolving turret closed behind him. He double-checked they were shut tight; if they were slightly ajar he would sit for hours in a body-numbing draft. But for now he was snug in his own Perspex-encased world, alone with just his four .303 Browning machine guns and his thoughts. Six feet tall, he cursed his height each time he settled in. "My head was just about touching the top of the turret and my shoulders were nearly at the edge. In front there was only enough room to get your hands round the triggers of the guns. Your legs were virtually locked in one position—you couldn't stretch them more than an inch or two without hitting the metal sides or the pedal that turned the turret." It was so tight that a gunner wearing a wristwatch could easily smash it against the side. One broke three before he switched the face to the inside of his wrist.

Pierson prepared himself for his job—to defend the plane and its crew from attack. He was the eyes in the back of their head. For the long hours ahead, from takeoff to landing back home, he would protect their tail. He could swivel his turret through a half circle and track slowly backward and forward, eyes constantly staring out into the night sky, above, below, to left and to right, looking for the silhouettes of enemy fighters, hoping to spot them in time. Lives—not least his own—depended on it. His only contact with the rest of the crew was on the intercom, and then, if the captain was being strict that night, only for essential communications. Chatter, human contact for contact's sake, was not encouraged. The psychological pressure was immense, as the enemy knew. German bombers were specifically designed so that no one member of the crew was isolated in this way. It was considered bad for morale.[5] But RAF tail gunners were expected to cope.

"For the rest of the crew there was the comfort of seeing other people, but in the back we never had that. The skipper might check in with everyone from time to time—'All right in the rear, Bob?'—but there were long periods of silence, and if the intercom packed up [broke down] you could be very lonely, on your own and traveling backward through enemy territory."

The loneliness of the long-distance rear gunner deterred many airmen. Miles Tripp tried flying in the back once and found it unnerving: "being dragged backward in a goldfish bowl," was how he described the sensation. And frustrating: "You sit in silence while the others speculate about what can be seen ahead, and when at last you see what they were discussing and can give your opinion, everyone else has lost interest."[6] He decided to stick to being a bombardier with a seat in the nose of the aircraft and a view ahead. But a natural-born rear gunner like Peter Twinn loved it. "You were out on a limb but you were the king of your own castle."[7] For another, Chan Chandler, there was a strange and awe-inspiring beauty in being alone, perched on the edge of eternity. He watched marvelous sunsets. "We set off at dusk, heading into the dark, and as we gained height so the horizon behind us extended, you could see a second sunset. This would slowly fade to just a purple line with blackness below and light above. It was indescribably beautiful and gave the most eerie sensation. It felt as if I was going clear over the edge of the world, like a lost soul flying out into space, never to return."[8]

A man's thoughts could easily wander and Bob Pierson remembered having to concentrate hard to stay awake, kept on his toes by the Benzedrine tablets he had swallowed—"wakey-wakey pills we called them." But, as his bomber reached the assembly point in the sky and linked up with hundreds of others before heading out across the North Sea, there was one last chance to dream of home. He and Joyce were engaged, but her father had refused to let them marry. There was a war on, he had told them, as if they needed reminding. Who knew what was going to happen to any of them? They had already lost Joyce's cousin, Billy, another airman, who had died in the wreck of a Wellington while training. And besides, the pair of them were only nineteen—"just kids, really," as Pierson himself acknowledged with a wry smile years later. "That's all I was, just a schoolkid." He carried a lock of her red hair as a lucky charm, tucked in the pocket of the blue serge battle dress underneath his flight suit. But they never talked about dying or mentioned it in their letters—except in that last one, of course, the one he hoped she would never have to read. When they parted she never said goodbye. It was bad luck; it might come horribly true. Instead it was a cheery, hope-filled "See you!"

It would be many years before he discovered the truth about how much Joyce worried about him. She tried to push the thoughts to the back of her mind, "but when I went to bed at night, I lay there in the dark thinking about him and what he was doing. Was he over Germany at that very moment? We were being bombed in London and he was bombing towns in Germany—it was all dreadful and I knew that he was thinking the same as me: Is there no other way to bring peace forward, than to be killing people?"[9]

The cold in his face brought Pierson's mind back into focus. There was a chilling chink in the rear gunner's armor. The Perspex canopy tended to frost up or smear with dirt and oil, clouding his vision, so one sheet had been removed at eye level, on orders from on high, leaving the turret open to the air. Pierson's face was exposed to the slipstream—the temperature of which plummeted the higher they went. But it was better for him to freeze than lose sight of the enemy. Some men greased their cheeks with lanolin to ward off frostbite. "We would be flying at 250 miles an hour and the wind tore through the gap continuously. I was often in temperatures of minus thirty and minus forty degrees. My breath froze into an icicle in front of me. I waited until it was three or four inches long before breaking it off with my hands. They at least were warm, thanks to the four pairs of gloves I had on—a white silk pair underneath, then mittens and a pair of ordinary black gloves, and finally gauntlets. My trigger fingers were twice their normal thickness!"

His flying suit was electrically heated. A wonder of early-1940s technology, it plugged in to the aircraft like an electric blanket—but it was a mixed blessing, if a blessing at all. Chan Chandler complained that his was so hot at ground level it would burn his skin and so useless at twenty thousand feet he wondered if it was working at all. Pierson never used his. "It had no thermostat and would never remain at a steady temperature. The danger was that it would get too hot and send you to sleep." And sleep could kill. Luftwaffe fighter pilots patrolling the skies, snapping at the heels and the flanks of the vast waves of bombers sent over Germany, looked for the turret which was still, where the guns were not moving, where the gunner was dozing or dreaming. Drawn to the weakness, they came in from behind, cannons blazing. A sleeping air gunner was a dead man. His crew, too, most likely.

The skipper's voice over the intercom told him they had passed the coast of mainland Europe. They were now over enemy territory, in the war zone. "Keep your eyes peeled, Bob." He strained for a glimpse of an enemy fighter. It could be a flash of light or the very opposite, a black shape darker than the night sky around it. "We were trained to spot different silhouettes, the shape and size of their wings. In the classroom they flashed slides in front of us for two seconds, and we were supposed to know instantly if it was friend or foe. But it was very different 18,000 feet up in the pitch black. You see something. You know instantly it isn't a Spitfire or a Hurricane. Your heart jumps. This is for real. But you can't just blaze away. You have to think clearly. If you fire, the tracer will give your position away to the enemy for sure. And, anyway, you might hit another Lancaster in the stream. Plenty of planes were knocked out by someone on their own side panicking. You know, too, that the odds of shooting down an enemy fighter are tiny. Our .303s were like peashooters against their cannons. So you wait. And it gets closer, until you can make out a head and shoulders in the cockpit. Is he going to keep coming? Is he going to start firing? Sometimes he suddenly peels away out of sight, and that's the worst moment of all. All you can do is sit tight and wait and pray he's really gone away, that he hasn't dived below you and is coming back underneath with his guns blazing away at you. The horror was waiting and not knowing, wondering if you were about to die.

"If an attack came, I would yell, 'Corkscrew, skipper,' and he would throw the Lanc into a steep dive. When a bomber corkscrews, the worst place to be is in the back. As the wings go down, the tail comes hurtling up. Facing backward, you go up, too, and then you plunge back down as the skipper pulls back on the stick and the plane climbs steeply in the opposite direction. The g-force clamps on your head like a ton of concrete. Your chin is pressed hard into your chest. And all the time you are still trying to fire at the enemy fighter on your tail."

Nearing the target—whichever German city with its factories, marshaling yards, and acres of homes had been picked personally by Air Marshal Sir Arthur Harris, the commander in chief of Bomber Command, for them to hit that night—the bombers were generally safer from enemy fighters. The Junkers and Messerschmitts would not follow them down into the flak, the antiaircraft fire coming up from the ground defenses. But then again, the bombers were now at their most vulnerable because they were flying straight and level with their bomb doors open and were easier for the ack-ack gunners to get a fix on—especially if they had caught a plane in their searchlights. Being "coned" was an experience that wrenched the guts with fear. "One moment you are in a complete blackout and the next you are caught by beams of intense light," Pierson recalled, "just as if someone has flipped a switch in a dark room. The thought that floods your mind is that you're the one—you have been picked out of all the other aircraft around you. And you know what happens next because you've looked out and seen it all before—seen other planes suddenly illuminated, then hit by shells from the ground. Balls of flame come from the engine, then from the fuselage, and you see it going down and down until it disappears into total blackness again."

The flak was what Bob Pierson feared most. Not the enemy fighters—he had fewer brushes with them. But below there were close on a million German men, women, and boys manning the Reich's ground defenses. All over Germany, fifty thousand big guns were pointing upward at aircraft crossing into its airspace.[10] A direct hit would destroy a plane, but most damage was caused indirectly by shrapnel from the exploding shells hitting the aircraft's fuel and hydraulic lines, oil system, or engines. And its crew. Concentrated flak produced a curtain of high explosive into which Pierson, in his rear-facing position, was swept blind. "The rest of the crew could at least see it ahead as we flew into it, but all I could do was wait for it to explode around me. All of a sudden there would be red fire flashes and orange explosions on either side of me, lighting up the inside of the turret. It comes horribly close, and there is nothing you can do to protect yourself. Instinctively I tried to cover myself with my arms, but that was silly. So I would grip the guns, just the way you would desperately cling to the seat of a runaway car, hanging on, dreading whatever is going to happen next and knowing there is nothing you can do about it. Each time the plane was hit there was a huge, hollow bang. I can still hear that sound now. It's imprinted on my mind. Again, it was as if you were in that runaway car but now somebody was throwing stones at you as well—and each stone was smashing against the windshield, making holes in the side and shaking it so violently you thought you could never survive. I once had three-quarters of my turret blown away by shell fire over Dortmund and I came back with my gloves peppered by shattered Perspex. I counted two hundred holes in the aircraft."

Over the target, with the bombardier calling his instructions to the pilot—"Steady, skipper, hold her straight"—and shells bursting all around, every second felt like a week. Sitting in his rear turret, Ron Smith used to will the bombardier "to drop the bloody bombs and let's get the hell out of it." He thought it but never said it, not wishing to betray his fear.[11] This was a time to suppress the instinct to flee, to let the training take over, to do their job, to let the bombardier do his. They hung there for an eternity, or so it seemed, desperate to hear the cry of "Bombs gone!" and feel the Lancaster, thousands of pounds lighter in an instant, instinctively leap up and away. In the relief of that moment of release, as they swung round and headed westward, the job done, some thought about the poor devils below. Chan Chandler looked down on Cologne one night and saw with sadness and compassion "the whole town like one obscene boiling mass beneath us. Men, women, children, babies, cats, dogs, rats, mice; nothing would live down there. All would be incinerated, the ashes covered by the falling buildings."

Others would think of the devastation wrought on British cities by the Germans and rejoice in the fact that they were taking the war back to their sworn enemy. Some never allowed themselves any sentiments. Peter Twinn remembered sitting in the rear, looking back at a city they had just bombed and still seeing the fires burning an hour later, from 150 miles away. "But I never thought about the destruction. It didn't enter my head. I was miles above the earth and not part of what was going on below. You couldn't see anybody and you couldn't hear anything. The whole thing was impersonal. We had done what we were supposed to do. I know it sounds heartless and cruel, but I'm afraid that's how it was. We were not philosophers."

On the way home, there was no letup for the rear gunner. In fact the return trip could be more dangerous than the outward one because the enemy now knew where the bombers were. German fighter defenses were thinly spread, and every effort was made to fool them. Dummy runs were made by small groups of bombers to try to lure the fighters away from the real target. But that was academic after the target had been hit. The Luftwaffe would wait to ambush returning Allied bombers. Nonetheless, Chan Chandler found it hard not to relax a little when the target was well behind them. He would take off his oxygen mask, light a cigarette, and take a swig of coffee—cold by now—from his Thermos flask. But one hand stayed on his gun and he kept the turret turning. Too many of his comrades had "been killed thinking they were safe once they had crossed the enemy coast on the way home, only to find the fighters had chased them anything up to thirty miles out to sea." Some of the more daring Luftwaffe pilots even hung around in clouds over airfields in England to hit the planes at their most vulnerable—on the flight path in to land.

A wise rear gunner remained on the alert for attackers until that moment of relief when the wheel beneath him hit solid ground again. "The front wheels touched down first," Pierson recalled, "and I would just sit there holding on for dear life waiting for that terrific bump. Because I was tall, I banged my head on the Perspex every time we landed. But that bump meant I was safely home. The feeling was indescribable. We were supposed to stay at our posts until the skipper brought the plane to a halt but I was always straight out of my turret and waiting at the side door. I'd open it as we were taxiing off the main runway, just to get a bit of fresh air after all those hours in the sky. We'd been on oxygen the whole way and there was also the constant stink from the Elsan toilet. It was great to breathe properly again. I gulped it in. It meant we were alive. Very tired but safe."

For Chandler, the moment of relief and release was not until the pilot switched off the engines. He luxuriated in the quiet after "those four bloody Merlins shut up." He often felt too tired to leave his turret. 'I'll just sleep here. Oh no, there's bloody debriefing to get to, isn't there? Legs won't work—numb from all those hours without moving. Crawl across the spar and along to the door; stick my feet out backward. Jimmy, the wireless operator, guides them on to the ladder and helps me down. A flight van rolls up. We all fall into it and it takes us off to debriefing. One more for the logbook—how many more will we manage, I wonder?'

Pierson relished debriefing for its sense of coziness and companionship. "The padre and the girls were there to welcome us with rum and chocolate. We sat at a circular table and in the middle there was always a big bowl of raisins and currants for us to help ourselves from, and packets of cigarettes, Thames cigarettes, the cheapest you could buy in those days. And we would sit waiting until it was our turn to describe what we had seen to the intelligence people. Afterward, back in my hut, I would lie on my bed, drained out, but thinking. "That was a job well done." Better still, none of us got hurt or injured. We didn't talk very much to each other. Everybody just got on with their own thing, writing a letter, reading a book, listening to music on the radio. Ann Shelton was my favorite singer. But at the back of our minds we all knew that tomorrow we were going to have to do it all over again." At the back of their minds, too, was that there might be one tomorrow too many.

It was a sentiment that U.S. tail gunners echoed. Staff Sergeant Eddie Picardo had little expectation of his life lasting very long. He had no illusions about how dangerous it would be fighting a war in the tail turret of a B-24 Liberator, and when he arrived in England for active service, he did not expect to see his homeland ever again. A third-generation Italian American, he had taken out as much life insurance as he could. His death would at least make his family back in Seattle $10,000 better off. But he also sought divine protection—he had his rosary and on the night before each mission, he recited his prayers five times, the way his grandmother had taught him as a child. Not that he thought even they could save him. "There is no way I will live through this experience," he told himself, "no way. I figured I might survive one or two missions, but then I would be history, blown into a thousand pieces in the skies over Germany." His life, he reckoned, with a conscious nod to Bogart in *Casablanca,* didn't amount to a hill of beans.[12]

Just like the British Tail-End Charlies, the American rear gunners were totally isolated in the back of the B-17 Flying Fortresses and B-24 Liberators. That fact alone very nearly killed nineteen-year-old Charles Sibray. From his perch, he saw smoke and flames shooting from under the port wing and called the pilot on the intercom to tell him. The order to prepare to bail out was given, and Sibray took off his headphones and unhooked his oxygen line while he reached round for his parachute and clipped it on. He then reconnected himself to the aircraft. In those seconds, the captain had ordered everyone to jump, but Sibray had missed it. He sat at his guns, waiting for the order that, unknown to him, had already been given. He tried to get through to the flight deck on the intercom but there was no reply and he *assumed* they were all just too busy coping with the emergency. Then he looked out and saw that the smoke from the wing was diminishing and *assumed* they were getting the problem under control. He stayed at his post for thirty minutes as the Fortress flew on. Then he saw flak bursts close by and radioed the pilot to maneuver away. When there was no response, and the plane continued on its steady course, he at last realized something was wrong. Sibray crawled out of his turret and back down the fuselage. There was no gunner in the waist position. He kept going. The radio room was empty. Finally, he reached the flight deck, to find it deserted. The Fortress was on automatic pilot and, not as badly damaged as had been thought, had kept going in a straight line. He had been alone in an unpiloted plane for the past 150 miles and so remote from the rest of the crew that he did not know it. Fortunately, since the bomber was on the return leg of the mission, those extra miles had brought him over Allied territory and when he at last bailed out he fell into friendly hands. The others had exited over Germany and spent the rest of the war as prisoners.[13]

But, isolated as it was in the back of a B-17, there was always the prospect of seeing the face of the enemy, which was something that almost never happened to British crews. The Eighth Air Force flew in daylight instead of under the cover of night, which was when their counterparts in the Royal Air Force's Bomber Command did their work. The American aircraft bristled with guns—from the nose, from the rear, and from the middle, known as the waist. The drawback was that the enemy could see them, too. Shoot-outs in the air, eyeball-to-eyeball confrontations between gunners from the Bronx and fighter pilots from Berlin, were normal.

Casualties were fearful. Bob Andrews, a Southerner from Georgia, was just nineteen when he arrived in England, drawn to the fight by a piece of death-or-glory propaganda. "One night, I saw a movie where good ole John Wayne shot down three-fourths of the Japanese air force. I was thrilled and immediately recognized my calling."[14] He went to gunnery school and after graduating was sent to kill Germans in Europe rather than Japanese in the Pacific. His first mission was a cakewalk—"No fighters, no flak, no nothing, but I still had a really great feeling to be in combat at last." He adopted the swagger of a veteran. Then, two days later, he really grew up. "It was an aging experience. There was tons of flak and many German fighters, one of which shot at us; I shot at him. To my total amazement he did not go down. As he barrel-rolled by, I had an almost uncontrollable urge to pee. I observed other planes, some with engines out or smoking, others out of formation. I wondered if everyone was experiencing the same subdued terror as me. On the way home I decided that it wouldn't be a bad idea to pray a little." On his first trip to Berlin, his plane was hit by flak and lost an engine. Then they were attacked by six Messerschmitts. "Their first pass shot our ball-turret gunner in the leg, their second hit him in the face. They also shot up the radio operator and the top-turret gunner. During all this melee, my guns jammed. One of the 109s apparently thought I was dead, because he came in real close, pumping cannon shells into us. I was sure I was about to die. I shouted to God for help and my guns immediately unjammed. The next time that fighter came in I fired on him point-blank. It came apart. We claimed and confirmed the destruction of three of them." The victory was hard-won: "The ball-turret gunner was on the floor with his hands over his face and what looked like an eye between his fingers."

It was no wonder that American rear gunners like Eddie Picardo let their hair down whenever they got the chance. He promised himself he would live life to the full while he could. He told any English girls he met—and there were lots—that he came from Hollywood. Movie stardom flashed before their innocent eyes. It certainly did the trick with one girl over a drink and a game of darts in a pub in London. "Boy, was she beautiful, a real tomato, with a great figure!" He was even ready to risk being late back to his base in Norfolk for her. He might be punished, "but what could they do to me anyway? There wasn't anything worse than being in the tail of a B-24 and flying over Germany!" He had always been a man to ride his luck. Called up to the air force for training, he had read in a magazine that the life of a tail gunner in combat lasted about seventeen seconds. "I said, 'Oh hell, I can beat that.' At nineteen I was so cocky I thought I could do anything, especially if I had the chance to kick the hell out of the enemy. I just wanted to be part of it all. I figured I didn't want to be a pilot because the training was so long and it would take a long time to get into action. I thought they could teach me how to shoot a machine gun in twenty minutes and then I'd be ready to go. I became a gunner because it was a way to get in quicker."

Now, flying at twenty-two thousand feet over Germany with a full bomb load in the belly of the B-24, Picardo wondered why he had been so eager. The realities of war hit home when, assigned to the 44th Bomb Group, he and his crew arrived at their new base just outside Norwich, "so wet behind their ears, they shone. An old hand came up to us and asked, 'Who's the tail gunner?' I told him I was, and he pointed toward a bullet-ridden plane on the runway. 'It got a direct hit in the tail today, and they're sucking out what's left of the tail gunner,' he said. It was a pretty stark initiation. But I told myself, that's not going to happen to me." He came very close. On more than one occasion he muttered, "Good night, sweetheart," to himself as the flak exploded around him and "I found myself alive though I could just as easily be dead." Getting back to base was always a moment of huge relief—"like being granted a reprieve from a death sentence. You started to live for the future again. You could make plans. I was filled with hope that I would see my family and friends again in Seattle or watch the Indians, my baseball team. I'd tell myself, one day I'm going to be sitting watching the guys again, nothing can stop me. Of course the feeling only lasted a short time. It was never long before you had to return to face death."

It is generally agreed that rear gunners like Eddie Picardo and Bob Pierson had one of the worst jobs of all the Allied airmen who took the fight to Germany in the Second World War. They were literally in the firing line, sitting targets for enemy fighters. Bombardier Campbell Muirhead thought the rear turret the most dangerous position in a Lancaster. "An attack usually came from behind, and the rear gunner received the full cannon blast. Sometimes he was the only one who got it. The plane would corkscrew to get away but it would be too late for him."[15] Military historian Richard Holmes maintained that the least survivable position was the rear turret and that Tail-End Charlies had "the coldest, loneliest, and most dangerous job of all. The extra demands made on the courage and endurance of rear gunners in the heavy bombers may well have been the most ever regularly required of fighting men. They were outgunned by the cannon-equipped German fighters, and even if they survived an attack that crippled the bomber, few managed to bail out, and aircraft were sometimes seen to crash with the gunners defiantly firing to the last."[16] It certainly took a special kind of bravery to climb into that rear turret night after night, to defy common sense and instinct and put your life on the line when everything in you screamed out not to go.

But every job aboard a bomber had its risks, and the simple, shocking truth was that death came pretty indiscriminately in the bomber war. The position a man sat in was largely irrelevant—they all died in droves. To fly in a bomber—whether as pilot or gunner, navigator, engineer, radio operator, or bombardier—was the most dangerous job of the Second World War, as risky as being an infantry officer in the trenches of the First World War. The odds were against survival. As a trainee B-17 pilot, Jim O'Connor recalled sitting in a hall full of boisterous recruits as an elderly officer tried to bring home to them the seriousness of the battle they were about to join. "All you young kids are thinking about is having a smoke and a Coke!" the officer, a veteran of the defeated Polish air force, called out to them in a thick east European accent. "But just look around you. Look to your right and look to your left. Only one out of the three of you is coming back alive! War is hell! I know, because I have been there." O'Connor remembered how they laughed. "We nudged our friends to left and right, but the fact was that, by midsummer 1944, only one out of three of us *had* survived."

Between 1939 and 1945 the bombing war launched from Britain against Germany claimed the lives of just over 55,500 airmen from the RAF's Bomber Command, around half its entire force. Its casualty rate was higher than any other section of the British armed services. The United States Army Air Forces (USAAF) had that same grim distinction among the U.S. forces. After its Eighth Air Force joined the battle in 1942, 26,000 of its officers and enlisted men died in combat. In all, more than 15,000 Allied bombers never returned, shot down by flak or by fighters or crashing as a result of mechanical failure or human error.[17] The sacrifice was enormous. On one terrible night 670 Bomber Command aircrew died in a matter of hours on one single raid. This was more than the RAF casualties in the whole of the months-long Battle of Britain.[18] If a bomber went down, the odds were that every one of its seven-man crew would die, unable to bail out in time. Even when there were survivors, in the vast majority of cases, fewer than half escaped with their lives.[19] The attrition was frightening. In January 1944 the death rate averaged 5 percent per mission—1,700 RAF men lost their lives in that one month. For the bomber crews of the Second World War, with a fifty-fifty chance of survival, every day was a D-Day landing; every time they took off they were "going over the top." And with most needing thirty operations to complete a tour of duty, a man didn't need a math degree to work out that, if he was going to live through this war, he would have to be very lucky indeed.

The extent of the slaughter is barely recognized. In a private room at the RAF archive at Bentley Priory in north London are kept the official documents of all the men who died and the missions that claimed their lives.[20] The filing cabinets line two walls of a room in sad, silent testimony. To stand there and try to grasp the individual lives—and deaths—recorded in front of your eyes is devastating. It takes one's breath away and gives pause for thought in the same way as does the Menin Gate monument at Ypres or the Vietnam War wall in Washington. But those are public cenotaphs;

Bomber Command's dead have no such memorial. They are filed away, as if they had done nothing to be proud of.

There are many groups of Allied fighting men who are rightly hailed as heroes—the D-Day assault troops who forced their way onto the beaches of Normandy; the Spitfire and Hurricane pilots who won the Battle of Britain; the Desert Rats who turned the tide of war in North Africa; the GIs who held out at Bastogne in the Battle of the Bulge. Such distinction is rarely accorded to the men who fought perhaps the most crucial battle of all—the bomber battle.

This is particularly so in Britain. A gracious and grateful nod may be made in their direction for the deeds of Bomber Command earlier in the war. Indeed, few would disagree that, after Dunkirk and after Hitler turned his military adventurism away from conquering Britain and looked east to Moscow, British (and, later, American) bombing *was* the war in the west, and it carried on being so for three years and more. Night after night, on Churchill's direct instructions, bomber crews took the battle to Germany because only they could. They were his gesture of continuing defiance, their regular raids all that prevented Hitler from peacefully enjoying his conquest of the European mainland. Tens of thousands gave their lives letting the world know that Britain had not hunkered down behind its sea defenses, that one day the Nazis would be defeated.

While this was going on, popular opinion did not inquire too closely whether the targets chosen and hit were fair. "Fair" was not the measure. Bombing military and industrial sites was preferable, but squeamishness about hitting civilians diminished after the Heinkels and Dorniers of the Luftwaffe laid waste to large areas of London, Liverpool, Coventry, and Bristol. The scruples that had prompted one RAF leader early in the war to forbid the bombing of arms factories in Germany because they were private property belonged to a lost age. Total war meant just that, and the principal arguments about bombing centered on how accurate and effective it was rather than whether or not it was ethical. Thus, an Air Ministry directive in 1942 ordered Bomber Command to focus its activities on "the morale of the enemy civilian population and in particular of the industrial workers."[21] It gave carte blanche to hit their homes as well as their places of work. A year later, after a summit meeting between Winston Churchill and the U.S. president, Franklin D. Roosevelt, in Casablanca, Bomber Command and the American Eighth Air Force were jointly instructed to make their primary objective "the progressive destruction and dislocation of the morale of the German military, industrial, and economic system and the undermining of the morale of the German people to the point where their capacity for armed resistance is fatally weakened."[22]

Harris, the head of Bomber Command since February 1942, took this order at face value. His target was German cities, and he never wavered from that thought. He continued with it throughout 1944 and into 1945. It has made a monster of him in the eyes of his many critics. They argue that area bombing, justifiable when survival was at stake, became terror bombing when victory was in sight. They claim that thousands of airmen's lives were sacrificed needlessly in pursuing a pointless vendetta against the German capital, Berlin, which did nothing to break the morale of the people or hasten the end of the war. They see the slaughter at Dresden in February 1945 as tantamount to a war crime.

We will come to these arguments in due course. For now, let us just say that Harris's men saw things—saw him—differently. With a few exceptions the men of Bomber Command we have spoken to or whose stories we have uncovered supported their commander in chief wholeheartedly. Bob Pierson is unshakable in his belief that Harris was a great leader who acted honorably. "I admire him. Giving the orders he did was a terrible responsibility, sending men like me to die. But in his mind it was the right thing to do." Arthur White, a navigator in Lancasters, made his first sortie to Germany in October 1944, long after the critics of Bomber Command say the outcome of the war was no longer in doubt and the continued bombing of German cities was unnecessary. He took no pleasure in what he was doing. "I was awestruck at the devastation we had helped to create," he said. But he felt justified then and he still does now. "Those who have tried to discredit Bomber Command should look at war as it really is. Despite Hague and Geneva Conventions, there are no rules of war. It's the aggressor who decides how you have to play, and Hitler opted for total war. Bomber Command didn't do anything the Luftwaffe hadn't done. We simply did it better."[23]

This is an accurate assessment, though acknowledgment of it has only ever been grudgingly given. Even before the war ended, the aerial bombardment of Germany was being treated as a guilty secret. Churchill distanced himself from it—and, shamefully, was the first to do so—though for years he had been happy to give Harris free rein. Six weeks after Dresden

Churchill decided, as he put it in a minute to the chiefs of staff, that "the moment has come when the question of bombing German cities for the sake of increasing terror, though under other pretexts, should be reviewed. . . . The destruction of Dresden remains a serious query against the conduct of Allied bombing."[24] It was a betrayal, the more shocking for its insouciance, as if this had never been anything to do with him. Yet, as we will see, Dresden was Churchill's baby, however much he was now keen for someone else to adopt it. Nor was it conscience that prompted the prime minister. He was thinking of postwar realities—if the destruction went on, "we shall come into control of an utterly ruined land." Although the minute was withdrawn after protests from the chiefs of staff and redrafted in a less accusatory way, its tone of moral indignation had done its damage to Harris and the men under his command. The slur on their reputation has never gone away, partly because no one stopped to hear their side of the story. Now elderly men, they need to be heard before it is too late, before there are no more of them left to tell us what really happened, why they did what they did, how it felt to be living at that awful time of death and destruction. If we are to understand them and their times, we must make the mental leap back to 1944 and 1945, to understand what it was like to live through those anguished years. And the most important step of all is not to assume that an Allied victory was a mere formality or a certainty. Too many commentators on the activities of Bomber Command and the Eighth Air Force in the last fifteen months of the war have let their judgment be colored by what they know was ahead. That most eminent of classical historians, C. V. Wedgwood, once wrote: "History is lived forward but it is written in retrospect. We know the end before we consider the beginning and we can never wholly recapture what it was to know the beginning only." But if history is to be fair to the forgotten men of Bomber Command and the American Eighth Air Force, we must try to recapture the moment— *their* moment. Only that way can we be truthful to those who lived it.

In 1944—where this story begins—the war had been going on for five years. Everyone wanted it to be over. But no one expected the end imminently, and the fighting men were understandably skeptical. In July that year, Campbell Muirhead recorded in his diary: "Forecasts that it could be over by Christmas. But I seem to remember such forecasts back in 1939!" He was right to be cautious. The Allied armies were on the European mainland but were stalled in Normandy and in Italy. V-1 bombs were raining on London and civilians had been evacuated from the capital for the first time since 1940. They did not know it, but ahead lay the serious setbacks of Arnhem and the Battle of the Bulge. Meanwhile, from their Lancasters and B-17s, bomber pilots and their crews gasped in amazement at German jet planes streaking across the skies at speeds they had never seen before. Jim O'Connor, copilot in a B-17, remembered coming under attack from two of them, "looking out of the cockpit and observing two blurs fly past with our tracer bullets trailing behind them. The gunners could not track them fast enough, even with their hydraulic turrets. They were Me-262 jet fighters—we called them 'rocket ships.' They made one pass at the formation, and then disappeared, their flying time in the air being limited. But the significance of the attack of these first jet fighters was like the rumble of a distant drum." This was a war that was far from over.

Bob Pierson had no sense of the end being close, whatever the historians might tell him now. "Our flying operations got longer as we penetrated farther and farther into Germany. On the ground we knew our armies were advancing. It had to come to an end sooner or later, but we had no idea when, and we were never overconfident about it. And I never had any doubt that we had to carry on doing what we were doing if we were to bring it to an end. What if we had stopped bombing and the war had then gone on for years and years? Then I suppose all those atrocities the Germans were carrying out and which were not uncovered until it was over, they would have continued as well. No, we were right to do what we did."

It was not until 25 March 1945 that Churchill stood with Dwight Eisenhower, supreme commander of the Allied forces, on the banks of the Rhine and declared: "My dear general, the German is whipped. We've got him. He is all through." As late as January of that year, General George Patton, a soldier of normally unbounded optimism, had written in his diary: "We can still lose this war. The Germans are colder and hungrier than we are but they fight better."[25] That is why Harris kept his men at the task he had given them of bombing Germany to its knees. Military experts have put forward plausible arguments that Hitler had in effect lost the war in 1941, when the United States joined in, in 1942, when the tide turned in the desert, in 1943, when Paulus's army surrendered at the gates of Stalingrad, or in June 1944, when Rommel failed to stop the Allies clambering onto the beaches of Normandy. So much for twenty-twenty hindsight.

The men of Bomber Command and the Eighth Air Force, with only their twenty-twenty vision to save them from dying, had no such comforting insight, only the uncertainty of tomorrow. In a fight to the finish, at the tail end of the most brutal of wars, they did not have the luxury of seeing into the future. They dared not even try. For too many of them, there would be no future at all.

FLYING FORTRESS BRITAIN

"We could have had no better brothers in arms. The American bomber crews were the bravest of the brave."
—SIR ARTHUR HARRIS

AS THEY SAT IN TROOPSHIPS CROSSING THE ATLANTIC OR ON FRESH-FROM-the-factory Boeing bombers hopscotching the polar route via Greenland and Iceland, American airmen en route to Britain were instructed in what to expect of their new home and how to behave toward its inhabitants. Don't look down your noses at them, don't show off, don't get too upset if they smell a little—they're running short of soap!—and don't ever say "bum," because it means something different over there. A little handbook prepared by the War Department in Washington and given to each man to read on the journey tried to be a gem of tact as it introduced Americans to bobbies, pubs, cricket, and guineas.[1] But its unmistakable underlying theme was that Britain was small—"You will find the British care little about size, not having the 'biggest' of many things as we do"—and impoverished, its people unfriendly and slow, their ways and customs (not to mention their language) unfathomable.

But be a good guest, the arriving airmen were urged, and don't criticize your hosts. If the British people looked "a little shopworn and grimy," it was because they had been at war for several years.

Remember you are coming from a country where your home is still safe, food is plentiful, and lights are still burning. But you are now in a war zone. British soldiers and civilians have been living under a tremendous strain. They have been bombed night after night and month after month. Thousands of them have lost their houses, their possessions, their families. Every light is blacked out every night. Gasoline, clothes, and railroad travel are hard to come by, and incomes are cut by taxes to an extent we Americans have not even approached. Food and clothing are rationed. Soap is so scarce that girls working in factories often cannot get the grease off their hands or out of their hair. So stop and think before you sound off about lukewarm beer, cold boiled potatoes, or the way English cigarettes taste.

There was a summary of do's and don'ts:

The British are more reserved in conduct than we are. Be friendly—but don't intrude where you are not wanted.

You are higher paid than the British. Don't rub it in.

Don't show off, brag, or bluster—"swank," as the British say.

Don't make fun of British speech or accents. You sound just as funny to them.

Don't try to tell the British that America won the last war. Remember that nearly a million of her best manhood died in the last war, whereas America lost 60,000 in action.

Nor do the British need to be told that their armies lost the first couple of rounds in the present war. Remember how long the British alone held Hitler off without any help from anyone. NEVER criticize the King or Queen.

But what would trouble most American airmen when they finally arrived scarcely got a mention—the weather. Major (later General) Curtis LeMay recalled the shock of fog when he flew in to a British airfield for the first time from the United States. "Can you see the runway lights?" the control tower asked the pilot of his aircraft, to which the pilot replied: "Shit, I can't even see my copilot!"[2] The War Department guidebook slid over this little local difficulty: It promised that the English climate was no different from Boston's or Seattle's and that newcomers would get used to it "eventually." But many never did. Warm beer and unwashed women they could learn to live with. But not the cold, wet, cloudy, horribly unpredictable weather.

Sergeant Eddie Picardo recalled waking up in the morning to a brilliant sunrise, only for the clouds to roll in an hour later. "Every imaginable weather system could blow in and out of that island kingdom in a twenty-four-hour period."[3] Captain Billy Southworth scribbled in his diary that it had "rained every day since we've been here. Mud a foot deep in places. Cold, wet, and black nights, wind stinging your face while your feet just have that dead cold feeling."[4] And that was on the ground. In the air, the weather would cost the lives of flyboys who had trained for disciplined formation flying in clear western skies and had never experienced anything like this before. "We were green," LeMay, one of the first arrivals with the vanguard of the Eighth Air Force in 1942, noted. Southworth concluded: "We will win this war but it will take a long time."

The Americans arrived with their own theories about bombing, exemplified by the practice targets they had trained on in the California desert. These consisted of a concrete blockhouse, which was the bull's-eye, with concentric white rings radiating out from it to five hundred feet. This was called the "circle of error." The dimensions of this practice target contained an astonishing assumption—that from nearly five miles up in the sky a bombardier could hit a target on the ground within one-tenth of a mile. This ran counter to everything the RAF had come to believe from bitter experience. In 1941, after a year's experience of bombing Germany, a crucial Air Ministry analysis of photographic evidence, the Butt Report, had revealed that only 22 percent of bomber crews who claimed to have hit their target actually got within *five miles* of it.[5] In the more heavily defended Ruhr valley, Germany's industrial heartland, where the haze from smoke and pollution was an additional problem, the figure was just 7 percent. This meant that, in the area where the bombing was expected to hit hardest in order to be most effective, only one bomb out of every fourteen was getting remotely close to its target. The revelation changed the RAF's strategy. If precision bombing was impossible, then the only alternative—short of abandoning bombing altogether[6]—was area bombing. From then on, Bomber Command targeted cities because there was a fair chance of hitting them.

This was the policy pursued by Harris when he took charge of Bomber Command in February 1942, and it had Prime Minister Winston Churchill's blessing. Harris knew that taking the fight to the enemy in this way would be costly in machines and in men, and he had to build up his numbers of both before any real onslaught could begin. In the spring of 1943 he felt ready, and from the beginning of March, large formations of RAF bombers pounded the industrial cities of the Rhineland and the Ruhr with 50,000 tons of explosives.

Then he turned his attention to Hamburg, Germany's second largest city and its biggest port. In four raids spread over ten nights, the 1.75 million inhabitants felt the force of nearly 11,000 tons of bombs, a staggering 22 pounds of explosives for each citizen, and that wasn't counting those dropped in two American daytime missions. On the last night of the aptly named Operation Gomorrah, the heat and wind created a firestorm in which glass windows melted, sugar boiled in bakery cellars, and people escaping from underground shelters onto the streets were trapped in quagmires of molten asphalt. The death toll was between 40,000 and 50,000, with as many again injured.

Bomber Command's casualties were 130 aircraft, half what they had been in earlier raids, thanks to new, secret radar-confusing equipment. For the first time, the Lancasters and Halifaxes had carried thin strips of aluminium foil known as "Window." Dropped in bundles from the bombers, this "chaff" (as the Americans called it) turned the German screens tracking the bombers into snowstorms. The British aircraft flew in on their target undetected and largely unmolested, bringing the sort of success Harris had always claimed could be achieved by a sustained bombing campaign. Hundreds of factories were put out of action; workers fled the city. Morale was so fragile that Hitler ordered a news blackout and sent in SS troops to stamp on any signs of unrest. Some top echelon Nazis saw the writing on the wall. Albert Speer, the minister for production, recorded that the raids on Hamburg put the fear of God into him. With his saturation bombing, Harris's intention had been to shock and awe. He appeared to be succeeding.

But the Americans rejected the idea of area bombing. This was partly on the moral grounds that it was wrong to wage war on citizens, but also because they regarded it as wasteful and inefficient compared with picking— and hitting—precise targets. In 1941, four months before the United States went to war, the Air Corps Tactical School produced a report for General H. H. "Hap" Arnold, commander of the USAAF, listing 124 strategic targets whose destruction would bring Germany to its knees and end the war—50 power stations, 15 bridges, 15 marshaling yards, 17 inland waterways, and 27 oil plants.[7] The military and industrial analysts drew up the list and presented it with a certainty that out-Harrised Harris. Then the mathematicians got to work. They decided that actual battle conditions would decrease the accuracy achieved in training by precisely 2.25 times. Applying this plucked-from-the-air factor,[8] they concluded that it would take 6,860 bombers to obliterate all 124 targets in a campaign lasting six months. And, in its essentials, that concept remained U.S. air policy in the European theater of operations for the next two years.

That policy required building up a large force of bombers specifically designed to be able to defend themselves against enemy fighters—hence the B-17's six gun ports (against the three in British bombers) and its designation as the Flying Fortress. They would fly in tightly held formations, covering each other with their guns like circled wagons in the old West. As an aid to precision, they were equipped with what the Americans claimed was the best bombsight in the world—the Norden bombsight. But what was seen as the main contributor to accurate bombing was that their attacks would be in daylight. They could hit their targets, they argued, because they could see them. The Americans were dismissive of the RAF for bombing only at night—and if it ever came to a frank exchange of opinions on this, they were never shy to suggest that the British were too scared to expose themselves to daytime operations. Those misplaced opinions changed as heavy daylight losses mounted, but when the first American airmen arrived, whatever the official guidance they were given to button their lips, many of them could not disguise their sense of superiority—that they felt streets ahead of the "Limey" air force in equipment, training, tactics, and sheer guts.

Accuracy was their mantra. They claimed to be able to drop a bomb into a pickle barrel from any height. A popular New York cartoon in late 1942 had a bombardier looking up from his sights and asking the pilot, "Was that address 106 Leipzigstrasse or 107?" The British believed this was nonsense. RAF navigator Arthur White was scathing of the American claims that they would hit only factories, docks, marshaling yards, and the like, leaving everything else untouched. "Sure, if they flew along singly in perfect conditions, they might be able to get a direct hit. But not with hundreds of them in strict formation, bobbing up and down and rocking in their own slipstreams and caught in a box barrage of exploding flak? No chance!"[9] Precision bombing, as historian Anthony Verrier explained, was never more than "an aspiration which *some* crews in certain conditions *occasionally* achieved."[10]

But the Americans stuck to their theory, even when the reality proved to be a long way short of the ambition. There is nothing to show that B-17s and B-24s were significantly more accurate in their bombing than the British Lancasters and Halifaxes. Indeed, the reality of sending large formations of bombers over Germany made the sort of precision the Americans claimed practically impossible. Often only the lead plane was equipped with the superaccurate Norden bombsight, and the ones behind simply dropped their bombs at the same time as the leader, even if they were flying miles behind it at the time. Inevitably, they would fall over a wide area. As a result, there was very little difference between what each air force actually did to Germany, how much damage they inflicted, how many lives they took. The Americans aimed at precise targets—and devastated whole cities in the process. The RAF devastated whole cities to be sure of destroying strategic targets. The difference was largely semantic, but the American position had one main advantage—by claiming to be precision-bombing and dissociating themselves from the taint of area bombing, the Eighth Air Force stayed out of the bitter moral argument that would eventually engulf the RAF and Bomber Command.

Many commentators dwell on the differences in theory and ideology between the two air forces and the fact that they were never resolved. They consider it a small miracle that the gaps were papered over. But the differences can blind us to the fact that the two forces worked in tandem if not always in complete harmony. The commanders—Harris of the RAF, and Carl Spaatz and Ira Eaker (and later Jimmy Doolittle) of the USAAF—got on well personally and saw no purpose in arguing. Harris, who had been the RAF's head representative in Washington for the first year of the war, knew the Americans well, and, as he wrote to a colleague when they arrived in Britain, "I and they can amicably settle things with the least inconvenience to anyone."[11] Each had an independent command. One was never subordinate to the other. They never trod on each other's toes. They also had a common problem—keeping at bay their respective military overlords, who were constantly disputing their faith in bomb power, trying to redirect their efforts, steal their crews, and generally interfere with what they were doing.[12] And they learned from each other. A U.S. intelligence briefing document when the war ended acknowledged how "these two great air forces, which started out with such entirely different ideas as to how they should operate, became more and more alike as each began to recognize its own shortcomings and the virtues of the other's methods. From different molds came similar results."[13]

The key fact was that the two entirely different approaches complemented each other, particularly since one force was flying daytime operations and the other at night. This meant round-the-clock bombardment of Germany—something on which both agreed.[14] Harris wrote to Eaker that "the effect of linking up precision bombing of selected targets in daylight by the Eighth Air Force with intensified night bombing by the RAF will unquestionably cause damage to German material and morale on a scale which the enemy will be unable to sustain."[15] Harris would later pay a handsome tribute to the Americans. He wrote in his memoirs in 1947: "If I were asked what were the relations between Bomber Command and the American bomber force I should say that the word is inapplicable to what actually happened. We and they were one force. The Americans gave us the best they had, and they gave us everything we needed as and when the need arose. We could have had no better brothers in arms. The American bomber crews were the bravest of the brave."[16] With typical self-assurance, as if that clinched the argument, he added, ". . . and I know."

The respect shown by the commander in chief was echoed down the ranks. Arthur White may have been dismissive of American claims to superhuman accuracy, but he acknowledged the bravery of the B-17 and B-24 crews. "Not many of us in the RAF relished the idea of flying in daylight to targets deep inside Germany."

To begin with, however, there were major concerns about whether the Americans were actually going to play much of an active role at all. Despite all the confident promises of 1941 and 1942, the buildup of the Eighth Air Force in Britain was slow. By the start of 1943 the Mighty Eighth had struck targets in France and Holland but had not managed to drop one single bomb on Germany, and by the middle of that year still had fewer than 300 bombers it could call on—a far cry from the 6,000-plus its deskbound Washington planners had reckoned it needed to win the war. Larger numbers were vital, given that the American planes carried a bomb load that was half that of a Lancaster. It never ceased to amaze Eighth Air Force crews how the British planes managed to struggle into the air with so much weight on board. But they had to concede that it would take two B-17s to carry as much firepower to the enemy as one Lancaster.[17]

When the B-17s and B-24s did go into battle, another major problem presented itself. The notion of the self-defending bomber formation was quickly (and literally) blown to bits. The "fortresses" proved alarmingly pregnable. Daylight operations—as the British had always reasoned—might mean the target was more visible and easier to hit, but so, too, was the bomber. The Luftwaffe fighter squadrons were having a field day. American air tactics, devised in training by LeMay, were based on the "combat box," a V-shaped formation of eighteen bombers at staggered heights, which joined up with two other boxes to form a combat wing. And a wing would have as many as six hundred .50 caliber machine guns protecting it. "The idea was to interlock fire and to create an impenetrable wall while moving unquestioningly forward in step with the man to the left and the man to the right."[18] But the thinking behind it was barely more sophisticated than eighteenth-century squares of infantry, and it had the same disadvantage—it was fine only as long as the ranks held solid.

Maintaining the integrity of the ranks proved difficult even before they came under attack. When Bert Stiles, copilot of a B-17, arrived in England in 1944, he quickly realized how little practice he had had at flying in formation. He was right to worry. The skill and discipline to maintain height and distance when all hell was breaking loose around you could not be learned in the clear, friendly skies of Texas. When he experienced the reality, it shocked him. "From the ground," he recalled, "a formation is always static and always beautiful. It looks deadly and simple and easy." In reality, chaos was always close to breaking out, "with pilots screaming at squadron leaders, 'Get us out of here, we're in prop wash,' and group leaders pleading with the wing leaders, and the wing leaders weaving in and out to stay in formation. A low squadron overruns a lead squadron and a high squadron leader chops his throttles and almost piles his wingmen into his trailing edges." In these conditions, B-17s were hard work. "She's a dream girl if you can set up the autopilot and coast along. You can have a cocktail party in the nose and a dance in the bomb bay and she will just go on flying until the gas runs out. But formation flying is something else. Then you dream of anything little that flies by touch, a glider even, anything but this big, heavy monster that has to be heaved around the sky."[19]

When the formation came under attack, it was even harder to maintain shape. Over France and Germany, as stragglers fell behind and nerves faltered, it was too easy for the high-speed German fighters, the FW-190s and Me-109s, to blast through the ranks and break them up. Luftwaffe pilots quickly learned to attack head-on and from twelve o'clock high, hurtling in at terrifying closing speeds of around 600 mph in the knowledge that they had the agility to pull away at the last minute. It took a brave Fortress flier to maintain his course and not duck and dive away—breaking the formation in the process. American aircrew soon came to realize they were up against a tough and resourceful enemy. When a propaganda poster was put up on U.S. bases mocking a new German fighter with the caption "Who's afraid of the new Focke-Wulf?" some grim joker wrote "Sign here," and everyone in the group put his name down, including the group commander.[20]

The Germans were also accelerating their production of fighters. Output in 1943 was increasing every month, and there were fears that, before long, as many as three thousand would be lined up against the Allied bombers. And the Americans had nothing to counter them in the air. The original U.S. strategic plan had called for ninety-eight groups of bombers to be sent to Britain but only ten groups of fighter planes to defend them, and even then their role was envisaged as protecting the bases rather than escorting the bombers on their missions. Now more were going on escort duties—backed up by RAF Spitfires and Hurricanes from Fighter Command—but their limited fuel capacity made them ineffective. They could ride shotgun on the streams as far as the German border but then had to turn back, leaving the bombers unprotected for the business end of their missions. The Eighth Air Force—its men popularly dubbed by the British as overpaid, oversexed, and over here—was in reality understrength, underprotected, and under constant attack.

Casualties soared. Statistics showed that the average crewman of an American bomber would be lucky to complete fifteen of the twenty-five missions that comprised a tour. Captain Billy Southworth noted in his diary that his group was down to half its original strength after three months. Captain John Regan recalled his group losing 113 crews—more than 1,100 men—in this early period. Replacements came and went with mortifying speed. "One evening I met a gunner who had arrived from home only that day and I said I was really sorry but there was a crew short of a gunner and he would have to fly the next day. He went on the mission and was shot down."[21] Even the generals got scared. One crew carried "Iron Ass" LeMay on an operation, and they were surprised when he came on board wearing *two* parachutes, one on his chest and one on his back. Then, as they arrived at the target and came under fire from Messerschmitts and flak, a voice that the crew swore was his could be heard over the intercom yelling. "Get us out of here! Get us out of here!" It went on until the flight engineer yelled back "and tells him to shut up or he'll knock his teeth down his throat. When it's all over the general wanted to know who said it but nobody would say." The crew didn't feel critical of the general. "Hell, we were all scared." But they were a little nonplussed when they later read in *Stars and Stripes,* the service magazine, that he had received a Silver Star for his part in the mission.[22]

Despite the mounting losses and LeMay's firsthand experience, there was no turning back for the USAAF chiefs. In the face of growing skepticism, Spaatz stuck to his guns, inadequate as his men's weapons were proving to be. He was under intense pressure from Harris to abandon daytime bombing and join Bomber Command in nighttime operations. Together they would fill the night skies of Europe with Allied planes and reduce the enemy's cities to dust. Spaatz declined the invitation. He wrote that he was "just as convinced as ever that the operations of the day bombers, if applied in sufficient force from the United Kingdom, cannot be stopped by any means the enemy now has."[23] But he was running out of manpower, as was clearly shown when a proposal was made to increase the number of missions necessary to complete a tour. It was rejected only because of the serious effect it would have on morale. The limit of twenty-five was proving academic anyway. The first crew to reach this figure was given a massive publicity boost. The men of the *Memphis Belle* became heroes in mid-1943 and were flown home to be fêted and celebrated. To the cynical, their singular achievement begged a terrible question: What had happened to the hundreds of other crews who had started out before them? One bomb group, the 306th, had lost twenty-seven of its thirty-five crews in eight months. In the words of historian Gerald Astor, in the summer of 1943, "Survival of the Eighth Air Force as a bomber weapon was by no means assured. It hardly offered the prospect of a long life to its members." A change of policy was essential.

In June 1943, the Joint Chiefs of Staff in London and Washington came to the conclusion that Germany could not be knocked out from the air unless the Luftwaffe was knocked out first. A new interim target was laid down in what became known as the Pointblank Directive—to check the growth and reduce the strength of the German day and night fighter forces. This would be done by direct attacks on the industries on which they depended. Harris interpreted this as consent to continue his policy of bombing German cities and stepped up his campaign against the Ruhr, Germany's industrial heartland, before switching his attention to Hamburg.[24] The Americans took it as an instruction to concentrate their "precision" bombing efforts on factories making aircraft frames, engines, and ball bearings. This new order was a tall one, however, since many of these vital factories had been evacuated to locations deep inside Germany and far beyond the point to which the bombers could fly under the protection of their own fighters. More lives would have to be sacrificed now to save lives in the future. It would be a race against time to see if the Americans ran out of bombers and crews before they had caused enough damage to slow German fighter production.

The first missions were far from encouraging. In one week, 100 planes were lost in attacks on Germany, leaving the Eighth Air Force with barely 200 operational bombers. A daring, long-distance attack on an oil-refining complex at Ploesti in Romania ran into savage opposition, and fifty-seven planes failed to return. Replacements flown in from the factories in America could hardly keep up with the losses. But 376 B-17s were scraped together for an attack on an aircraft plant at Regensburg producing 200 new Messerschmitts a month. The formation was ambushed by 200 German fighters, some armed for the first time with rockets. Sixty Fortresses failed to return, and another twenty-seven limped home so badly damaged they never flew again. The loss of life was terrifying, as was the effect on morale. The crews in a fifth of the planes that took off for a subsequent raid on Stuttgart found reasons to turn back before they reached the target. Casualties continued to mount. In October 1943, a trip to bomb a ball-bearing factory in Schweinfurt resulted in another sixty B-17s lost, a casualty rate of more than 25 percent. If this continued, new crews would be lucky to last five missions.

As so often before, on the Schweinfurt raid the Germans struck after the American P-47 fighters escorting the formation—our "little friends," as the bomber crews called them—had turned for home, their fuel situation critical. One pilot recalled: "German fighters were suddenly on us from every point of the compass." Bill Fleming remembered a brief and awful silence after the "little friends" had gone.

We were a hundred miles inside Germany and we heard that about 200 enemy fighters were coming in on us. We expected them to attack for thirty to forty-five minutes before they had to break off to land and refuel. That was what usually happened. They duly hit us, took out several of our planes and left, and we all relaxed. Then someone hollered, "My God, here comes another wave!" and this continued all the way to the target. We bombed, turned, came back and the same thing happened as on the way out, one wave after another. It was one huge fight for six hours. Finally we ran out of ammunition and all they had to do was come in and shoot down what was left of us because there was nobody to fire back. But evidently they were just as tired as we were because they broke off. That day was the one time I got so scared I vomited all over myself.[25]

October 14, 1943, went down as "Black Thursday" in Eighth Air Force annals.

Its generals claimed the attacks as victories and in messages to Washington said the targets had been totally destroyed. This wasn't so, but that didn't stop Arnold from claiming that "we are wearing them down." The truth was expressed by Lieutenant Colonel Beirne Lay, who had flown on the fateful Regensburg mission: "Without fighter escort all the way to the target and all the way back, heavy bombardment can't operate in daylight against this type of opposition."[26] The message was clear—the Eighth Air Force would have to contemplate switching to night operations, losing enormous face in the process but also ending the round-the-clock nature of the Allied bombardment of Germany. If this happened, it would be a serious double blow to the war effort. The Pointblank Directive had ordered the skies cleared of Luftwaffe fighters not just to enable Bomber Command and the Eighth Air Force to bomb German cities unhindered. The Allies also had to have command of the air to ensure success for the planned invasion of the European mainland (now seen to be an inevitability by all except Harris and his American counterparts, still convinced that air power could finish the job alone). The Combined Chiefs of Staff had set May 1944 as the deadline for Pointblank to be achieved in order for that invasion to go ahead in the summer. The task now looked hopeless.

Over the winter of 1943–44, the Eighth Air Force rethought, regrouped, and reinforced. Long-distance targets beyond the range of escort fighters were abandoned. Bremen, Cologne, and the Ruhr became the effective limit of penetration. New battle technologies were tried out, notably chaff, the antiradar smokescreen of tinfoil which the RAF called Window, and experiments made with anything that might give the bombers some more protection so they could continue the assault on Germany while they awaited the arrival of the long-range fighters that, in the end, would be the only real solution to their problems.

Priority was at last given to increasing the range of existing fighters. P-47 Thunderbolts and P-38 Lightnings were equipped with extra fuel tanks that could be jettisoned when empty, a simple enough idea but one that had taken an inordinate amount of time to implement. Some of this could be put down to stubbornness on the part of USAAF commanders, reluctant to admit that their impregnable Fortresses were in need of fighter protection. Bureaucracy—of the sort that in Whitehall provoked Harris into asking British civil servants whose side they were on—hindered rather than helped. Drop tanks for the Thunderbolt had been under discussion since late 1942 and there had been lengthy arguments among officials over the size—200 gallons, 125 gallons, 100 gallons?—the composition—steel or paper?—and where they should be made—in the United States or in Britain, where they were needed? The upshot was that it was not until the end of 1943 that the supply of the tanks came anywhere close to meeting the demand.[27] While pen pushers postcrastinated bomber formations had been flying undefended into Germany and aircrew had been dying in their thousands.

As 1943 turned into 1944, matters improved dramatically. Replacement men and machines poured across the Atlantic to join the fight. Recruiting sergeants were less choosy. They took Ira Weinstein, though he was only five feet tall and every time he went in a plane the controls had to be specially adjusted for him. Weinstein, from the Chicago Jewish community, was desperate to join the war against the Nazis and a slot was found for him as a bombardier.[28] John Cadden remembered that during his training there must have been an urgent need for gunners because "being color-blind didn't seem to matter too much. They had some balls of yarn and asked you to pick out the red one. If you got the wrong one, they'd say: 'Now, you know it's not that. Try again.' "[29] More and more of the new bombers were the very latest B-24s, carrying a payload a third larger than the aging B-17s and with twice the range. Its purpose was expressed in its nickname—it was "the Liberator." Thirteen new bomb groups arrived in Britain to swell the ranks, and more agricultural land in eastern England was commandeered. Airfields with lengthy runways and makeshift accommodations sprang up almost overnight. Within months, forty thousand English acres had been transformed into miniature American townships; in all, forty-three airfields were now in operation. The Eighth Air Force, having been fought to very nearly a standstill by the Luftwaffe in the autumn of 1943, was pulling out all the stops to make sure it won the spring 1944 campaign.

The growing armada was largely grounded by atrocious weather for the first seven weeks of 1944, but then, in the final week of February, the now mightier Eighth, supported by the RAF's Bomber Command, went in search of the German aircraft industry. Clear weather was predicted for the operation, and American commanders fumed, as they always did, when the forecast faltered. But the raid went ahead and, in what became known as "Big Week," formations of up to a thousand bombers took off through snow flurries and headed east to pound cloud-covered Messerschmitt factories in distant parts of Germany. Almost an equal number of fighters equipped with 150-gallon jettisonable tanks flew beside them, and the bombers and the fighters engaged the Luftwaffe in a bloody battle along the way. And those who returned home in one piece set off the next day to repeat the process in worsening weather conditions.

In five days the Americans dropped more bombs on Germany than in the whole of 1943. Their targets were deep in Germany, places such as Leipzig, Brunswick, Gotha, Augsburg, and Stuttgart. The fight was hard—157 bombers and 33 fighters from the Eighth Air Force were lost, plus a further 58 bombers from the 15th Air Force, based in Italy, a terrible toll.[30] In backup night operations, RAF Bomber Command lost a further 140 aircraft. But the enemy lost more. It was claimed that 600 Luftwaffe fighters were shot down, 1,000 half-built planes destroyed on their assembly lines, and a further 1,000 not produced while the factories were rebuilt or relocated. The figures were almost certainly exaggerations, but it is undeniable that the balance had at last tipped in favor of the Eighth Air Force. Its bombers would not be forced to abandon the daylight skies over Germany after all. General Arnold later reported to Congress that "the week of February 20 to 26, 1944, may well be classed by future historians as marking a decisive battle in history—one as decisive and of greater world importance than Gettysburg."[31]

For the Germans, the loss of pilots was more devastating than the loss of machines. Fighter production was set back but not halted, and it would pick up again within months, most of it now driven into underground factories. But men could not be turned out on conveyor belts in the same way. The Luftwaffe was scraping around to find trained pilots. Rest periods for sick and wounded airmen were slashed on Hitler's direct instructions. Encouraged by intelligence reports of rising German losses, the Eighth Air Force switched tactics again. It had pulverized Luftwaffe production on the ground. Now it would take on its fighter planes in the air. A major attack on Berlin shortly after "Big Week" was designed not to avoid enemy fighters but deliberately to lure them into an engagement, to come out and be shot down. This was a war of attrition, and the Eighth Air Force was determined that, with all of America now pouring its trained aircrew into battle, the last man standing would not be German.

The difference had been made by the arrival in large numbers of the P-51 Mustang fighter. When fitted with a British-made Rolls-Royce engine, the type used in the latest Spitfires, this was 50 mph faster than an FW-190, could turn tighter than an Me-109 but, more importantly, had a range that would take it—and the bomber formations it protected—right into the heart of Germany, to Berlin and beyond. The first of these fighters were used in December 1943, but it took a while for production to build up. Their impact was instant. Jim O'Connor, a B-24 copilot, thought it a momentous day in his war when, in July 1944, his squadron took to the air and saw they were being escorted by Mustangs. "To hear the cry of a Wing or Group Commander: 'Bandits in the area!' over the radio, and to see the Mustangs drop their auxiliary wing fuel tanks and hurry to the scene of action, was a beautiful sight. They were largely responsible for the continuation of the bomber offensive and the saving of numerous crews."[32]

The Luftwaffe lost 10 percent of its fighter pilots in one month, and those who survived were increasingly reluctant to be drawn into a gunfight. Secret high-level military messages intercepted by British intelligence talked of critical shortages of men and materials. The Japanese naval attaché in Berlin reported to his masters in Tokyo that that Allied claims to have destroyed a fifth of German fighter plane production were accurate. The Germans were "being crushed by overwhelming superiority." The result, according to the official history of British intelligence, was that, by the beginning of April 1944, the USAAF had established daytime superiority over western Europe, including the Reich itself, which the Allies were to retain for the remainder of the war.[33] It was a remarkable turnaround from Black Thursday less than six months earlier. But the victory was still a long way off. The battalions of airmen flooding into Britain from the United States had turned the tide. Now, alongside the men of Bomber Command, they had a war to win.

In that summer of 1944, Walter Hughes, a farmer's son from Santa Barbara, California, found himself approaching the coast of Northern Ireland and flying through cloud so thick he could not even see the wingtips of his shiny, brand-new B-24. It was a worrying moment, not least because a little over a week earlier he had signed for it at Hamilton Field, near San Francisco, agreeing that if it was lost through his negligence, the War Department could come after him for its $237,000 cost (plus $15,000 for the on-board equipment). With his crew he had flown it from the western to the eastern seaboard of America, that alone a big adventure for a boy who had never left his home state of California before. From the sky he looked down for the first time on the country whose interests he was about to risk his life in battle to protect. Then they were pointed northeast, across the icy wastes of Canada toward Great Britain. It was a well-worn trail. Thousands of bombers and their crews had been delivered in a similar way. They were now flying over to Britain at a rate of 450 a month. Not all of them made it. A tragically large number were lost, crashing somewhere in the frozen wastes of the remote North Atlantic, their newly qualified pilots unable to cope with the conditions or their newly built aircraft proving defective.

Hughes landed in Anglesey in north Wales, where the plane he and his crew had come to love was taken away from them. Thus far they were just delivery boys. An experienced crew would get this mint-condition machine, not a bunch of rookies. When they went to war, it would be in older aircraft, "combat-weary clunkers," as Hughes called them. "We were never again to find a ship so richly endowed as the one we flew over. We often yearned for her powerful new engines."[34]

Jim O'Connor was flying a bomber making that same crossing. As they flew into Gander, the stopping-off base in Newfoundland, Canadian antiaircraft gunners were firing practice rounds into the sky. The crew looked at each other nervously, knowing this was just a foretaste of what lay ahead. Leaving Gander and heading out across the Atlantic, O'Connor heard a soft farewell from the control tower. It was a woman's voice wishing them "Goodbye and good luck." He was touched. "Flying into the unknown, it felt good that somebody cared." The trip was one long nightmare. Bad weather closed in, ice formed on the wings, and they plowed on in eerie silence, each of them aware that, with no stars for the navigator to steer by, they could easily drift off course and miss the landfall entirely. Six hundred miles out at sea, they picked up a homing beacon from Northern Ireland. That was comforting—unless it was a fake radio signal they had been warned about, sent out by German planes to lead them the wrong way. But they followed it—what else could they do?—and as the sun came up they looked down on lush green fields.

They landed at a base near Belfast, handed over their plane, and took a flight on a transport aircraft to the mainland. They arrived on a typical English summer day—cold and rainy—and were sent to a transit camp close to London. "At night, off in the distance, we could see the prowling searchlight beams and the bursts of antiaircraft shells over the city, which was under attack from V-1 flying bombs." Now there could be no doubts. They really were in what until then had just been a set of initials—ETO, the European Theater of Operations. As the sentry at the gate said to them: "Welcome to the combat zone, guys!"

The starkness of this could be sobering. To Bert Stiles, the realization that the rehearsal was over and the curtain was about to go up on the main show came very hard. Shortly after his arrival on his operational base, he was woken one night by the noise of a drunken airman from another crew being carried in by two of his friends.

That guy really had the bright stare of death in his eyes. He looked at me and said: "So you made the team, eh?" and then he just laughed until the whole room was shaking from it. His friends took him off to his bed but then they came back and one of them said: "That baby's got it bad. He won't last much longer. He's seen too many guys go down." When they had gone, I lay there for a while. I thought about all the guys who had slept in this same bed in the last four months. Apparently there had been eight of them, and they were all dead or in some German prisoner-of-war camp or hiding in a French ditch somewhere.

But I wasn't scared. I was just wondering what I was doing here at all. I'd been building up to this for a long time. At school, I would sit drinking Cokes with some girl, reading airplane magazines and dreaming of this. And now we were really here, ready to go to war, to knock off the Germans. Yet I knew nothing about war. I didn't feel like some Polish pilots I had met who wanted to kill every German in the world. I'd never been shot at or bombed. War was something I knew about from books and movies and magazines. It wasn't in my blood. But now I was here, and the whole idea was to blow up as much of Germany as possible, and to do so from way up high, so I wouldn't know if any women or little kids got in the way. The more I thought of it, the uglier it seemed. What I really wanted to be doing was wading out into the surf at Santa Monica and then lying in the sun all afternoon. Instead I would soon be beating up a town, or an oil plant, or a steel factory. It seemed a pretty futile way to live.

There was an even more disturbing welcome for Walter Hughes when he finally got to his destination in East Anglia that summer of 1944, one that sent shivers down his spine.

My crew and I were in our hut listening to Axis Sally, the American woman who broadcast propaganda from Berlin on the shortwave radio. Suddenly we heard her say: "We welcome Lieutenant Hughes and his crew to the 93rd Bomb Group. We wish to assure them that we are planning a much warmer welcome when they come to Germany." I was shocked! How did they know about me when everything was supposed to be secret? I discovered others had had the same greeting. Apparently German intelligence was really good, partly because they had so many prisoners after each mission and they pieced together the little bits of information they got from them.

But those eerie words from Berlin played tricks with his mind and did little to settle him as he fought to find his feet in this strange country he had landed in. He felt desperately homesick. The base he had arrived at was on flat farmland and was little more than Nissen huts, seemingly thrown up almost overnight, grouped around a runway. The living quarters were spartan, the food reassuringly American but out of cans. He rarely ventured beyond the gates of the base to find home comforts. He preferred the comforts of this American island to the charms (or horrors) of the bigger island outside. The England he had glimpsed on the way in—where small boys scrabbled in the gutters for pennies thrown by "the Yanks"—seemed to him to be rather a primitive place.

Jim O'Connor, on the other hand, quickly felt at home when he arrived at Knettishall, the village in Suffolk around which his American air base was built, and was soon getting on with the locals.

You only had to climb over a wall from our barracks to be in the center of the village. There was a row of stone cottages whose housewives did our laundry for a few shillings and a bar of American Family soap. It also had a deserted medieval church and one pub, which had a couple of wooden benches and one keg of nut-brown ale. The local farmers farmed the land all around us. A field of beautiful red poppies carpeted the pastureland during the summer and early autumn.

It was England's rabbits that Ira Weinstein, a bombardier based at Tibenham in Norfolk, liked. As he drove to headquarters with his bomb-strike photographs, "I would sit on the bumper of the jeep and shoot them. I'd bring back a dozen at a time for the mess hall sergeant, and in return he would give me a can of steak, which I loved, whereas I couldn't stand the mutton he usually dished up."

Life on the base was pretty easygoing. O'Connor remembered there was a rigid hierarchy based on respect rather than rank, depending on how many missions a crew had flown.

The standard put-down to newcomers like me was "Get some missions in, Rookie!" But it was all good-natured. Everyone happily went about his business doing his particular job, from the cooks to the combat crews to the long-suffering ground crews who worked day and night, sleeping in tents on the flight line with their particular beloved bomber. Military discipline was reasonably relaxed. On my crew there was little if any distinction between officers and enlisted men and we were all on a first-name basis. Generally, morale was high, flying efficient, and everyone was gung ho to win the war, survive, and return home.

The bases were set up like mini-Americas with all the comforts of home. This was the result of a deliberate decision by General Eaker. He had contemplated the idea of the incoming Americans being put on pretty much the same footing as the British in terms of food and facilities. But he recommended instead that his men should be able to buy American tobacco, candies, sandwiches, coffee, and toilet articles on their bases. Precious space would be found for these items on the overstretched convoys bringing supplies from the other side of the Atlantic. This was not in order to coddle the U.S. soldier, he explained, or show him special consideration. Even less was it to emphasize the disparity between American standards of living or scales of pay and the British. It was because he recognized "the paramount importance of morale for air combat and maintenance crews and appreciate some of the more important factors in keeping it high."[35] Just as important, he also insisted on rubber boots for every man arriving in Britain because of the rain and the mud.

On their homes-away-from-home, the boys could play baseball outside if the weather was good. If not, it was an endless poker school inside. There was plenty of entertainment provided—films, music, clubs to relax and drink in—and stars visited from home regularly to boost morale. Eddie Picardo remembered the thrill of dancing to Glenn Miller and the Army Air Corps band. He was torn between jitterbugging and jiving with the girls he dated or dancing cheek to cheek with them. "I liked holding them close because you never knew if this might be the last time you would ever be so lucky to have a woman in your arms." And Picardo had had a lot of women in his arms in his time, though he had never expected English girls to be among them. Being in Britain was a great surprise to him. He had always set his sights on fighting the Japanese. Their assault on Pearl Harbor had angered him and he wanted revenge. Democracy thwarted his ambition. In the final stages of training, his B-24 crew was given a choice of the Pacific or Europe. "I wanted badly to go to the Pacific but eight of our crew were dead set on joining the Eighth Air Force in England, so England it was."

He left behind in the United States a string of brokenhearted girls, one, it seemed, at every one of the training bases he had been at. The best had been the sexy Italian girl with a scary mother, who "would scrutinize me as if to say: 'No monkey business. I want my daughter back just the way you found her!'" Picardo had other ideas, and so, it turned out, did Gina, the girl. They went to a dance and drove home to park in the basement garage under her house.

I turned off the car lights, disappointed, thinking that was the end of our date. Then she said softly, "My mother's sleeping. We can do it here." I yelled out, "What! Are you crazy?" What if her mother came down and found us! We would be in a helluva lot of trouble. But Gina didn't care. She unbuttoned her blouse, took off her bra and got in the back seat. I figured, what the hell, sooner or later everyone dies. But when we were finished, I got the hell out of there as quickly as I could. *I was more scared in that garage than I ever would be in flak over Germany.*

Picardo was determined not to be tempted into a serious relationship. Going off to war, he did not want a wife or a girlfriend waiting for him. The girls had been queuing up for Billy Southworth, too, but he felt the same way. On his last night before setting off for England he wrote in his diary: "I'll never marry Helene, hard as she's trying. Babs proposed persistently to me last night, second date. She's very pretty but I wouldn't have her on a silver platter. There's Ann, wealthy in looks but lacks something. Ruth had everything but was too fond of herself. Betty a swell gal but too set in ways and lacks oomph. Cliffy might be a possibility, haven't known her long enough. I'd like to get into this damn war and return so I can settle down."[36]

From their bases in East Anglia, most of the Americans ventured to London, to marvel at the history around them. Many would tell later of running into friendly locals who made them welcome, of taxi drivers who drove them round the capital for free, claiming "it's the least I could do for you Yanks." Ira Weinstein tracked down a Jewish delicatessen where one could still get a corned beef sandwich—virtually unknown in the war. But to a regular Lothario like Picardo, London meant girls. It was in a pub there that he met his "real tomato!"—a girl named Becky—and spun her his usual line about coming from Hollywood. It worked. It always did.

"We dined and danced and made love. I remember our first night to-gether, hugging on the bed. I told her, 'You're about to be kissed by a tail gunner with pork chop lips. I'm going to put a smile on your face that will last you the rest of your life.' " Only later did she tell him of the sadness that not even his kisses could make better—her fighter pilot husband had died in the North African desert. "I never met anyone in England who didn't have a tragic story to share," he reminisced ruefully years later.

When she told me about him there was nothing I could say except "Sorry." So many of my buddies were meeting the same end. I thought to myself, I could be next. I wondered if he had carried a picture of her around with him. Boy, I know I would have done if I had been lucky enough to be her husband. I hope he looked at her photo one last time be-fore he got in his fighter the day he died.

Or maybe she was lying. After all, I told her I was from Hollywood and I wasn't telling the truth. Maybe her husband was not killed and was away and she just wanted some fun before he came home on leave. Who knows? Maybe we all lived a lie in those days. We were all ships passing in the night. But in the middle of war, you had to live as intensely as pos-sible. There was always a danger of instant death. You went on a bomb-ing mission and you didn't know if you were coming back, but also you could go on a pass to London and be killed by a German buzz bomb.

He knew this for a fact. After a night together, she left the hotel they had stayed in ahead of him, walked out into the early morning gloom, and turned right down Piccadilly. He came out thirty seconds later, turning left out of the door, racing to the station to get a train back to base. The explo-sion of the V-2 rocket sent him reeling flat on his back.

I looked up to see one side of the hotel weaving back and forth. I thought I was going to die. I got up and ran as fast as I could.

I never heard from Becky again, and I had no address, so I couldn't contact her. I didn't know if she was alive or dead. But that was the way it was then. You met somebody, had a good time, then simply never saw them again. She disappeared from my life. I've never stopped wondering if that V-2 missed me and got her instead. It exploded two blocks away from the hotel and she had left half a minute before me. That could have made all the difference. Who knows? I hope she still had a smile on her face . . .

The presence of the Americans on British soil would touch many people. And now, individually, they would be staying longer. The powers that be of the USAAF had finally bitten the bullet, risked a slump in morale, and increased the length of a tour. It had been upped first from twenty-five missions to thirty, then shortly after to thirty-five. Various official reasons were given, but they all came down to one thing—too many experienced crews were being lost for the veterans to be allowed to go home when there was still a job to finish. It was not a popular move—except for one twelve-year-old English boy by the name of David Hastings. He was obsessed with the Yanks and their huge planes and spent all his spare time hanging around the bases. Eventually he was adopted as a mascot by one B-24 crew and, in particular, by its pilot, Al Dexter. By the middle of 1944, Dexter should have completed his tour and been safely back home in St. Paul, Minnesota. Now he was forced to stay longer, and young Hastings would get more precious time with his hero.

The lad had been aviation mad all his life. His father, who had served in the Royal Flying Corps in the First World War, had arranged his son's first flight at an aero club at the age of six. Then the growing boy had watched dogfights in the skies over their home in Norwich during the Battle of Britain in 1940. He had also seen action closer at hand when he was bombed while playing cricket at school. "A German plane came over, machine-gunned the field and dropped a bomb which demolished the scout hut. I threw myself into a slit trench and was in trouble when I got home because my cricket whites were covered in mud." He knew how lucky he had been—"A house five doors up from us was hit and everyone was killed. They were great friends of ours."[37]

In the spring of 1944, the news that B-24s were arriving at RAF Horsham St. Faith, a base just outside Norwich, sent Hastings and a school friend racing there on their bicycles. "We watched them land and then waited and waited until the evening when the gates opened and out came all these smart-looking Americans. We were open-mouthed in amazement when one guy came straight up and said, 'Here, kid, have this,' and gave me a silver quarter. That was my first experience with Americans." The introduction was worth the caning he got at school next day for having played hooky. Nor did the drubbing cool his enthusiasm. "Their being here gave me an amazing feeling. We had been through black times, what with Dunkirk and the Blitz, but their arrival was like a bright light at the end of a tunnel. You suddenly thought that if these young men were willing to come thousands of miles to help us then there was no way we were going to lose the war."

It was at Hethel, another Eighth Air Force base on the outskirts of Norwich, that Hastings met the man he would come to idolize.

I was standing by the fence waiting for the bombers to return and the ground-crew chief, who was waiting too, came over to chat. Then, when his plane had landed, he sent the pilot over to me. This lieutenant strode toward me and said: "I believe you would like to look at my airplane," and he picked me up and lifted me over the fence. We started to walk toward the B-24 when a military policeman rode up in a jeep, and I thought I was going to be thrown out. But, to my amazement, the pilot stood up for me. He told the policeman: "Sergeant, you have a choice of three things—you can arrest me, and that's great because I won't have to fly any more missions, or you can shoot me, and I don't think you'll do that, or you can get your goddamn ass out of here." The military police never bothered me again after that!

The lieutenant showed me round his B-24. The truck had already arrived to take him and his crew to debriefing but he made them wait—which was an amazing thing to do for someone who had just come back from a dangerous mission over Germany, who had just put his life on the line. And then he said anytime I wanted to come back I would be welcome. It was unbelievable. I had been adopted by a crew. They were so friendly. You could never get onto RAF bases but the Americans loved showing us kids around and even allowed us on the airplanes. They would let us sit in the cockpit and the gun turrets. And when the plane came back from a mission we were allowed to go through it from nose to tail collecting up the boxes of boiled sweets [hard candies] and chewing gum they had all been issued with when they set out. We could keep whatever was left. I also went back to the mess hall with them, and had ice cream and chicken, things we hadn't seen for years.

Some mornings I would go out to the base early and see them off to France or to Germany, and, if it was in school holidays, I would wait there all day until they got back. The return could be very sad because they took some awful losses. You would suddenly realize that the B-24 from the next stand hadn't come back and that meant a whole crew was gone, a crew I'd probably talked to, just wandered over to and nattered to. I prayed hard every day that Al's plane would be there in formation coming home and I breathed a great sigh when I spotted her. As soon as she landed we would run to see her. Al would always put an arm around my shoulder and walk me around the aircraft showing me any battle damage. It became a tradition, and I discovered years later that the crew regarded me as their lucky charm. On days I wasn't there when they got back they used to worry. I'm glad I didn't know at the time, because that would have been a heavy burden for a small boy. But when I was there, Al never changed that routine, even the time one of the crew was killed.

When they landed that day we could tell something was wrong because the crew were all very quiet and we weren't allowed to go through the plane collecting up the sweet boxes. I could see from the holes and the blood that somebody had been badly hurt. It was the top gunner, Mike. I saw blood all over his dome and I watched him being carried away. I thought he had just been wounded and I was stunned when I was told he was dead. It hit me hard. He was the baby of the crew and not much older than me. He had lied about his age to join up. He'd only been out of school a couple of years.

A sight that never failed to thrill young David Hastings was hundreds of B-17s and B-24s assembling in the skies over East Anglia. He remembered watching bomber after bomber rise from the ground and "go round and round over Norfolk, forming up into squadrons and then into wings and then into groups and finally into the division." There had been hours of meticulous preparation and strict military routine before this point was reached. The pre-op drill began the day before a mission. Details of crews on standby were posted at the squadron office in the morning and that afternoon warning lights would flash in the crew quarters to indicate that the mission was on. The whole airfield switched to combat mode. All personnel were confined to the base, and the camp's bars and clubs shut up shop. No alcohol would be served from then on. That night the crews did their best to sleep—some did so easily, like babes; others fretted. Four hours before takeoff, they were woken up by an orderly. Walter Hughes recalled: "Outside we could hear a muted roar as the ground crews preflighted the engines. Wash, shave, dress in regular uniform and head for breakfast—stale eggs, greasy fried baloney, toast. I preferred sweet biscuits and the occasional apple or orange that I kept in my hut. It meant I got an extra hour of sleep and it didn't make me sick on the mission as the greasy stuff did."

Picardo hated those early starts, a flashlight shining in your eye and rousted out of bed while it was still dark. The earliest he recalled was 2:00 A.M. "We would dress ourselves still half asleep. Then a truck would come by and take us over to the mess hall for breakfast." But O'Connor relished those predawn moments, "cycling to the mess hall with the cool damp night air clearing our brains. Always there was a coldness in our bones, even in summer. The big deal before a mission was two real eggs for breakfast, instead of mushy powered eggs. They were cold storage eggs from the States and of some antiquity. Occasionally a sleepy-eyed chick would look up at you."

After breakfast came the briefing. In Picardo's mind, they were always doom-laden occasions. "Too many American fliers learned at those briefings where they were going to die. It was difficult to come to terms with the knowledge of what the day might bring—we all knew some of us might not be around in a few hours' time. Sometimes you could see people looking around the room—wondering who might not be there for the next brief, or the one after that."

Hughes, on the other hand, as a pilot and skipper of his crew, had too much to take in at those briefings to spend time worrying.

Mission briefing for officers was an hour and forty-five minutes before takeoff. Everyone had to be in and seated when the Group Commander walked in. "Ten-hut!" Everyone popped to attention! "At ease!" He spoke for a few minutes about any problem that needed attention, then he turned the meeting over to the briefing officer, who announced the target and had the curtains pulled away from a large wall map at the end of the room. The course was shown by red string to the target, with a pin at each point where a turn was made. The weather officer gave the forecast for clouds and winds. The intelligence officer briefed us on expected opposition—fighters, how many guns and what size—and on our own fighter escorts, who they were, when they would pick us up, and where they would leave us. The armaments officer told us what bombs we had on board and whether they had special fuses which had to be activated when we were in the air.

As they filed out, often in silence if the target seemed a particularly risky one, some men peeled off to the chaplain's office. Picardo was a regular visitor to the Roman Catholic priest and always received Holy Communion and the last rites before taking off. "The priest would deliver the 'Our Father' and also a short prayer asking for God's special protection for us on the mission. After this, we went to get our parachutes. I never worked out which was more help—the priest or the parachute." The crews drew their combat gear from supplies—a large zippered flight bag which contained oxygen mask, parachute, and harness, helmet, Mae West flotation vest, and plenty of warm clothing. "The B-24 was a cold ship," Hughes recalled. "It had a heater on the flight deck but we rarely used it because it burned raw gasoline and was a fire hazard. So we dressed up as warmly as we could in electrically heated suits, boots, and gloves." Once they were kitted out, the copilot drew escape-and-evasion kits for everyone, and the bombardier picked up the bombsight, carried it to the plane, and installed it. Meanwhile the gunners were mounting the guns while the pilot and copilot completed final checks. The navigator was usually the last man on board, as he calculated last-minute flight data.

Inside, the American bombers were slightly roomier than the British Lancasters and Halifaxes, which made movement easier. But with a crew of ten instead of seven, it was still cramped inside. A medical officer of the time graphically described in his memoirs the conditions under which pilots—many of whom presumably became his patients, which is how he knew—had to do an extremely complex job. The flight deck

was lined—front, sides, ceiling, and part of the floor—with controls, switches, levers, dials and gauges. I once counted 130. The coordinated operations of all these gadgets would be difficult in the swivel-chair comfort of your office. But reduce your office to a cube five feet by five feet by five feet, engulf it in the constant roar of engines, and increase your height to around five miles, and that will give you an idea of the normal conditions under which these men worked out the higher mathematical

relationships of engine revolutions, manifold and fuel pressures, aerody-
namics, barometric pressure, altitude, wind drift, air speed, ground
speed, position and direction.

The job was both physically and mentally demanding. "It put driving an
automobile into the kiddy-car class."[38]

With the crew on board and settled and all checks made, they waited for
the signal to start up the engines. "All planes of the squadron fired up at the
same time," Hughes recalled. "The engines were warmed up for about five
minutes and, on a signal, we began to line up on the taxiway in assigned
takeoff order." The first task was to form up in battle order in the sky, the
complex maneuver that so thrilled David Hastings as he watched from the
ground. It was potentially highly dangerous, and new pilots arriving on base
were made to practice for many hours before being sent up for real. One
rogue rookie could cause a whole formation to fall apart. Walter Hughes
quickly discovered that "it was important to follow the standard climb and
turn rate to avoid collisions, and it was always prudent to keep an eye out
for another B-24 cutting across your climb to get into position." Problems
arose when there were cloud—which, of course, was the norm—but, once
above it, he would look down delighted and amazed as "I saw yet another
B-24 pop out of the clouds, from the same spot, every thirty seconds."

It took between forty-five minutes and an hour to form a group at mod-
erate altitude: fifteen minutes to get thirty planes off the ground and thirty
minutes for the last one to climb to six thousand feet and get everyone in
place. Then the wings and groups from numerous airfields all over eastern
England would come together into a formation of as many as 900 planes, creating a stream seventy-five miles long that then headed eastward to Germany.

Hughes's first encounter over enemy territory was hair-raising.

As we crossed the Rhine somewhere between Frankfurt and Cologne, an
antiaircraft battery opened up on us. The first burst was about a hundred
yards away, ahead and to my side. I was scared. I shook and shivered and
tried to squeeze my whole body up inside my flak helmet. I had no idea
that it would be like this. Nothing in my training had prepared me. A few
more bursts and we were left in peace, but I was still shaking from that

first burst when we landed. Luckily, the intercom was not functioning, so each of us kept his own secret of how he felt to himself. As captain, it was important for me not to show fear. I had to hold in my feelings and to make sure nobody else in the crew was going over the edge. I was twenty-two and I had this mighty responsibility on me.

On his second mission, he had his first close-up view of other planes going down around him, and he watched helplessly as comrades struggled for their lives. "Three chutes came out of one but its bomb bay was blazing like a torch and, unable to escape through the flames, another man climbed out of the top hatch almost directly into the whirling propeller. To our relief, he missed it by a whisker and fell safely away." Back in training, Hughes had convinced himself that he would be able to take control of any situation, that he would never be the one to make a mistake or suffer a fatal lapse of concentration. "Now I realized I had no control. If something happened to me, there was nothing I could do to avoid it. It was a strange feeling. We returned home to count the holes in the plane and eat what food our stomachs could stand."

A deep sense of comradeship kept crews going in these morale-sapping conditions. The men became inseparable. Picardo remembered the time he and the bombardier on his crew were grounded for a mission because of frostbite. They had to watch their crew leave for Germany without them. He could not relax while they were gone and rushed on his bicycle to the landing field when he heard the sound of engines in the distance. "We knew that thirty-six bombers had taken off, and we started counting. Some were firing yellow flares indicating they had wounded on board and got priority to land. Ours, thank God, was not among them. But where was she? Then we spotted her and the relief was fantastic. They had made it back." The reunion on the ground was full of ribaldry and didn't-miss-you-at-all ribbing but it disguised real emotions.

It was such a relief to see them back again. I would have been devastated if they had not returned. It would have been just like losing your family. We were extremely close, as you might expect of a group of men who entrusted their lives to each other's hands almost daily. I believe you can measure someone's character by the degree to which you can trust them in a life-and-death situation, and by this criterion the men in my crew were some of the best people ever assembled.

Off duty, they were just as close.

Laughter was an important antidote to the possibility of death. We played pool and drank beer, sometimes to excess but not often. I truly can't remember any of the crew getting mad at one another. To be sure, we teased each other unmercifully, but everyone gave as good as they got. We liked each other so much that when we showered we would wash the other guy's backs. It felt great.

Most men of the RAF had nothing but sympathy and understanding for their American cousins. But they also relished the rivalry. When British and American airmen came in contact, it was usually a mutually fascinating encounter. They were like pool—or billiard—balls that touch gently, more a kiss of cultures than a clash. RAF sergeant Reg Davey remembered his crew flying their Lancaster into a nearby American base so that they could all take a look at each other's aircraft.[39]

Our pilot did a very low pass over their airfield, just to let them know we had arrived, and then, more by luck than judgment, brought our Lancaster in for a perfect landing. They formed an orderly queue to file through her while we went across to inspect one of their Fortresses. It was the height of luxury compared with our stark interior—padded seats, individual heater outlets and the like. We exchanged reminiscences and we marveled that they flew over Germany in formation and in daylight, while they thought we were quite mad to fly at night and at a much lower height. Then we went to their club for coffee, Coca-Cola and delicious chocolate and cream cakes, the like of which we had not seen for several years, plus packets of Camel or Chesterfield cigarettes at rock-bottom prices. There was also a fruit machine [slot machine], which our mechanical wizard of a flight engineer managed to fix with his penknife so that we could play without putting any money in. When we walked back to our Lancaster for the homeward flight, our blouses were bulging with legally purchased cigarettes and candy bars, and our trouser pockets filled with illegally gained shilling pieces. We made about eight shillings each— nearly a day's pay! We reported a highly successful operation to our CO and very sportingly the Americans, who caught on to what we were up to, made no complaint. Nice guys the Yanks—I like them!

RAF navigator Boris Bressloff never forgot the Americans jazzing up the town hall dances in Downham Market.[40] "Normally we had what passed for an orchestra, with the vicar playing the violin very badly and another man on the banjo. Then the Americans brought in their own thirteen-piece band. It was fantastic. The joint was jumping with everybody jitterbugging until half the roof fell in. Afterward there was a big notice in the town hall—'No stamping dances allowed.'" Then the Americans came to the RAF base for tea on the lawn outside the officers' quarters, an old vicarage. They arrived in their flying gear, some of them with pistols in holsters round their waists. A game of croquet was in progress and the Americans stared in astonishment "at the sight of languid young Englishmen daintily sipping tea on the lawn of an ancient house, the silence broken only by the clink of cups and croquet balls. The mess president asked them to leave their guns with the steward. 'We're rather nervous of firearms,' he told them with mock horror."

Despite all the warnings the Americans had been given in advance about the hardship in Britain, they did not always grasp the point. A couple of U.S. airmen invited to the officers' mess saw a jug of milk on the table and swigged the whole lot between them. They had no idea that fresh milk was strictly rationed and that they had just consumed the day's allowance for the entire mess. But when they were told, they reacted with typical generosity. They came back next day with supplies from their own base and, Bressloff recalled, "we had ice cream and milk for weeks. They had everything."

The British social system was another mystery that many visiting airmen never fathomed. The booklet introducing them to Britain assured them they were coming to a country with democratic traditions as great as their own and that, though "many of the titles held by the lords (such as baron, duke and earl) have been passed from father to son for hundreds of years, others are granted in reward for outstanding achievement, much as American colleges and universities give honorary degrees to famous men and women."

That explanation of British social equality didn't stop Bert Stiles wondering what it would be like to marry a duchess and live in a palace. Subtler social distinctions caught Lieutenant Ralph Golubock unawares. His plane was forced to make an emergency landing at an RAF fighter station, and he and his crew stayed the night.

When I awoke and began dressing I realized my GI boots were gone. I assumed someone had stolen them. What a rotten thing to do, to steal a man's shoes when he was asleep. I was furious. Then I discovered my shoes just outside of my door, all polished and looking new. Then I remembered the English have the custom of leaving their shoes for their batman to clean and polish. I laughed. Imagine cleaning and polishing a lousy pair of muddy, scuffed GI shoes! Still laughing, I went down to an excellent English breakfast. The British really know how to live![41]

But it was Bert Stiles who got to the heart of the British way of life in that wartime era. He found a sense of comradeship he had never expected. On leave, he had taken himself off to London, as he had done many times before, but this time:

I was alone and feeling it. I had dinner at the Savoy and drank a whole bottle of wine, which, on top of the scotch I drank all afternoon, deepened the loneliness. The buzz bombs were coming over steadily and a hellish pressure seemed to be on everyone. The world was pretty shaky. I needed someone to look at across a table, someone just to talk to. In the end I went down in the underground and took a tube. I got off at Bond Street station and almost stepped on a little girl. She was asleep. Then I looked around. The cave dwellers were getting their cave ready for the night. The bunks were all taken and most of the floor space was covered with blankets and coats. An old man with a beard was reading a book in the harsh light. The double-decker bunks along the wall were all full. A weary-faced woman was looking at me. I tried to smile, but it didn't come off very well and she didn't smile back. Maybe she was out of smiles by this tail end of the day. I looked down at the little girl and said: "Hello, I nearly stepped on you." She didn't say anything, just kept looking at me. I figured she was about three. "How old are you?" I asked. "Five." Her voice was sleepy. She sure didn't look five. "Want some gum?" She shook her head, but a boy in shorts, with the dirtiest knees in London, said, "I do." I gave him a whole packet of Beechnut. "Thanks, Yank," he said before disappearing to sleep.

The little girl needed to go to the bathroom and Stiles volunteered to her mother to take her.

I lifted her up on my shoulders and we were off. I took her up one side of the escalator and down the other. She was laughing all the time but silently so as not to wake anyone. Meanwhile the trains were roaring by every few seconds. Two women, sitting with their backs to the wall knitting, smiled up at me. A one-legged man reading Proust looked up at me and there was friendliness in his face. Then the little girl tapped me on the ear and pointed me to a sign that said "Women." I put her down and she went in. She was soon out again and we set off back but I had a bad time finding my way to the right blanket and the right mother. But eventually I got her back to her family. Her mother was asleep, her arm thrown slackly over another child in a gesture of complete exhaustion. The little girl lay down again on the cement and covered herself up with a coat. Then she closed her eyes. I stood over her and my mind moved back to a time in my life when there were beds and sheets and blankets, and moonlight and a fresh wind coming through the window into my room, a time a thousand years ago when there had been laughter and peace. I looked around. Peace was just a word here in London, just a wish, a prayer to the new dawn. But for a little while there had been the quiet laughter of a little girl who didn't want to wake anybody, while trains screamed through the tunnels, deep below the war outside. Love pressed in on me, stronger than the fear or the deadly tiredness or the smell of so many people. And I found the loneliness had gone.[42]

It was a rare moment of tranquility, and it was fleeting. The worries of war would flood back all too soon. But Stiles had seen at first hand the grit of the British people, the material deprivation, the constant fear they lived under, the way the war brought death and destruction to their very backyards.

These were circumstances that American families back home—three thousand miles and more away from this front line—could barely envisage. U.S. servicemen like him had come to the rescue, like the Seventh Cavalry in a cowboy movie, crossing from the New World to the Old to help sort out its troubles. They came as professional fighting men with a job to do and their motives were of the highest order. For the airmen of the Royal Air Force, though, this was not just a war of principle. It was a war of survival.

3

BOYS INTO MEN

"And should you weep for him, if so inclined,
 Then mingle knowledge with your gift of tears."
—WALTER CLAPHAM, "REQUIEM FOR A REAR GUNNER"

THE WELCOME WAS EFFUSIVE. WHEN EACH MAN JOINED THE RAF FOR AIR-
crew training he was sent a personal letter from Archibald Sinclair, the secretary of state for war, which told him he was now part of an elite corps.
"The RAF demands a high standard of physical fitness and alertness from
its flying crews. Relatively few attain that standard, and I congratulate you
on passing the stringent tests." They had a great task to perform, he told
them. "The honor of the RAF is in your hands. Our country's safety and
the final overthrow of the powers of evil now arrayed against us depend
upon you and your comrades." He urged them to "keep fit, work hard, live
temperately." Nothing was mentioned about the fact that the majority of
them would be lucky to survive.

Indeed, there was a cautionary tale hidden in the history of that letter.[1]
One version of it was written in 1942 and went on to explain that there was
huge pressure on training places. Most of them would have to wait awhile,
and in the meantime they should get on with their civilian jobs until told to
report. Some waited a year or more. By 1944, there were no such delays.
The rapid expansion of the force under Harris had seen to that; so had the
high mortality rate. As experienced crews finished their tours of duty and
were taken off frontline duties, fresh young meat was needed to feed the
military machine. Some who went through this grinder felt like cannon fod-

der. But if the demand seemed wearily insatiable, it did not show on the faces of the recruits. Most arrived brimming with confidence, eager for battle. And more than eager. When they got to their squadrons in 1944 and 1945, many of them had one fear—and it was not of dying. It was that they were too late. One of the paradoxes of wars is that those who fight them are often torn between the dread of being involved and the dread of being excluded.

New recruits came from all classes, which was a change from the earlier days of the war. The initial RAF recruiting drive had been for upper-class boys, in the belief that the best sort of chap would make the best sort of flier. And since the men doing the recruiting were from the same background, they would know how to spot them. Leadership, sportsmanship, and a knowledge of hunting were what they freely admitted they were looking for. One medical officer said that in finding the ideal aviator, "background is important. Breeding very definitely is of great importance. It is unlikely that the son of a coward would himself become a hero, for it's remarkable how heroism often runs in families."[2] Such archaic restrictive attitudes were not going to win a modern war. The demand for crew was too great to be confined to an old elite. Social barriers were bundled out of the way. Dickie Parfitt was working class, a Kent miner who had left school and gone down into the pit at thirteen. He found himself alongside solicitors, surveyors, and "university types" in the ranks of recruits and told himself, "I am quite capable of matching any of them."[3]

Bill Kiley was one of those who came straight from university.[4] He had had six months at Cambridge, his time divided between studies and the University Air Squadron. "I always wanted to fly. It was the up and coming thing and it got into your blood. It was exciting." He had also spent long hours listening to his infantry-officer father talking about trench warfare during the First World War. He was not the only recruit who chose to fly rather than flounder on the ground. He remained in ignorance about the massive losses in the force he was joining.

Our instructors at Cambridge didn't go into detail about what was happening in Bomber Command. Remember, too, that we only ever saw tour-expired people, the ones who, by definition, had survived, who hadn't been shot down. There was a boy from my school who was a pilot, and he came on leave but he never mentioned anything about casu-

alties. He was always cheerful and happy. Frankly, the losses didn't figure in my mind. I think when you are eighteen it is all just an adventure.

Bill Carman, eighteen-year-old son of a London publican, admitted to
total ignorance about what it would be like to go into battle. "All we young
chaps were dead keen but pretty naïve. We just wanted to get in and have a
go."[5] They were naïve about more than just the realities of war. During basic training, Bill Low was given a talk by a medical officer about the dangers of gonorrhea and syphilis and had not the faintest idea what he was
being told.[6] Campbell Muirhead, from a strict religious home, learned the
meaning of the words "prick teaser" when he was billeted at a guesthouse
in Blackpool and lusted after the landlady's "smashing" daughter as she
flashed her eyes and her legs at him. He took her out but, as he noted in his
diary, "nothing doing." But he was happy enough just being away from
home. "From the moment I joined the RAF, boredom became a thing of the
past. Now I was free—from office routine, from going to night school to
obtain a bit of paper, most of all, from my parents. The discipline of the
RAF was a form of freedom when, once off duty, you didn't need to account to anybody for your movements. It was a massive breakthrough into
the life I was missing."[7] Boys like him became men almost overnight.

But not all. Carman turned up at his local recruiting office, ready to do
or die, only to be sent away and told to come back "when I started shav-
ing!" That was "a severe and dampening blow to my youthful enthusiasm."
Undeterred, he got his father to have a word with a wing commander he
knew, who explained that he had been turned down because he was under-
age for aircrew training. He should apply to join as a ground-based wireless
operator and transfer to flying duties later—which is what he did. This time
the recruiting sergeant put his arms around him and welcomed him in.

Many of those joining at this time felt they had a personal grudge to settle with the Germans. The commander in chief, Air Marshal Sir Arthur
Harris, had famously stood on the roof of the Air Ministry in London
watching a German air raid in 1941 and commented: "They are sowing the
wind."[8] This is often interpreted as indicating a personal sense of vendetta
that would skew his judgment. But he was far from alone in such sentiments. Ken Newman had been on a school trip to Germany in 1938 and
shared youth hostels with members of the Hitler Youth. Having stared Nazi

militarism in the face and disliked it, he felt its full impact two years later when his family's semidetached house in south London was blitzed.[9]

> We were just in time getting to our shelter in the back garden. As I was closing the door we heard bombs screaming down. I thought our end had come. I counted three explosions very close by, accompanied by splintering wood and smashing glass. The shelter rocked like a small boat in a rough sea. When it was quiet again, I opened the door and was hit by a thick fog of brick dust. Our roof was in the garden. We had taken a direct hit. We no longer had a house. I was extremely angry because there was no reason for bombs to have been dropped in our area, which was entirely residential. There were no factories producing war-matériel, or anything else for that matter.

After that, he was desperate "to get my own back. Revenge was high in the minds of a lot of people who lived in big cities that the Germans had walloped." Aged eighteen, he volunteered for the RAF, knowing that if he waited to be conscripted at nineteen he would not have a choice of which service to join. It wasn't just a matter of avoiding the army and the navy, he was also attracted by the novelty of airplanes and the glamour of flying. The idea of becoming a pilot was "beyond my wildest dreams." His mother was more down-to-earth when he told her that not only had he enlisted in the RAF but he had also been accepted for pilot training. "As far as she was concerned, the war was dangerous enough without adding to the risks."

On the other side of London, another lad was spurred into joining up by the destruction he saw around him. Reg Davey remembered digging a hole in his back garden in Tottenham to house an Anderson air-raid shelter on the day war broke out.[10] It was his seventeenth birthday. It lay unused even when the bombing began in 1940. It filled with rainwater, and the family preferred to crawl under a table in the dining room or run to the nearby tube station for shelter. At night, Davey would look out and see the glow in the sky from the docks on fire ten miles away. In the morning he cycled through shattered streets to his workplace in Westminster. His brother's girlfriend and a pal from school were killed in the raids. The war also split up his family when his younger brothers were evacuated to the country. He joined the RAF "to do my bit and to repay the Germans for what they were doing to myself, family and country."

As a Jew of Russian extraction but born in England, Boris Bressloff had amassed more reasons than most to want to fight.[11]

We knew right from the beginning what was happening, that Jews in Germany were being beaten up and discriminated against. I wanted to go for that reason, but also because I was patriotic and I still am. I love this country. I think anybody who is born in England is very lucky and should remember that. Working in London I had seen the Blitz—seen buildings bombed, people killed. I had done fire watching in the West End and doused incendiary bombs with sand or water.

But what pushed him into actually donning a blue uniform was a girl putting his manhood to the test. Bressloff was a ladies' hairdresser in a Mayfair salon—a suspect profession for a man.

One of the girls in the salon pointed at a magazine advertisement for fighter pilots. It showed this young man with a helmet and goggles looking up at the sky, alongside the words "Are you fit and keen to fly? Join the fighting comrades of the sky." She said to me, "You'll never get into that," and I was so annoyed at the insinuation that I wasn't man enough that I went round to the recruiting center that very day and joined the RAF. Little did I know what I was letting myself in for.

Little did any of them know. They were joining a glamorous elite at a time when aircraft and flying verged on the exotic. Very few of them had ever been anywhere near a plane in their lives, let alone flown in one. It had been less than forty years since the world's first flight, when the Wright brothers had struggled airborne in their aircraft built of wood and muslin. In the two interwar decades, aviation had been a pursuit for pioneers, for ocean-hopping record seekers such as Charles Lindbergh and Amy Johnson. Flying as a means of transport had been restricted to the rich and fa-

mous. Now, in a few short years, it was at the cutting edge of military technology and anyone could join in. But the men who flocked to it generally
did so in ignorance and out of bravado and exuberance. They had little idea
of the casualty rates, and no one was about to tell them. Thousands,
alarmed by what they knew of trench life in the First World War, joined on
the assumption that it had to be safer than going over the top at Ypres. In
time, they would discover that it was not.

In time, but not yet. For now there was the long haul from joining up to
qualifying for battle. It began with several weeks of initial training—drill,
lessons in elementary navigation, and Morse code, and lots of hanging
about doing nothing—followed by aircrew selection, which took place at
the commandeered Lord's cricket ground in London. Dickie Parfitt, the
miner from Kent, sat in the famous Long Room in the pavilion, staring out
at the field and remembering all the times he had listened on the radio to
commentaries of international cricket matches being played here. Recruits
were housed in requisitioned apartment blocks close to Regent's Park and
many recall being marched to and from London Zoo—devoid of animals,
which had been evacuated to another zoo out in the country—for meals en
masse in the huge café there. Few forgot standing in line with their trousers
down waiting for FFI inspections—freedom from infection—by the doctor.
Parfitt recalled the medics in muffled and prolonged discussions over one
particular man, which left the rest of them standing and shivering in their
seminakedness waiting for their turns. The chap was taken aside afterward
and made to confess his problem—he had a mole on the end of his penis.
The others made sure he was at the end of the line for all future inspections
of this sort. They also gave him a suitably cruel nickname—"Knobby"
Clark. There were other, more rigorous, medical examinations—eyesight,
hearing, lungs, etc.—and those who passed these A1, and who also did well
in the leadership tests for pilot training, then found themselves heading
overseas for up to a year. Some went to the United States, others to the
edges of the British empire. They would learn their flying skills in the cloudless skies and the low, flat landscapes of the Midwest, Canada, and South
Africa—and return home to fight a war in overcast, mountain-dotted Europe. It would be a moot point how well prepared they were.

Ken Newman was packed off to South Africa in a crowded troopship,
which took several weeks to get to Durban. Then there was more hanging

around before he finally found himself putting on his flight suit for his first outing in an open-cockpit, single-engined Tiger Moth trainer. It had been exactly a year since he had joined up. The clothes were a disappointment. He and his fellow trainees had expected to be given sheepskin jackets, the jaunty trademark of the Battle of Britain fighter pilots they all wanted to emulate. A zip-up canvas suit did not have the same cachet any more than the embarrassing silk-and-wool long johns they were expected to wear underneath. "They were the old-fashioned sort our grandfathers wore. We could not imagine we would ever have any use for them." Later, high over Germany in subzero temperatures, he would feel their benefit. Twelve weeks of rigorous training began, heralded by a warning from the commanding officer that half of them were destined to fail.

Newman had the arrogance to believe he would not be one of them, despite the fact that he (and most of his fellows) had never driven anything before, not a car or a motorcycle. Unlike young people of their age today, at ease with speed, this was a generation of novices when it came to mechanical power. They started from scratch, and after a week of training, Newman, like any new learner-driver, began to doubt that he would ever get it right. "I just did not seem to be able to master the aircraft; it was mastering me." But then, just as he thought he was about to flunk the course, he made his first successful solo flight. It was two days before his twentieth birthday. For others, the station commander's prediction was coming true. Newman's best friend—they had been mates since joining up—failed to make the grade and was shipped off to train as a navigator. "I never heard from him again."

For Newman and the other survivors, training went up a gear— aerobatics, forced landings, night flying. He began to feel confidence in his fingertips—"I was no longer hanging onto the joystick for dear life; I felt in control." It was time to graduate from Tiger Moths. In a twin-engined Oxford, he learned more skills—gunnery, aerial photography, practice bombing, cross-country navigation. Newman was thrilled to complete a night flight over the veldt before dropping in to land at Kimberley. Only later did it dawn on him that, back in blacked-out Europe, he would have to manage his landing lights-off and without the illumination of the city to guide him in from miles away. But with 160 flying hours now logged, he was well on his way to qualifying as a pilot. His wings were pinned on him at a ceremony in March 1943, a few weeks short of two years since he had joined up. His sergeant's stripes went on his arm at the same time. Two months later he was back in England.

It would be another full year, however, before Newman was operational. In South Africa he had learned how to fly. But he was a long way from being ready to fight. It was back to school for a familiarization course, which meant unlearning his South African experience and practicing in true north European conditions. "Flying in South Africa was totally different from flying here. In South Africa there were miles and miles of nothing. A railway line was a significant feature. But back here the landscape was so much more detailed and confusing. We flew around Shropshire and Wales just getting used to finding our bearings." And a crucial decision was awaiting him: Which branch of the RAF was he going to serve in? Until this point, all pilot training had been standard. But now came the choice: Would he be sent to Fighter Command to fly Hurricanes and Spitfires, to Coastal Command to patrol the Atlantic for enemy submarines, to Transport Command to fuel the supply lines, or to Bomber Command? He had no say in the matter. Bombing Germany was London and Washington's declared priority. He was posted to a bomber training unit. "My fate was sealed."

Bill Carman's route to frontline duties was just as long and a lot more tortuous. He trained as a ground wireless operator at the RAF radio school in Wiltshire and was then posted to RAF Farnborough. But he longed to fly. In his off-duty time he would hang around the flight office, chatting to the pilots and trying to cadge a ride. They took pity on him and he got his wish to be airborne. One suggested he should volunteer for a posting to the specialist unit that flew planes towing practice targets for antiaircraft gunners, and soon he was sitting in the back of a Hawker Henley hauling a line of red flags across the seafront at Clacton while gunners on the promenade tried to hit them. It was, he recalled, "a hairy experience." He smelt the cordite as he and his crew flew through black puffs of smoke "and I began to wonder what I had volunteered for."

But it was a different hazard that nearly killed him. One day the engine in the two-man Henley cut out a mile offshore and they plunged toward the water, Carman terrified because he could not swim. Somehow—how often would that word "somehow" figure in such incidents?—the pilot pulled out of the dive and got them to dry land, clearing the beach and promenade at three hundred feet with the towrope still trailing behind and snagging on a chimney or two before breaking free. They headed for a soft sandy beach before a voice over the radio told them it was mined and the pilot veered away to come down in a field of panicking cows. "As we hit the ground at over 70 mph, a trapdoor in the floor burst open and acted like a demon lawn mower, scooping up and showering the inside of the aircraft with clods of grass and earth and stones. I was sitting with my legs well astride and my feet braced on the struts as these lumps started to bombard my nether regions." The plane then hit an irrigation ditch and slewed to a halt on its nose. "We scrambled out, badly shaken, but had the sense to stay where we were. Sure enough, we were in a minefield after all. Eventually a line of troops gingerly made their way toward us in single file, led by a none-too-happy-looking officer closely studying a map of the area." It was the first of a number of times Carman would cheat death, but, undeterred, he clocked 130 flying hours with the target towers before being sent for proper aircrew training. There he would join wireless operators who had taken a more direct recruiting route.

Meanwhile, gunners were completing their training at gunnery school, navigators and bombardiers at theirs. The time it had taken to get to this point varied, depending on whether a man had chosen his trade right from the start or whether he had been assigned to it after washing out from pilot training. But from joining up to the completion of training was rarely less than a year, more often two, and sometimes three. Whichever direction they came from and however long it had taken, pilots, navigators, bombardiers, engineers, wireless operators, and gunners reached the end of their specialist instruction and were ready to come together. For each of them, the next stop would involve the most crucial decision of his young life—choosing the comrades in whose hands he would place his survival.

In both the Royal Air Force and the United States Air Force of the twenty-first century, a good deal of deliberation goes into deciding who should fly with whom. There is a degree of psychological profiling and matching, even if it is of the low-tech variety in which a commanding officer reckons that Flight Lieutenant X and Flying Officer Y will make a good team. The men and women themselves have little or no say. Not so in the RAF sixty years ago. Bomber Command's new recruits decided for themselves who they were going to live or die with. "Crewing-up," as it was called, was one of the most extraordinary asides of the bomber war—an activity quite unexpected in such a centralized command structure as the RAF and one that was so alien to everything in the British character that it is hard to believe that it really happened like this—but it did.

Airmen, fresh from their various training camps and schools, would assemble at one of the twenty-two Operational Training Units around the country in batches of around 140 to 200, enough to make up between twenty and thirty crews. At some, like children on the first day of school, they would all be thrust into the "playground"—in this case usually a giant hangar—to make friends. A pilot would seek a navigator, a bombardier would pick a couple of gunners, and so on. It could be a complete free-for-all. "You just wandered around and went up to people and chatted," said English rear gunner Bruce Wyllie. "I approached a group of Australians, introduced myself and said: 'I'm looking for a skipper.' We talked for a few minutes and then one of them said: 'Would you like to join us, Bruce?' and that was that. We were crewed up in a couple of hours."[12]

For others, the procedure was drawn out, and for good reason. Flight Sergeant Miles Tripp likened it to a marriage market, "and yet the choice of a good flying partner was far more important than a good wife. You couldn't divorce your crew, and you could die if one of them wasn't up to his job at a critical moment."[13] He felt

like a girl at her first dance. I cringed at the thought of being a wallflower. At first, pilots, navigators, wireless operators and air gunners stayed with their own kind but as the morning passed men from each group began to circulate and a jocular insecurity pervaded the cheerless hangar. Every so often one would hear a happy cry, "Hey, Bill, I've found a navigator!" The day dragged by and when the time came to close the hangar I was still a wallflower. That evening I went to the village, had a few drinks and sat down to play the pub piano. A sergeant navigator with a pint of beer in his hand came and stood by the piano. After a while he offered to buy me a drink. Like me he was uncrewed. I bought him a return drink and we agreed to team up. On the following day he came to me greatly excited. He had found a pilot who had already crewed up with a wireless operator. The four of us met.

And so the mating session went on until everyone was in a crew. They knew little or nothing about each other. Instant judgments were made—on a man's bearing or his accent, a smile, a look in his eye, or the way he talked. A distinctive regional brogue could be an asset or the opposite. Tripp called it an "arbitrary collision of strangers" and could see merit in it. It meant, for example, that "those who were too sensitive, diffident or withdrawn to respond to these conditions would eventually be crewed up with others of similar temperament."

Some men went into crewing-up knowing precisely what they were looking for. There were crews entirely of teetotalers or churchgoers, because they had sought each other out. Pilot Robert Wannop was one who wanted nondrinkers like himself, and he was prepared to take his time to find them.[14] He, too, was conscious that the procedure resembled a marriage, especially, he thought, the bit about "for better or for worse" and "until death us do part"! He put up a notice—"R. E. Wannop of Liverpool requires crew members for all positions. Teetotalers preferred."—but the response was disappointing. Other pilots openly scoffed at him for what they interpreted as prissiness, but just when he had given up hope he was approached by a navigator who saluted and introduced himself. The two of them walked and talked for a while and "we began to warm to each other. He had the qualifications and attitudes I was seeking." Eventually Wannop got his crew of nondrinkers and felt all the safer for it, and pleased that he had not let himself be rushed into decisions. For him crewing-up took several days, but at the end he felt he had the right team, one in which they could all rely on each other's skills to survive.

Some were seekers, others preferred to be found. Wireless operator Bill Low was "found." At his OTU, there was a variation of the hangar routine. "All of the wireless ops were in a room and all the pilots walked in and wandered around until they liked the look of somebody. One came up to me and said: 'I say, old boy, would you like to fly with me?' I was pleased because he was a squadron leader, and I said: 'Certainly, sir.' " At Ken Newman's OTU, the procedure was reversed. He was assembled along with all the other pilots and then an equivalent number of navigators was sent in. "I chose a flying officer on the assumption that as he had gained a commission he might be better than average. He was also a married man, like me, and I felt that our joint will to survive would be stronger. Then the bombardiers were sent in and we rather liked the look of a fresh-faced Welsh sergeant."

By this haphazard method, fighting crews came together. They now had to learn to operate as a unit and then to train for warfare in aircraft more akin to the ones they would actually fly over Germany. Ken Newman clambered into the cockpit of a Wellington for the first time. It was twice the size of anything he had flown before—"a real operational bomber and not just a training aircraft." The power as the Hercules engines roared into life excited him. He took her for a trial run with an instructor on board and a gunner in the rear turret. Standing orders insisted on this in case they ran into a marauding enemy fighter. However unlikely, this was another indication that training was ending and the serious business of war was beginning. Then, with a full crew, they practiced evasion tactics, fighting off mock attacks in the air by trainee fighter pilots, and live bombing runs over a range in Staffordshire. Night flying was next on the training agenda, along with a timely reminder that a turning propeller was impossible to see in the dark. A member of another crew walked into one and was literally sliced into pieces. Newman learned the lesson—never start the engines without being sure everyone was on board.

For some the lessons came too late. Bill Carman watched in horror as the training Wellington ahead of his taxied round the perimeter track and ran into the back of another. "The unfortunate gunner, one of our course mates, was chopped to pieces. One minute he was there and the next he wasn't. Only his legs were left. We realized we were now at the start of a serious business." The boys who had joined up were quickly becoming men.

There was one last stage before they were allocated to a squadron. Seven trained men had become a crew; the crew had been trained in air skills and tactics. Now the crew learned how to fly the type of aircraft they would go to war in—which for most arriving at the latter end of the war was the Lancaster. The culmination of all the years of preparation was a short stay at a Heavy Conversion Unit and then they were posted to a frontline station. The theory was over. The practical was about to begin.

Some thought the lengthy training they had received was superb. Navigator Boris Bressloff found it stimulating, absorbing, and largely enjoyable.

We were stretched to the limit and made aware that our lives and the lives of others, not to mention a lot of valuable equipment, would be in our hands. The information and skills we learnt were staggering. We were required to have a grasp of the workings of engines, bombs and components, gunnery and the maintenance of equipment. I did a moving target bombing course and advanced ship recognition with the navy at Scapa Flow and an RAF regiment assault course.

Bill Carman agreed that the training was outstanding. "Look at the hours we put in." It did not seem that way to some on the other side of the fence. Tom Tate was a wireless operator and gunner who had finished his first tour and spent most of 1944 training recruits.[15] He felt that he was simply helping to churn out men "like a sausage machine." Training barely prepared a man for actual operations. "We only gained efficiency as we gained experience." Another instructor, John Wynne, came to the conclusion that all he was doing was teaching young men to fly to their deaths. "As a flight commander on a training unit, I knew that 70 percent of my course would be dead in a few months and there was nothing I could do to change that. They had little chance of survival."[16] He was scathing in his criticisms of the system—starting with himself. He had spent two years flying Wellingtons over the desert in North Africa. Then he was sent back to England to teach young men how to stay alive over the very different terrain of northern Europe. He was desperate to be posted to a frontline squadron so that he could acquire the direct experience of air operations in Europe to pass on to his trainees. Instead, he was then allocated to a post teaching new instructors, fresh from squadron duties, how to instruct. He was staggered by how little they knew.

These were chaps who'd finished their thirty operations and I was shocked at the standard of flying. Unbelievable. These were meant to be the instructors yet how they ever finished their tours I didn't know.

I was worried for the young aircrew in my care. I knew they weren't properly trained—they had so few hours. They were being thrust into the face of the most sophisticated air defense system in the world and they had only twenty to thirty hours on four-engine aircraft and only a small percentage night flying. These chaps were barely safe. If anything went wrong, they'd had it.

Wynne got his wish for frontline operations, and then discovered how little he knew about the realities of this war over Germany. Why hadn't he been taught to differentiate between types of flak? Or the best way to deal with a searchlight—whether to try and run from the cone or fly straight down the beam to 4,000 feet until you lost it? "The first time many experienced these real, incredibly important, tactical decisions they didn't know what to do. And there was no time then to think about it." He tried to do his thinking beforehand.

The squadron had an intelligence library where you could read up on things like this but it was usually empty. You could go into the coffee bar and it would be full of chaps rolling dice on the floor. I used to look at these buggers and think they were mad. In the air they would be playing for the highest stakes ever—their lives—and yet they were frittering their time away for a couple of shillings when they could actually be loading the dice in their favor in that intelligence room. But it wasn't their fault— there was no organization. They weren't made to go and read and learn.

Wynne concluded that the RAF was rushing as many men through the training as possible in the shortest time and cutting corners if necessary. Once, he was flying with a student pilot and a trainee gunner in the rear, who had a cine camera mounted on his turret to record his "hits" in a mock gunfight with a fighter plane. The gunner would be marked on the number of frames in which he snapped the Spitfire. Such war games— fighter affiliation exercises, as they were officially known—could be dangerous. One airman recalled in his memoirs seeing a Hurricane fighter slice off the tail of a Lancaster bomber in midflight.[17] All on board the Lancaster died, as did the Hurricane pilot. Wynne decided to replicate real battle conditions—for both the pilot and the gunner—and, as the attack plane came in, he ordered the pilot into a corkscrew.

When we landed, my flight commander was absolutely furious. The gunner hadn't got a single frame of the attack plane on his film. "What the bloody hell were you doing? You wasted two hours up there and we haven't got a single picture." I realized that I wasn't supposed to teach this pilot how to fight. All I was there to do was to help the rear gunner pass his course. It was almost a negligent way to prosecute training. The hierarchy in the RAF was more concerned with pushing numbers out, regardless of the quality. Only volume mattered.

He thought Harris looked on bomber crews as nothing more than "the teeth on a blade of a chain saw" and just as easily replaceable.

Combat losses were certainly mounting at an alarming rate. The second half of 1943 had been bad for Bomber Command after Harris, emboldened by his success in devastating Hamburg, Germany's second largest city, turned his attention to the capital itself. Brimming with confidence, he predicted he could "wreck Berlin from end to end. It will cost Germany the war." He promised a winter campaign of such ferocity that the Germans would surrender by April 1944.

But Berlin was an altogether tougher nut. Flying there involved many more hours in the air over enemy territory. Zig-zag courses were necessary to avoid flak, but this meant more miles, more fuel on board, and fewer bombs. Bigger, more widely spread, and more vigorously defended, Berlin was not to be knocked out in a short, sharp campaign. Moreover, the destruction at Hamburg had awakened the Germans to some harsh realities. Defenses were sharpened, and the night-fighter force was reorganized and its tactics streamlined. "Window" was counteracted. Bomber Command would not have that edge again.

Harris also had to vary his targets. To fly to Berlin every night would have been too obvious, and he had to intersperse raids on the German capital with raids on other cities. More diversionary targets were also needed to throw the Germans off the scent. All this spread his force too thinly. He had hit Hamburg with between 750 and 800 bombers at a time. In sixteen raids on Berlin, he rarely mustered more than 500.

They did enormous damage to the German capital but at great cost. A loss rate of 3.4% on the night of November 22–23, 1943 was up to 8.7% a fortnight later. As 1943 turned into 1944, each trip was getting more and more dangerous. Routinely, 40 bombers or more failed to return from Berlin or Brunswick or any of the other cities targeted in this campaign. Unknown to the British, the Luftwaffe was using a new and deadly secret weapon.

Jazz music was loathed by the Nazi regime. Its rhythms were considered primitive, and distinctly non-Aryan. Goebbels, the minister for propaganda, declared it banned. It was curious then that "*Schräge Musik*" ("slanting music")—as close as the German language could get to a word for the American "jazz"—should have been chosen as the code word for the weapon that in early 1944 gave the Luftwaffe a devastating (if temporary) edge in the battle of the bombers over Germany.

It was a simple enough device: two upward facing machines guns pointing out of the top of the cockpit of a fighter in addition to the cannons mounted in the wings. It revolutionized tactics. Until then the fighters had closed in on the rear of an enemy bomber at around 300 mph. This gave the pilot three seconds to line up his target and squeeze the trigger before having to pull away to avoid a high speed collision. Pinpoint accuracy was difficult.

Now he could dive beneath the bomber from the rear and, totally unseen, shoot up at the wings from a distance at which it was hard to miss. The bomber crews, as their aircraft burst into flames around them and the lucky ones bailed out, had no idea what had hit them. The first use of *Schräge Musik* was in May 1943 but the Luftwaffe then proved extraordinarily slow in equipping its fighters with this new weapon. Its existence was therefore still largely unknown when, at the end of March, 1944, Harris directed his bombers to the southern German city of Nuremberg.

At this stage, Harris's Berlin campaign was faltering as casualties multiplied. His deadline of April for the Germans to throw down their arms was nearly upon him, and yet the Berliners were as defiant as ever. In London and Washington, the focus of military planning had shifted to Operation Overlord, the invasion of German-occupied France—the step Harris had always argued would be unnecessary because Bomber Command would do the job of defeating Hitler from the air. Soon his men and aircraft would come under the orders of General Eisenhower, supreme commander of the Allied Forces, to make its contribution to the D-day landings.

But there was time for one last big raid, one last throw of the dice. As he considered his options on March 30, 1944, no doubt Harris would have preferred a final shot at Berlin. But the weather ruled out northern Germany as a target. He would have to go south.

The list of possible targets put in front of him that day included Nuremberg, the medieval Bavarian city which was the symbolic heartland of Nazism. It was also an industrial, administrative, and communications center, which made it a legitimate military target, but above all, it was, as a Bomber Command document described it, "one of the Holy Cities of the Nazi creed and a political target of the first importance."[18] But Nuremberg was a risky target. It involved a long trip (more than 1,500 miles, eight hours there and back), and the weather was not the best. Clear skies under a bright moon were forecast, and the bombers would be very exposed.

On the other hand, there was a possibility of a brisk tail wind and high cloud banks edging down from the north. A bomber stream could use that cloud as cover to fly high, straight, and fast to the heart of Germany, slipping through the twenty-mile gap between the heavy searchlight and flak defenses of Cologne and those of Koblenz while the German night fighters were still on the ground trying to work out which city they were heading for. Then they would turn south to hit Nuremberg by the last of the moonlight. With the moon down, it would then be a clear run home under cover of complete darkness.

That was Harris's plan. Bold, elaborate, clever—perhaps too clever, depending on too many variables. Colleagues argued just that, but he brushed them aside as he had often done before. "It was a gamble on the weather and on the reactions of the German night-fighter controllers, but then so was every raid that Bomber Command carried out."[19]

On thirty-nine airfields up and down the eastern edge of England—from Yorkshire in the north to Essex in the south—crews of close to 800 aircraft began their preparations. At their briefing they were told they were about to strike a massive blow to German morale, but the length of the trip ahead and the route clearly caused some alarm. Sergeant W. J. Blackburn of 12 Squadron sat in the briefing room at RAF Wickenby in Lincolnshire and saw "uncertainty and plain simple terror" on the faces around him. Flight Sergeant Lesley Nugent of 78 Squadron observed a similar attack of the jitters around him. "There we were, 112 of us, all thinking 'Will I live or die?'" A Liverpudlian, Nugent remembered a voice in his head nagging him: "Don't do this one, Scouse, you won't make it back."

Shortly after 9:15 P.M., the first Lancaster rumbled down the runway. A hundred Pathfinders led the way and behind came the main force of 700 bombers, split into five waves. They crossed the coast of mainland Europe at around 20,000 feet, to find themselves lit up by the shocking brightness of the moon. "It was as clear as day—there was no need to worry about searchlights," according to "Scouse" Nugent.

That night it was not just the moonlight that conspired against Bomber Command. The wind veered, pushing the stream too far north, and lessened, slowing it down. The formation began to string out. Meanwhile, the Luftwaffe was trying out a different plan of attack. Its normal routine was to wait to assess which city the bombers were heading for before sending up the fighters. The new tactic was to get in among the bombers early. The Ju-88s, FW-190s, and Me-110s homed in on a beacon between Cologne and Koblenz—in that very gap the RAF stream was heading for.

The Luftwaffe arrived at that point at the same time as the main bomber force. Their tanks still full enough for two more hours of flying, their *Schräge Musik* at the ready, their pilots eager for the fight, the Germans entered the stream about two thirds of the way back and then proceeded to work their way forward, killing as they went. In the next sixty minutes, the worst hour of Bomber Command's war, 59 aircraft with close to 500 men on board were shot down.

They were sitting ducks, picked out in the cold light of the moon—but also exposed by another freak of the weather. Vapor trails normally did not appear below 25,000 feet, but for some meteorological reason that night, they strung out behind bombers flying as low as 16,000 feet. It was as if each one was hauling a banner behind it announcing its presence and inviting attack.

Aircraft were exploding and going down in flames everywhere. Flight Lieutenant D. F. Gillam climbed to 22,000 feet to escape and looked down on a Lancaster being chased by a twin-engined German fighter. "It overtook him, got underneath and then there was an explosion and the bomber blew clean in half. There were no parachutes. My stomach turned over and we tried to get even higher. I was feeling angry with the powers that be for sending us out on a night like that."

Flight Sergeant S. Welch felt the heat of a bomber blowing up just twenty yards away on his port side. "The blast nearly threw us onto our back and I thought we were going down too." The images of death were unforgettable that night. Sergeant E. Wilkins saw a crewman bale out of a crippled Lancaster, only for the top of his parachute to be caught by a stream of burning gasoline from the ruptured wing tanks. The parachute burned to nothing and Wilkins watched the man fall earthwards from 22,000 feet. Flight Sergeant R. Rhodes felt "as if I was sitting on a platform overlooking the end of the world." Flight Sergeant F. A. Taylor, though not a religious man, simply repeated the 23rd Psalm—"The Lord is my Shepherd"—endlessly to himself.

The remnants of the stream struggled on, made the turn to Nuremberg and then ran into thick cloud. All night the clear skies had made them vulnerable. Now the cover they had longed for hid the target instead. The Pathfinders, unaware of the carnage behind them, laid their colored Christmas-tree flares to mark the way but clouds swallowed them up, and the main force bombed blind. Most of them missed. High explosive bombs and incendiaries peppered the countryside but left the city largely untouched. There was so little damage that many of the city's fire and rescue units stood idle that night, not needed.

Back in England, as ground crews and squadrons waited for the return of their planes, the reality of what had happened was slow to sink in. The first crews to return had been at the front of the stream and they reported nothing out of the ordinary. As the first of the crews caught in the fight landed and told the debriefing officers what they had seen, they were not believed. A pilot officer who said he had seen thirty bombers shot down was told he must be wrong. The intelligence officer put down eight instead. An exhausted wing-commander blurted out that it had been "the biggest chop [killing] night ever" and was told to get a grip on himself.

But as more and more crews checked in with horrific reports, the reality became impossible to dodge, and as the sun came up that morning, the terrible truth dawned, too. Ninety-five aircraft had gone down. Six hundred and seventy men were dead or missing. The casualties in just one night were greater than in the whole of the Battle of Britain. Nuremberg was Bomber Command's equivalent of "Black Thursday" for the Americans.

Harris has been the subject of excoriating criticism for Nuremberg. The official RAF history of the bomber war[20] put the disaster down to "bad and unimaginative operational planning," though adding the palliative that this was "uncharacteristic" for Bomber Command. After the event, it was easy to judge that the raid was a disaster waiting to happen. The moon, the winds, the route—what did Harris think he was playing at?

But Harris was not playing. He made deadly decisions all the time, and sent men out in conditions that carried an element of risk. Martin Middlebrook, an expert on the history of Bomber Command, pleaded in Harris's defense: "An admiral might fight one major battle in his lifetime. A general might fight three such battles. Harris committed the whole of his front line force to combat ten times in each month for three and a quarter years. Many successful raids would never have taken place if he had waited for perfect conditions. On this occasion, he took one chance too many."

Harris himself said little about Nuremberg—except once, turning the issue on its head. "Given the meteorological conditions pertaining in Europe, we were very lucky that there weren't half a dozen Nurembergs," he said.[21]

As for the overall battle of Berlin, most historians and commentators would judge that he had lost it. RAF losses were too high and the damage caused too slight. German industry was hit but it recovered. In the air, the fighters beat the bombers. On the ground, the German people were bruised but unbowed.

Although the German capital lived to fight another day, the morale of its people was sorely tried. The instruments of a fascist state kept it together. Defeatist talk was silenced by the SS and the Gestapo. Yet German morale was perhaps more fragile than has been imagined. In London, Air Intelligence received secret reports from visiting foreign businessmen and the like of widespread apathy among the people, which, though not breaking out into actual unrest as yet, was unpredictable. Harris had not managed to awe the Germans into surrender, but shock them he most certainly had.

As for what lay ahead, he had no doubt that the Allied victory would still be built on the dead and maimed bodies of his airmen. They knew it, too, and some reacted gloomily. Ken Newman was nearing the end of his training and was facing the stark reality of going to war. Aware of Bomber Command's losses in the battle of Berlin, he felt as though

we were just waiting in the wings for our turn. I came to the conclusion that the commander in chief and his staff at Bomber Command—and Churchill, too, come to that—regarded us as expendable. I don't think the top brass had any respect for us, none at all. We called Harris "Butch" because we regarded him as a butcher—not a butcher of the Germans but a butcher of the RAF. Losses didn't seem to matter to him, only achieving the objective.

As the men got closer to going operational, they felt the screw being turned on them.

Morale was very high up to that point. I was flying a Wellington with my new crew and felt on cloud nine. Then we were sent to RAF Lindholme to convert to the Lancaster and the whole atmosphere changed. They treated us like shit. We were all apprehensive about the future but they acted as if we were all about to desert. They were very heavy-handed. It was such a shock.

To make matters worse, Newman then heard that his sister's husband, a navigator, was missing in action on his first sortie. His Halifax had been shot down over Magdeburg. Newman had been the best man at their wedding. He had been a step or two behind his brother-in-law in the training process. Now his sister was a widow, and five months pregnant, too, and he himself was on the brink of being blooded. "Victor's fate made the risks I would soon be facing all too starkly clear." Newman was a newlywed himself. He decided not to tell his wife, Mollie, how close he himself was to going operational.

He became even more disillusioned after an encounter with a stranger on a train. On his way back to camp after leave he was sitting next to a civilian of his own age.

He told me that when he was called up for military service he arranged for a sick cousin to attend his medical examination, with the result that he was exempted. Now he worked in a factory where he was permanently on nights—not night work exactly, for he said they played cards until midnight, then went to bed, and this was all paid at time and a half. I was unsure whether to believe him or not, but the fact that dockers and miners went on strike even during the darkest days of the war showed that there were many civilian workers who were ready to put personal gain before patriotism. This episode did nothing to make me feel any better about the prospects ahead.

Nor did the fact that training was moving on to procedures for ditching and bailing out and exercises in how to avoid capture. But then came the introduction to the aircraft he had been eagerly awaiting—the Lancaster bomber. "I liked her from the first moment I climbed aboard—a decent-sized access door and a sensible cockpit layout with everything a pilot might want within easy reach." It was a quick romance. Newman had just short of ten hours' flying time to learn the ways of his new love, just three of those hours at night. Others recall just six "circuit and bump" flights before they were declared operational. Then they were off to fly night sorties into hostile territory. As a bus took him to his new squadron, Newman was both excited and fearful at the same time. I was looking forward to giving the Third Reich good measure in return for the hurt they had inflicted on my family in general and my sister in particular. I was going to pay the bastards back for that. At the same time I realized that we were going to fill dead men's shoes. I couldn't help wondering how long it would be before another crew would be sent to fill ours.

Arriving at his new squadron at Downham Market in Norfolk in that same summer of 1944, Boris Bressloff was greeted over tea by Squadron Leader Ian Bazalgette, DFC. "Welcome to 635," he said. "I think you will be happy with us, we are a happy squadron and a good squadron. If you just do what you have been trained to do, you should come through OK. I wish you luck." Days later, Bazalgette was dead. He was the master bomber directing a raid on a V-1 flying bomb site in France. His Lancaster was hit on the way in and caught fire, but he refused to pull out of the action. He continued marking the target, ordered the rest of his crew to bail out, and then stayed himself when he discovered two of them were wounded and could not escape. With only one engine left, he tried to crash-land but the aircraft exploded on touching the ground. He was awarded a Victoria Cross, one of nineteen won by Bomber Command in the war.[22] His death devastated the newcomers. Bressloff recalled: "He was such a nice guy. It was a pretty awful introduction to operational life. It also brought home that there still was a hell of a lot of work to do."

Generally, the veterans on the squadron ignored the new boys. It was like the first day at school all over again. "They didn't want to know us," Bressloff said. One such veteran, Campbell Muirhead, admitted as much.[23] "On the whole we didn't do very much to make life easier for them." He remembered what he called "sprog crews" at his squadron. In the summer of 1944 those young men fresh from training were arriving almost daily as replacements. With a terrible war-weariness, he wrote in his diary:

They don't know, and can't be expected to know, a thing about operational flying. They ask the inevitable: (a) How many have you done? (b) What's it like? (c) Do you get scared when the night fighters trail you? To which we answer: (a) the truth, (b) fucking awful, (c) yes, with the word "shitless" added. Which is not very fair, really. But that was us only a short couple of months ago, wasn't it? When, just like them, absolutely green and scared, wondering what we'd done to get ourselves in a situation like this, we arrived here to find they'd allocated us the oldest, clapped-out Lancasters on the unit because you don't get a top-notch one until you've proved you've got a reasonable chance of not losing it the very first time you take the thing abroad—and you get around to wishing you simply had not joined.

We feel sorry for them. We all had that same romantic feeling as they do—oh, it's terrific to be prancing around with your flying brevet and your sergeant's tapes, or your pilot officer's rings, thinking, yes, I'm a hero and the girls are all aflutter and life's just absolutely bloody wonderful. But now it's the payoff. Because, when you crawl into your pit, the word "life" jerks you right back into the realization that "this is it." For that is just what is now forfeit—your life. Unless you amass luck in large quantities. Maybe they'll make it, and if they do, then it'll be their turn to feel sorry for the next lot of newcomers.

The official introduction to squadron life was hardly encouraging. Bressloff and the other newcomers were given a lecture on personal hygiene from the medical officer which began with pictures of diseased, rotting genitals and the warning that "That's how you guys are going to look if you get syphilis." The MO was just as blunt on the topic of first aid—there was almost nothing useful they could do for a wounded crewman, he told them. "If you have to deal with injuries, the best you can do is stanch the bleeding and then give a morphine injection. If you do that, don't forget to make a note of this so the medical people know when you get back. But since there won't be time to write out labels, just dip your finger in some blood and write 'M' on their forehead. Don't worry, there'll be plenty of blood for this." He had another gut-wrenching word of warning. "In the case of a really nasty abdominal wound, if you open the flying suit, the entrails will be protruding from the wound. Whatever you do, don't try to put anything back. You mustn't go rummaging in the plumbing." Bressloff was shocked. "It didn't inspire us with confidence," he recalled.

But he found his new home a cheerful and efficient place to be. "We were comfortably quartered, well fed and warm." There were pubs in the nearby town and a café where they could get decent coffee and—occasionally, in those days of rationing—cakes, some filled with "pineapple" jam (a stray pip or two revealed that it was actually made from vegetable marrows). But when these men-boys really wanted to let their hair down, they tended to confine their antics—"our notorious roistering"—to the mess.

The officers' mess, particularly, was run like a good club. It was spacious and well furnished; an armchair was always vacant to read or doze. It had a games room and a cozy bar stocked with plentiful supplies of wartime beer. It was weak—only two percent—but it lubricated the carousing, which was our way of shrugging off the stresses of operational flying. We loved a singsong—bawdy ditties, sung as loudly as we could. The padre, no mean pianist, would sometimes accompany us on the battered barroom piano. I always admired the stoical detachment with which he played, seemingly oblivious to the lyrics, although he would wince if they became too blasphemous. Both he and the Doc—our medical officer—could knock back a glass or two with the best of them. Sometimes a twinge of conscience would induce them to try setting a good example and they would stand at the bar nursing a glass of orange squash, but not with any evidence of enjoyment.

We had various games. One was the public school "Jimmy Knacker Up against the Wall," [akin to "Johnny on the Pony" in the United States]. One team would bend down and form a line from a wall with each man's head between the legs of the man in front. Then the other team would run the length of the mess, one after another, and jump as hard as they could onto the line until it collapsed under the weight. It was all very hilarious, but pretty stupid. Necks could break doing that kind of thing. Another favorite prank was to plant footprints on the ceiling. You mixed soot with beer and then painted this all over your feet. You made the imprint by swinging from the rafters until your feet could be firmly planted on the ceiling. Our CO was the champion. Somehow he managed to imprint his bare buttocks up there.

Such high jinks were the very stuff of squadron life, whether in the officers' or the sergeants' mess. Woe betide the man who sat in an armchair and spread the broadsheet *Times* in front of him to read. For some it was an irresistible temptation—creep forward, strike a match. The reader leapt up cursing as his paper erupted into flames and he stamped out the burning mess on the floor. At RAF Wickenby a notice went on the board banning this practice—the mess took just two copies of *The Times* and they were not lasting past lunchtime. There were more copies of the *Daily Mirror* and the *Daily Mail*. The firebugs were requested to redirect their activities. The *Mirror,* however, had a fireproof quality about it—thanks to Jane, the skimpily clad cartoon character it featured. How little would she be wearing today? Reg Davey recalled: "We all went into battle wondering whether or not in the next day's *Daily Mirror,* Jane would lose her bra or knickers when caught up a tree by a ferocious Alsatian dog."

Pranks built comradeship and killed time, and if there was something juvenile about them, then that just reflected the youth of those taking part. But they were also a vital safety valve for men under pressure, a way of blowing off steam. "Station life provided a necessary antidote to the terrors of operational flying," Bressloff recalled. "Some people drank too much, used alcohol to try to drown their fears or their sorrows, but we certainly didn't drink if we knew we were on the battle order and we never touched spirits." His faith that his fellow airmen knew when to stop was not shared by everyone. Reg Davey had a flight engineer on his crew who had to be sent away to dry out. He never returned to flying duties. Dennis Steiner's pilot got roaring drunk one lunchtime, ahead of a night operation. "His roommate and I filled him with black coffee, dunked him in a cold bath and bundled him into bed for the afternoon. When he attempted to get up we sat on him, but he soon fell asleep. At briefing—which was for a trip to Happy Valley [the Ruhr], he kept nodding off." Steiner had an impossible choice to make. "Should I report him as unfit to fly—which would have meant a court martial—or chance him being sober enough not to endanger us all on the operation? Fortunately, by the time we got out to dispersal, he was almost normal and went aboard the aircraft to inhale lungfuls of oxygen, a good cure for a hangover. All then went well, much to my relief." The pilot's problems turned out to be a woman rather than fear of flying, but whatever drove him to drink, this was an uneasy time for his crew. Ken Newman recalled how his navigator brother-in-law, Victor, had consulted him about the pilot in his crew. The man was a heavy drinker who, to hide his fears, spent all his off-duty time in the pub and was seldom totally on top of his job the next day. They were just reaching the end of their training. Should Victor tell his superiors? Should he ask to be recrewed? Newman's advice was clear: "While I could understand Victor's reluctance to pull out the rug from under his pilot, he would be unwise to do nothing about it." It was shortly after this that Victor died; his plane crashed on his crew's first operational sortie. No wonder Robert Wannop had gone out of his way to surround himself with teetotalers.

As for Bressloff's assertion that crewmen generally stuck to beer, Eric Banks, a wireless operator, recalled "seeing off large quantities of spirits on several evenings each week." Admittedly this was during stand-down. He and his crew had twenty ops under their belts and had been anxious to race to the required thirty. But bad weather and other circumstances left them grounded for weeks on end. The waiting was "doing our heads in." Later he realized they were getting through a bottle of whiskey each at their drinking sessions in the mess.[24] At some stations, senior officers kept an eye on drinking by running their eye over mess bills. Drink was always logged separately, and Campbell Muirhead remembered that if the amount under this heading became excessive, the mess president would have a quiet word. Muirhead was never taken aside in this way, but he did notice that the bills started coming more frequently. Then he realized the mess secretary was making sure of prompt payment, "given that so many of his customers were unlikely to be around too long to fork up." Muirhead also commented that his bills seemed to be on the increase—"I suppose we are all drinking and smoking more as the tour progresses."

Some had the money to do so, especially the officers. As a flight lieutenant, Roy Day was paid £1 4s. a day,[25] which, after deductions for tax and postwar credits, left him with between £26 and £30 a month in his pocket. It was a "princely sum" for a young man to have at his disposal, "particularly with beer at one shilling a pint."[26]

Life on most squadrons swung between exhaustion and anticipation, recovering from the last sortie and getting ready for the next, celebrating your survival and moaning. Not surprisingly, aircrew were susceptible to niggling medical complaints, and an enterprising mess sergeant could boost his pay by supplying liver salts, nasal inhalers, even cod-liver oil, under the counter. Nervous stomachs and ear, throat, and sinus infections from flying in draughty aircraft at subzero temperatures were common, but few men ever reported sick with such minor ailments. To do so might mean being grounded and thereby left behind by the crew you had come to depend on, and who had come to depend on you. If you missed three operations with your own crew you became a "spare bod," a drifter who could be assigned to any crew short a man. But the worst thing about officially going sick was that the powers that be might suspect you of malingering, or, worse still, of being too scared to continue, for which, as we will see later, the consequences could be terrible.[27] So men forced themselves through pain barriers in order to keep flying. They coped with these outbreaks of what today would be deemed stress-related illnesses by dosing themselves with quack or patent medicines. They handled the other major health problem—exhaustion—by popping the Benzedrine tablets that appear to have been freely available on most (but not all) stations. To Miles Tripp these "wakey-wakey" pills were "the answer to every flier's problems." He thought they were supposed to be issued only occasionally and under careful medical supervision, but his own experience was that they were handed out on request after every briefing session. Flight Lieutenant Dennis Steiner recalled the medical officer at his squadron standing at the briefing-room door and doling out pills that staved off sleep. Writing his memoirs in 1989, he concluded they were taking drugs that would "no doubt be banned today." Bob Pierson thought the pills also suppressed the need to urinate, which was of great advantage to a rear gunner like him, almost welded into his turret, with little room to move.

Superstition and ritual were also part of everyday life on a squadron, and pretty well anything that helped a man to get through the ordeal of staying alive and staying sane was acceptable to his fellows. Miles Tripp carried four good-luck charms with him—a silk stocking, a Women's Land Army brooch, a pink chiffon scarf, and a tiny bone elephant. Another member of his crew had his girlfriend's brassiere in his pocket, and the pilot refused to take off unless his hat was on a ledge behind his head in the cockpit with the peak facing forward. Harry Yates carried perhaps the most idiosyncratic charm of all. "It was the wishbone of my favorite hen, Blackie, whose demise enriched the family table on Christmas Day 1942. This hallowed relic was garlanded by my mother with a sprig of dried lavender which she fixed by means of some black wool. I never left the ground without it. And there was no doubt that luck proved a true and constant friend."[28]

It was a small, slightly mad world they all inhabited. Johnnie Clark felt as if he and the men he fought alongside were isolated, cut off even from other squadrons who shared the same airfield.[29] "The squadron became your whole way of life, an enclave which occupied every member of it. There was a life going on outside the main gates but we knew little of it. Our days revolved around the battle order, which was circulated each morning. Our days off were spent in catching up with sleep or roistering in the mess." He recalled an Australian member of the squadron announcing:

"Let's have a party tonight!" "Why tonight?" someone asked. "Because it's Monday," he replied, "and there's only one Monday in the week." But not everywhere was there that much fun to be had, and for some at the more remote airfields, it was virtually nonexistent. Peter Marshall remembered RAF Strubby—brought into commission late in the war—as a place of unremitting bleakness.[30] The wind howled across the flatlands from the North Sea. It was five miles to the nearest village. "But there was a little farmhouse on the other side of the airfield where you could pop in and the farmer's wife did lovely egg sandwiches." On such small treats was the war endured.

Miles Tripp fell in love with a WAAF. There were around 38,000 women in uniform working in Bomber Command, most of them in clerical jobs, in the operations room, as orderlies, or packing parachutes. But there were many, too, who did technical jobs as engine fitters, electricians, and mechanics, anything, in fact, which would leave the men free for flying duties. They often drove the tractors towing trolleys of bombs from the arms dump to the aircraft. Then they would switch to three-ton trucks to pick up the crews from briefing and take them to their aircraft. Eric Thale remembered "their quiet efficiency and shy caring for us."[31] When the boys got out of the truck there was always a cheery call from the WAAF driver: "I'll be waiting for you lot when you get back." It was no good being a shy WAAF. Morfydd Brooks from South Wales recalled:

> We had to endure a barrage of good-natured banter from the aircrews as they swarmed in for breakfast after returning from an operation— "How's your sex life?" they would ask, or "I dreamed about you all night," or "Please serve us in the nude," or just a straightforward "Will you sleep with me?" Then one of them would ask: "What is the collective noun for WAAFs?" and they would all answer, "The collective noun for WAAFs is a *mattress* of WAAFs." And they would erupt into laughter. We took it all in good part because we knew the great strains they were under and the dangers they faced.[32]

The women's social life was a full one, if they wished. Eighteen-year-old Pip Beck was told when she arrived at her first posting at RAF Waddington in Lincolnshire: "This is a bomber station and you'll have a good time. You can have a different boyfriend every night if you want to. It's wizzo [splendid]."[33] She couldn't stop herself falling for the dashing young men she met. "They were young gods, fabulous beings. I admired and hero-worshipped them." Nor could she stop herself blushing in their presence—she was glad no one could read her thoughts. But there were dangers in being so easily swept off her feet. Her first boyfriend was killed, and when her tears had dried she told herself to be more careful with her emotions. From then on, for a special man she would iron his shirts, find little ways of helping. "Removing the creases from a shirt seemed little enough to do given what they went through. Then you would go on duty one day and discover he hadn't come back from the night's op. That was how it was. We accepted it, shrugged, and said, 'That's it.' But underneath, we each had a nagging ache of sorrow." She developed uncanny instincts: "Once I was dancing with a Scottish sergeant pilot and suddenly I knew he was for the chop [going to be killed]. I wondered if he had any suspicion himself. Sure enough, on his next operation he didn't come back. It made me very sad."

Some airmen thought (or bragged to each other they thought) the WAAF girls good for only one thing. Bawdy squadron songs celebrated members of the Women's Auxiliary Air Force in ways that would have made even the most worldly of them cringe. The women resented the collective slur on their character. Pip Beck hated "the derogatory labels pinned thoughtlessly on us all—as 'aircrew comforts' or 'Officers, for the use of.' It was most unfair. We consoled ourselves that those who knew us would not subscribe to such views."

Miles Tripp certainly had no such low thoughts. His Audrey, he recalled, was "fragile and fawnlike, even in severe gray uniform." She was on a meteorological course in London, and he risked his career to see her as often as he could. He would race there on his motorbike, technically absent without leave, and when the bike broke down he had to hitchhike back, desperately hoping that a snap op had not been called. His pals covered for him as best they could with the authorities but were unhappy among themselves at having a lovesick and potentially unreliable crew member.

He was just over halfway through his tour of thirty ops when he met her, and "the daily threat of death made my love of life more acute. All senses were extended and magnified." He spent all of a seven-day standdown with her and saying goodbye was agony. They were among countless couples going their separate ways at "sad, shadowy" Liverpool Street station. He noticed how "all the women's faces looked strained, even when they smiled." When she could, Audrey would travel up from London and book in at a hotel near the camp and he would stay with her overnight unless an urgent phone call had him rushing back for a briefing. Landing after a night operation over Germany in the small hours of the morning, he would hurry to be with her before daylight, popping wakey-wakey pills to stave off his tiredness. "It seemed wasteful to go to bed with an attractive woman and then promptly fall asleep," he recalled.

At least navigator Bill Kiley's WAAF was on the same base as him. Pat was a typist in the station headquarters and they fell into each other's arms at a squadron dance. From then on, he had only to walk past the window of her office to see her. Each morning he would take her a breakfast of toast, jam, and coffee scrounged from his mess. She would give him a kiss and cuddle before he flew on a sortie, but they never talked about precisely what he was doing. "It was so difficult seeing him go off, knowing he was putting his life in danger. But I didn't let it affect me. When he came back I never asked him if he was scared or if it had been a bad raid. We just lived for the day." Another taboo subject was marriage. They knew instinctively that it was best to wait for the war to end.[34] Bombardier Dickie Parfitt's instincts were completely the opposite. Realizing that if he was killed, his widow would get a pension, he decided it was a good time to marry his girlfriend, Ed. Bolshie ex-miner that he was, he told his commanding officer: "If I'm going to have my backside shot off for King and country, then I expect King and country to look after my widow." Not long after joining up, he had a few days' leave for the wedding at home in Kent. Their families had been saving food for months for the reception, a friend gave them a present of white flour for the cake, and Parfitt's Uncle Charlie killed a pig. The party broke up at 9:00 P.M. because that was the time of the last buses home, and the remaining guests went to the shelters when an air-raid siren sounded. Two days later, Parfitt was on his way back to camp. He did not see his bride for another two years, not until he returned from his training in Canada in August 1944, and then it was just for a week. But Ed never had any doubts that he would be coming home for good one day. His mum had told her: "You don't have to worry about our Dick. He'll be back."

Many other wives waited in vain. Many young husbands would never come home. Their plight was poignantly recorded in a poem that surfaced after the war. Its author was named Walter Clapham, and the intimacy of the recollection suggests he was either aircrew himself or related to someone who was. "Requiem for a Rear Gunner" captures so much of that lost generation:

> And should you weep for him, if so inclined,
> Then mingle knowledge with your gift of tears,
> Bare not your heart alone—unveil your mind
> Upon the history of his nineteen years.

> He kicked a ball in narrow London streets,
> Then pedalled groceries round Walthamstow.
> He learnt of love in cheaper Gaumont seats,
> Set it to jazz-time on his radio.

> He had a wife for seven magic nights,
> His eyes grew softer in a small hotel.
> They shared a dream of London, rich with lights
> And all the things that Woolworths has to sell.

> Against his shaggy head he brushed a sleeve,
> Within the barber's shop considered "pride,"
> Bought contraceptives in the hope of leave,
> Then flew to Nuremberg that night, and died.[35]

The war was hard on wives, even those whose husbands survived. Their natural anxiety was not eased by bureaucratic incompetence. Three times, Mollic Newman was informed that her husband, Ken, was missing, presumed dead. No wonder many men preferred to stay single and not to get too serious in their relationships with the opposite sex. Bruce Wyllie, although on a sergeant's pay of only 14s. 6d. a day, had his own car, an old Ford Y, and it was a girl magnet, he said with a twinkle in his eye sixty years later. He remembered with fondness a particular WAAF who he thought wanted to marry him. But he had always told himself it was a wartime romance, like a holiday romance, intense but not serious, not the real thing. After all, war wasn't real life, was it? Many airmen preferred to eye up and chat up the local "talent" and, being away from parental restraints for the first time, they had as free and easy a time as was possible for unattached young men of their generation. Sergeant Bill Low couldn't wait to get off the base at Metheringham in Lincolnshire. "There wasn't much life in the camp. I don't remember going to any event there at all. And anyway, we were billeted in Nissen huts some miles away from the main buildings. We had bikes, and we tended to go out to the villages at night. I struck up a good partnership with the flight engineer on my crew and we would go off together to the local dances or for a drink. We were just young people enjoying ourselves. There were lots of Land Army girls around, and they all had backache from picking beets, so we used to massage their backs. But it was all clean stuff, pretty innocent. We didn't get up to the things that youths get up to today."

Whenever they could, off-duty aircrew would venture farther afield, taking a train or bus or driving by car to try the pubs in the larger towns and cities in eastern England. Cambridge, Lincoln, York, Norwich, Bury St. Edmunds, all got used to an influx of airmen looking for a good time. The adventurous went to London. Those with friends or relations living in the capital had places to stay. The well-off put up at hotels. Those with less money to burn had to rely on hostels and clubs. A bedroom to yourself at the Victoria League Officers Club in South Kensington cost 5s. 6d. a night, though there was little chance of a dog-tired airman getting a long lie-in there. Rooms had to be vacated between 10:00 A.M. and noon for cleaning. The men were pushed out on the streets, where they went in search of what young men of their age were always looking for—beer, a chance to chat up a pretty girl, maybe a dance, perhaps a little loving, too.

But love and war made uneasy bedfellows. When lives were constantly on the line, being close to someone was a blessing and a curse. There were WAAFs whose men never came back, and if it happened to a girl more than two or three times, she would find herself shunned by the others on the base. No one wanted to go out with a "chop girl," as such women were cruelly called. Arthur White recalled a WAAF radio operator nicknamed "Jinxy Jean" because three of her boyfriends had been killed in action. When one of his crew revealed that he was taking her out on a date, the others revolted. "You take her out and you can find yourself another bloody crew!" he was told. Superstitious and cruel such an attitude might be, but everyone who flew a Lancaster knew how low the chances of survival were. They needed every last bit of faith and good fortune they could muster, not just to survive but to conquer the greatest enemy of all—fear.

4

FLYING IN THE FACE OF FEAR

"You can only live once,
It's a matter of months,
And it doesn't take long to die."
—SONG OF 100 SQUADRON, RAF

DEATH AND THE FEAR OF DEATH WERE DAY-TO-DAY REALITIES FOR MANY of the British and American airmen charged with taking the war to the very heart of Germany in the tail end of the Second World War. They lived their lives with the knowledge that each day could be their last, but while death would most likely come in an instant, fear was a constant companion. Miles Tripp called it "the eighth passenger" because it always accompanied the seven men of a Lancaster into battle.[1] Campbell Muirhead could even describe fear—a dry throat, a tightening of the stomach, a dull ache that wouldn't go away, and a voice in the head that kept asking, Why did I let myself in for this?[2] It was a perfectly natural reaction, given what they were asked to do.

A Bomber Command doctor who dealt with thousands of combat airmen had nothing but admiration for the way in which these men coped. "Some drew upon their resources of courage and determination. Many turned to their friends or the inspiration of good leadership."[3] Curiosity and bravado got most through their first few clashes with the enemy, and the worst period of stress tended to come between the eighth and sixteenth sorties. By then, even the most phlegmatic had realized the nightmare of their job and the odds against survival, while completing the tour seemed unattainably far away. "Nonetheless, the vast majority, though inwardly terrified, maintained sufficient morale to carry on." But the effect of such constant stress was hard to disguise. The doctor was haunted by "their pallor, the hollows in their cheeks and beneath their eyes, and the utter fatigue with which they lolled listlessly in chairs in their mess." They were young, but their faces wore "the mask of age."

Not all of the men faced with the harsh realities of war reacted the same way. Tony Iverson had been shot down while flying Spitfires in 1940, been an instructor pilot, and then returned to combat as a bomber pilot. He remembered little real fear from the time. "Personally, I would call it a 'niggle.' To go on a series of operations and not expect anyone to get into any kind of trouble would have been stupid thinking. On my time on 617 Squadron I think we lost about eighty aircrew. It may seem strange to outsiders but I think we just took it in our stride. That might sound a bit blasé, but you do cope; one just accepted it as part of life."[4]

Most aircrew went about their duties with quiet courage, and the heroism shown by many bomber crews was rewarded with countless awards for bravery. Though they kept quiet about moments of fear at the time, many relived them in their memoirs and their memories. Pilot Alexander Adams (later an air vice marshal) recalled coming under fire and not being able to steer the aircraft away. The rudder would not move. "Beads of sweat broke out on my forehead. My heart began to pound . . ." Then he realized that, in his blind panic, he had forgotten to switch off the autopilot. By then the firing had stopped—and the crew came on the intercom to congratulate him on keeping his cool! "I let it pass. No sense in telling them that I had panicked."[5] The experience taught him to be sympathetic about fear in others. One night Adams took a group captain from Fighter Command as a guest on a bombing raid to Berlin. As they approached the German capital in the last wave of the attack, they looked down on a scene of chaos—"myriad searchlights, hundreds of small clouds of smoke from shells, the crack of lights from exploding bombs and the carpet of fires below. Airplanes were silhouetted by the light of the battle, some on bombing runs surrounded by bursting shells, others diving away, some in trouble." The veteran of Spitfires and Hurricanes had seen nothing like it. "Alex, surely we're not going in *there!*" he yelled. But that was precisely where they were going, and as Adams steered toward a colored marker for his bomb run, he held out his hand to his companion. "I knew how terrified he must have been. He took my hand and wouldn't let go as we made our bombing run." That was how frightening it was to be on a bombing raid: Even fighter pilots trembled.

Bill Carman simply didn't believe anyone who claimed not to be "shit-scared" on a raid.[6] The struggle—the true courage—was controlling it. And shit-scared could literally be just that, though only, it seems, on very rare occasions. Reg Davey remembered one man who came with his crew just once as a "spare bod." "It was a nasty raid to a town in the Ruhr, and after we landed I could smell that he had messed his trousers. Despite popular belief, this was most unusual."[7] But to climb into a bomber night after night or day after day in the knowledge that you might never come back and still to retain control of body, bowels, and mind took extraordinary strength.

That strength came in different guises. Some men chose denial as a way of coping. "We knew about the heavy losses," flight engineer Freddie Cole recalled, "but no one talked about fear or our chances of survival. You told yourself it would never happen to you. You couldn't think any other way, really. How could you go through a tour thinking, 'Is this my day to die? Is it my turn yet?' I always believed I would see the war through, that I wouldn't get the chop. And the more missions I got under my belt, the more I felt bulletproof."[8] Eighth Air Force navigator Arthur Prager's biggest fear was of fear itself. "I was worried about measuring up. Suppose I was a coward and others weren't. Could I ever hold my head up again. To twenty-two-year-olds like us, war and the missions were like a series of high school football games. We wanted to win and show ourselves as stars."[9]

Others conquered their fears by confronting them. "The only way to survive is to make believe you're dead already" was a far from unusual sentiment among aircrew. Boris Bressloff, for one, came to terms with the possibility of being killed.[10] "Statistics weighed the odds against our survival. When I saw my name on battle orders, I had to rush to the lavatory. I know some people say they were never afraid, but I think it's unnatural for a human being to face the sort of things we went through without knowing fear. The vast majority of men I knew were afraid. I saw them and I know." But he, too, hid his feelings, and very successfully. "I never told anybody I was scared. When you are young it seems a shameful thing to admit. People suppress their fears—particularly English people with their stiff-upper-lip attitudes." After the war he discovered that the others in his crew thought he had steel nerves.

At a reunion, our wireless operator admitted to the fact that he was afraid and said to me, "You never were, you never showed any fear." I put him straight, told him I was constantly afraid, but he refused to believe me.

"But you were always joking," he said, which was true. I was renowned for getting drunk and singing bawdy songs in the mess. At briefing I was a bit of a clown, too. I would go into the ops room and the curtain would be drawn over the map showing our target and I would have a peek before the CO came in and then fall flat on my back in a dead faint. But the joking was my way of covering up the fear.

He was not unusual in this. Humor had a huge part to play in calming the nerves, diverting a man's attention. Never was the saying truer that if you didn't laugh you would cry. More often than not, airmen's humor was of the gallows variety, from the lips of condemned men. "If you're shot down, can I have your egg for breakfast?" was a common request to novices.[11] The sicker the joke, the closer to reality it was and the funnier it seemed. There was a regular repartee with the girls who handed out the parachutes. "What do I do if it doesn't open?" the men going into battle would ask. "Bring it back and I'll give you another one," the girls would reply, and everyone would crack up, knowing full well that parachutes could indeed fail at the vital moment, and then it would be no laughing matter. They had all felt sick to their stomachs at seeing someone bail out of a stricken plane and the silk canopy fail to mushroom out. Falling to the ground like that, would you be headfirst or feetfirst? Would you black out before impact? Or would you see the ground rushing up to meet you? The thoughts went through every airman's head but were never resolved. Who was alive to give them the answers? Humor filled that void. "We never talked about dying," American gunner Eddie Picardo said. "Each morning when we got together we would be talking about crazy things, making one another laugh. You didn't want to talk about the reality of what the day was going to bring, absolutely not."[12]

But humor could also slip over into madness. Chuck Halper from Chicago, a pilot with the 385th Bomb Group, had what he thought was a fun way of brightening up dull hours in the cockpit. He would take a lungful of pure oxygen, put a cigarette in his mouth, "tap my copilot on the shoulder and when he turned toward me I would exhale and the flame would shoot within inches of his nose." Halper—not surprisingly nicknamed "Idiot" by colleagues—confessed his playful habit to a medical officer who told him he ran the risk of burning out his lungs if he accidentally breathed in instead of out. Looking back, Halper concluded: "Sanity was slowly slipping away."[13]

Some tried to drown their fears. Fresh out of training, Reg Davey found himself in the crew of a Stirling with a pilot who drank heavily. "Sometimes when we were taxiing out he would spew out of the window. He was all worked up and his stomach was a mess. He was sick from drink and sick from fear—mainly fear, I think." Davey, a navigator, used rigid discipline to see off his own demons.

I did my job, checked myself, checked everything again and again to the extent that I became a bit of a zombie. The only people I ever talked to about my fears were my mum and dad. My father was very good about it. He said: "Well, you just carry on, mate." But my mother cried every time I went back from leave, though she tried to hide it. She kept a very straight face and wished me well but every time she thought she would never see me again. That scene must have been reenacted in so many families.

Tom Tate was another who told himself he had a job to do and he had better get on with it, perform his duty to the best of his ability, and try not to think too much. That attitude got him through terrible moments.

I remember the night our captain was hit by shrapnel. Fortunately we had a second pilot on board and he took over, but we were still in trouble and it looked as if we would have to abandon the aircraft. I heaved the captain to the escape door, put his parachute on him, and attached a rope to the rip cord, then dangled him over the edge waiting for the order to push him out. Looking down, I could see the flak. The searchlights were coning us, and the inside of the aircraft was all lit up. But you can only be terrified so much. Things were happening so fast I didn't have time to think. I was just concentrating on getting the skipper out. But then the stand-in pilot regained control and we were out of danger. I shut the escape door, put a tourniquet on the captain's arm, and gave him a prick with a needle to kill the pain. You just carried on. It was the same seeing other aircraft exploding around you. There was nothing you could do about it. And, of course, we never discussed it. You didn't have to, because we all shared the same fears.[14]

Tate did not expect to survive more than nine operations, and he wrote to his "lady friend" at home to tell her not to make any plans involving him. But even he was shocked when his commanding officer briefed the men to fly low into the flak and bomb the Ruhr from 8,000 feet one night rather than the usual 13,000. "What are a few miserable lives compared with hitting the target?" the group captain demanded, a glint of madness in his eyes. The men—feeling their lives "miserable" but precious nonetheless—were outraged by his cavalier attitude, and the CO later apologized, excusing his tactless outburst on the grounds that he was depressed by all the losses his men were taking. Tate could understand this. For all his determination just to do his job and not to let his imagination run riot, there were times when he felt he couldn't take any more. Like a small child, he would bite his own lip "and hope that I would bleed to death. Sounds ridiculous now, but I just wanted to put an end to all the dreadful experiences. Even when we didn't fly it was hellish. We would go through all the drama of being briefed for an operation and then it would be canceled. It was a relief not to go, but then you only had to go through it all over again. The cycle of emotions was relentless. I was completely demoralized a lot of the time."

Nightmares dogged the sleep of many during their tours of combat, and for some they never stopped. Standing by helplessly as a friend died could blight a man's life forever. In his mind, navigator Boris Bressloff never fully recovered from a disastrous raid on a heavily defended synthetic oil plant at Gelsenkirchen in the Ruhr.

It was a frightening place to go. I had been there twice already and each time I was more scared than before. This time we ran into a solid wall of flak, the sort you just want to run and hide from, except there is no hiding place. I heard a *klonk* as one of the engines was hit and it caught fire. The aircraft was bucking and Alec, the pilot, was trying to steer toward an area where the flak didn't seem quite so bad. We made the bomb run, we dropped the bombs, and then we were hit again. We were losing height and that brought us within range of the German light antiaircraft guns, which were much more accurate. They did their best to polish us off. Bits were coming off the aircraft. The astrodome went for a Burton [vanished] and a piece of flak thumped me in the back. It was bloody terrifying, but we maintained our discipline. Nobody cried out. But I knew the rest of the crew were as frightened as I was because I could hear their heavy breathing through their microphones.

As we crawled home, we were still being hit by flak and were down to just two engines. The skipper was calm, even though the starboard fin and rudder had gone—I looked out and could see them flapping uselessly. I couldn't see how he could possibly land the aircraft. We pressed on, heading for Woodbridge in Suffolk, an emergency airfield with an extralong runway.[15] We crossed the coastline at one thousand feet and were still losing height. By this time we were down to one engine and the aircraft was totally out of control, with everything shot to ribbons. We weren't going to make it to the airstrip, so Alec spotted a field and aimed for it.

We crashed through a line of saplings—I could hear them snapping—and pancaked onto the field. Earth was flying everywhere. Then there was a loud crash as the aircraft broke its back, came to a halt, and caught fire. I rushed to the rear of the plane, which was full of flames and smoke. Oxygen bottles were burning and I knew that the fuel tanks in the wings were going to explode any minute. For a moment I was trapped behind some broken metal where the fuselage had caved in, and as I tried to work my way round the obstruction I saw the upper escape hatch was open. I struggled through it, out and onto the wing. From the corner of my eye I caught a glimpse of what could have been a man's leg lying under some debris, but I had no chance to stop. The wing tanks must have gone up a split second later because I was blown off the wing and I found myself in the field.

The plane was burning and the ammunition was going off and we all retreated to a safe distance. That was when the engineer told me: "Jimmy's bought it, he's been blown up with the aircraft." That leg I had seen on the wing had been our wireless operator's, Jimmy Crabtree. He must have got tangled up, and the blast killed him. I knew I couldn't have done anything to save him. If I had stopped, I would have been dead, too. But the truth is that I sort of died with him. I kept thinking I should have stopped and done something, anything. I was racked with guilt. I always have been, I shall die with it. When Alec heard about Jimmy, he started running toward the aircraft, even though he was hurt and his head was streaming blood. I went after him, shouting, "Alec, there is nothing you can do, Jimmy's had it." I managed to stop him—ammunition was shooting off all over the place, and I wasn't sure if there was a bomb waiting to go off. All of a sudden a lady came from a farmhouse bearing a tray of tea and cakes and she walked through all this exploding ammunition as though nothing was happening at all and said, "Would you boys like a cup of tea?" Suddenly you go from fear, panic, death, guilt to just being glad you are alive and having a cup of tea.

That night we waited to be flown back to our base. We were all quiet, we couldn't talk, we were all shattered by the loss of Jimmy. We all withdrew within ourselves, alone with our own thoughts. Then Alec said to me, "I wish we could have saved Jimmy," and that was when I cried. Alec tried to console me. "It was all too quick; there was nothing you could do," he said. He urged me to forget it. But I couldn't. I felt that I owed Jimmy Crabtree something. He was a sergeant and I was a flight lieutenant, and we had been outside a dance once when a drunken airman took a swing at me. Jimmy, who was an ex-policeman, a big guy, stepped in and knocked him down. I always felt guilty about not having stood up for myself, having let him defend me. And now I had let him die.

I was so traumatized that when a plane came from the squadron to take us back to base, I put one foot on the ladder and was suddenly paralyzed with fear. It was only a short trip and not even a combat mission, but I had to struggle with myself to get on board, and all the way I was shaking. Back at base we were sent on leave and then came back and we went back on ops again. I was really glad to be going back on ops. It was some kind of palliative for my feelings of guilt and inadequacy. Many times I wished I were dead during those remaining operations. It was this terrible pain of feeling responsible for Jimmy's death. I didn't talk about it. I couldn't. We never did.[16]

The end of the war brought no respite for his troubled conscience. Bressloff could not settle into civilian life and eventually found another war to fight in.

I joined the Israeli air force and did twenty trips on B-17s as a navigator. I needed to face conflict again, and if I had been given the chance I think I would have gone on until I was killed. That would at least have been relief from this guilt. It took me years of depression and nightmares to come to terms with my mental agony and find peace of mind. I would try to work out in my mind what I should have done, whether I could have saved him if I hadn't been so selfish and tried to save myself. Could I have stopped and grabbed him? I would wake up weeping and my wife would have to comfort me. The nightmares went on for a long time. Other people might have been able to forget, but Jimmy's death that day in 1944 left a mental scar on me that has never healed.

It was hardly surprising that on some men a cloak of fatalism descended, as if they accepted they were doomed. Their fears then seemed to shift away from themselves to how those they left behind would cope with their loss. Flying Officer Henry Medrington, an English public school boy brought up, by his own admission, in a stiff-upper-lip culture—"I'm not usually one to unpack my heart"—was one such man, and he was greatly concerned for his mother. "It is people like her who suffer from wars, not we who fight them. For her the whole business is inexplicably painful." He wrote from the officers' mess at RAF East Kirkby in Lincolnshire to ask his Uncle Norman to try and be with her if and when the fateful telegram came.[17]

"And please have no illusions about the chances of her receiving this," he wrote. "We are quite definitely losing more than we were." He set out his own situation baldly.

I have completed twenty-three sorties at the time of writing. Together with endless foreboding calms, last-minute cancellations and unceasing conjecture and rumor, they have left my nerves in a [poor] state, if only from the effort involved in putting a face on it. I have always been far more afraid of the possibility of my own panic or the revelation to the rest of the crew of my own fear than any flak or fighters that we have seen. The strain of suppressing my feelings has been considerable and left a mark on me.

If *that* telegram came, his uncle was to know the following—and Medrington, a navigator, elaborated on what would happen next with the certainty of a man who had studied the prospects of living and dying:

Once reported missing, the chances of survival are about 6–4 against. Most of our casualties are caused by bombs dropping on aircraft from another at a greater height or from attacks by fighters. In either case, you haven't a hope in hell. If you are hit by flak there is a fair possibility [of survival]. Flak has hit us often enough and we have so far returned with only two slight casualties. But a shell immediately underneath the aircraft will more or less disintegrate it, and a stray piece killing the pilot would probably settle the whole crew since the aircraft would dive too fast to be righted. Still, 40 percent get out, and of those 40, a good 25 return to this country without ever being captured. This is an established and incontrovertible fact.[18] Understanding the details, grim as they are, you will know what line to take with mother.

Fatalism was accompanied by melancholy. *Dulce et decorum est pro patria mori*[19] was the sentiment of another war, not this one. Medrington was skeptical about the sacrifice. Was victory really worth the price of their lives? Would the world really a better place? Perhaps it did not matter, because they would not be part of it.

An appalling number of my friends have been killed, people I loved and respected have been slaughtered without either deserving it or gaining anything for anyone else by it. I see no chance of improving conditions after this lot is over. For my friends who have died I feel no pity because I believe they are well out of it. It is for their parents, whose whole lives were centered around them, that I am desperately sorry.

For others who surrendered to fate, it helped that they put themselves in divine hands. Bob Pierson, a practicing Catholic then and now, used to pray, "asking God to look after me. I can't be sure about the rest of my crew because we never discussed religion, but I have a feeling a lot of them prayed, too. It was private, like your fears. The only person who ever said anything was the padre. He would come over and say, 'Everything OK? Godspeed.' "[20] Pierson also felt he had a guardian angel protecting him—a disabled girl who lived next door to a pub where he and his crew drank.

The family's name was Lancaster, which of course made them special to us, and she was called Sally. She was fifteen and had been in a wheelchair from birth, but she was a cheerful soul, always smiling. Every time we went to the pub, she would be sitting in the window in her wheelchair and knitting little patriotic red, white, and blue dolls. One night she said to me: "This will take care of you," and gave me one of those dolls. I wasn't ever superstitious as a person, but there was something about her, and I was very touched by her gift. I carried it pinned inside my battle dress all the way through the war. I promised her that I would always go flying with it and I always did. And it must have worked because I'm still here.

But for every survivor, there was an airman who never came home. Having watched so many comrades die, Eddie Picardo could not help pondering how they had met the moment—and how he would meet his own death. He watched a B-24 in the formation take a hit and explode. "Their nose gunner, Jim, had sat across from me at breakfast only that morning. He was alive one second and dead the next. It was almost impossible to come to terms with. Was he scared, did he scream, was it quick and painless? *How would it be for me?*"

The loss of friends had usually begun in training, and been all the more traumatic because the men were unprepared for it. Danger and death were not on the curriculum. Reg Davey said, "The instructors didn't talk about the horrors of war, about losing friends or anything like that. They talked about successful operations only." But the realities became apparent when he was ordered to complete the will form in his pay book. For Bob Pierson, the fate of a fellow gunner named Peter brought him up with a start. "He and I learned our trade together. Then he went on an exercise, a cross-country flight, and they crashed. I was a pallbearer at his funeral and I'll never forget the coffin going down into the ground. I met his family—mother, father, a brother, and a sister. There was nothing you could say, just mumble your condolences. He was only nineteen, the same as me."

The deaths came quickly and regularly once they became operational, but they were never any easier to stomach. Acquaintances drifted into your life and were just as quickly gone. Eric Banks got talking to a fellow wireless operator and they had a great evening in the mess laughing and drinking. "He was Australian, his name was Mac and he said he would join me and my crew again later in the week, if we were available, if we didn't mind. The days passed and I had forgotten about him but then one morning at breakfast I mentioned I had not seen him around. 'In Baker's crew wasn't he?' someone said. I nodded. 'Went for a shit Tuesday evening.' " To anyone who thought that particular euphemism for dying was coarse or cruel, Banks explained: "It was the only way such tragedies could be accepted by those surviving. There could be no mourning and no pause for discussion or inquest, whatever our private thoughts and regrets. If our job was necessary—and we all fervently believed it was—there could be no stopping to count the cost."[21] But he did the counting in his head—of the eight men he had started out with in advanced training, five were dead. "What a filthy and horrible business this is!"

It was the incongruity of the beauty of flying and the ugliness of death that troubled American airman Bert Stiles. Over enemy territory on his first operation, he heard the pilot of another B-17 calling for help on the radio, terror in his voice. "I'm going down. Our oxygen's gone and my navigator's shot to hell!" Stiles thought: "Up there, somewhere in the soft blue sky a navigator was dying. It was pretty hard to believe."[22] Safely back home, through his baptism of fire, no longer "a virgin," as he and his crew put it, he told the padre it had been easy, a milk run. The padre told him two squadron planes had not made it. Stiles had briefly met one of the dead men—a copilot who had laughed like a maniac and drunkenly mocked him the night before,[23] an airman who drank to forget and who would now never drink again. "Now he was just blood and little chunks of bone and meat, blown all over the sky. Or he was cooked, burned into nothing. I thought about him all through interrogation [debriefing] and couldn't get him out of my mind." He grabbed a bicycle and sought solace in the open air and physical exertion. "It was so good to be moving, to be riding down a road and breathing and laughing, not knowing where the road led, nor caring. The world was big and endless and so green and soft . . ."

Stiles flew eight missions in the next twelve days and felt "like an old man. I looked in the mirror and a haggard mask of a face stared back at me. The eyes were bright, the veins were cleanly etched in the whites and the pupils were distended. We were all like that. It seemed like the sun had gone out of the world." It seemed even darker when a close friend—"the best guy to talk to I've ever known"—did not return from a mission.

When a guy goes down, it doesn't mean anything at first. You just say, Mac's gone, he's had it, but you don't really believe it. Everything goes on. You keep waiting for him to come back from leave. And then you wake up some night after you've been arguing with him in a dream. And you walk into the mess hall and save a seat for him before you remember. It hits you slowly, like cancer. It builds up inside you into something pretty grim and pretty ugly. Why did it have to be him? Why? For a while I was going to write to his mother. I even started a letter. But there was nothing to say. He could fly an airplane, sock in close in formation and hold it there all day long. He knew plenty about engines and flaps and landing gear. He wasn't the best-looking guy in the world but plenty of women thought so after they saw his clear brown eyes. He had a mind and was the kind of guy the world could use after the war. *All he lacked was luck.*

Sometimes that luck ran out horribly early. Campbell Muirhead had an Irishman and a Welshman billeted in his room and never got beyond calling them Paddy and Taffy (and they calling him Jock) before they were killed, dead on their first operation. "Their two beds have now been removed and I'm on my own again. Oh Christ! To get it on your very first!" Arthur White recalled a tall, cheerful-looking Canadian skipper who poked his head into his hut one day and said: "Hiya fellers! We've just been posted here. Is it OK for my crew to bunk down in here with you?" They were invited in but "we never even got to know their names. The squadron was briefed for an attack on the oil refineries at Zeitz near Leipzig. Ten Lancasters were lost. The next morning a sober-faced officer and a couple of lads from the orderly room came into the hut and quietly removed all the young Canadians' possessions."

The ritual clearing of dead men's belongings was one of the most harrowing memories for all those who survived the bomber war. "It was pretty horrific, seeing somebody's life being taken out of his locker to be sorted into personal items for his family to collect and the official things, which went back into stores," Reg Davey recalled. But it was often the sight that greeted brand-new crews arriving on squadron. When newly qualified radio operator Peter Marshall arrived at RAF Strubby, he and his crew were directed to a hut billet, only to find slept-in beds and clothes and equipment strewn everywhere. A flight sergeant sent them all to the mess to cool their heels. "Sorry about this," he explained, "but those two crews in there didn't come back last night. You'll have to wait until we have cleared all their kit away."[24] Ron Smith didn't even have the luxury of orderlies, policemen, or padres removing the personal possessions of the previous crew. "At the side of the bed I had chosen, its sheets turned down, were photographs of a pretty girl with a signature and sentiment to the absent previous occupant. We tidied up, placing all the items together for collection."[25]

For Bomber Command casualties, disposal of their property was the responsibility of what was termed a "committee of adjustment." Some stations had staff permanently assigned to this job. At Ken Newman's, they operated from a Nissen hut in the woods—"deliberately hidden from view so as not to remind aircrew what might happen to them."[26] Possessions were stored there until they were moved to a central RAF storage depot for safekeeping until a man's fate had been confirmed—dead, missing, or a POW.[27] But at other squadrons, fellow airmen were called on to perform the awful task of packing up a missing man's belongings. Sometimes it meant making sure that a man's death did not cause his family any greater pain than they were already enduring, as Campbell Muirhead discovered when he was detailed to carry it out for a navigator who had failed to return.

You sift through everything in his locker so it can be returned to his next of kin but you've got to be careful. For example, you wouldn't return French letters [condoms] to some fond mother who had never for a moment thought her son would indulge in that sort of thing. Same for pornographic photographs. And you had to read the letters he had kept to see what was in them and who they came from. This particular guy was married. Extremely handsome—looked like Errol Flynn. And as randy as hell. Any attractive girl was a challenge to him—he went all out to shag her. He used to say that he was certain he would buy it during the tour and that accordingly, even though married, he was going to "do" every woman he could. We found enough French letters to kit out the entire squadron. All the letters went into the fire. We checked and double-checked that nothing which was returned to his wife would give her any impression other than that of a devoted and faithful husband.

A few weeks later Muirhead noted in his diary that the officer in question had in fact survived and was in a POW camp. "No nooky for him there," Muirhead commented. He was glad that his experience of a committee of adjustment had ended up without tragedy. "Most don't. One pilot told me it was the most upsetting job he'd ever been handed. He knew the bod [man] had been killed because he had seen his plane hit by flak and explode with nobody getting out. He found going through the dead chap's effects numbing. He was almost unable to read the letters from his parents with phrases like 'We pray for you every night. May God protect you and return you to us safely.' " Often a man's only real possession was his uniform, and Muirhead wondered if his own parents would want his back "if I get the chop. What on earth would they do with it? It would, I think, be a constant, sad reminder to them that I once wore it." If a man's parents didn't want their son's suit, he presumed it would be put up for sale in the mess. "But would the mess forward the proceeds of such a sad sale to the parents? Doubt it. It wouldn't seem right. Must find out about that some time."

Other airmen recalled the possessions of the departed being auctioned or claims being put in that so-and-so had been promised the dead man's bike or car or whatever. Muirhead was sure of one thing, however: No one on a committee of adjustment would take any item for himself, no matter how trivial. "Even if your uniform was on the scruffy side and the deceased's was brand-new and a perfect fit, you'd never think of switching. That would be ghoulish."

Sometimes a dead man's locker held a sad secret. Davey remembered a rear gunner who was found to have two logbooks—one the official log of his tour, verified and signed each month by his flight commander, the other a fictitious account listing dozens of German night fighters he claimed to have shot down, "presumably to impress his girlfriend and to obtain free drinks in his local pub when on leave!"

One airman left a note in his locker for the men charged with removing his property if the worst happened:

> *To the Committee of Adjustment. Dear Sir, Hoping sincerely that I have caused you as little inconvenience as possible. Please accept this meager gift for doing a job that receives no thanks. I was yours sincerely,*
> *Michael C. Skarratt.*[28]

What the "meager gift" was is unknown, but the officer reading the letter must surely have been moved that here was a young man, prepared, even expecting, to die for his country but concerned that the disposal of his few possessions would be a trouble to the authorities.

When death came, it was not always at the hands of the enemy. Accidents claimed many lives[29]—one in seven of Bomber Command's fatalities—and when this happened it seemed more pointless than a loss in battle. Too often a heavily laden bomber lost power on takeoff and crashed. The fireball from a full load of fuel and a full bomb bay was spectacular, surpassed only if two aircraft collided. On his second operation, Arthur White looked out and saw two Lancasters in the forming stream ram into each other at the first turning point on the English coast. "They exploded in a holocaust of red and yellow flames and black smoke long before they had even reached operational height." Fourteen men dead in an instant. With hundreds of aircraft, sometimes a thousand, in the sky at the same time, the risk of such collisions was immense. It was a miracle there were not more. Eric Thale remembered the chaos as the Lancasters and Halifaxes jockeyed to get into position in the darkness.

> Aircraft that have got ahead of time for the rendezvous are trying to reduce speed, pulling back on the power and hanging on the "props," others are flying a dogleg track, while inevitably some clot [blockhead] will do an orbit, scaring the hell out of everyone who sees him coming at them head-on. All this is happening in total darkness so any sightings are split-second affairs. We seldom see another aircraft, but their presence is felt as we wallow through their slipstream.[30]

Under the stress of going to war, mistakes were easily made. Human error almost killed Eighth Air Force pilot Lieutenant Bill Dewey after the Luftwaffe had tried its best and failed. He had nursed a shattered B-24 back from Germany, its tail shot off by enemy fighters and the fuselage full of holes, and made a landing at an emergency runway on the Kent coast. Three of his crew were badly wounded. He was given a couple of shots of whiskey to settle his nerves and then another aircraft to fly back to base. He forgot to go over the checklist. "We went roaring down the runway, but the aircraft wouldn't lift off. I had left the control box locked, and I couldn't move the control column. I stood on the brakes, and we screeched to a stop with the brakes on fire. It was such a basic error that nearly killed us. I hadn't been thinking straight because I was still so shaken up by being shot up over Germany and only just making it back. And I should never have had that whiskey on an empty stomach!"[31]

Even being on the ground was no guarantee of safety. Jack Watson remembered a foggy night at RAF Upwood in Cambridgeshire when a Mosquito, a fast twin-engine bomber often used as a Pathfinder to mark the route for the heavyweight Lancasters, returned from a mission to Berlin dangerously low on fuel, hit a brick bomb shelter, and then plowed into some living quarters.

I was just on my way to bed when we heard this terrible crash and rushed out to see the quarters ablaze. Up in a window we could see three of our lads who had just come back from a raid. They still had their uniforms on. They couldn't get out and we couldn't get in to help them—and there was nothing anybody could do. Then they disappeared into a cloud of flame and smoke as the building collapsed on them. I then came across the bodies of the Mosquito pilot and navigator. They were still in their flying kit, but that was all that was holding them together. They were all smashed up, and when each body was put in a blanket, it just folded up into a ball as if there was nothing left of them. Now *that* really shook me.[32]

Sights like that could turn a man's stomach and then his mind. B-24 copilot Jim O'Connor went to a wood near his airfield after seeing one of his squadron's Mustang escort fighters crash into it. "My buddy and I helped two doctors who were collecting the remains of the pilot. I found a GI shoe with a foot still in it. At the base of a huge smoking tree, one of the doctors lifted up a pile of intestines like a string of steaming sausages. He said we each had twenty-nine feet of them inside us. Up in a tree we saw the victim's skull, rib cage, and spinal column wrapped round the trunk. Just about all the flesh had been blown off the bones."[33]

So this was what it meant to fall from the sky. O'Connor had only five missions left to fly to complete his tour, but was this how he, too, would die? He poked through a pile of wreckage and found the pilot's dog tags. "The next of kin stamped on the plates was a woman from South Carolina. In my mind's eye I saw a telegram from the War Department with red stars on it being delivered to a little house on a quiet, shady street." O'Connor's own parents had received just such a telegram a few months earlier telling them their older son, Tom, a fighter pilot, had been shot down in action against the Japanese in Burma. His body was never found. O'Connor had grieved then, and he grieved now for this young fighter pilot whose end he was witnessing. "My buddy and I headed back to base and passed through a village just as the sun was going down. We stopped at the pub and drank a pint of ale in silence."[34]

It helped to deal with events like this if you could tell yourself you didn't care. John Wynne developed a matter-of-fact attitude to death after risking his own life to try to rescue two men who, it turned out, were beyond saving. He was on watch at the end of the runway when a Wellington touched down and then blew up in

a bloody great white light. I ran to the plane and at the rear end there was a bloke sitting in the rear turret. I banged on the fuselage and indicated to him to turn the turret around to get out. Then an airman came up to me and said, "He's dead, sir." I climbed up on the wing and looked in the astrodome and there was a bloke lying on the floor. His leg, still in a flying boot, was on the floor next to him. The aircraft was on fire and leaking fuel, but I chopped a hole in the side with an axe and took him out and parked him on the ground.

The doc came up in his little truck and I told him: "He's lost his leg. It's in the airplane. Do you want it, sir?" but he said: "No, I don't think so." And I said: "Are you going to give him some morphine?" And the old doc looked at me and obviously thought I was a bloody squirt. He said, "No he'll be dead in a couple of minutes," and he stuffed his hands in his pocket and went off. I looked at the airman on the ground and thought, poor old bugger, he's not even worth a shot of morphine. I thought there is nothing I can do about this, so I went back to work.[35]

Had the doctor been callous? Had Wynne been indifferent?

But this was life in those days. Today we are a totally different society. We put out bunches of flowers, have little vigils, hold hands, and have counselors to tell us all what to do. It was totally different then. The world events were so monumental that you had no time to think about the people who had fallen by the wayside. If we had had today's attitudes, we would never have won the war.

It was not just the thought of dying that caused consternation to aircrew. Some fates were seen as worse than death. Campbell Muirhead met a fellow bombardier whose horror was of being blinded.

He told me that, if hit about the eyes by flak or cannon, he would dive out of the escape hatch and drop down to a quick death rather than spend the rest of his life blind. I couldn't agree with him—you could be hit across the face and *think* you were blinded but in the event not be. No, I wouldn't do that. Still, a terrible thought, to be blinded for life. All those beautiful things you'd no longer be able to see. Doesn't bear thinking about. Want to forget it.

Many were horrified by the thought of being burned. Before he joined the RAF, Bob Pierson had seen airmen with faces disfigured by burns at a special hospital in Kent. He remembered their smiles but also the awful nature of their injuries, the swollen lips and raw-scarred skin, the gimlet eyes, the stumps of ears. Bill Kiley had come across a similar group of men in a street in Cambridge in 1942. "They were in uniform, chatting away, laughing and talking, but their faces were terrible, and one had no hands. I was never really worried about dying—that seemed almost unreal. But I did worry about being burned. That was the one thing I was afraid of."[36] Chan Chandler witnessed a man burn to death—heard it, too.[37] The bomber had blown up on landing—a "flamer" the men called it—and all but one of the crew had scrambled out. From the pyre came a sound "unearthly and mind destroying, like an animal screaming from some unbearable torture." No one could get near the flames to rescue him. They could only stand and wish he would die quickly. If Chandler had had a gun, he would have tried to shoot the poor wretch to end his misery. When the silence came, probably only seconds later, though it felt like an eternity, it was even more agonizing.

A veteran airman told him that in flames like that the eyes burnt out first, then the hands, and a man would be too disoriented to save himself. If you didn't get out in the first half minute you had probably had it, and if you did get out after that, then you would probably wish you hadn't. A nurse told Chandler of changing the dressings on badly burnt men. She had wept just thinking of their agony. "The only treatment is to scrub off any burnt skin or infection every day until they are stable. It's terrible, but it's all we can do. If they get septicemia, nothing can save them. It's not so bad for the ones who are unconscious, but for the other poor dears, they get terrified every morning when they see the clock getting round to nine o'clock, the time for bandage changing. It's awful, awful."

The thought of bailing out also terrified many airmen, to the point where they chose not to think it could happen to them. There was little or no parachute training, and the first time a man jumped it was likely to be the real thing. Most men worked out their escape route in their heads and knew split seconds would be the difference between life and death in a bucking, diving, fire-filled fuselage. They put thoughts of hitting the tail, being sliced by the prop, or thudding into the ground at terminal velocity beneath a burnt or broken parachute out of their minds. Nor would they want to know that if they jumped at high altitude there was every chance of severe frostbite and oxygen deprivation. And that was if they could get out at all. Training in a Halifax, Ken Newman had grave doubts about ever being able to bail out. "Five members of the crew were jammed into the nose, where there was just one escape hatch. It was in the floor under the navigator's chair, and in an emergency he and his chair had to be moved out of the way, and there was very little room to do that. Only after the navigator, the bombardier, and the wireless operator had clipped on their parachutes and exited could the flight engineer and the pilot get down from the upper part of the nose and escape."

In a Lancaster, the escape route was through an even tinier hatch in the floor of the bombardier's position at the front of the plane. It was twenty-two inches wide—barely more than the width of the average man's shoulders and "almost criminally too small," according to one aviation specialist.[38] For all the many joys and benefits of a Lancaster, it was a death trap in an emergency, the escape rate an appalling 15 percent compared with 50 percent in a B-17 and a B-24.

For once, Tail-End Charlies sitting in the rear gun turret had an advantage over the rest of the crew. In extremis, they had their own way out of a doomed aircraft. They could swing the turret to a right angle, open the doors and tumble out backward. But this advantage was canceled out by the fact that a rear gunner had to get to his parachute first. In an emergency—in the panic, in the dark, with smoke choking him and flames at his feet—he would have to remember to grab the brown pack and clip it on. Some men kept theirs close to them—Sergeant "Titch" Wyllie was small enough to be able to sit on his.[39] Others, especially tall men like Bob Pierson, had no alternative but to hang theirs on a hook just inside the fuselage and pray it would never be out of reach. Realistically he knew that, if they were hit, "I would never have got out; it was just not possible."

Chan Chandler was of the same mind. "If you had to bail out, you had to line your turret up, open the doors, and get half out of your turret to get your chute, clip it on, get back into the turret, swing it ninety degrees, then fall out backward. I could never figure out how you could do that and be certain not to get your legs trapped." Few could expect the sort of miracle that saved Flight Sergeant Nick Alkemade, whose Lancaster was shot down returning from Berlin. The pilot ordered "Abandon aircraft," Alkemade hurriedly docked his turret, opened the doors, and reached inside the fuselage for his parachute, only to be hit by a blast of heat and flame that singed his face and hands. The rubber mask of his helmet began to melt. The parachute—out of his reach anyway—was ablaze. He hauled himself back into his turret, slammed the doors behind him, holding the flames back temporarily. Then, deciding on a quick, clean death rather than burning alive, he rotated the turret, opened the doors, and dropped out. He was eighteen thousand feet above ground. Free falling, head down, eyes closed, he blacked out. Three hours later he came to in a snowdrift in a pine forest. He lit a cigarette and waited for the Germans to find him.[40]

Most men who ended up in German hands had little idea of what to expect. Many were startled and frightened by the hostility of German civilians, to whom the bomber crews were *Terrorflieger*—"terror fliers"—who firebombed cities and massacred women and children. If they survived their initial capture—and, as we will see, not all did—they would eventually be taken to prisoner-of-war camps, another fate which few of them had properly contemplated or been trained to deal with. They had written orders on what their responsibilities were as POWs, but these were almost entirely concerned with not giving away any information to the enemy. Stick to name, rank, and number and don't trust a soul was what this amounted to. Of life in the camps and how to cope with it, they received little guidance. Their ignorance of what awaited them was shown by men like Boris Bressloff, a Jew, whose identity disc made clear his religion. He was fully aware of the Nazi regime's persecution of his race, but it seems not to have occurred to him that he would be in extra danger if shot down. Nor was it in the interests of the RAF authorities to remind him or remove him from danger. While some airmen made elaborate escape kits and had emergency plans in case of landing in enemy territory, most do not appear even to have talked among themselves about what they would do in such an eventuality, any more than they discussed dying or their fears. These were taboo subjects.

Their commanders were happy to connive in this silence. The less said about casualties the better. Sir Charles Portal, chief of the air staff, even instigated a ban on releasing figures. In a top-secret memorandum he expressed his extreme anxiety "that statistical information relating to the chances of survival of aircrews should be confined to the smallest number of people. The information can be so easily distorted and is then so dangerous to morale."[41] The men had only to look around their empty huts and mess halls to see the truth for themselves. Nonetheless, discussion of figures and rates and percentages was forbidden at squadron level, and all correspondence on the subject went through secret channels. There would be no careless talk about lives lost. And if a man could be encouraged to think that he stood a good chance of getting home unscathed even if he was forced down in the heart of Germany, then so be it. Let them believe the myth.

Nor did the authorities do anything to dispel that other strange myth of the bomber war—"scarecrows." As casualties mounted, stories were told among the airmen that the Germans had developed a special shell, a firework that simulated a plane exploding in midair. Memoir after memoir mentions these. Dickie Parfitt called them "spoofs," and he said they had tiny parachutes inside them which deployed when the shell exploded and from a distance looked like a crew bailing out.[42]

The explanation of "scarecrows" and "spoofs" was that they were an attempt to demoralize Allied bomber crews by exaggerating casualties. After the war the Luftwaffe and the commanders of the German antiaircraft batteries were found to have no records of such a mysterious weapon. Parfitt returned from the lethal Nuremberg operation and reported seeing lots of "spoofs," until a straight-talking intelligence officer told him: "They weren't spoofs; they were our boys."

Others worked out the truth for themselves. Reg Davey felt sure that the Germans didn't fire up scarecrows at all. "What we saw going down were actually Lancasters and Halifaxes. Somebody told us they were scarecrows to try to get us not to worry about these things." The issue has never been completely resolved, and the debate still continues among the dwindling number of bomber crews. But it suited the authorities not to dispel the "scarecrow" rumor, to pretend that casualties were not as bad as they really were. The truth is that the bomber crews themselves were happy to believe that, too—that, in the face of all the evidence, they might, after all, get through this bloody war.

Such faith was not, however, granted to all the men who fought the bomber war. For some, the relentless journey to the front line night after night became too much. Jerry Jackson, Tail-End Charlie in a Lancaster skippered by American pilot Nicky Knilans, was one such man. One afternoon Knilans was called to see his wing commander. "He told me Jerry had been in to see him. The strain of our previous combat raids had become too much for him. His position in the aircraft was the most isolated and the coldest. He had to stare out into the darkness hour after hour. He knew enemy fighters were stalking him most of the time. He wanted to be taken off flying duties."[43]

But what had really got to Jackson was a telegram that day from his wife in Scotland telling him he had a newborn son. He was a father—and desperate to live, not die. The wing commander congratulated him and reminded him he was due for leave in a week's time and that he could see the baby then. In the meantime, he had to keep flying. The wing commander had persuaded Jackson to carry on, but he thought Knilans needed to know that his tail gunner was a man on the edge.

I deliberately said nothing to Jerry. He did not need to know that I knew. As we assembled around the aircraft before takeoff, we congratulated him about his son. He was a chain-smoker anyway, so no one thought of his nervousness as anything out of the ordinary. He seemed less despondent as we took our stations. We were at 19,000 feet over Germany and turning for our target when the wireless operator spotted blips on the radar screen. Suddenly a stream of tracer cannon and machine-gun bullets came through the port wing and thudded into the fuselage. I dived to starboard and yelled down the intercom to Jerry: "Can you see him?" There was no reply.

The fighter disappeared. Knilans steadied the Lancaster and resumed course for the bombing run despite one engine being out. Hitting the target, completing the mission, was always priority. "Press on regardless" was the standing order. As they pulled away after dropping their load, he could now think about the casualties. Heading for home, he dropped to twelve thousand feet so the crew could move around without their oxygen masks and sent his flight engineer back to find out the damage. Crawling to the rear, the flight engineer came upon devastation. The turret was at an angle and the doors were out of reach. He reported to Knilans that Jackson was "tipped forward inside and not moving."

The flight home was a nervous one. The mid gunner was also wounded and the plane was defenseless. Fortunately they ran into no more enemy fighters, and back on the ground the crew raced to the rear. Knilans forced the doors of the turret apart with a screwdriver and pulled Jackson out by the collar of his flying suit. It was obvious to them all that he would never see his baby son.

His body was stiff as I lowered it to the ground and took off his goggles, oxygen mask, and helmet. His still features were unmarked. I brushed back a fallen lock of hair. His forehead was icy cold. The middle of his flying suit was bloodstained and badly torn. We put him on a stretcher and into an ambulance.

I stayed behind in the darkness, depressed at losing my friend. When I got to the briefing room the squadron doctor told me Jerry must have died instantaneously. He gave me two sleeping pills, but I gave them to a WAAF who was overcome with grief. She was a good friend of Jerry's, and he had given her his personal effects to send to his parents if he failed to return. Before drifting off to sleep, I prayed that God would see Jerry into heaven.

Jerry Jackson had been forced to go on one operation too many because the RAF offered no honorable exit for brave men who lost their nerve. Quite the opposite, in fact. With a war still to win, Bomber Command afforded few concessions for those worn down by flak and fighters and fear. There would be no compassion for those it termed cowards.

5

NO EARLY RETURNS

"We just thought: poor sod."
—KEN NEWMAN, ON THE SUICIDE OF A PILOT

BLOOD AND SWEAT, FEAR AND DEATH. THESE WERE THE EVERYDAY REALIties for the airmen of the Eighth Air Force and Bomber Command. How did one cope with such horror? How did one force one's mind and body to press on amid the trauma of watching friends blasted out of the sky or seeing the remains of bloodied colleagues washed out of their aircraft? Some simply couldn't. American tail gunner Eddie Picardo remembered: "We could quit at any time. There wasn't any disgrace in the USAAF about saying that you had had enough. We were volunteers—they wouldn't do anything to you. If you said you couldn't go flying anymore, you were well treated." But that didn't mean a man could pick and choose when to fly and when to play safe. Picardo recalled briefings when the announcement of the target—particularly if it was a heavily defended place such as an oil refinery—would lead to a lot of men suddenly reporting sick.

They were sick all right, but it had nothing to do with the flu. They were queasy because they figured there was a good chance they wouldn't be at the next morning briefing. But the commanders got wise to this, and as the war progressed, they changed the procedure at briefings. Instead of jumping right into describing the target and what level of resistance we could expect, they began by asking if anyone wasn't up to flying that day. If no one spoke up at that point, the doors would be locked and every airman in the room was flying, oil refinery or no oil refinery. I attended plenty of briefings where guys wished they had spoken up early rather than find out that they might be blown out of the sky.[1]

Of course, once in the air, it was possible to shirk one's duty, but even men who did that were treated with compassion. USAAF pilot Walter Hughes knew one airman who found it impossible to force himself over the target. "He'd just slide out of formation, fly round the flak, and join us on the other side. They simply grounded him and gave him a desk job."[2] Bill Dewey had a fellow pilot who quit after bringing back a plane with his bombardier beheaded. "He came to our hut and said, 'Bill, I'm not going to fly anymore. I'm turning in my wings.' He'd had it." There were no re-criminations, either from fellow pilots or from the authorities.[3] Both Hughes and Dewey thought the American way of dealing with those who couldn't go on humane and correct. After all, what else could be done? The Royal Air Force had a very different view.

The flak was light as the Lancaster swept in and bombadier Campbell Muirhead lay flat on the floor, waiting to line up his sights on the V-1 launch pad in northern France.[4] With such a comparatively easy run-in, it was surprising, then, that there were anxious cries from the crew over the intercom: "Turn back, for God's sake!," "Mummy!" and "I don't want to effing die!" All of it was duly noted on a pad by the wing commander who had come along as a passenger. Muirhead and his crew were putting on a performance—though the twenty holes they later found in the aircraft might have been reason enough for the apparent outburst of emotion. But their fear was phoney this time. The "guest" was a psychiatrist—a "trick cyclist," as the crew disparagingly called him. He had asked to fly with a seasoned crew so he could assess behavioral patterns in combat conditions. Muirhead himself had begun the put-on. As they waited to board the bomber, "I started biting my lower lip and nervously informed the skipper that I wasn't going. He entered into the spirit and said if I didn't get into the kite, then I would face a court-martial. We then squared up to each other. The mid gunner then did a bloody good impression of throwing up." Five days later, the crew was called in by the squadron commander and rebuked. He waved the psychiatrist's report at them. "You bloody idiots," he cried. "Consider yourselves reprimanded. Now get out!" But they could hear him laughing his head off the moment the door was closed.

The crew's attitude reflected the general view in Bomber Command, from top to bottom, about those who dared to delve into their minds. And yet never has there been a body of men whose thoughts, emotions, and behavior were more worthy of study, and who deserved all the help they could get. Their position was uniquely stressful. They went from tranquillity to the chaos of battle and back to tranquillity again in a matter of hours. One pilot remembered crossing the English coast at Selsey Bill and knowing that his wife and children were in a cottage somewhere below him. One clear morning, returning from delivering mayhem to Berlin and after being coned in searchlights and missing a midair collision by just feet, he even picked out the house—"a thin spiral of gray smoke rising from the chimney, my wife no doubt astir and the children disturbed from their sleep by the drone of the returning bombers, unaware that Daddy was up there thinking about them."[5] How hard it must have been to keep a grip on reality. They confronted death, saw friends die, knew their own chances of survival were slim. And yet time after time they climbed into confined spaces, braved the air (itself a considerable psychological barrier for some) and the elements, aware that they were riding on top of tons of fuel and bombs that could blow them to kingdom come in a split second. On the journey, they were caught in bright lights, shot at, shelled, and pursued. And when they weren't doing this, they were worrying about doing it, being briefed to do it, waiting to do it. Here was a recipe for madness. And psychiatrists could have provided some genuine help for stressed-out airmen—if only the culture within the RAF had allowed it. But it did not. The prevailing view was that fear could not be openly admitted; otherwise how else would cowardice and desertion be contained?

It had not always been so. Indeed, the special stress felt by fliers had long been understood in military medical quarters. An article in the *Lancet* in 1918 stated: "There is no branch of the services where losses are more keenly felt. One of the greatest strains on the pilot's nerves is when he sees one of his friends go down in flames or learns that so-and-so is missing. After this occurs with monotonous regularity it is very hard for him to maintain his mental equilibrium."[6] A War Office inquiry into shell shock after the First World War heard air force doctors declare that, whereas soldiers often broke down suddenly under fire, for fliers there tended to be a gradual buildup of tension—"They get more and more nervous until somebody sends them on leave or they crash." It was even stated by no less an authority than the head of the RAF Medical Services that all airmen would break down in time when their endurance and determination were used up.[7] Such sensitive thoughts did not last. By the time war broke out again in 1939, the RAF had filed away shell shock as irrelevant. A good stiff chat and a spot of leave would sort out any flier feeling the strain. Psychiatrists would do more harm than good.

This was unfair to men such as Squadron Leader David Stafford-Clark, a Bomber Command medical officer who observed four thousand airmen and, like the wing commander who accompanied Campbell Muirhead's crew, went on fifteen combat operations himself. He wrote after the war: "From firsthand experience I can confirm that the supreme factor in stress among aircrews was fear—natural, normal human fear. The more imagination you had, the more inwardly terrified you were a great deal of the time, and the more strained, tense, anxious, and apprehensive you were apt to become at the prospect of the job you had to do."[8] That job, he concluded, became a "waking nightmare" after the first few missions. Each man was in a constant emotional struggle—"a conflict between his desire to do his duty and thereby maintain self-respect, and his instinct for self-preservation."[9]

No one knew better than their commanders that this was a personal struggle that could be allowed to have only one outcome. The will to do one's duty had to win. Fear had to be conquered, defied, denied, whatever. Otherwise the war would be lost. Sir Arthur Harris knew that the best and bravest would never be more than a quarter of his manpower. But battles could not be won by them alone. The less bold and the less committed had a job to do, too. He once wrote in a note to his boss, Sir Charles Portal, chief of the air staff:

It is inevitable in war that the best are the keenest to go back to operations and they are the ones who, when they get there, hit the target. There are perhaps 20 to 25 in each 100 who can be classed as the best. The remaining 75 to 80 divert the enemy effort from the destruction of the best and receive a certain number of casualties, so saving the best from being picked off by the enemy. At the same time, the weight of bombs they drop, some of which hit the target some of the time, all help to add to the damage but to a smaller degree than the bombs of the best, which will normally land on the target. This is true in any service in any war and in any operation, e.g., in the infantry there are a certain number of the not-so-good who confuse the enemy and make it difficult for him to pick off the best men only.[10]

Sixty years on, this might seem a cold, inhuman way to view one's subordinates, but this was total war, and the task at hand was to make sure the majority did not desert their posts. They had to be made to conquer their fear. And the way to do that, or so the reasoning went in the higher echelons of the RAF, was to make them fear something else even more. And that something else was the fear of being exposed as a coward.

What was reenacted night after night on Bomber Command stations in England was the equivalent of sending men over the top in the trenches of the First World War. Then it had been achieved by brutality. Those who refused to fight and die were tied to posts and shot—a scandalous disregard of the horror of war that could not be repeated a generation later. Yet the same result—sending men to what they knew was near-certain death—had to be achieved in the bomber war against Germany between 1942 and 1945. And with men who were volunteers. The RAF prided itself that all its flying personnel had chosen to do what they were doing. They were not conscripts, forced to join the fighting. A man *chose* the RAF and, within its ranks, a man *chose* to put himself forward for flying duties. What could not be allowed to happen was those same men choosing when they would fight and when they would stay at home. At the end of the war, Harris could claim that morale was never a problem among his men. He was right. The dropout rate was tiny. Though official figures are hard to come by because of the RAF's continuing sensitivity and secrecy about this issue, the number of Bomber Command airmen who refused to fly has been calculated by one expert to be around 200 a year and fewer than 1,000 for the entire war.[11] A further 8,000 were deemed incapable of flying because of some form of mental breakdown, removed from duties, and sent for hospital treatment.

Harris's supreme achievement was to persuade the rest of the men under his command routinely to risk their lives on his say-so. High morale, team spirit, and sheer bravery were key elements. But so, too, was coercion. Harris took a strong line on those he called "weaklings and waverers."[12] He followed what one historical expert has described as "the prevailing philosophy in Britain during the Second World War—that soldiers or airmen who broke in battle were innately weak or cowardly, and that courage was a function of background and breeding. Men of strength and character were judged immune from emotional disorder."[13] In the RAF, those who had lost the will to fight—or never had it in the first place—were classified as LMF, Lacking Moral Fiber.

The threat of being branded LMF was used as little short of a terror tactic, a sword of Damocles that hung over every airman. And it worked. From his training days, Miles Tripp felt "haunted" by those dreadful initials:

> It wasn't so much the admission of fear and loss of self-respect that deterred men from going LMF, it was the awareness that they would be regarded as inadequate to the pressures of war in a country totally committed to the winning of war. In this atmosphere, the man who opted out was a pariah, an insult to the national need. He was conscious of bringing shame to his family, and that most of his friends wouldn't wish to recognize him, or at best they would be embarrassed and awkward on meeting. Nobody cared about the explanations of the psychiatrists about stress-induced illness.[14]

Harris himself could not have put it better. Jack Watson, who saw one of his own crewmen crack up, said: "Some people carried on flying absolutely scared out of their wits because they were more scared of being called a coward than they were of flying."[15] Even talking about your fears could be a mark against you. Bill Carman, who had no doubt that every man was shit-scared going into a raid, and rightly so, constantly worried about being accused of LMF. "You didn't talk about the dangers, not even with your crew mates. People might think you were going LMF."

The pressure was applied softly and even subtly to begin with. Peter Marshall, a wireless operator, assembled in a hall with other airmen shortly after crewing up to be addressed by a wing commander.[16] "Well, gentlemen," he began, "what you are about to undertake is going to be very dangerous." He told them losses were quite high and their chance of surviving a tour of thirty operations was one in six. "So anyone who now wants to get up and walk out of the door can do so. There will be no stigma." They would, of course lose their sergeants' stripes and their coveted flying brevet and be returned to a ground trade, "but there will be no repercussions."

Then came the threat. "However, when I get off this stage, there is no getting out. You are *in* and that is it." It was the point of no return. Marshall recalled: "Nobody left the room—it took more courage to leave than stay." Only later did he cotton to their having been misled about their statistical chances of survival.

It was at a similar stage in his training that pilot Ken Newman remembered the attitudes of senior staff becoming "intimidating and unpleasant" with constant references to LMF.

> They began to treat us all as potential deserters. We were told that anyone who refused to fly on an operation, no matter how many he had already completed, would suffer the consequences—a court-martial with cashiering (i.e., dismissal in disgrace) for an officer or immediate reduction to the rank of aircraftman and military imprisonment for those who were not commissioned. Both would have their records annotated "LMF" and be given the dirtiest jobs in the RAF. It was also made clear to us that we were not to complain about anything. We were warned that anyone who stepped out of line or who was considered "difficult" could be sent to what was called the Aircrew Corrective Establishment, where for a week or a fortnight we would be given "disciplinary" training—drill and PT from early morning to late at night.

Newman felt insulted by the threats. "I wasn't daft. I realized that one or two chaps might have got to that stage of getting cold feet. But to treat all of us as if we were just about to mutiny was awful. *I expected encouragement not coercion.*"[17]

The pressure increased as crews went operational. Virtually every briefing for a mission at every squadron and airfield would end with the station commander's: "Good luck! Good bombing! *And no early returns!*" However cheerily it was delivered, it was a threat. Fail to complete the job, turn back before reaching the target for whatever reason, and you would have to account for yourself to a commander whose inclination would be to believe you had chickened out. Arthur White recalled: "There could be dozens of reasons for aborting an operation—engine failure, radio and radar faults, crew sickness, or a variety of mechanical problems and inexplicable malfunctions. But any early return was investigated most thoroughly. The skipper would be interrogated and an investigation might even be carried right up to Group."[18] The result was what the chiefs of Bomber Command wanted—men were reluctant to turn back. White would fly a long-haul mission to Munich—nine hundred miles there and back—one engine out of action virtually the whole way, navigation instruments not working, and the oxygen supply defective. To every suggestion that they should turn back, the skipper replied: "Let's give it a shot. We'll press on a bit and see how she goes." Forced off the bombing run by a German fighter, the pilot even went round a second time—a very risky maneuver—rather than have to explain later that he had missed the target. Harris would have been proud.

The commander in chief's strategy worked. Men who did turn back felt guilty. Roy Day suspected he was getting distrustful looks in the mess after he aborted a trip because of problems with the rear turret. "We were an hour and a half out over the North Sea when the rear gunner called me up and said the turret operation was intermittent, and his guns would not fire. I asked the crew if they thought we should go back, and when most of them said we should, I fell in with the majority."[19] This was something that Harris and others at the top of Bomber Command particularly feared—democracy breaking out in an aircraft on its way to war. But this was a danger, they recognized, when the skipper was a recently promoted sergeant like Day. Behind the high-level concerns about LMF lay the dead hand of British class consciousness. The officer class—preferably public-school educated—was thought of as having the right qualities of leadership, backbone, and moral strength needed to pursue a war. Those from a lesser background were suspect—would they fight or would they run?

In the early stages of the war, RAF selection procedures favored the traditional officer class. A typical selection board interview went along the lines of "Do you ride a horse? Do you drive a car? What school did you go to?" But then the net had to be cast wider to meet the demand for more recruits. And conventional military thinking was that a wider net would inevitably throw up some pretty strange and unreliable fish. Roy Day was one such catch, and his decision to abort out there over the North Sea was no more than was expected. He had very recently been promoted from sergeant to acting flying officer in the equivalent of a battlefield commission. Heads would have nodded knowingly in the armchairs of the RAF Club in Piccadilly. But Day did not need his betters to tell him where his duty lay. He knew his decision was a weak one as soon as he made it. He should *not* have asked the crew's opinion. "I had never done it before and I have regretted it ever since," he wrote. "A faulty rear turret was not sufficient cause to turn back. Back in the mess the CO gave me a very funny look. I think he might have had second thoughts about my promotion and might even have had thoughts about LMF." Day was aware that he was under scrutiny. The squadron doctor may well have been detailed to keep an eye on him.

Station commanders expected their medical officers to be alert for waverers. "It is possible for a good doctor to anticipate the onset of stress and to encourage and assist some individuals through a passing phase of slight loss of confidence," Harris advised. They would mix with the crews, especially at debriefings, on the lookout for indications of stress.[20] One medical officer recalled the signs—"remarks by friends that a man's general behavior was changing; crew members' concern about his ability to do his job properly; reporting to the MO rather frequently with obscure symptoms; responsible for his plane aborting missions for reasons that ground crew were later unable to confirm."[21] A man identified in this way might be taken off flying duties for a day or two, encouraged and cosseted, dosed up with sedatives and allowed to sleep.[22] Perhaps he would be bullied, too. A bombardier recalled how, after flying eight or nine operations, he felt exhausted. He was so lacking in energy that everything he did required a great effort. His skin was also going an unpleasant shade of yellow. Returning from his eleventh operation over Germany, he was violently sick and decided he really must report to the doctor because his condition was threatening not only to himself but to the safety of the whole crew. The medical officer listened to him as he recounted his symptoms and then said: "I think you're frightened of flying and that's the reason why you've gone yellow. There's nothing else the matter with you."[23]

A man could expect more sympathy from his fellow airmen. Arthur White thought being overcome by fear could happen to any member of a crew at any stage and he was happy for such a person to be removed from duties because "apart from anything else, he was a danger to the rest of the crew." But he disapproved very much of the stiff punishment that was handed out.

What everyone in Bomber Command feared was public disgrace for cowardice. Dickie Parfitt remembered being called into a room one day with thirty or forty others to witness a ritual dismissal. "We watched this guy being stripped of his rank and having his badges ripped off. The air force police did the necessary. I just felt sorry for him."[24] Campbell Muirhead was another airmen made to watch the "sad, sad sight" of a comrade being humiliated for having had enough. In his diary in June 1944, he recorded:

The entire strength of the station was on parade. By order. No exceptions. This sergeant had refused to fly an op. He had been accused and found guilty of LMF. There he was standing out in front, all on his own, in full view of every person in the unit, to be stripped of his wings and then his sergeant's tapes. They had all been unstitched beforehand so they came away easily when they were ripped from his uniform. He was immediately posted elsewhere.

Muirhead's crew were split on their reactions. "Vernon [the pilot] says he feels sorry for the guy. Horsfall [mid-upper gunner] says it serves him bloody well right—that the RAF had spent a packet on training him, and the time to chicken out was before you find yourself in the kitchen." But Dickie Parfitt thought the treatment of men branded LMF was utterly unfair—and counterproductive. "A person should have been able to go to the CO and say I can't do it anymore. It would be only sensible, because if he couldn't do his job properly then he was putting the other crew members in danger. I actually think it was brave to admit that they were too scared. I think a lot of people wished they had the courage to say, 'I'm too scared to go on.'"

Tony Iverson, a flight commander on 617 Squadron, could see both views.

There were obviously occasions when most of us would rather have gone back to bed. Two o'clock in the morning on a bleak airfield, a twelve-hour flight into unknown conditions with a German fighter squadron waiting for you isn't nice. It's not a Sunday afternoon trip along the Thames. But I think if people had been allowed to say "I'm sorry, I can't go," it would have spread. If one chap was allowed to pull out of ops, then why not another? We were at war, it was a tough business, and unless someone was really medically unfit we all simply had to soldier on.[25]

What did it take to push a man over the edge? And why did some manage to pull themselves together where others could not? Parfitt recalled returning from the terrible raid on Nuremberg and "while we were eating our egg and bacon in the mess, another crew came in. The rear gunner sat with us and his hands were shaking so much that his cup of coffee rattled in the saucer. His nerves were frayed. And I could well understand it. But he was all right after a few beers! He didn't go LMF. He stuck it out." To the RAF authorities, the answer was imply that some men had character and strength of mind and others did not. Lack of moral fiber implied a flaw in a man's makeup. But it was never that straightforward.

Some men realized early on that they were not cut out for battle and had the sense to admit it. In initial training, Robert Wannop's closest friend was a man called Len. Like tens of thousands of others, they were sent together to Canada to learn to fly. But there were accidents during training, and men died, four in one month. Len decided at that point that he could not do what was being asked of him. Wannop recalled: "We had just returned from the funeral of a comrade killed in a midair collision when he said he wished to speak to me confidentially. We walked outside the camp and he broke down. He'd lost his nerve and he had decided to quit the course." Wannop tried to argue his friend round,

> but no amount of cajolery could persuade him to change his mind. "If I'm afraid now, how could I ever be in charge of a bomber with other men's lives dependent on me?" he concluded. I warned him that the powers that be would crucify him, and crucify him they did. Every menial job was his. He was shunned, treated like a leper. And one day he was gone. Out of sight, out of mind. But not out of my mind, for he wasn't a coward to me. He had acknowledged his shortcomings, and his subsequent action took a lot of guts, and, who knows, maybe even saved other men's lives.[26]

The precise fate of those deemed cowards is still shrouded in mystery. The last their comrades ever saw or heard of them was their hurried departure from the squadron, with or without the public disgrace of being cashiered. Whether by accident or design, accounts of their treatment after that are rare. But after the publication of *The Eighth Passenger,* his book about his war, Miles Tripp received a letter from a man who would identify himself only as "Bob N." Forty years after the events he described, he was still too ashamed to give his full name, rank, and number, except to say that he had been an air gunner. He went LMF after his tenth operation, convinced he would not survive the eleventh. His crew took off with a spare gunner in his place and did not come back. His premonition had been correct, but he was punished for it. Stripped of his rank, he was sent to Eastchurch, a bleak RAF station on the Isle of Sheppey in the Thames estuary. There he met others who had also been sent away from their squadrons in disgrace. One was a sergeant who had been shot down in Europe, evaded capture, and made it home. He must have subsequently refused to fly, but his record behind enemy lines clearly did not save him from being demoted to aircraftman and, as Bob N put it, "dumped." Tripp's anonymous informant went on: "One Warrant Officer pilot shot himself while I was there and the atmosphere was ghastly." But the mystery of where men who went LMF finally ended up remains unsolved. Eastchurch was, apparently, a receiving center from which those in disgrace were then posted to a destination where they could be safely and secretly deposited, in Tripp's words, "rather like nuclear waste, without fear of contamination to others."

For others whose nerve had gone, however, there was compassionate treatment available. Dennis Wiltshire was a man whose bravery could not be doubted. In training in Canada, he had survived a terrible crash, holed up in a wreck in subzero temperatures for two days, and was in the hospital for two months recovering from frostbite and snow blindness. Yet, having so narrowly cheated death once, he still went on to get his wings as a flight engineer and return to England to fight. He did two operations over Germany and then took off for Cologne in March 1944.[27]

All of us on G-George that night were anxious, alert, apprehensive, but no more than before as we took off, headed for the coast and then on to Germany. It was a dark night, no moon and a little broken cloud some thousand feet below. Ahead I saw a pale orange glow in the sky. The Pathfinders were doing their job. My stomach went into knots. I longed to be going home to base. I began repeating the Lord's Prayer to myself.

We moved ever nearer the target zone. Searchlights were beginning to pierce the darkness along with antiaircraft shells with flares. I was very nervous. I had been scared before, but this was different. The flak seemed heavier and very close. They had us well targeted. I felt naked and defenseless. The fear was building but no one was saying anything. They were all at their stations doing their jobs. My problem was that, as flight engineer, I had no specific duty during the actual bombing run. I had done what I had to do and was waiting now until we were heading home. I tried to concentrate on something else, to keep my mind occupied. What I didn't realize until later was that fear and the knowledge of the danger you are putting yourself in can build up gradually in you until it snaps.

In a calm, steady voice, the navigator called "Three minutes to ETA [estimated time of arrival]," followed almost immediately by the bombardier, "Keep her as she is, Skip." We were now feeling the blast from the ack-ack shells. Les had his eyes fixed out to portside, mine to starboard. I was feeling pretty awful—in a cold sweat and very light-headed. The skipper almost screamed at the bombardier, "For Christ's sake, Jim, hurry up!" Then it was "Bombs gone!" The skipper made a steep turn for home, but we were now in the thick of a heavily defended area. Shells rocked us continuously. I felt frozen to my seat. Then something crashed through the Perspex window behind me, screamed past my head and buried itself in the cockpit floor. There was a sickly smell of burning and phosphorous. It brought me out of my fear. I had to deal with this. I released my harness, leapt from my seat, and stamped on the object to put the fire out. Then the bombardier suddenly screamed: "For God's sake, *my suit's on fire!*" He had been hit. He crumpled up and blood was pouring from his nose, mouth, and ears. He was dead. A horrendous, blinding flash shook the whole aircraft. Glass and oil were everywhere. It was chaos in the cockpit, but Les remained calm. He winked at me, gave me a smile of encouragement, but I had that feeling we were not going to get back. I looked out and saw a Lanc, minus its tail end, with all four engines on fire, hurtling to earth. I was really scared then, seeing all of them going to their deaths, if they weren't dead already. And that was the last thing that I really remember. From then on my mind is a blank.

He woke up in a bed

with wonderful snow-white sheets, beautiful soft white pillows, a nurse seated at my bedside in a beautiful crisp, blue and white uniform. "Doctor! Doctor! He's awake!" she called out and the doctor, in white, but his shoulders bearing RAF epaulettes, asked: "Well, laddie, and how are we today?" I replied: "Confused, sir. Confused, hungry and very weak, thank you, sir."

Wiltshire was in an RAF psychiatric hospital in Derbyshire, a forbidding-looking institution with twin turrets, high on a hill overlooking the town of Matlock. It had been the Rockside Hydro, a 160-bed spa hotel, before being requisitioned when war broke out. Now, with unforgiving bluntness, the locals (and its inmates) called it the Hatter's Castle after the Mad Hatter character in *Alice's Adventures in Wonderland*.

Over the following weeks he pieced together what had happened to him. He had lost his mind in the Lancaster, left his post, pulled off his helmet, and strode off to the back of the aircraft. The others yelled at him to go back to his job but he ignored them. Then he tripped, fell to the floor, and lay there motionless and speechless until the aircraft landed back at base. "Apparently an ambulance took me to the sick quarters, where I stayed for the next four days. I had no wounds, no broken bones, and no physical disabilities, but I could not stand or sit. I ate nothing. I drank nothing. I did not seem to understand any spoken word and, despite attempts by the medical staff, nothing would register in my mind. My crew came to visit me but I was never aware of their presence." He was then sent to Matlock.

I have no idea how long I was there. My life was just a blank. A part of it just disappeared and, now I am almost eighty years of age, it's pretty certain it's gone forever. And that's very disconcerting, to have lost part of your life. I am told that once a nurse accidentally knocked a dish of medical instruments on to the floor and the noise made me leap to my feet screaming "There's another poor sod going down. Let's get the hell out of here. Look at the flares, look at the flares, shoot the bastard down, they're coming closer, for God's sake shoot the bastard down!" I then collapsed. I do recall having electrical convulsive treatment—ECT. This treatment is supposed to alleviate pressure on the brain if that is what is causing you problems. It's pretty frightening. People having it go into terrific convulsions and some throw up, some nearly choke. I remember little of the sessions I had except that they were awful. I don't think the treatment worked for me. To be fair, though, I think the doctors and nurses there tried to help us.

Penny Chapman was one of those nurses. Arriving there in 1944 and stepping through the large oak front door into the grim, gray Victorian building, she was struck by the faces of the young men, "masked in melancholy, their minds shattered like the planes they had flown."[28] Rest was deemed one of the best cures, and men would sleep for days on end with the help of drugs. Those showing signs of recovery were allowed out to walk in the dales or take tea in the town with local families. But some would never leave their rooms, and others were under twenty-four-hour observation in case they tried to harm themselves. "The quiet ones were the ones you had to watch," she recalled. "They were suffering from melancholia and never spoke, whereas others could at least be encouraged to try rug making or painting as therapy." There were extreme cases. One man she treated had parachuted into France and been helped by the Resistance to get home. But he was constantly tormented by thoughts of being chased by German soldiers. He would suddenly flee in panic, scampering on all fours like a dog under the rows of hospital beds. At those times it took two male orderlies to restrain him. For some, the hospital could offer no release from their demons. One patient killed himself, jumping from the window of his room in his pyjamas onto the stone courtyard. But it is said that a third of the inmates recovered sufficiently to put their uniforms back on and return to their duties.

Dennis Wiltshire recalled talking to virtually no one.

Life at Matlock was very miserable. There was no conversation. We were all in a world of our own. You didn't want to talk to others about why you were there and nobody was very lucid anyway. Perhaps people were ashamed to be there, especially given those infernal initials LMF, though I didn't think that was what was supposed to be wrong with me. I wasn't branded LMF. After many weeks of treatment at Matlock, I was subjected to tests, questions, and cross-examinations by senior medical officers, psychiatrists, neurosurgeons, and representatives of the RAF Mental Health Board. Some weeks after this inquisition I went before another medical board where a squadron leader medical officer read something to me from King's Regulations, which sounded like a load of mumbo jumbo. Later he came to see me in the ward, said that I was being discharged as a result of psychoneurosis but with an unblemished service record.

It was important to me to leave with an unblemished record. I was happy to be going home. I didn't want to go back onto the front line—to go back on operations. I had had enough. I felt I had done my bit. I felt no sense of shame. I hadn't let anyone down. The only thing I resent is that on my discharge papers it said I was "unfit for further military service but fit for employment in civil life." Well, I wasn't. I was quite a sick man when I left the RAF, and afterward I had five years of hospitalization and treatment in mental institutions. I wasn't fit for discharge from the air force. But I was of no use to them. That's obviously why they got rid of me. They never offered me a pension for my military service. I was just out, thank you, and goodbye. I thought it was mean-minded.

The idea that cowardice has to do with lack of character simply never took root in the American services. The lessons of the First World War had been learned. "Shell shock" was real and not a fabrication of the "trick cyclists" and the pacifists. Fear was natural, and even the bravest of the brave could be pushed beyond his limits. In fact, "operational fatigue" was to be expected and should be dealt with by treating those who succumbed to it as sick men rather than shirkers. The U.S. airmen were happy to use terms such as "flak happy" about themselves or their comrades and not to bottle up their fears and their feelings as their British counterparts were prone to do. They were also happy to take extended breaks from the base at "flak farms," as they called the dozen or so country houses and hotels that had been set aside for rest and recreation. Eddie Picardo spent seven days at a small castle near King's Lynn.

It had enormous, huge bedrooms, bathrooms with multicolored tiles and an acre of lawn reaching down to a small river. The first thing the organizers did was give us civilian clothes. It was wonderful to be out of uniform for once. In the afternoons we would play baseball or soccer. Then, after dinner every evening, local girls were bussed in. They were very polite and some were rather shy. We would dance to records, and have punch and some kind of snack. But there was no booze. At other times, we had movies, or we would pile into trucks and go into town for a dance or visit a pub. The war seemed so far away. There were no air-raid sirens, no enemy bombers, no V-2 rockets, not even the sputter of a buzz bomb. It was like heaven.

But, as Picardo discovered, heaven has its downside.

It was heartbreaking to have to leave. Giving back those civilian clothes was hard to do. But we had had our morsel of civilian life, and now it was back to the bitter taste of war and the chance that you might go on a mission and die. It had been too easy to relax and forget that the war was on. When reality set in again, it hurt. If I had it all to do over again, I would have settled for a three-day pass. It would have been easier psychologically.

Nonetheless, after a couple of missions he felt back to his old self. Warlike again, just not so war-weary.

It should be said that the Americans' relaxed attitude to those who could not take the stress of war failed to convince the British. Air Commodore Sir Charles Symonds, a Harley Street neurologist serving in the RAF, criticized the Americans for letting airmen think that nervous tension in combat conditions was perfectly natural. It gave them an easy way out, too easy. But if that was so, the numbers taking that easy way out were very few. Eighth Air Force statistics show just 2,000 out its 100,000 flying crew were permanently removed from flying duties because of stress or refusal to fight, and 700 because of LMF. These figures do not suggest that men had been shirking their duties in the absence of a heavy-handed, authoritarian approach to shell shock and combat fatigue. So was the big LMF stick wielded by Bomber Command really necessary? Did the disciplinary regime need to be quite so strict? In Harris's defense it should be said he was fighting a war in which Soviet commissars turned machine guns on their own soldiers if they retreated. Soon SS troops would be patrolling behind the front line in Germany and hanging deserters and defeatists. In that context, merely threatening men with the stigma of LMF appears benign rather than bestial. The real mark against it, however, is that, in the end, it may have been counterproductive. How many men forced themselves beyond their endurance, endangering the lives of fellow crewmen in the process? Almost every airman accepted that it was better for a man at the end of his tether to be replaced. The system, however, did not encourage the honesty—and the bravery—to admit defeat.

That personal dilemma cost lives. Ken Newman remembered a young flier he played snooker with.

He was rather quiet by nature. He told me that his father was the vicar of a country parish. Sadly, his body was found under a hedge in the field behind the mess. He had shot himself in the head with his service revolver. He left a note to say his conscience would not allow him to undertake any more operational sorties as a bomber pilot and he could not face the shame of being branded LMF, which would have resulted in a court-martial and being stripped of his rank and pilot's brevet.

Although I could understand Bomber Command's intransigence toward those who refused to carry out operations, I thought the policy was sometimes applied much too rigidly. I felt very sorry for his parents and hoped they were not told the truth. It was just such a hideous position to get into. We just thought: poor sod.

6

ORDERS FROM ON HIGH

"He took full responsibility. The strain on him must have been enormous."
—BOMBER COMMAND OFFICER ON HARRIS

IT WAS JUST AFTER TEN O'CLOCK IN THE MORNING WHEN THE PHONE RANG in the office of Wing Commander Alexander Adams, the officer commanding 49 Squadron.[1] He picked up the receiver to hear the familiar voice of a WAAF corporal in the operations room. "We're working tonight, sir," she said. Nothing more. But those four words were the prearranged code that meant it was time to prepare his crews for another dangerous night ride into enemy territory. Up and down the country, squadron commanders like him were receiving similar alerts. At other bases, it might be delivered differently—"There's a war on" was another commonly used phrase—but the message was the same. A signal had been received from Bomber Command headquarters at High Wycombe after the morning conference there. The squadron was under battle orders. In the ops room at RAF Fiskerton, the WAAF was repeating her simple message to half a dozen other key sections of 49 Squadron—the armament officer, navigation officer, flying control, weather officer, signals, sick quarters. From the coded signal in front of her she knew what they were yet to learn—that the target was to be in the Berlin area, a tough one, and that headquarters, probably "Butch" Harris himself, had designated it "maximum effort." When wasn't it?

Adams arrived in the operations room. He read the signal, questioned his intelligence officer, and then set to work. He would not be flying with the squadron tonight, not this time. Men like Adams carried the burden of responsibility; sometimes they had to fight their war from a distance, coping as best they could with the mental and emotional strain of sending young men out to die, writing the letters of bereavement to relatives, then sending more to meet the same fate.

In the next few hours more details arrived from Command—the route, bomb load, fuel, tactics, timing. WAAFs set up maps. A teleprinter chattered with the latest weather reports and forecasts. The young weather officer looked anxious—when didn't he? In reply to Adam's question he said, "It's going to be cloudy, sir. Poorish visibility most of the night. Here and over *there*." Adams turned to the adjutant. "How many aircraft have we serviceable?" "Eighteen, sir." Together they looked at a board on the wall on which all the crews were listed—their photographs, too—together with their aircraft letter. The flight commanders arrived, and all four men began running through the names of the men they would send out to their possible deaths that night. Not that it was ever put like that. They were too professional for emotion. But every squadron commander knew that the decisions he made meant life or death to others. Any such thoughts in Adams's head were interrupted when the armaments officer arrived for instructions. Prepare full loads, Adams ordered.

Over in the operations room, another signal had arrived from headquarters detailing the route. A tape was fixed on the large map of northern Europe covering the whole of one wall, ending at Berlin. Red spots on the map indicated antiaircraft gun concentrations—with so many grouped around the German capital it looked like a measles rash. They had been offered a choice of routes home, and Adams picked the one his experience told him would be marginally safer, especially for the rookie pilots.

Outside, the airfield was frantic with activity. Trolleys of bombs were snaking out to the dispersal areas. Fuel trucks were filling up. Engines were being tested. Adams sat quietly and double-checked all the data for distance, fuel, payload. Lives depended on careful and correct planning. A mistake now and someone would pay the penalty. "What about food, sir?" The adjutant needed to warn the cookhouse. "They'll be taking off between 1615 and 1630," Adams said, "so they'll have lunch as usual and then sandwiches to take with them, and coffee." It was easy to forget the importance of the right food to fill anxious stomachs. There was a station commander who, on taking over his new post, had made his first task a visit to the kitchens. He had told the girls working there: "Your job is vital. If you stop cooking, or cook badly, the danger is that the boys may stop flying or the aircraft don't get looked after properly and the war suffers."[2] It was a wise thought.

There was more food for thought when Adams tuned in to a speaker-phone conference with headquarters and all the other stations involved in that night's operation. There were words of encouragement for "a good attack" from an air vice marshal, a voice from the third rank of Bomber Command's hierarchy but as close to the top of the tree as anyone could ever expect to hear, given that the commander in chief, Air Marshal Harris, tended to keep to himself. Fog over the target would keep the enemy fighters on the ground, the AVM assured them. Adams would try to pass on that optimism to the skippers of his crews when they assembled for the first briefing. They were already waiting for him, attentive, pencils in their hands, ready to jot down information to pass on to their crews. To an outside observer, they appeared supremely calm and confident. Only someone like Adams, who had been down this route himself, flown through the skies over Germany under fire, could guess the turmoil inside the heads of men about to go into battle. He gave them the information they needed, straight and direct; this was no time for prevarications or games. His final instructions: "Gain maximum height at the enemy coast. Bomb at twenty-five thousand feet. OK, fellows." He then left them to talk among themselves so he could join in the tail end of the navigators' briefing, which had been going on simultaneously in the main briefing room. The navigation officer was taking the navigators through their calculations, helping them plot the route on their charts, answering questions, giving instructions, like a math teacher with a class. It wasn't long since many of them had been schoolboys studying for exams. Now their very lives depended on getting their sums right.

Then all the crews came together for a last briefing, a final word of encouragement from the commander. His job was nearly done. The success or otherwise of the operation was moving out of his hands and into theirs. He knew a commander of a neighboring squadron who at this point in the pre-op briefing always insisted on playing to his men a particular Andrews Sisters song on the phonograph—"The Shrine of St. Cecilia," it was called. Somehow it brought his boys back, kept the losses low, or so he wanted to believe. And they listened every time because they wanted to believe it, too.

As Adams's crews filed out of the final briefing, the squadron doctor—"the traveling quack shop," as he called himself—was standing at the door, his pockets bulging, offering pills for the sleepy, the airsick, and the nervous. But pep talks were just as important as pep pills, so Wing Commander Adams hopped into his car to drive to the dispersal area. He went from aircraft to aircraft. "Everything all right?" He helped a gunner fasten his yellow flak suit. "Goodbye, and have a good trip." And then the crews were gone. Up through the hatches and into their planes. For them the waiting was over. Engines roared. Adams's wait was just beginning. He stood by the trailer at the end of the runway as each Lancaster taxied up and then thundered away. He waved. From the rear turret, each Tail-End Charlie gave him a thumbs-up.

And now all he could do for the next seven hours was sit in a becalmed officers' mess. When the crews were away, you could easily find a spare seat or a paper to read. The snooker table was usually free, too, not that anyone seemed anxious for a game. Nobody spoke, all too aware that the action was elsewhere. Hundreds of miles away, in the black night, the men he had ordered out, *his* men, were in a battle. In his mind he flew every mile with them, counted every minute, saw the flak and the fighters, looked down on the enemy's capital and thought of little except their getting home.

He would be keeping half an ear open for a drone in the sky outside that meant an aircraft was returning early. Then he would have to play the tough man. It was his duty to find out what had gone wrong, hope there was nothing untoward, be prepared to take action if he had the slightest suspicion. It cannot have been easy, suspecting his own men, but it was the price of command. But this time there were no early returns to concern him. Instead, he could now worry about how many wouldn't return at all.

As the hours ticked away, Adams was out pacing the airfield, his eyes fixed on the eastern sky. Then he called in to the control tower, where the girls sat waiting for the crackles and the scratchy, breaking-up voices over the radio that meant some, at least, of the squadron were back in range. The first aircraft called up: "U-Uncle, upwind. Over." And now the silence was broken by the jabbering of call signs and messages and requests for clearance to land.

Down in the operations room, the loudspeaker was pouring out a babble of reports from headquarters and from other stations and squadrons. Adams waited in the debriefing room as his men came in for interrogation. They chattered away, still high on adrenaline but higher still on the joy of having survived another operation. As they drank mugs of strong tea and sat in semicircles of chairs round the tables to be debriefed, he wandered among them, picking up snatches of how it had gone. "No fighters . . . target obscured . . . very few searchlights." Occasionally he asked a question of his own. "Good trip?" "It was pretty quiet, sir. Fighters didn't get off. I think we were bang-on. Large fires were starting as we came out."

The men wandered off, their job done, beginning to simmer down, thinking now of breakfast, bed, sleep. Tomorrow? Another day, a long way off. But for Adams there was still a watch to be kept. The situation board showed three aircraft had made emergency landings at other airfields in England. Transport would have to be organized to bring the crews back. The damage that had forced them down would have to be assessed. But still one was missing—O-Oboe—now dangerously overdue. He looked at his watch and made the calculation in his head that her fuel situation would be critical, if she was still in the air. A few more hours went by and there was still no sign. The commander gave his last order of the operation—the worst order of all—and he watched, a grave look on his face, as a WAAF stretched up and, against O-Oboe on the board she chalked the word "Missing." There would be seven painful letters for Adams to write later that day, aware that whatever anguish he felt in composing them was nothing compared with the grief of those who were to receive them. He mourned comrades; they wept for sons and lovers. In consolation, all he could tell himself was that it could have been worse. On other operations in the past few months, a quarter of the squadron's aircraft and their crews had failed to return. For now, though, he had better grab a few hours' sleep—before that bloody phone rang again.

For officers at the next level of command, it was just as hard when men in their charge failed to return. Group Captain James Pelly-Fry stood on the balcony of the control tower at RAF Holme-on-Spalding-Moor in Yorkshire, counting the aircraft home. He was station commander and therefore one step removed from the boys of the squadron. His responsibilities covered the entire base and its 3,500 personnel. But he still insisted on being there when the Halifaxes of 76 Squadron were due back. Each one that landed was logged with a small disc on a blackboard. "How I hated that board," Pelly-Fry recalled. "It was the devil's harbinger of bad news. After nearly every operation one or more discs were absent."[3] Three discs missing meant twenty-one young airmen down somewhere in Europe or in the sea, "and there's nothing we can do about it. There are no emotional scenes, no tears, not in public anyway. Just a bit of silence and a soft-spoken sympathetic comment. That's all." He was amazed by the courage of the crews.

"Why they opted to go flying by night over hostile Germany still mystifies me," he wrote more than fifty years later.

Nor could he ever get used to how thin was the thread on which their lives hung. In the early hours of one morning, keeping watch in the control tower, he and other senior officers had logged in most of the flight but, as time went by, virtually given up on A-Apple. Then she appeared and was given clearance to circle and land.

From the balcony I watched the white tail light begin to descend steadily from 800 feet, down and down. Then, somewhere beyond the aerodrome, there was a huge flash followed by an awful noise of rending metal. I sped off in the direction of the fire, realizing that the chances of rescue were virtually nil, but I had to go. I found a route across the fields but the Halifax was burning furiously. Nothing could be done. Those boys were too low to bail out so all of them had perished, and I stood there silently on the verge of tears. It was the first fatal bomber crash I had witnessed and the impact on my emotions was profound. Poor fellows, they had returned all the way back from Germany only to be killed within moments of landing.

Pelly-Fry carried out an investigation into the crash and discovered an even greater horror. Because of an engine malfunction, a propeller had sheared off on the very last leg of the flight, hit the cockpit, killed the skipper, and doomed the aircraft. "At low altitude, the crew had no choice but to wait for the inevitable crash. It was a quite dreadful and horrifying affair to contemplate."

The burdens of command were clearly hard enough at squadron and station level. How much more must they have been for the man at the very top of Bomber Command, Sir Arthur Harris? Pelly-Fry had some inkling because he knew Harris well. He had worked beside him as his personal assistant before the war. He met him again soon after Harris took over Bomber Command and found him "determined, dedicated and utterly convinced about the correctness of his views." Harris ran Bomber Command from secret headquarters not far from the town of High Wycombe, thirty miles west of London—sited "nowhere in particular, hard to find by road and invisible from the air," as one regular visitor described it.[4] Code-named "Southdown," the complex contained a country mansion which housed the officers, and a rather less elegant barracks for the men. But the heart of this hive was a three-level bunker carved into the Chiltern escarpment, topped by two grass-covered mounds that might well have been Neolithic barrows and screened by groves of beech trees. Around it, bluebells grew in profusion, and there was the constant chatter and shrill of birdsong. It was quintessentially English—something that Harris was not. Though born in England in the twilight years of Queen Victoria and schooled there, what moulded him was that entity that, win or lose, ironically was doomed by the very war he was fighting—the British empire.

His father had been an engineer and architect in the Indian civil service, an expatriate who saw his son only on the rare occasions he came to England on leave. Parked in second-rank schools and spending holidays in the homes of strangers, Harris grew up with that peculiar sense of never quite belonging that often went with being part of a colonial family. As soon as he could, he went in search of roots. At eighteen he left school, and in defiance of his family, he went to the wide-open spaces and limitless possibilities of the British colony of Rhodesia in southern Africa. He farmed there in what was very much a pioneering period, and would soon have had his own tobacco plantation if it had not been for the outbreak of the First World War in 1914. There were Germans to be fought in South West Africa (modern Namibia), and he joined up, was briefly an infantryman, and then arrived in London, where the newly formed Royal Flying Corps attracted him. From then his career was marked out. But those four years in Africa also marked him for life. Thereafter he would always think of himself as a Rhodesian. His experiences there gave him his resilience and his self-assurance. There was always the air of a self-made man about Harris, a certainty of purpose and a sense of having proved himself to himself and therefore not having to prove anything to others. Bullheaded and bullying was how it might look to some. But in times of crisis—such as 1940s Britain—it was the sort of conviction that others could rally around.

There were few of the social graces about Harris when he was doing his job. "Sometimes his manner seemed to be almost a calculated rudeness," according to Major Charles Carrington,[5] the army's permanent liaison officer at Bomber Command headquarters. It was an unenviable job given Harris's combative attitudes to the other services. Two words guaranteed to raise his hackles were "combined operations," while his views on admirals were as unrepeatable as theirs on him. Carrington should have been a hostile witness, yet he was filled with admiration for Harris, describing him as "the most dominating personality with whom I became acquainted in the Second World War." The major sat in daily on conferences at Southdown, speaking only when spoken to, like everyone else. He felt in awe.

> Harris never played for popularity, like some commanders I might mention, never wasted words or time on mere civilities, but he instantly made his presence felt. As a horse knows by instinct when his rider holds the rein with a firm hand, so Bomber Command knew that it had a master. Under him, the whole machine tautened up, seemed to move into a higher gear, and this though he rarely visited the squadrons and scorned to give pep talks.

The commander in chief's morning conferences were among the unique set-piece tableaux of the war—like Churchill holding meetings in his bath or Montgomery gathering his youthful aides-de-camp around him in his battlefield trailer. "Down the hole," in the large underground operations room at High Wycombe, the complete battle order of Bomber Command was drawn up on a huge blackboard stretching across an entire wall. Groups and squadrons were listed with their aircraft numbers and crew strengths. There was also a huge map of Europe and a list of the code names for targets, all of them fishy because Harris's number two[6] was a keen angler. Berlin was "Whitebait" and Cologne "Trout." In front of this was a single table and chair which, according to Carrington, looked as though "it might have been borrowed from a servant's bedroom." Harris would sweep in at 9:00 A.M. and sit down at it without a word or a smile. What the irreverent termed "high mass" had begun.

His first question was inevitably, "Did the Hun do anything last night?" He never minced his words about the enemy—"the Boche," the "Herrenvolk," anything derogatory would do. The officers grouped around him in a half circle would, when called on and not before, step forward and give their reports—casualties of the previous night, prospects for the day, squadron readiness, weather forecast—and answer his questions. Woe betide the man who was late, absent, or slow coming up with an answer.

There would be a roar that was likened to that of a wounded elephant—though it was rarely heard, because no one ever dared be late or hesitant. Harris would then scan a list of priority targets drawn up by the intelligence officer, choose the ones for the night, and then turn to his weather officer for a report. This brought the only moments of comic relief in the crisp, businesslike meeting. According to Group Captain John Searby, who was on Harris's staff, "Harris had a feeling for the weather and rarely accepted the forecast without putting Dr. Spence [Group Captain M. Spence, the chief weather officer] through the hoop. Occasionally he endeavored to nudge the forecast in the direction he wanted but Spence stood firm and Harris would smile faintly and give up. I think he enjoyed this kind of delving but he never overruled the met officer."[7] And then Harris would rise and leave the room without a word. The meeting was over. It had taken a few minutes, no longer. He had made the decisions that mattered, and the details he left to his deputy and staff officers.

There would be another, smaller conference later to brief Harris on those details, and then a final weather conference at midday at which the decision to go or to cancel would be made. It was Harris who made it, an awesome enough task for a man if he took a decision of that magnitude just once in his lifetime. Neville Barnes Wallis, the scientist whose bouncing bomb made the Dambusters' raid possible, was consumed with guilt at having sent fifty-six airmen to their deaths on just one operation. The strain of high command had General Eisenhower smoking eighty cigarettes a day in the run-up to D-Day and even brought from him a plaintive cry of "I hope to God I know what I am doing." Harris smoked incessantly, too, as he made life-and-death decisions *every* day. As Searby observed: "He fought a set-piece battle most nights in the week and took full responsibility. The strain must have been enormous." But because the responsibility was so great, he would not delegate it. He took no leave in three and a half years. At home in his official residence—a sprawling Georgian house called Springfield, five miles from Southdown—at night he was kept informed by telephone about operations and, though usually in bed by 10:30, seldom slept until he knew the raid was over and most—though very rarely all—of the crews were home and safe.

Eighth Air Force general Ira Eaker would also find it difficult to sleep at night. He was once asked: "What does it do to your guts when you know you have to send men out, and by the thousands they're going to be killed?" He replied that he knew to expect losses and that they would be disastrous at times because of the weather, operational conditions, and enemy concentrations. "You have to be prepared to take that without changing your plan or changing your morale, or you won't last long as a general and you'll be sent home." He knew all about fear, he said, because he had experienced it himself. There were two types. One is physical, "and I've had it many times during my flying career, when death appeared imminent. It had no effect other than to spur me to quick action and decision, such as getting out of a plane in a flat spin at 200 feet." He had found fear like this relatively easy to get over by, as it were, making sure he got straight back on the horse. "I always flew more rather than less after disasters or near disasters in the air." But then there was mental fear, and this is what most affected him as a commander.

This mental fear has two principal phases. One is making a decision that will cost men their lives. The other is making a decision that leads to the failure of a significant military operation. Both these things wear you down. They will keep you from sleeping well at night as you lie there thinking about every possible aspect of a mission and what you might do. Then after an important mission like Schweinfurt, for example, you wonder if you might have taken other courses of action that would have prevented heavy loss of lives. This mental fear has to be combated very carefully. I always said to myself, if I worry too much about the past, it will decrease my ability to deal with the future. So when I would get morose over a past decision or a past engagement like one of the great raids, I would change my attitude by thinking about what I should do in the future. That's the way I coped with it.[8]

Eaker was being painfully honest. Harris, on the other hand, said little about the pressures of his work. When it was over he did once write how he had been "borne down by the frightful inhumanities of war."[9] He put it forward as an excuse for having been curmudgeonly from time to time. In his memoirs, he spoke fleetingly of "the frightful mental strain of commanding a large air force in war" and wondered simply if anyone could understand it unless they had experienced it for themselves.[10] But he went into no detail about what that strain involved. There was no soul-baring, carping, or self-pity. He had done what he had done, and it had been hard. That was all. His most recent biographer, Henry Probert, set the strain of sending men to their possible deaths alongside all the other matters the commander in chief had to deal with:

> the overall direction of his Command and the incessant pressures to which he was subjected from all quarters, from the Prime Minister to the Air Ministry downward. We may find it hard to believe today that he could have driven his Command and himself the way he did, and that higher authority allowed him to do so. There were, however, no ground rules for how one should lead an unparalleled campaign in an unprecedented war of national survival, and Harris was utterly determined to spare no effort to do the job with which he had been entrusted to the very best of his ability.[11]

Moreover, he did all this while nursing a duodenal ulcer he had had since before the war. No wonder he could be irascible.

Harris himself admitted to being "crotchety and impatient,"[12] and his moodiness and personal rudeness were undoubtedly factors in the breakdown of his first marriage.[13] But how bad-tempered and unreasonable he actually was when doing his job is subject to contradictory evidence. He never held back his opinion of Air Ministry civil servants he considered pettifogging and obstructionist, and was renowned for facetiously asking those he did not like what they had done to help Hitler win the war that day! He had an almost unrivaled capacity for making enemies. Soon after assuming command at High Wycombe he clashed with Lord Selbourne, minister of economic warfare, who, not unnaturally, given his governmental brief, wanted a say in deciding Bomber Command's targets. Harris would have nothing to do with him or his department. He must also have been spectacularly rude to Sir Wilfred Freeman, vice chief of the Air Staff and his superior officer, on one occasion because the offended man wrote to Harris that he could put up with his truculence and hyperbole but he drew the line at being accused of "deliberately proposing to risk human lives in order to test out an idea of mine which in your opinion is wrong."[14] The issue was unimportant. What mattered was that Harris was unrepentant and even more rude. He challenged Freeman to give him a direct order so that he could register his official protest. The hyperbole that Freeman commented on was also very much a Harris device. He never knowingly underplayed an argument or soft-pedaled a point of view, and in the end it was this that prevailed in the memories of many of those who crossed swords with him.

Charles Carrington knew young officers, brave men with battle honors, who were terrified of Harris. "I have seen bemedaled wing commanders trembling on his office doormat like naughty schoolboys outside the headmaster's study." Once inside, they were subjected to another headmasterly device—deliberately left standing while Harris ignored their presence, his head buried in whatever he was writing or reading, before glancing up menacingly over his glasses. Carrington had seen it all before and was not put out. Others quaked. They were reacting as much to the reputation as to the reality, a mistake that Harris's secretary, a rather fearsome character herself, very nearly made when he arrived at Bomber Command. She doubted she wanted to work for such a person. Instead she found him kind and considerate, a man who would listen to all sides of any argument before making up his mind. She saw nothing of his fierce temper, nor did the other WAAFs in his headquarters office, some of whom thought him a teddy bear, once they had got used to the fact that he never said thank you or offered praise. But they knew when he was happy with the job they had done and when he wasn't—and those who didn't meet his high standards were simply posted elsewhere.

He also had great charm, which he employed socially with the many politicians and other dignitaries he and his wife entertained at Springfield. Throughout his period at Bomber Command, Harris ran a public relations offensive to put over his point of view to those whose support he valued. He had Churchill on his side, but most of the War Cabinet were also guests at one time or another. Even the occasional admiral was invited. By all accounts they were splendidly convivial occasions, and he was a relaxed and considerate host. One visitor recalled him as "witty and amusing, a humorous, if somewhat cynical observer of the human comedy, and never pompous or self-admiring."[15]

One of the mysteries we have to grapple with over Harris is how this master of spin during the war completely lost the public relations battle afterward and allowed himself to be so thoroughly demonized while others with less to boast about were canonized. But, then, Harris was full of contradictions. He was a wonderful father, according to his daughter, Jackie, born when he was forty-seven. She was a lively toddler around Springfield for all of his time at Bomber Command, and he was enthralled by her. Wing commanders who trembled in his presence could not believe the sight of "Butch" being led tenderly by the hand by a four-year-old. She herself remembered his "great sense of humor and fun" and how "he taught me to ride my pony and stand on my head."[16] But so many of the bits and pieces that make up the complex personality that was Arthur Harris seemed not quite to fit together, and even in his delightful family life there was the enigmatic and the contradictory. This doting father of little Jackie erased his three other children—the fruits of his first marriage by the wife who divorced him—from his life story, as told to and by his first biographer.[17]

If Harris was the sort of man to be careless with the very existence of three of his family, why should we believe he gave a fig for the lives of the men he led? But he did. The accusation is often made that Butcher Harris sent his lambs to the slaughter without a second thought. The charge does not stick. He knew there was an awful job to do and the airmen of Bomber Command would be the ones to die doing it. His job was to minimize the risks they had to take while still pursuing the war. Of course, he could have kept more of them alive if he had grounded the force except when conditions were perfect. As he pointed out in his memoirs, "Our climate being what it is, I should have been able to justify myself completely if I had left the whole force on the ground and done nothing whatever on nine occasions out of ten. *But this would have led to the defeat of Britain in the air* [emphasis added]." He was always balancing the demand for success against the risk to lives. He noted the difficulty of having political masters who demanded victories but were the first to complain if casualties mounted.[18]

In this context, it is significant that, as Searby witnessed, Harris never overruled his weather forecaster, even if he did press him hard at times to modify his assessment. The safe return of his men was top priority. One night a raid on the Ruhr was scheduled. Harris had named his target and authorized the attack, and there should have been no going back. But as the time for takeoff approached, the duty group captain was worried by an updated forecast of fog on the way back that would make landing difficult and dangerous. He took it on himself to abandon the operation at the last minute. On this occasion, the weather outwitted the lowly group captain. The expected fog did not appear. The operation could have gone ahead—as everyone knew, the group captain in particular. As the minutes ticked round to 9:00 A.M. the next morning and Harris took his seat for "high mass." The inevitable question came—who had ordered the cancellation? The group captain confessed. "I did, sir. I was not satisfied we could land them back at base, sir—the visibility was deteriorating rapidly." The silence that followed was broken by Harris's verdict: "Quite right." He did not need to question the man further. It was enough that the group captain had exercised his judgment as he saw fit and with the safe return of the crews his priority.

Harris knew the courage it took for his men to carry out the tasks he set them. He wrote at the end of the war:

> There is no parallel in warfare to such courage and determination in the face of danger over so prolonged a period. It was, moreover, a clear and highly conscious courage, by which the risk was taken with calm forethought, for the aircrew were all highly skilled men, much above the average in education, who had to understand every aspect and detail of their task. It was, furthermore, the courage of the small hours, of men virtually alone, for at his battle station the airman is virtually alone. It was the courage of men with long-drawn apprehensions of daily "going over the top."[19]

The courage of the small hours—only a commander who really understood the special nature of what he put his men through could have written that.

From the moment the Americans joined the war, Harris welcomed their air force generals into his command headquarters at High Wycombe in an open-handed gesture of cooperation and friendship that would not always—or even often—be the case between four-star fighting cocks from opposite sides of the Atlantic. Eaker was happy to take up residence at Southdown, if no other reason than to avoid being trapped under the same roof with army generals, who were all too eager to rein in the air force. He was still having to watch his back for those who would chip away at his independence and autonomy. With Harris and company he was among friends and equals. Nor was the hospitality merely for work. Eaker became a live-in guest at Harris's house, Springfield. They were an unlikely combination—the gruff Harris, always prone to self-importance, and Eaker, a soft-spoken Texan who was naturally modest and retiring. But they got on well. Over a fine dinner—though sadly lacking the turnip greens and black-eyed peas that were the general's favorite vegetables—they could continue their daily discussions about the war and how to win it. Sometimes little Jackie Harris was there at the table, joining in the conversation with the tall and handsome man she called "Genewal Ika" because she was having trouble with her r's.[20] The Americans were amazed at the generosity of the British, prepared to share bunkers, homes, equipment, *and* intelligence. Eaker would gratefully note: "They turned over to us all of their experience; they kept no secrets. I don't believe there was ever a more thoroughly co-operative effort in warfare than the RAF and our air effort."[21] Of course, the Americans were soon to need a place of their own, and the agreement that staff would attend each other's daily operational conferences dictated that the place they chose would have to be close by.

Within a five-mile radius of Bomber Command's headquarters was Wycombe Abbey, a girls' school set in historic, ivy-clad buildings inside a sixty-acre private park. On first viewing, Eaker was all for requisitioning it, but the Air Ministry in Whitehall was reluctant. The abbey was no ordinary academy—it was the alma mater of many women of influence in the land. It would be like turfing out the boys of Eton. But despite stiff resistance from the formidable spinster who was the school's head mistress, turfed out the girls were. After all, there was a war on, as the British were fond of saying, and with Wycombe an obvious target for enemy air raids, they were probably safer anyway in schools in Oxford, thirty miles away. The Americans moved in, giving their new headquarters the code name Pinetree. Any place less deserving of such a Wild West epithet it would be harder to imagine. The abbey was mock Gothic with battlemented stone walls, miniature turrets, and mullioned windows and almost as old as the United States. Before the house became a school, four British prime ministers—Pitt, Disraeli, Gladstone, and Rosebery—had stayed there. The dormitories each had a brass plaque on the wall which read: "Ring bell for mistress." In the coming years, hundreds of hopeful young American officers would ring in vain. Down on the ground floor, the library was converted into the war room, the books removed and the carved oak paneling covered with pinboard for wall charts and maps. Outside, camouflage netting was hung over the courtyards, while the lawns, once used for cricket, became arenas for touch football and volleyball. Tents and Nissen huts were erected in the rest of the grounds of what was officially designated Station 101. At its height, the site was like a small town, accommodating 12,000 headquarters staff. In time, the war center moved to a bunker built into the side of a hill, covered by ten feet of concrete and twenty-five feet of soil. The side walls were six feet thick and surrounded by a void designed to absorb the shock of any blast. The bunker had gas-tight doors, an air filter, and its own emergency power and water supplies.[22]

Eaker fostered good relations with the locals. He allowed the head-mistress to remain in her office at the requisitioned school with one of her assistants, and she stayed for the duration, helping to sort out problems while also protecting as best she could the buildings that would be returned to her charge once the war was over. At the general's invitation, too, the mayor and the police chief would pop by for drinks in the mess. In the town, the general took his place in the queue at the barber's waiting to have his haircut. Every day he drove out to one of his bases and on the way back in his limousine, a Humber, he would give lifts to British soldiers, a courtesy not always extended by class-conscious British officers. Certainly there are no stories of Harris stopping on his high-speed dashes to and from London to do the same favor for a lost GI. Early on in his time in High Wycombe, Eaker won many admirers when he addressed two thousand British servicemen in the town hall. Instead of the braggart Yank some of them might have expected, they heard a man of modesty tell them he wasn't going to do much talking "until we've done more fighting. After we've gone we hope you'll be glad we came."

Like Harris at Springfield, Eaker entertained VIP guests at Pinetree, among them the president's wife, Eleanor Roosevelt. James Parton, an Eaker aide, recalled how she then went to the nearby Bovingdon airfield to inspect a Flying Fortress:

Entrance to a B-17 was through a small door near the tail. She nimbly shoehorned her lanky body inside, noted the gunnery ports and the ball turret beneath, asked searching questions in the compartment shared by the navigator and radio operator and then gamely insisted on tottering on high heels up the narrow steel catwalk through the bomb bay to the pilot's and bombardier's stations in the nose. On the way back down the catwalk her eye was caught by a black rubber funnel and hose clamped to the rear bulkhead. "What is that?" she asked. Told that it was for "the convenience of the crews during long flights," the First Lady declared, "How clever!"[23]

As a VIP visitor himself, Eaker always knew what he was looking for. When he dropped into Eighth Air Force combat bases, flying his own twin-engine plane if the weather allowed, the first place he headed for was the mess hall. He would inspect the cupboards, talk to the cooks, make sure the pans were clean. He told his staff that as a former cavalryman he had been taught that feeding and grooming the horses were his first priority. He believed the same principle applied to the men under his command. But he could inspire them in military talk, too. He had a reputation as a top pilot, and that in and of itself won the men's respect. He would personally debrief returning aircrew, hand out medals for bravery at impromptu parades, and inspire the men with talks in his American drawl. They felt all the better for his commanding presence.

Eaker chose to spend as much time as he could with his fighting men, but Harris, in Bomber Command, felt differently. He cared greatly about the men under his command, but he tended to stay aloof from them, even those he worked next to on a day-to-day basis. Charles Carrington recalled how little the staff at Bomber Command saw of the boss. "Apart from the inner ring of courtiers, what the rest of headquarters saw was his black Bentley car, marked with a lighted 'Priority' sign, which he drove, very skillfully at a furious pace, down the Chiltern lanes. Rumor said that, if in a hurry, he blasted his way through all the red-light traffic signals between Southdown and London." He loved to drive fast—a habit he had picked up as a young-ster in the wilds of Rhodesia. It could be risky when repeated in the Home Counties of England. On one famous occasion, Harris was stopped by two policemen for speeding along the A40 highway one night and warned that he was in danger of killing someone. "It's my business to kill people," he apparently told them. "Germans!"[24] This story is often told against Harris, as a mark of his pomposity and his callousness. In fact, it was the irony that he was drawing attention to. When the policemen realized who they had stopped—"Are you Air Marshal 'Arris, sir?"—they saluted, but not be-cause they felt intimidated, rather out of respect for the man and the job he was doing. They leaped back on their motorcycles and gave him an outrider escort home at speeds Harris himself had not even attempted before.

But if the staff at headquarters saw little of Harris, the men he sent into battle saw even less of him. Unlike Eaker, he rarely visited bomber bases.

Not for him the morale-boosting sessions so loved by commanders such as Field Marshal Bernard Montgomery, never happier than when gathering his troops around him, talking to them man-to-man. It has been suggested that Harris could not face the thought of meeting men he would have to order into battle. This was always a difficulty for commanders. Eisenhower visited U.S. troops on the eve of D-Day and was troubled by the experience. He told Kay Summersby, his driver and confidante: "It's very hard to look a soldier in the eye when you fear that you are sending him to his death."[25] But Harris does not seem to have had any trouble looking any man in the eye. Some historians view him in the same light as First World War generals—as a donkey leading lions, sitting safely and smugly behind the lines, sending the other ranks over the top to die on futile missions. What gives the lie to that picture is that Harris's boys—his "old lags" as he called them—felt like knights, not pawns. The very few visits he did make to bomber stations—scarcely half a dozen are recorded—were emotional occasions. The pilots of 57 Squadron banged the tabletops and cheered, though he had just told them one in three of them would be lucky to survive what lay ahead. One pilot recalled how Harris paused at the briefing-room door on his way out and turned to face his men. "Suddenly silence returned to the room. Butch half opened his mouth but no sound came out. Instead he took a short step forward, lifted his arm in a smart salute, turned on his heel and was gone."[26] A flight engineer from 103 Squadron, honored with another of Harris's rare personal appearances, thought him "older and kinder than I had imagined. But there was no doubt he had a cool, calculating brain and his whole bearing suggested he would be utterly ruthless when occasion demanded. It was obvious that he was proud of us." The flight engineer felt he was in safe hands, that Harris was "no mere figurehead, content to sit at headquarters and pull strings, but that he could slug it out with the boys and valued an honest opinion, be it expressed by a group captain or a sergeant. I felt his one ambition was to batter the enemy into an early submission and that he believed Bomber Command, given a free hand, was powerful enough to do it."[27] Given that his visits could have such a powerful effect on morale, it is a wonder Harris did not get out and about more. It puzzled a mere bombardier like Sergeant Campbell Muirhead, who noted in his diary: "Why does 'Butch' never visit his bomber squadrons? We'd be delighted to see him. Most of us don't know whether we like him or not. They say he's not a very friendly type."[28] But that was

not his reason for staying away from close contact with his men. It was because he thought he could best protect their interests—and pursue the war
successfully—by concentrating his own efforts at High Wycombe and
Whitehall. Pelly-Fry once tackled him on visiting the troops. "I told him it
would please his aircrews no end if he could spare a day on one of his air
stations. His reply was that he would be delighted to do this. 'The trouble is
that if I leave my office for even half-a-day, when I get back the chances are
that I will find that I have lost some of my squadrons to some other damned
outfit that thinks it needs them more than I do.'" That was Harris speaking
in 1942, but he never shook off the feeling that other services were just
waiting in the wings to pick off the juiciest bits of Bomber Command.

Interservice rivalry was intense, and the army and navy were never short
of schemes to dismember the RAF, in their eyes the third and junior service.
The navy wanted to commandeer bombers to attack submarines and protect North Atlantic convoys. The army came up with a plan for airborne
troops that would have meant switching 215 squadrons over to its
control—with the proviso that the RAF could have them back for their normal operational missions "at times when they were not required by the
army"! An independent RAF irked the commanders of the other services.
They would have much preferred the United States setup, where the army
and the navy had their own air corps to deploy and order about. Harris's
first battle was always to ward off those who threatened the independence
of the RAF, his second to keep at bay those within the RAF who threatened
the independence of his command. If that now sounds like petty squabbling
fouling up the war machine, then it can only be said that a general who
could not hold together his own troops and maintain the integrity of his
own command was hardly likely to beat the real enemy.

Harris fought his corner against all comers. Relaxing at Harris's home
one evening, Pelly-Fry heard one side of an earnest telephone conversation
in which Harris was refusing to part with six Lancaster squadrons. Pelly-
Fry knew the C-in-C was talking to someone very senior because he kept
using the word "sir" as he gave his reasons. Then Harris said, "Good night,
sir," and hung up. "He then looked at me and said, 'That was Winston.'
With feigned casualness I said, 'What does he want?' Harris said, 'The
damned sailors are at it again. They are trying to get the PM to bully me.
No luck though—as you heard.'" Pelly-Fry, having witnessed firsthand
what was clearly a not unusual argument in Harris's life, commented in his

book: "Now I appreciated just what he meant about never leaving his head-quarters."[29]

There were often major disagreements among the American generals, too, not so much over bombing policy—on that they were at one—but over supplies. One of the reasons for the slow buildup of the Eighth Air Force in Britain was that men and machines were often being diverted to other theaters of operation, notably, of course, the Pacific. And for all its industrial might and seemingly limitless manpower, the United States was stretched to the limit in fighting on two continents. Eaker would write bitter letters to General Hap Arnold, the overall commander of the USAAF, in Washington, complaining that he was being kept short of the planes, men, and supplies he needed to take the fight to the Third Reich. Arnold replied that he had eight theaters of war to service and told Eaker in no uncertain terms to get on with his job and stop moaning. It may have been this clash that led to Eaker's being moved. He was transferred away from England to become head of U.S. air operations in the Mediteranean. In his place the Eighth got Jimmy Doolittle, who would be their commander for the rest of the war. Doolittle arrived brimming with confidence, a message from Eisenhower in his pocket in which the Supreme Commander congratulated him for "services of inestimable value to our country."[30] He failed to live up to this early promise—or so it appeared to his immediate superior, General Carl Spaatz. Doolittle was dogged by the fickle English weather from the start of his command. The very first combat mission he ordered was a fiasco. Sitting in the operations room at Pinetree, he heard his meteorologists pointing out a nasty front approaching slowly from the west. He calculated he could get a force of 500 bombers into the air, onto targets on the German coast and in western France and back home safely before the weather closed in. His biographer[31] takes up the story: "The bombers roared into the dawn, and Doolittle sat watching the weather map. Two hours passed, and now he knew that his bombers would be over enemy territory, evading German fighters, being subjected to the merciless and accurate flak thrown up at them by the excellent German antiaircraft defenses. Then his weather experts gave him a nasty shock. The slowly moving low-pressure front had suddenly begun racing madly toward England."

A vital call had to be made. Which would reach England first—the storm or the 500 bombers and their 600 fighter escorts returning from their mission? If the storm won the race, then as many as half those planes—and the close on 3,000 men on board them—could be doomed. At the same time, if he recalled them when they were virtually on their targets, his first operation as commander of Eighth Air Force would be logged as a terrible failure. A million and a half gallons of precious gasoline would also have been expended for nothing.

The three division commanders whose planes were participating in the raid all checked in with Doolittle on the phone from their bases. They too had seen the weather front pick up speed. Now they waited for instructions, all secretly glad that the decision was not theirs to make. In the Operations Room at High Wycombe, all eyes were on Doolittle as he stared at the map. Then he turned his head and snapped out one word: "Recall." Aides reached for the phones to relay the word to the division commanders. Within a matter of half a minute the pilot of every one of the 1,100 planes heard the terse message to abort the mission. Some were already over their targets, others very close to theirs. But an order is an order so they all turned and headed for England.

It had been a brave as well as a humane decision, played by the book. Rightly, he had refused to put his men at risk when it could be avoided. But Doolittle's difficulties were not over yet.

He kept watching the weather map. The low-pressure area was close now. It would cover east England in another two hours but by then Doolittle knew all of his chickens would have come home. Then, suddenly, the freakish English weather played a heartbreaking prank. As mysteriously as the front had spurted forward, it now stood still. Then it turned south to dilute and lose itself in the faraway regions off the African coast. Doolittle walked out of the Operations Room. The sun was high now, smiling benignly, and there wasn't a cloud in the sky. The bombers and fighters all returned in perfect weather, their pilots wondering what manner of man the new commanding general was.

Within the week, a similar situation occurred, and once again Doolittle aborted at the last minute. There were mutterings on the combat bases. The division commanders were uneasy that what could have been highly successful missions were called off because of . . . What word should they choose? "Overcautiousness" was the most generous. There were other terms less gracious or forgiving. The disquiet was picked up by Spaatz, now in overall command of the U.S. strategic air forces in Europe. He had been a friend and colleague of Doolittle's for twenty-five years, and what had happened seemed totally out of character. But it was not unknown for even very senior leaders with impeccable records of valor to lose their nerve when called on to make instant life-and-death decisions. Doolittle's biographer again takes up the story:

Spaatz called Doolittle to headquarters, and without any preliminary conversation said coldly, "It looks as though you haven't got the guts necessary to run a big air force." Doolittle stood there, stunned. A reproach of this nature was invariably reserved for commanders about to be relieved in disgrace. That this reproach should come from a man he liked and respected as much as he did Spaatz made it more bitter. The normally combative Doolittle calmed himself. Then he said quietly: "You may be right, General, but I'd like to explain how things looked to me." He then told of the two accidents of weather which had resulted in the two recalls, pointing to a map on the wall to show where the two fronts had been and explaining his calculation that he fully expected them to reach England long before the returning bombers and fighters of the Eighth. His judgment turned out to be wrong, but he added: "You know I never take an uncalculated risk, General, and I refused to allow these men of the Eighth Air Force to engage in a gamble with the weather."

Spaatz was clearly unconvinced by the explanation. "That will be all," was all he said before dismissing Doolittle from his office, and Doolittle left headquarters convinced that he was finished. Back at his own HQ, he got on with his job as best he could but certain that his days in charge of the Eighth's bombing fleet would soon be over. Then, with no warning, Spaatz turned up one day and said he wanted to tour some of the bases in England,

Doolittle was to come with him. They set off in Spaatz's own B-17, flown by his personal pilot, an old and trusted hand by the name of Lieutenant Colonel Robert Kimmel.

As they were about to leave each base after their visit, both Spaatz and Doolittle, in the tradition of old pilots, checked the weather. At the last base they visited they received a "Weather fine" report. They walked out of the Operations Room to be greeted with lowering clouds and heavy rain. "We'd better head for home," Doolittle said. They took off, but were only airborne ten minutes when they found themselves in the midst of heavy fog. Kimmel, at the controls, queried a dozen air bases but found they were all closed in. The weather had completely contradicted the optimistic report of the meteorologist. The pilot tried to go above the front. It was clear enough at 18,000 feet, but there were no airfields up there. He went down again, but the fog extended right to the deck. "I can't locate a base, General," Kimmel said to Spaatz, "I'll just have to hedgehop, hoping to find a field where we can set down." Calling upon all of his experience and skill, the pilot finally managed to sideslip the airplane blindly into a field. By sheer happy chance there were no trees, no cattle, no overhead wires and no barn in the path of the big B-17. Finally he brought it screechingly to a stop just a few yards from a stone wall that would have completely wrecked the plane and lost the United States Air Forces in Europe their two highest-ranking officers.

Wordlessly, Spaatz and Doolittle climbed down from the plane. The gloom had deepened. Spaatz turned to Doolittle and said quietly, "Jim, I see what *you* mean now. You were absolutely right. I've changed my mind." Doolittle grinned. "I just hate uncalculated risks," he said, "even when a pilot like Kimmel is at the controls. And remember, most of the kids flying our heavies don't have anything like his experience." A month later Doolittle received his third star and the rank of lieutenant general.

There was no doubting Doolittle's courage or his leadership after that. It was under his command that the Eighth went on the offensive against the Luftwaffe. When he arrived to take charge, the pilots of the P-47s and P-51s had been used to acting as guard dogs, shepherding the bomber formations to and from the European mainland. A motto on the walls at fighter bases proclaimed that "The first duty of the fighters is to bring the bombers back alive." Doolittle had the signs taken down and replaced with "The first duty of our fighters is to destroy the enemy's fighters." His new orders were for the fighters to go out in front of the main force, actively seeking the packs of Messerschmitts and Focke-Wulfs, not waiting for them to initiate battle. "Tell the men to chase them all over the sky, chase them down to the ground and then destroy them on the ground," he ordered. It was an instruction his fighter crews were happy to follow. They were less pleased with another of his orders—that the number of missions needed to complete a tour of combat missions should be raised from twenty-five to thirty. He explained himself thus: "It takes a bomber crew about ten missions to learn its trade. Very few crews do accurate bombing during those first ten missions. Then a crew does a pretty good job during its next fifteen missions. By the time it's had its twenty-five missions it has really reached its peak of maximum efficiency. Then we take it off the line. That just doesn't make sense. A crew that has been through twenty-five missions knows how to take care of itself; it knows the tricks of evading flak and of getting away from German fighters." Later he would raise the requirement to thirty-five missions.

Unlike his British counterparts, Doolittle was also determined to lead from the front. Harris would never let his headquarters staff go into combat, and he never showed any hankering to be up in a Lancaster himself. This was not cowardice but practicality. He had been a fearless leader of his fighter squadron in dogfights over the Flanders battlefields in the First World War, undeterred by a crash landing in which he was lucky to escape with his life. But that was then. Now his job was to lead and to direct. Doolittle had been a pioneer of aviation in his younger days. He was the first pilot to cross the United States from coast to coast in less than twenty-four hours. He had led the formations of B-25s that took off from the aircraft carrier *Hornet* to hit Tokyo in 1942. He had also flown in the bombing of Rome. Now he wanted to follow that by leading an attack on the other enemy capital—Berlin. His superiors were all in favor of the Eighth making daylight raids on Hitler's principal city, but they were against Doolittle taking part. His intention to go was discovered just a few days before the first Berlin mission. Eisenhower forbade him to fly. Doolittle was angry and frustrated, according to his biographer. He appealed to Spaatz to help him persuade Eisenhower to relent. But Spaatz agreed with "the Boss." "We cannot allow you to go because of the risk of Pentothal," he told Doolittle. "What the hell is that, and what does it have to do with hitting Berlin?" Doolittle replied. Spaatz spelled out the harsh facts. "Pentothal is a truth serum which is being used by the Germans to make our captured airmen talk. No one has any defense against it. You know far too much about the forthcoming invasion of the mainland. You know the time, the place, and the strength we will throw against the Continent. If by any chance you were shot down, they'd give you a shot of this drug and you would spill everything you know." Reluctantly Doolittle accepted the order and stood himself down. But his deep desire to be in the front line with his men typified the remarkable esprit de corps at the heart of the Mighty Eighth.

That same exceptional esprit de corps marked out the British bomber crews, too. Of all the groups of fighting men in the Second World War, Bomber Command was second to none in its sense of comradeship and purpose. Men pushed themselves beyond the limits of bravery and endurance time and again. Putting their lives at risk was a nightly occurrence. They knew how small their chances of survival were, and yet, as we saw in the last chapter, the dropout rate was minuscule. Was it fear or respect that drove them to such heroic deeds? Whichever, the commander must be given credit for inspiring them. Yet, as we have seen, Harris led neither from the front nor by example. To cut such a distant figure was a strange form of leadership. And it is hard to disentangle what his men really thought of him at the time from their sentiments about him after the war. His old lags only really got to know him when he met them at squadron reunions, usually for the first time. That was when they rallied round him, protecting his reputation from attack and their own as well. Chan Chandler declared after meeting Harris on one of those occasions: "I felt in the presence of a great man, a man of affection and a humanitarian."[32] But the actual feelings about Butch among aircrew as they climbed into their Lancasters and Halifaxes and headed for the skies of Germany are harder to pin down.

Some recalled adoring Harris. Chandler, just eighteen years old when he became a tail gunner, thought of the commander in chief as "a mystical figure" who gave him a tremendous sense of purpose. "He was a commander of quality, vitality, and drive and we were all proud of him. When he issued his orders, they were lucid and straightforward—no messing about and no pussyfooting. When we arrived back at base after an operation we felt he really appreciated our efforts. His short 'Well done' messages were a tonic to us all. We knew what he wanted and that he was more than aware of what he was doing." But for most, he must have been a distant authority figure (and a fearsome one at that), a man they respected but knew little about, except by reputation. Bill Low thought of him as "just the guy in charge," someone he knew of but never saw and never thought much about. Now, however, he is very protective of the commander's memory: "I don't like any criticism of Harris or of RAF policy. We did the right thing. It was what we had to do at the time."[33]

At the time, Harris's great skill was not in being popular but in leaving his men in no doubt that he knew how the war could be won, and how they could be the ones who won it. His principal belief was that in every war there was one new weapon that would be decisive, and once it had been correctly identified, it had to be used without restraint. Harris believed the First World War had been the war of the submarine but the weapon had not been properly employed because of naval commanders, on both sides, who still wanted to play with battleships. The Second World War he identified as the heavy bomber's war. It had to be exploited to the full. But it was also a new and largely untried weapon, and its limits should never be assumed until they had been demonstrably reached, and that point, he was adamant, had *not* been reached. He did not believe the power of strategic bombing was limitless, only that its limits had yet to be fully tested because he (and the Americans) had never had the chance to build up a big enough force of aircraft, men, and equipment to do the job he was convinced they were capable of doing. Batter the Germans long enough and hard enough in their own backyards and they will surrender, he maintained. Their morale would collapse along with the industries they needed to fight the war.

Critics of his theory that a people could be broken by bombing said that Britain had not given up under the Blitz but had, on the contrary, been stirred to battle on. Why should it be any different for the German people? To which Harris's reply was that Hitler's mistake had been to call off the attacks at precisely the point when he should have persisted with them. As he watched German bombs fall on London in 1940 and felt momentarily vengeful, it was the misses that caught Harris's eye as much as the hits. He wrote later:

> Even on the worst night the majority of the German aircraft failed to reach the actual target area and the weight of bombs they dropped was a mere nothing compared with our subsequent attacks on German cities. If the Germans had gone on and if the majority of aircraft had got to the target they would have had the whole of London in flames. The fire tornado would have been worse than anything that happened later in Hamburg. The whole of London would have gone as Hamburg went.

Standing on the Air Ministry roof that night and seeing London burn before his eyes, the lesson Harris learned was to send more aircraft, to bomb on target and never, never to give up. He wrote in his memoirs: "I was convinced that a bomber offensive of adequate weight and the right kind of bombs would, *if continued for long enough,* be something that no country in the world could endure." (Emphasis added.)

But it was from the German bombing of Coventry that Harris took his most important lesson. The Luftwaffe had targeted it as an industrial center producing weapons for the war, and had succeeded in damaging output quite considerably. But loss of production was due as much to the interruption of public transport and utilities and the absenteeism of workers caused by the destruction of their homes as it was by direct hits on factories. From this Harris inferred that hitting a whole city—homes as well as factories—was the way to cripple its industries. There was one further part of the thesis: Coventry's production was restored within a couple of months, and it could be said that the same would apply to any German city hit in the same way. Harris argued that Coventry was soon back in business because Britain at that time had battalions of soldiers available with nothing else to do. In Germany, if soldiers were rushed in to restore a shattered city at home, it would have to be at the expense of some other front. Damage would be done just in repairing the damage done by bombing.

It was a credible argument, but then so was much of what Harris said, once you discounted the hyperbole and the sarcasm he was prone to indulge in. In fact, Harris's mind and his understanding of history were altogether more subtle than his critics ever credit him with. To see just how subtle, let us fast-forward for a moment to the aftermath of the war. In 1947 Harris wrote his memoirs, in which he looked to a future in which the bomber he had loved so much was obsolescent. He did not mourn its passing. It had had its day—though, as he pointed out, RAF commanders stuck in the past would cling to it as the means for delivering the newfangled nuclear weapons. Harris looked beyond planes and missiles as a means of devastating cities in the future. "Wars will be mainly taken over by the scientists, the diplomats and the cloak and dagger men," he wrote. "An ordinary embassy official or a commercial traveller or a tourist will eventually prove just as good a purveyor of atomic explosives as any aircraft, rocket or machine. There is no reason why an atomic bomb should not be brought in bit by bit by seemingly innocent people and assembled in an attic, lodging or in a ship in a harbor. The threat of its presence could then be used to back an ultimatum."

Harris's vision did not extend to seeing terrorism as the force of the future, but, that apart, what he was describing back in 1947 was the pattern of warfare we are now told to expect in the twenty-first century. Harris foresaw weapons of mass destruction in suitcases, the specter that has just begun to haunt the military analysts of today. It was astonishingly perceptive of him and should make those critics who considered Harris a blockhead with tunnel vision think again. Harris was a clever man. The ideas he persisted with in 1944 and 1945 in the face of much opposition cannot just be dismissed as the stubbornness of a bigot.

To understand those days, we have to make an imaginative leap and try and grasp how new, untried, and untested air warfare was in the 1940s. Who knew for sure what bombing could and could not achieve? It was only twenty-five years since the main role of the United States Air Corps had been to chase the Mexican bandit-revolutionary Pancho Villa back across the Rio Grande. Since then, Guernica, Ethiopia, Warsaw, and Rotterdam had demonstrated the terrifying offensive potential of aerial bombing. The London Blitz may have failed, but it was the only air onslaught to have done so (and for very particular reasons). In 1944, therefore, there was no reason at all to conclude that the bombing of cities was a strategy that had run its course. Quite the opposite. Nor was Harris alone in believing that strategic bombing could break the morale of the enemy. As Harris pointed out in his memoirs, "The Americans were so impressed by the achievements of strategic bombing in Europe that, in their conduct of the Japanese war, they decided to put a far larger share of the national resources into air power than had previously been intended." Tokyo, flattened by conventional bombs, and nuclear-annihilated Hiroshima and Nagasaki, were part of that strategy. And the belief that a country could be bombed into submission has persisted in U.S. military circles right into the twenty-first century—through Vietnam to Serbia and Iraq.

It should be said, too, that Harris accepted in a way others refused to do that modern warfare inevitably involved civilian populations. To pretend that you could fight a "total war" that could be ended by only "unconditional surrender," as the Allies had agreed at Casablanca, and yet to be sentimental about civilian casualties was nonsense. Harris put the issue in his usual robust way. "The point is often made," he wrote in his memoirs, "that bombing is specially wicked because it causes casualties among civilians. This is true, but all wars have caused casualties among civilians." In the past, warfare had involved the besieging of cities, ending with soldiers and civilians alike being put to the sword. "What city in what war has ever failed to receive the maximum bombardment from all enemy artillery within range so long as it has continued resistance?" he asked. These were uncomfortable arguments for people to accept, but they were true nonetheless.[34]

By and large, the men he sent to do the job for him, to visit the front line over Germany night after night at the risk of their own lives, believed in him and what he asked of them. Bombardier Campbell Muirhead wrote in his diary in June 1944: "Harris has dedicated himself to laying Germany absolutely flat. It's a worthwhile dedication. The bastards deserve all they've been getting and what they're going to get. Wonder if they still support Hitler as much as they did before all that destruction started descending from the skies on to their cities." He lay on his bed listening to Lord Haw-Haw[35] on the radio, "telling me what a swine I am dropping bombs on innocent civilians. Jesus wept! There's nothing innocent about that bloody nation. No talk about swine when bombing Coventry or that dreadful raid on Clydebank. They're getting what they deserve. And I'm glad to be one of those dishing it out." Muirhead was further incensed when on a mission over Germany a Luftwaffe controller broke in on their radio frequency and denounced the raiding party (in a beautiful Oxbridge accent) as "English terror fliers." Muirhead yelled back that he was a *Scottish* terror flier— "One doesn't like all the credit to go to the Sassenachs." At other times, though, he hated the idea that he was bombing women and children. "God, it's a terrible killing time." He decided he "really can't afford such brooding. I know nobody can stop it until the Germans surrender."

But not all agreed with Harris's strategy. Some of his men worried deeply whether what they were doing was right. A raid on Hamburg in July 1944 made Boris Bressloff question the morality of bombing cities. "It wasn't one of the big firestorms, but it was still pretty awful. I saw the bombs going down and the fires starting, and I thought, this is terrible. I felt guilty, like a small boy throwing a brick through someone's window." Bressloff was Jewish and aware of what the Nazi regime was doing to people of his race, "but I was sensitive enough to know that there were innocent people down there, women and children who had nothing to do with it."[36] There was a moment, too, when Robert Wannop thought he had become inhuman. Dropping bombs on Saarbrücken,

I pondered on the dreadfulness of it all. Here was I, a young man with a wife and a beautiful baby daughter, raining death and unbearable horror on similar wives and children. Yet the worst part of it was that I felt no guilt, no feelings of repulsion at the enormity of my deed. My heart didn't bleed for those poor innocent children huddled terrified in rat-riddled cellars and shelters far below. I had no feelings at all for their misery and fear. I just felt quite remote and aloof to all the suffering. God! What monsters had we all become![37]

Wannop's conscience would be further troubled,[38] but for now "a burst of flak put paid to my musing. Flying shrapnel rattled like a handful of pebbles against a stout window, penetrating the Perspex cover over my head. Too bloody close for comfort!" The delivering of death and horror was not just one-way. He switched his mind back to the job he had to do, his personal conflict set aside but not resolved.

Those German cities were about to get some respite. Harris might think them his only proper target, but in the early summer of 1944 he was instructed to switch the efforts of Bomber Command to supporting the forthcoming D-Day operation. He never wavered in his belief that the invasion was a mistake. To the end of his days he remained convinced that if only he had been allowed to stick to his task, "we should never have had to mount an invasion on anything like the scale that proved necessary," as he wrote in his memoirs.[39] There had been so many attempts to divert him to what he saw as "panacea" targets. Some bright spark was always coming up with a sure-fire, quick, and easy way to end the war. Bomb the synthetic oil plants, destroy the ball-bearing factories, remove this one component on which the whole Nazi edifice depended, and it would all be over by Christmas. Opinion in Downing Street encouraged the boffins and the dreamers. Churchill, with his butterfly mind, loved eccentric schemes, and was always one for letting a thousand flowers bloom. Harris preferred to plow the furrow he knew and believed in. He would shake his head and say no unless and until a higher authority directed him otherwise. And then, as Harris wrote world-wearily after the war,

whenever we did successfully attack such [panacea] targets, we were always told, just when the enemy ought by rights to have been surrendering unconditionally, that some other manifestation in that particular war industry had just been discovered or that there was some other material which the enemy was using as an alternative. Had I paid attention to the panacea-mongers who were always cropping up and hawking their wares, Bomber Command would have flitted continually from one thing to another and the continuity of the offensive as a whole would have been irretrievably lost.

Harris never took his eye off Germany's cities, which he considered his real objective. For now, though, it was the middle of 1944 and he was under specific orders to divert his attention to France and the needs of Operation Overlord. Whether he approved or not, the invasion of Nazi-occupied Europe was about to begin, and he and his men had a vital part to play.

D-DAY AND BEYOND

"The more of these 'easy' efforts we do, the happier we'll all be. We'll settle for French docks and U-boat pens any time."
—CREWMAN ON D-DAY SUPPORT OPERATIONS

USAAF NAVIGATOR AUGUSTUS BOLINO'S WAR WAS AN INTENSE ONE. HE went out on his first mission in May 1944 and his last in July. He was back home in Boston by August. But in the few months he took to complete his tour, he was involved in desperately dangerous missions while also experiencing one of the most memorable events of the entire war. The impression those hundred bittersweet days made on him would last a lifetime. Sixty years later the memory of them would draw him back to the East Anglian countryside and the reunion and the dedication of a memorial to the fallen with which this book began. Berlin, the biggest target of all, was his second mission. The Eighth Air Force had kept its distance from the German capital until its commanders were sure they had enough firepower and fighter cover to pound Hitler in his own backyard without disastrous losses. Even so, when the attacks were finally made on "the Big B," the casualties were high. Bolino watched "planes falling out of the sky everywhere. It was truly a flying circus. The flak was thick, and black puffs of smoke were circling all around us." On another mission he saw the two lead planes in his group shot down in front of him. His own skipper was next in line and took charge, rallying the group and completing the mission. Over Bremen, an ack-ack shell pierced the wing, and only a miracle prevented it breaking off and sending them spinning to oblivion.

But Bolino's greatest day was D-Day—the invasion of France by the combined Allied forces on June 6. "This was what we had been working toward," he remembered proudly.[1]

It began for us the day before when we bombed a giant German gun in the Pas de Calais area. This was a diversionary tactic to make the Germans think that the landing was going to be in the north of France when, of course, it wasn't. It was 150 miles further south in Normandy. Then, on D-Day itself we were up very early, at 2:00 A.M. or 3:00 A.M., and at the briefing the colonel told us that, if we got into trouble, there would be absolutely no possibility of ditching in the Channel. We were kind of puzzled as to what he meant—until we saw the Channel. It was full of thousands of ships of all sizes. It was the most awe-inspiring sight I've ever seen. The sky was also filled with planes of every conceivable type and shape. Below us were the gliders carrying our soldiers behind the German lines. And below them, of course, this vast armada. I doubt if, in the history of the world, there will ever be another group of ships and planes amassed as there was on June 6. We bombed the coastal defenses in front of the ships and then headed back to base.

New Yorker Martin Garren, a copilot, was very young to be in the air at the controls of a B-17. He had had his nineteenth birthday shortly before D-Day. He had joined up straight out of high school in White Plains after falsifying his birth certificate to make himself two years old than he was. "It was important that I go to war before I started the rest of my life," he recalled. "We were exposed to a lot of propaganda that glorified war, but my motivation was family values. Honor and duty were basic things to me. In the long run I felt I was defending my mother and my sister from invasion by our enemies."[2] At briefing that night he knew straightaway that this was the big one. The place was alive with visiting generals and colonels. When the men were officially told that D-Day was finally here, they went wild with excitement.

We were briefed to hit the defenses in the Utah Beach area fifteen minutes or so before the landing boats came ashore. That meant taking off around

3:00 A.M. and assembling in the dark, which was very hazardous, and there was a lot of apprehension since we had never practiced that kind of thing. The tail gunner had an Aldis lamp which he kept flashing to indicate this is the tail of a B-17 here and don't bump into it. We also took off with wing lights, which would have been of great help to German fighters if there had been any around, but we turned them off as soon as we were airborne because the sun was already in the sky and we could see each other. We assembled into our thirty-six-ship formation, then the 108-plane combat box of our wing, and headed for Utah Beach to bomb the concrete fortifications the Germans had built. Just before we went in to bomb, I looked out to the right and left and suddenly saw what looked like the entire Eighth Air Force, maybe, 1,500 planes almost in a line abreast like the kickoff of a football game. We had expected the Luftwaffe to put up everything they had against us, but we did not see a single enemy plane or a burst of flak.

After bombing we were given a specific course to fly over France and then make a big, wide U-turn for home. We passed over the town of Ste. Mère Eglise, where a few hours earlier our paratroopers had dropped, and I found myself thinking of what might be happening to them—anyone who came swinging down in a parachute was likely to be shot at. Suddenly, we developed a fire in our control panel, and we all thought, "My god, what a place to have to bail out." But the fire was put out and we returned to base without further incident.

By then, Nicky Knilans, an American-born pilot serving in the RAF's famous 617 Squadron, had long ago completed his vital contribution to D-Day. In the early hours of the morning, along with the rest of his squadron, he had flown his Lancaster bomber in the tightest of patterns over the Channel off Calais, throwing out continuous showers of Window (chaff), the aluminum strips that deceived German radar. They had been practicing this maneuver, one requiring immense discipline, for a month. Height had to be constant, as did the distance between the planes. So much concentration was needed that a reserve crew was on board to share the flying. But the cumulative effect was worth the effort. The picture building up on the enemy radar screens was a solid block, indicating an invasion fleet fourteen miles wide and heading directly across the Straits of Dover at a speed of seven knots toward the flat sandy beaches of the Calais-Boulogne coastline, miles from the real action.

This sort of deception was vital. Even as Allied troops were clawing their way onto Utah, Omaha, Sword, Juno, and Gold beaches in Normandy, Hitler was convinced this was a decoy and the main force would still come in the north. He refused increasingly desperate requests from his generals on the spot to send troops from the Calais area to shore up the Normandy defenses. As Knilans was able to congratulate himself later: "617 Squadron's ruse worked to perfection. Most of the German army remained in the Pas de Calais to repel the imaginary invasion armada. I was especially pleased because my brother was one of those Yank soldiers landing in the south."[3] As Knilans flew back to his base in Lincolnshire, he dropped to one thousand feet and virtually skimmed the Channel so as not to run headlong into the droves of Allied gliders and aircraft in the air corridors above carrying tens of thousands of paratroopers to the fight in France.

A few hours earlier, Campbell Muirhead had been lying prone in the bombardier's position of his Lancaster and directing it in at seven thousand feet over the coast of Normandy before releasing six tons of explosives on a German heavy gun battery at the hamlet of Crisbecq overlooking Utah Beach—where in just a few hours' time crafts full of American troops would be trying to land. Along with Bolino's, his was one of more than two thousand Allied bombers that dropped more than five thousand tons of high explosives on the coastal defenses in those vital hours just before the invasion, doing their bit to guarantee the success of Operation Overlord. The briefing before takeoff had been emotional—they had been told the guns had to be silenced even if it cost them their lives, otherwise "the invasion might well be affected to a frightening degree." He thought he had done his duty—"I made a good run-up and am pretty certain I obtained some direct hits."[4] He was right. Later he heard the battery had been obliterated and gave no problems to the ships anchoring offshore to unload troops. Other B-17s, B-24s, and Lancasters targeted the actual beaches where the troops would land, trying to flatten the massive defenses, obstacles, pillboxes, and barbed wire and to obliterate any human defenders. The barrage ceased only minutes before the first landing craft ground to a halt in the shallow water. On the cliffs, startled German soldiers—those who survived the air attack—put their heads out of their bunkers to see lines of ships approaching the shore. Above, the skies were patrolled by Spitfires and Hurricanes, Mustangs and Lightnings, all enjoying complete superiority over the Luftwaffe, thanks to the battering the German air force had suffered from the combined efforts of the Eighth Air Force and Bomber Command in the spring. At the controls of one of the thousands of fighters in the air that day was General Jimmy Doolittle. The commander of the Eighth could not resist the temptation to see for himself. He also had the satisfaction of roaming those skies over the Channel and the French coast without running into a single enemy fighter. Here was the proof of what a good job he and his men had done in the past six months with their ferocious assault on the German aircraft industry. On D-Day the Luftwaffe failed to turn up. This was a victory in itself.

Not surprisingly, the waves of optimism on D-Day revived thoughts of an early end to the war. Wil Richardson of the 94th Bomb Group recalled how at briefings everyone was shouting that the war would soon be over.[5] Bill Low, a wireless operator and air gunner on Lancasters, even dared to think of the future. "We had been waiting for this moment for so long, and finally this was it—not the end of the war but the beginning of the end. We talked of a new era, a chance to live normal lives again. I started making plans about what I would do after the war—I wanted to go into the Civil Service and have a cozy, secure, quiet job."[6] Even at the time, Low knew he might be tempting fate.

The end of the war was far from Augustus Bolino's thoughts. He and his crew had fallen into their beds exhausted after their bombing run on the Normandy coast but were roused a few hours later. "The invasion's in jeopardy," he and his men were told. "The Germans are pushing our soldiers back into the sea. You've got to go in again." They were soon back in the air and over the Channel to bombard the German defenses. "I remember how difficult it was to make the second trip that day," he recalled. "We had only had three or four hours sleep in two days." He was so drained he could barely swing himself up through the hatch and into the Fortress. A boot from behind helped him on his way. There was no alternative. They had to go back to the beaches. Somehow the boys on the ground had to get a foothold in the sand, otherwise the war would never end.

Wil Richardson from Long Beach in California was in that second wave, too, his five-foot eleven-inch frame crammed into the ball turret slung beneath his B-17. The ball was less than four feet in diameter and, as he recalled, "you had to double up on your back with your knees up by your eyeballs. You looked between your knees and feet through the side and through the round window at your feet. It was a very tight fit. There was no room for a parachute or a flak suit." But from this vantage point, he had the best view of the action below. "I saw the battleship *Texas* firing her big guns across the water to the target areas just beyond the beaches. Hundreds and hundreds of boats were still coming across the Channel while thousands were already lined up along the beach."

While 150,000 British, American, and Canadian infantry stormed onto the beaches or parachuted inland, 10,000 of them dying to secure that precious, precarious foothold in France, Campbell Muirhead's squadron had been stood down. They spent much of D-Day at a tantalizing lecture. Home from destroying the coastal battery, they had been summoned to an aircraft recognition lesson. They lolled around in chairs in a darkened briefing room as slides flashed on a screen. As minds wandered, the instructor would drop in the occasional nude, his usual device for keeping the men's attention. He promised more "once we've done *ship* recognition." A few destroyers and pocket battleships later, as Muirhead recalled, "On came a shot of an orgy in full flight. 'You've got it the wrong way up,' someone shouted. 'No, it isn't—you have to turn your head sideways,' someone else explained." But these men of Bomber Command deserved their lazy, mildly licentious day away from the fighting. For two months they had done little but fly operations to soften up the French hinterland. The Americans channeled their efforts into attacking Luftwaffe airfields and radar stations in France while Bomber Command concentrated on transport links, arms dumps, and factories. It had meant many sorties to areas that would be untouched by the invasion—the Germans had to be left guessing where and when it would come.

The invasion was an event that Harris, commander in chief of Bomber Command, and Spaatz, his American counterpart, had always claimed would be unnecessary because their bombing alone could bring Germany to its knees. Events had overtaken them, though they remained unrepentant in their views, insisting even as they prepared for it that the invasion was a huge risk which did not need to be taken and fearful of the consequences if it proved to be a disaster. They had been given their part to play in ensuring that it was not. Since early April, Bomber Command and the Eighth Air Force had been placed at the disposal of the supreme commander of the Allied Expeditionary Force, General Eisenhower. Harris and Spaatz, for all their misgivings, had thrown their bombing forces enthusiastically into this new work.

The raids Bomber Command carried out were significantly smaller than the attacks on big cities in Germany had been. Only rarely were there more than 220 aircraft in the attacking force, but they were required to be more accurate in their bombing. Killing enemy civilians as a consequence of carpet bombing might be excusable. Reducing the cities of France to rubble was not. At the very least it ran the risk of alienating the very people the Allies were liberating. This requirement meant no change in practice by the Eighth Air Force. Regardless of the reality, its generals had always claimed their bombing was precise, whatever the target. But Harris had always doubted that such precision targeting was possible—it was why he backed area bombing in the first place. Now he was called on to train his men to do the impossible.

They proved him wrong. Their response to the new demands on them was excellent, and, with the increased use of master bombers to lead and direct operations, the success rate was high. The crews were said to be delighted to be associated with the planned invasion, a turning point in the war, and also more settled in their minds because their targets were now more obviously of a military nature. But what really made the crews happier was that they were getting in more operations in a shorter time and running fewer risks. Although a total of 250 bombers were to be downed in the pre–D-Day campaign, these operations clearly carried fewer risks. The sites were poorly defended compared with German cities, and the shortness of the sorties generally meant the Luftwaffe fighters had little time to get into the air and cause any damage.

Campbell Muirhead, arriving at his squadron at the end of May, began his tour with two such jaunts to France—"a very gentle blooding," he recorded in his diary. "No tightening of the stomach muscles, not even a faint quiver. Tell myself not to feel so cocky, that when we get briefed for an op on Germany those wretched muscles will start working overtime." He counted his blessings. If it had not been for an attack of appendicitis toward the end of his training and a two-month stay in hospital, he would have arrived on station in time to fly—and probably die—in the fated Nuremberg raid. "Odd the part luck plays in it all," he noted, "luck, nothing else." He was glad not to have become "a statistic over Nuremberg." Instead he was skipping across the Channel to bomb railway junctions and radar installations. "Rumor hath it," he wrote, "that 'Butch' [Harris] isn't at all happy at his 'heavies' being diverted from their task of laying waste the Third Reich to engage in this kind of work. As for me and the crew, we're all for it. The more of these 'easy efforts,' the happier we'll all be. We'll settle for French docks and U-boat pens any time."

There was something else that Butch wasn't happy about. The raids on factories, railway marshaling yards, arms dumps, and coastal batteries in France and Belgium could not be equated with sorties to Germany. It seemed unfair to him that these easier, shorter operations should count equally toward the number needed to complete a tour. He was not alone in his misgivings about what was happening. Navigator William Lovejoy, just starting his second tour, was appalled at seeing new boys in the squadron "clocking up three short daylight operations totaling rather less than one trip to Berlin in flying hours."[7] For Harris, more than just fairness was at stake. Unless the quickies across the Channel were discounted, he risked rapidly running out of crews as their tours of duty ended in a matter of weeks rather than months. He therefore proposed—and the Air Ministry agreed—that each sortie to a "soft" target in France and Belgium should be deemed just one-third of an operation. The men themselves were horrified by this change. Some saw it as "a sentence of death." Bill Low echoed the thoughts of many: "As far as I was concerned people were still getting shot down and killed on a daily basis, and flying over enemy territory in France could be as dangerous as anywhere else." Exactly how dangerous, he was soon to find out.

When word of their discontent reached Harris, he did something unusual for him—he sought advice from his group commanders. One of them, Air Vice Marshal E. A. B. Rice of No. 1 Group, told Harris of the resentment growing among the men and warned of "a serious effect on morale" and loss of confidence in higher command. He did not use the word "mutiny" but it must have uneasily in the air as Harris read Rice's report at his High Wycombe headquarters. Rice presented a different interpretation of what was fair or unfair. "The old crews are fully prepared to 'take the rough with the smooth' and, having spent months attacking targets deep into Germany, which were certainly 'rough,' they now expect to be allowed to enjoy some 'smooth' raids to end their tours, and as a result they feel that they are being badly cheated in having to do three times the number." As for new crews just beginning, Rice went on, "they see the prospect of having to complete ninety raids during their tour, and feel that the likelihood of survival is slender." He ended his report: "I most strongly urge that the system of dividing up sorties should be discontinued, and every raid be counted as a full sortie, to ensure that the present very high morale of the bomber crews be preserved." Harris heeded the warning. He returned to the old system of all sorties counting as one, irrespective of the target. There would be no more fractions. In his diary, Campbell Muirhead welcomed "the end of *that nonsense*. Much to the relief of all of us. Off to Vaires tomorrow, knowing it'll count as a full one. It'll be our thirteenth. . . ."

Vaires was a railway yard near Paris, one of the many communications targets Bomber Command was hitting as part of its operations to support the invasion. Harris carried out close to a hundred raids in France and Belgium, implementing the transportation plan drawn up at Allied Supreme Headquarters (SHAEF). The theory was that knocking out a few key points in the railway network would prevent German reinforcements getting through. In the event, smashed junctions and marshaling yards were quickly repaired—usually with the use of slave laborers and gangs of POWs, of which the Germans had hundreds of thousands—enough for essential traffic to resume. Civilian trains were stopped, but vital military transports got through regardless. Harris always had his doubts about the transportation plan, thinking it just another "panacea." Whenever the opportunities presented themselves he chose to hit the German supply of arms at their source. In the run-up to D-Day, as well as bombing military targets in France, he also managed to send his force in large numbers to Cologne, Essen, Brunswick, and other cities across the Rhine.

It was at this time that Ken Newman made his very first operational flight to Germany. As he flew over the town of Duisburg in the Ruhr and heard the shout of "Bombs gone," his mind went back three and a half years to the London Blitz when his home had been destroyed and he and his family had narrowly escaped with their lives. "I had a sense of satisfaction, that I was paying the Germans back." His delight was tempered when, back at base, he learned that twenty-nine Lancasters had been lost that night, three from his own squadron. The next night he was back in the air again, another trip to Happy Valley. As they crossed into Germany the huge defensive zone around the Ruhr—"a forest of searchlights which seemed almost impenetrable"—could be seen from miles away. One of those lights coned Newman's plane, and he was thrown from his seat and smashed his head on the canopy cover as he corkscrewed away. He was lucky not to have been knocked out, with fatal consequences for all on board. He fell back into his seat, grabbed the control column, and forced the Lancaster to climb out of the cone of light. "Back in the blackness again I was in a cold sweat and shaking from both fear and physical exertion." But the danger was only beginning. Ahead, over Dortmund, the target, "the sky was filled with exploding antiaircraft shells and from time to time a burning aircraft—whether friend or foe I could not tell—plunged earthward in a slow and graceful curve of fire. I knew I had to run the gauntlet of this vortex of death and destruction and wondered if I would be able to get through unscathed."

He did, but he was shaking as he steered for home after dropping his bombs, dodging searchlights and flak until he was clear of Germany. Back at base, the news was that another eighteen Lancasters had been downed that night. Newman, thanking God his was not among them, tried to sleep but found it hard to shut out the sights and sounds of battle. What was worse was the thought that he had twenty-eight more operations to go— "that seemed like a very high mountain to climb."[8] Forty-seven aircraft had been lost over Germany in a little over thirty-six hours, and more than 340 men were missing, most of them dead.[9] Nor did the damage end there. A separate attack on Brunswick had cost a further thirteen aircraft and eighty dead. No wonder the men preferred the easier option of beating up railway yards in France.

Bill Low was certainly happy with his "easy" hop over the Channel on D-Day itself. The light was beginning to fade at the end of what was being termed "the longest day" when he took off to bomb the bridges at the strategic town of Caen, "a low-level attack, drop the bombs and come out. It would take about ten minutes from getting over Cherbourg—ten minutes there and back. It was only a short trip, a piece of cake. I didn't even put my flying boots on." They crossed the Channel at eight thousand feet before dropping down. Low could see the flashes of the guns in the fierce fighting below.

It was an amazing sight. We felt quite safe compared to the guys on the ground. But then, as we prepared for the run into Caen, all hell let loose. Out of the blue, German antiaircraft guns got a bearing on us and let fly. The aircraft was hit in the port wing and in the fuselage at the back. The skipper just shouted "abandon ship" and we piled out. My job was to go and tap the mid-uppers' legs, to tell him to bail out. Then I had to go down the back to make sure the rear gunner got out. But the back of the plane was on fire. There were flames everywhere and I couldn't get through. I sometimes feel I should have tried harder, but I just couldn't get there, so I fought my way back up to the front.

There he found the pilot about to dive out of the escape hatch.

> It was lucky for him that I came back at that point because I saw that the skipper's parachute was only clipped on one side. There was so much noise, flames everywhere, confusion, but I can remember stopping to say, "That's not right," and clipping him in properly. It can only have taken a few seconds but it seemed so slow at the time. We were meant to count to ten before pulling the parachute ring but we were so low panic set in and I pulled it as I dived out and there was the ground coming up to meet me.

He bounced off a roof and hit the ground hard, landing on his back and knocking himself out. When he came to, the pain was intense.

> I was quite frightened but also very surprised. I always thought that this was never going to happen to me. I took the parachute off and hid it and began to walk away. Suddenly I bumped into a German patrol, about eight of them. I was amazed. It felt unreal. This is what I had seen on films, but these were real Germans, not film Germans. One of the guys dropped his rifle; another ran away. I suppose they were more frightened than I was. The others took me inside a building, stole my cigarettes, my escape pack, and my chocolate, then they threw me down some stairs.

Bill Low's war was over. He had survived the massacre at Nuremberg only a few weeks earlier, yet now a "soft" operation to France had claimed him. He had fractured his spine and shattered most of his teeth on landing, yet he still regarded himself as one of the lucky ones. "I spent the rest of the war as a POW, but others were not so fortunate. Both gunners went down with the aircraft. The mid-upper always carried a special scarf for safety and part of it was found near the wreckage of our aircraft. He wore that scarf every time we flew. He said that it was part of the routine, to keep us all safe. It didn't seem to work that time."

———

In the weeks *after* D-Day, Lancasters and Halifaxes, B-17s and B-24s were constantly in the skies over Normandy, flying thousands of sorties to help the advance on the ground. This was much slower than planned because of intense German resistance. Having secured his toehold on the mainland, Eisenhower needed all the support he could get to make any strides forward, and Bomber Command and the Eighth Air Force were again called in to hinder the arrival of German reinforcements. Three days after the landings, Nicky Knilans found himself in a small raiding party of twenty-five Lancasters and three Mosquitoes heading for a railway tunnel at Saumur, a town one hundred miles south of the invasion beaches. The French Resistance had sent a message to London that a German panzer division was being rushed north by rail. It had to be stopped. The bombers were loaded with the latest "Tallboy" bombs designed to penetrate a hundred feet into the earth before exploding. These were dropped on the tunnel, which collapsed. Knilans directed his bombs on the mouth of the tunnel, leaving a fifty-foot crater where the railway line had been. The panzers were forced to find another route. There were also missions to arm the Resistance fighters in France, whose job was to harass the German forces, tie them up in local security operations, and prevent them being rushed as reinforcements to Normandy. Jim O'Connor took part in one such operation, code-named Zebra, by the Eighth, dropping supplies to guerrilla forces in the wooded hills of the south of France. Three hundred B-17s were loaded with canisters filled with guns, ammunition, and supplies. O'Connor recalled:

As we approached the rugged terrain at the foothills of the Alps beyond Lyon, we dropped down to several hundred feet. Three bonfires on three separate hilltops told us where to make the drop. We could see German sentries guarding bridges in the area and groups of French villagers in the towns looking up in awe at the armada of planes above. The supplies were dropped from about 500 feet into an open valley. Immediately the *maquis,* as the Resistance fighters were known, scurried out of the woods like a bunch of mice, gathered up the loot, and disappeared back into the forests. A handful of commandos also parachuted out to join up with the fighters below. All this happened on Bastille Day, the French equivalent of Independence Day. It gave us a warm feeling to have helped them celebrate that occasion. And it must have boosted their morale to see and hear the roar of several hundred American bombers overhead to give them support. They knew they were not alone.[10]

Operations like these required low-level flying—and more new skills for the bomber crews. From 2,500 feet, an unprecedented bombing height for him, Muirhead could clearly see the locomotives in the French marshaling yard below and the steam rising from their stacks. He was a railway buff and their destruction pained him, but that was his job. He presumed "they were troop or ammo trains. Doubt if any civilian trains would be allowed in these parts." He worried that some others in the squadron were not as careful as he tried to be. He knew the bombardier's temptation only too well— "they can't wait and their thumb drops on the button just that fraction of a second before the target is fully in the crosshairs and if one or two bombardiers act similarly the entire bombing effort 'creeps back' until it's the area before the target which is getting it." In this case, French families. "I wonder how many die as a result."

There was an unnerving change in procedure around this time, too. On some missions Bomber Command operated in the daytime instead of at night, as they had been doing for four years. One pilot recorded the joy of sitting in a warm cockpit and feeling the sun on his face, a new experience, but he thought it made it harder to face the prospect of dying "on such a beautiful day." William Lovejoy, a veteran on his second tour, actually *saw* the enemy coast approaching for the first time in his war and as he passed into occupied territory was left pondering the fact that "the green fields and hedgerows of this 'foreign' land were little different from southern England."[11] But when flying to bomb the docks at Boulogne, a ninety-minute hop across the Channel, Muirhead remembered feeling "naked—I would much have preferred to have done this in the dark." The sight of Spitfires escorting the bombers cheered him up, however.

Bomber Command's duties did not stop at logistical attacks. It was also called in to destroy German strongholds that were blocking the Allied advance. Harris had deep reservations about using his strategic heavy bombers for such sorties. A month before D-Day he had visited Montgomery at the headquarters of 21 Army Group and told the general and his staff bluntly about the limitations—and the dangers—of using heavy bombers over battlefields. The soldiers ignored the airman's advice; they wanted bomber support. In his memoirs Harris wrote: "It seemed to me that the army had no idea of the risk their troops would be running."[12] However, his views at this time were subordinated to those of Air Chief Marshal Sir Trafford Leigh-Mallory, appointed by Eisenhower as Allied air commander. On his orders, the Lancasters were sent in to attack enemy troop concentrations—requiring even greater precision by the bombardiers since the front lines were very close and slippage of even a few hundred yards could result in bombs falling on the wrong side. Muirhead, bombing less than two miles ahead of Allied troops, refused to drop his bombs because he was unsure. He ordered the pilot to go round again "and, God, the language which came over that intercom, interspersed with references not only to my complete inadequacy as a bombardier but also to my parentage. But there was no way I was going to drop 13,000 pounds of high explosives when there was the slightest possibility of the dreadful stuff killing our own troops."

Still the Allied advance on the ground stalled. The town of Caen, just ten miles inland from the beaches, was supposed to have been taken within hours of the invasion but was still in German hands six weeks later. It fell only after a massive air raid that flattened it, destroying many of its medieval buildings in the process. But still there was little progress, and an even bigger force—942 bombers—was deployed to blast a way through enemy defenses to the east of the town and free the British Second Army to break out into the Normandy countryside. Ken Newman was one of the pilots on this operation and remembered how keen they all were to help the soldiers on the ground. "We did not envy their situation." Flying back over Allied lines, he waggled his wings at the soldiers below and the crews of tanks waved back.

Nearly seven thousand tons of explosives were dropped that day. Watching them fall from a safe distance, one of Montgomery's staff officers likened the attack to "a swarm of bees homing in upon their hive. One appreciated the great bravery of those pilots and crew as they flew straight into the most ghastly looking flak. But I also thought how terrible it must be to suffer under the Harris technique in a German town."[13] Montgomery's own view as he watched was that "nothing could live" underneath an air attack like that. He was wrong. The line of German tanks dug in beyond Caen remained unbroken. From his observations six thousand feet up, Ken Newman attributed the failure to press forward to the fact that the massive aerial bombardment left the ground so churned up it was virtually impassable. Newman recalled: "Our bombs made hundreds of huge overlapping craters. It was several days before our boys could advance, by which time the Germans had regrouped." The limitations of using heavy bombers as tactical support—always Harris's fear—were evident. He still felt his bombers could be put to better use, telling Charles Carrington, the army liaison officer at High Wycombe, "I have dropped a thousand tons of bombs to get the army forward one mile. At this rate it will take me 600,000 tons of bombs to get them to Berlin. You can tell them I'm willing, *provided they let me start at Berlin and work backward.*'[14]

The Eighth Air Force was also called in to ease the way forward for the American forces on the ground. Jim O'Connor was in a fleet of 1,500 bombers pounding enemy defenses in St. Lô, another strategic town that refused to yield. He was carrying a huge bomb load in the bay and thousand-pounders slung under each wing as well. He peered through cloud and mist, and went round four times, finally descending to 15,000 feet, 10,000 feet lower than usual, before he felt it safe to drop without endangering his own troops. Others were not so careful. Bombs fell into the U.S. Army front lines, stark evidence of the dangers of battlefield bombing. The same thing happened the next day, this time killing 111 soldiers (including a general, Lesley McNair) and wounding nearly 500. With his air and ground commanders blaming each other, Eisenhower pledged not to call in the heavy bombers again.[15] The job had been done anyway. A hole had been punched in the German lines, and Patton and his men streamed through it, racing south to the River Loire. But the casualties to their own men caused the bomber crews great distress when they heard about it. Bombardier Irwin Stovroff of the 44th Bomb Group accepted that his plane must have been one of those responsible. They bombed on the smoke released by the lead plane in the formation but he believd the smoke must have drifted back over their own lines. Herb Shanker of the 303rd recalled dropping clusters of twenty-pound bombs and seeing the propeller wash from all the planes scatter them in every direction. But navigator Jim Hill put the incident in perspective. Allied lives may have been lost but "the carpet bombing of St. Lô made the breakthrough possible."[16] Meanwhile, the Allied bombers, relieved of battlefield support duties, found themselves directed at a new and more urgent target.

In London, the population had cheered the news of the D-Day landings, and then waited for Hitler to hit back. Would retaliation come from some new and secret deadly weapon? The whispers and worries went on for a week, and then the first flying bombs came out of the sky. There were only four on the first day. One exploded on a vegetable patch near Gravesend and another destroyed a railway bridge in East London. Apparently five of ten launched had crashed on takeoff, and another had disappeared into the Channel. It was a tame start, but three days later the real onslaught began. On the night of 15–16 June 1944, London was hit by seventy-three of these "phantom planes," as people called them at first. Londoners were mystified. Where was the familiar drone of fleets of heavy bombers above, which they knew from earlier Blitzes? Instead, they heard a sound more like a light aircraft, then silence followed by an explosion. What could this be? Those manning the antiaircraft batteries around the capital assumed they were ordinary planes and that *they* had shot them down. Their self-congratulations were ended when the wartime know-it-alls told them the truth: These were pilotless planes intended to fall to earth and explode.

Rumor disseminated the news, for there was nothing in the newspapers or on the radio about the attacks. The government, unaccountably taken by surprise, given how long it had known of this threat, imposed an information blackout. The barrage of V-1s continued for weeks from their launch pads in northern France and Holland, though it was a faltering display. The bombs were surprisingly inefficient. Many blew up on takeoff. Of the nearly seven thousand that made it over the coast of England in the following three months, half were destroyed before reaching the capital, intercepted by fighters, shot down by antiaircraft guns which had been moved from the outskirts of London to the south coast to catch them early, or caught in nets slung between barrage balloons. But those that got through, screaming in at 300 mph at heights of around 2,500 feet before their engines cut out and they fell to earth, were effective. They killed 5,475 people in all. More than a hundred died when one fell on a crowded pavement outside Bush House in the Strand and human flesh was left hanging on the trees. The chapel at the Guards barracks on Birdcage Walk next to St. James's Park was hit during Sunday service, killing 119. Many fell short of the center of the city, with the result that the southern suburb of Croydon took the heaviest pounding. Around 140 doodlebugs[17]—the popular name for the gasoline-driven missiles—dropped on the area, destroying and damaging tens of thousands of homes.

Churchill stoked up the anger when he finally made news of the flying bombs public in the House of Commons, more than three weeks after the first ones had fallen. He appeared to relish the new sense of danger they brought to the capital. Never squeamish about fully involving civilians in the war, he was happy for Londoners to feel as much in the front line as the troops fighting for every field and hedgerow in Normandy. Fear boosted morale. Aircrew caught up in the attacks while on leave felt their sense of purpose sharpened. Even the sceptical Ken Newman, wary of the RAF authorities and not always comfortable about his part in bombing German cities, was incensed. "This was a totally indiscriminate weapon—the launchers had no idea where their bombs would fall. The object was simply to terrorize the population."

And the terror clearly worked, because he admitted that he felt "safer flying a Lancaster over the Ruhr than being anywhere in the London area!" The writer Evelyn Waugh was chilled by the inhumanity of this new and dreadful weapon: "No enemy was risking his life up there. It was as impersonal as a plague, as though the city was infested with enormous, venomous insects."[18] American servicemen visiting London found themselves getting their first taste of being the target on the ground. Bob Seneym a ground crew chief, had prepared many planes for bombing missions to the European mainland. Now, after seeing a girl home after a date in London, he was walking through streets under attack. Taking shelter at a U.S. Army post, he watched the V-1s come into view. "We waited for the engine to cut out and then five seconds later heard the explosion. You knew more casualties had been added to the ever-rising total of dead and injured. I was given a bunk for the night at this army post and I slept for about an hour before I found myself being thrown three feet into the air with the bed coming back down on me. A V-1 had fallen less than a block away. I was fine, but it was a learning experience to be so close to the receiving end of one of those things."[19] Another factor adding to the fear was that the doodlebugs came at any time of the day or night. During the Blitz, there had at least been some respite in the daytime. But robot bombs kept all hours, and the relentlessness and the lack of warning shredded the nerves. The boost in morale Churchill had hoped for turned in on itself, and rumor spoke of 250,000 casualties and blamed the government for not doing more to stop the onslaught.

Behind closed doors, ministers were desperately worried about the V-1 menace, much more so than they would admit in public. The war was not progressing as well as it might in France, with the armies pinned down in Normandy. Now here was a threat to the home front that was utterly unpredictable. The V-1s begged the question of what other secret new weapons Hitler had up his sleeve—rockets, jet aircraft, supersubmarines that could stay underwater indefinitely and reopen the battle of the Atlantic? Military historians might argue that the outcome of the war was never in doubt once the Allies had secured a foothold in France, but there was little of that glad confidence at the time, among either the government or the governed. After the initial euphoria that greeted D-Day, uncertainty was the prevailing mood in the summer of 1944, despite the unfailing optimism displayed by the newspapers, and it would continue that way for the rest of the year.

The doodlebugs were certainly denting morale. John Gielgud wrote to Alec Guinness that London was "empty and sad."[20] A Home Office briefing to the Cabinet warned that Londoners were reaching the end of their tether. The capital's people would have been even more dispirited if they had realized how little was known in Whitehall about the V-1s. British intelligence had no idea how many were in production—they *guessed* it was around 7,000 a month when it was in fact nearer 2,000. They had a very hazy picture of how and where the missiles were constructed. Nevertheless, Bomber Command and the Eighth Air Force were instructed to obliterate sites where intelligence believed the bombs were being made or launched.

The first raid went in on 16 June in the Pas de Calais area, the size of the force—236 Lancasters, 149 Halifaxes, and 20 Mosquitoes—for such a small site indicating the urgency that was now being felt. The trouble was that launching sites, little more than a ramp resembling a ski jump, were quick and easy to construct and just as easily abandoned for a fresh site. They could be anywhere within an area of five thousand square miles. A dozen large-scale attacks, some involving more than seven hundred aircraft, were made over the next three weeks. Nicky Knilans, taking some leave in London after raiding V-1 sites in France, heard the constant bangs of antiaircraft guns trying to knock down incoming doodlebugs and wanted to reassure "the thousands of people lying on draughty, dusty underground stations that my squadron would soon put an end to their need to hide from the buzz bombs." He was being overoptimistic. As he discovered, the launch sites were tiny and well hidden, often with no more than a blockhouse visible, which from eighteen thousand feet looked like a "a white postage stamp." The sites were also well protected by big guns, and some were covered in so many layers of concrete that even Tallboy bombs made no impression.

The real breakthrough came only when Enigma code breakers found evidence that V-1s were being stored in large numbers in tunnels once used for growing mushrooms at St. Leu d'Esserent in the Oise Valley, thirty miles north of Paris. The entrance to the caves was hit on three occasions, but on the way home after the last raid the 208 Lancasters and 13 Mosquitoes were savaged by German night fighters. Thirty-one planes were lost, 140 men died, and 30 were captured. Bomber Command, along with the Eighth Air Force, was paying a heavy price to make London a safer place.

There would be dozens more attacks on launch sites and storage sites, and many more lives lost, before the threat of the doodlebug petered out and the attacks on London largely ceased at the beginning of September.[21] The official history of British intelligence[22] concludes that attacking the store at St. Leu and two other V-1 depots, Neucourt and Rilly, was effective but that the amount of energy expended on the launch sites was probably wasted. Intelligence, acting on reports from secret agents, also thought it had identified four other depots, and these were duly attacked. After the war, captured German documents showed these were not V-1 stores at all. The attack on one of these decoy targets, at Trossy-St.-Maxim, ended with Squadron Leader Ian Bazalgette crashing and dying at the controls of his Lancaster after giving four of his crew the time to get out (see page 92). He was awarded a posthumous Victoria Cross, the sacrifice of his life all the more poignant for having happened on an operation that, with the benefit of hindsight, was pointless. Trossy cost the lives of thirty-seven other airmen, and Bois de Casson, another dummy storage site, forty-four. Campbell Muirhead's Lancaster was peppered with flak over Trossy. An engine was hit and there were large holes in the port wing and the fuselage. "It really shook us, and in a way it was worse than the stuff they throw up over the Reich. And, of course, it's coming at you in daylight. Don't like flak at any time but it seems nastier by day."

He thought Butch Harris must be "more cheesed off than ever" at having his men diverted from flattening Germany for sorties like this. In fact, Harris always saw the V-1 sites as legitimate targets for Bomber Command. The panacea argument did not apply—they were a genuine threat that had to be forestalled, not a fanciful quick fix to end the war. Had Harris known the truth about Trossy, however, he would undoubtedly have given one of his elephantine bellows of derision. Everything he had ever thought about British intelligence would have been confirmed.[23] By any measure, its part in countering the V-1 offensive was *not* the intelligence service's finest hour.

But there was worse to come. Air intelligence dismissed rumors that the next stage in Hitler's retaliatory weapons—the rocket-powered missiles known as V-2s—was ready to be unleashed. The politicians, taken aback by the V-1 attacks and the damage they had caused, as much to morale at home as to people and property, were not so complacent. As the doodlebug assault on London was at its height, the minister of supply, Duncan Sandys, Churchill's son-in-law and the chairman of the Crossbow Committee, which had been given the job of handling the menace of German missiles, alerted his father-in-law to the even greater danger of the V-2s. Civil defense operations were urgently upgraded. Plans were drawn up to evacuate hospitals, factories, and 2 million people from the capital. What fueled the anxieties was the slow progress of the invasion forces in Normandy. How long would it be before they could break out into the north of France and overrun the V-1 and V-2 launch sites threatening London? Too long, was the depressing answer.

Meanwhile, little had been learned about the nature of the rockets. How were they powered, how big a warhead did they pack, and how far could they fly? None of these questions could be answered. Nor the most vital one of all: How many did the enemy have at his disposal? At the end of August 1944, the conclusion the Crossbow Committee came to, on frankly sketchy information, was that each rocket could *probably* carry as much as two tons of high explosives (twice that of a V-1 flying bomb) and that the Germans *probably* had around two thousand, enough to launch up to sixty a day on London for an entire month. Of two things it was sure—that it had little or no idea where the launching sites were and that the great speed and high trajectory of the rockets, once launched, made them unstoppable. The capital could expect to be bombarded with nearly twice as much firepower as had fallen on it during the height of the V-1 offensive. As for the start of the attack, it should be expected at any time.

But this alarmist scenario was put aside in favor of an assumption that the launching sites in France would be overrun before they could inflict much, if any, damage on London. And this was indeed the case. August saw the long-awaited breakout from Normandy, Allied troops pouring into the rest of France, and the liberation of Paris. The areas from which the V-1s had been launched were taken. Then the first V-2 rocket landed on London, in the western suburb of Chiswick, killing three people. It was said the explosion could be heard all across the capital. The horrified authorities allowed the rumor to spread that it had been a gas explosion but there were few takers for this theory. The wags made jokes about "flying gas mains."

It would be another two months before Churchill finally admitted to the public the truth about the rocket attacks.

The rocket had been fired from Holland, still held by the Germans. The Crossbow Committee had wrongly ruled this out as a serious possibility because no evidence could be found of sites being prepared. Sandys was so confident about this that he gave a press conference about the end of the V-1 threat, declaring that, except for a few last shots, "the battle of London is over." The very next day, Chiswick was hit. What followed was months of uncertainty. More than a thousand V-2 rockets would fall on Britain, half of them on London, over the next thirty weeks. Their destructive power was awesome—a single hit could demolish fifty houses. One struck Woolworth's in Deptford, killing 168 Christmas shoppers. Two babies in a pram disappeared without a trace in the blast. Another hit Smithfield market and 115 women queueing for their meat ration died. There was never any warning. Radar detected the missiles—whose initial trajectory took them out of the earth's atmosphere before hurtling back down at the speed of sound—less than a minute before they struck and there was no time even to sound a siren. Nor was there the audible warning of an engine in the air, followed by silence as the engine cut out, which had heralded a doodlebug. The rockets were silent and deadly. In truth, they only ever came intermittently, and the onslaught was never as bad as the pessimistic forecasters predicted. But then the public had been kept in ignorance of how gloomy some of those Crossbow predictions had been.

The government's worries were demonstrated by the fact that it was November before Churchill conceded that Britain was indeed under attack by rockets. He made no mention of the fact that his intelligence services still had only a sketchy idea where they were being manufactured, stored, or launched from. Nor did he reveal that a captured enemy document had indicated German plans to produce more than twelve thousand rockets and that the only known assembly plant was in a deep underground tunnel untouchable by any bomb. The heavy bombers were able to do very little to stop the rockets. A proposal to send them in against launch sites believed to be near The Hague was vetoed because of the danger that would be posed to Dutch civilians on flimsy intelligence. In the end, the V-2 bombardment of London continued on and off until Holland finally fell to the Allies. It had cost lives and spawned a sense of fear that hung over what turned out to be the final months of the war. The V-1s and V-2s did *not* alter the course of the fighting or change the outcome, but it is easier to feel that in retrospect than it was at the time. And an indication of how much concern there was about these weapons is to be found in one of the most bizarre experiments of the entire war, the top-secret Aphrodite missions.

The need to destroy the flying-bomb menace called for desperate measures. Ironically, it was their very robotic nature that suggested the solution. They were housed in underground bunkers that even Bomber Command's Tallboys, the so-called earthquake bombs, could not penetrate and only a massive direct hit on the entrances could guarantee destruction. But such a mission would be suicidal—unless a pilotless plane could do the job. It was the Americans who came up with the idea; surprisingly so, since they were not in the immediate firing line. But though it was London that was taking the brunt of the V-1 onslaught, the Eighth Air Force bases in East Anglia could just as easily come within the range of Hitler's missiles. And could worse be ruled out? With Washington's experts suddenly made aware that German rocket technology was much farther advanced than their own, there were wild concerns that perhaps, sooner or later, a missile was capable of crossing the Atlantic. In this climate of uncertainty, who could be sure it wouldn't happen? And so a hastily improvised plan was put together.

Lieutenant Fain Pool, a pilot from Oklahoma, had been with the Eighth Air Force's 388th Bomb Group in England for barely two months when

I was called in to an office by our group commander along with seven other men. What he was going to be discussing with us was top secret, he said, and not to be talked about with anyone outside the room or even among ourselves. He told us we were specially chosen. "I only ask our *best* pilots," he said, but I could tell he was buttering us up. Then he said he needed volunteers for a mission that involved a parachute bailout from a plane. Just that. Nothing more. He gave us a few minutes to think it over, adding that we didn't need to feel bad if we didn't say yes. I volunteered. I'd already flown twelve missions and bailing out didn't sound too dangerous or too harrowing. And I was curious. But I was the only one in the room. The rest said, "Thanks, but no thanks." The next day I was posted to a different base. My orders read, "for an indefinite period."

And at that stage, that was all I knew. I didn't know what the hell was going on."[24]

It was July 1944.

What Pool had volunteered for was a scheme to take old and battered
B-17 bombers, load them with ten tons high explosives and aim them at difficult enemy targets in what the Japanese termed kamikaze style. Except
that these were not to be suicide missions. A two-man crew would take the
plane up, fly it to the coast, aim it in the right direction across the Channel,
and then parachute to safety on English soil. The plane—by now a flying,
pilotless bomb—would then be directed to its target using the very latest
techniques of radio remote control from a "mother" ship, a fully equipped
and up-to-date B-17 tracking it from eighteen thousand feet above. It was a
crude response to the V-1s and V-2s, but with no advances in rocketry to
call on, it was thought better than nothing. Moreover, each "robot,"
"baby," "drone," or "weary Willy"[25] (all names used for the pilotless
bomber) would carry a payload more than ten times that of a doodlebug
and hit the target right on the button rather than land indiscriminately in
V-1 style. As newcomers to the Aphrodite project—for some unexplained
reason named after the Greek goddess of sexual desire—were proudly told
in a training film, here was the biggest single bomb in human history.

Ten war-weary B-17s were soon undergoing a dramatic transformation.
They had been beaten up on repeated flights to enemy territory and were
scheduled to be sent back to Boeing for complete refurbishment. Now each
would end its life in a big bang at the end of one final, never-to-return sortie. All nonessential equipment was stripped out—guns, oxygen, armor
plating—the bomb-bay doors sealed, and the fuselage packed with high explosives. State-of-the-art radio equipment—developed in secret by U.S. military scientists but largely untried and untested[26]—was installed in the
cockpit so the plane's autopilot could be controlled remotely. Special transmitters were installed in the mother aircraft, along with a control panel
which even included a miniature joystick to steer the "baby." Security was
tight. An Associated Press war correspondent who happened to be on a
base where the work was being carried out was heavily leaned on to make
sure he wrote nothing about it (and did not until the war was over).[27]

The first test flight had taken place only a week before Fain Pool was re-

cruited. In this practice, bags of sand were used in place of real explosive
and the pilot did not bail out but stayed on board the robot just in case of
problems. He successfully handed control over to the mother aircraft, and
for two hours the robot was directed in flight patterns over the Hertfordshire countryside. It worked—though there was an immediately obvious
problem. Clouds had rolled in and the gap between the two planes had to
be cut from 18,000 to 6,000 feet. For the mother to see and guide her infant warrior into battle from the safety of 20,000 feet, even though it was
painted bright yellow so as to be easy to spot, the weather would have to be
of a crystal clarity rare during a north European summer. There were other
teething problems to be sorted out too, but fundamentally the test was
judged a success. The theory translated into practice. Approved personally
by General Jimmy Doolittle, commander of the Eighth Air Force since the
beginning of the year, the plan moved rapidly ahead. No fewer than sixty-
five robots were to be prepared. Under conditions of the greatest secrecy,
the recruitment of crewmen like Fain Pool began, with the incentive that
one Aphrodite trip would count as five ordinary missions (plus a guaranteed Distinguished Flying Cross).

Pool had by now joined nine other pilots at Fersfield, a small and isolated
airfield in the Norfolk countryside surrounded by armed guards day and
night. Still none of them had any idea what they had let themselves in for. Information emerged but slowly. "We were told that we would be flying special B-17s that had been stripped of everything but pilots and that we would
be making some training flights in preparation for a special mission." There
was, as Pool recalled, no mention of twenty-two thousand pounds of explosives. The ten of them speculated endlessly about what the mission might
be—a raid to capture a secret enemy plane was one thought—but were always wide of the mark. The whole story, when it finally emerged, was quite
a shock. "When they told us the plane was going to be full of explosives, I
knew this was a one-way trip, and I realized I had better damn well concentrate on doing it right if I wanted to live much longer. But it didn't worry me
that this was going to involve flying bombs, hell no. The details were for the
scientists to figure out. All I had to do was take that sucker off and set it up
on automatic pilot and then bail out of it successfully." The only training he
got in bailing out, however, was watching a trained parachutist demonstrate
how to steer the canopy and rolling off the back of a moving lorry to learn
how to fall. There would be no practice jumps to perfect his technique.

By now the first targets had been selected—the V-weapon sites at Watten, Mimoyecques, Wizernes, and Siracourt, all concrete emplacements just the other side of the Channel close to Calais. All of them had been regularly attacked in conventional bombing raids but to little effect.[28] Could Aphrodite succeed where others had failed? It was time to find out. And there would be no dress rehearsals. The first outing, fully armed and fully targeted, would be the real thing. When weeks of foul weather relented in the first week of August, it was go.

They were sent up in pairs—tests had shown that radio signals became confused with any more aircraft in the air at the same time. Pool took up the first robot, accompanied by an electronics specialist, Staff Sergeant Phil Enterline.

> When they woke us up that morning, they said the weather was good, and so "It's on." I didn't have any fears or flutters in my stomach. We were just anxious to get it over with. We hadn't been allowed off base for weeks and we were getting bored as hell. After the briefing we collected our parachutes [they had two each, front and back] and climbed into the aircraft. This was the first time I had seen all the dynamite packed in, and I was shocked. It filled the aircraft, from the back right up to the pilot's seat.

Every spare inch of space was taken up by the explosives, piled in wooden crates and linked by dynamite cord so it would all go off at the same time. Ground crew had spent seven hours loading and fixing the detonators. Pool, settling in the pilot's seat, started up the plane's electrics and then watched helplessly as sparks flew from the alternator and nearly touched a trailing piece of cord.

> They missed by about six inches, that's all. The whole lot could have gone up. That was when I really grasped how dangerous this mission was. But it was too late to back out, even if I had wanted to, which I didn't. Then we taxied out to the runway and everything was jolting up and down, and I got a bit worried about the movement setting off the explosives. It didn't help when I looked out from the cockpit and saw people who had come to watch the takeoff suddenly start running for the bomb shelters. They must have seen the aircraft bouncing up and down and thought it was going to blow.

There was another moment of anxiety for him when he reached takeoff speed but the nose of the overweight B-17 refused to come up off the ground.[29] His number two had forgotten to put the flaps down. "So we were hurtling along but we weren't getting airborne—and that was a pretty scary moment. I used up about all of the runway but I made it and that was all that mattered. But the hairs were standing up on the back of my neck, I can tell you." They climbed to two thousand feet, making contact with the mother ship as they did and checking that all remote controls were working. "I was talking all the time. I wanted to be sure that I did everything right. I wasn't scared but I was supercautious." Then, at the agreed moment, Pool sat back in the pilot's seat, took his hands off the controls and let "mother" take over, guiding the aircraft round a fifty-mile rectangular course. There were some problems. The elevator control was stuck in the up position and the altimeter was faulty, but it was not serious enough to abandon the mission. It was time for the veteran B-17 to become an *unmanned* missile.

"I called out the code word to the mother ship to let them know that I was getting out of the pilot's seat," Pool recalled. "Phil had already gone but I had a lot of things to do before I could jump. I had to set a clock up on the instrument panel and then turn the elevator controls and put the plane in a dive. Then I had to walk back down the aircraft catwalk and pull all the arming wires to set the fuses on the explosives." This proved tougher than he had imagined. Seventeen wires converged in one big knot. In theory, all he had to do was pull this and all the fuses would be set. He pulled but nothing happened. As the plane bucked and time slipped away, "I had to put my foot up against the bulkhead and tug like hell to get all those suckers out in one go. This was something I had never practiced before in training. It was supposed to be easy."

Even then he was not ready to leave. He had to check that the electric arming device was working. He threw a switch and waited to see if a red light came on. If it did, the device was set. If not, he had another switch to try and if that too failed, it would be down to him to thread dynamite cord into a third, backup switch and hope not to blow himself up. He told himself to stay cool, to get the sequence right, not to panic. "It was a procedure that I had memorized." But he also knew that the aircraft was rapidly losing height and he was running out of time. Luck was on his side. A red light. It was his signal to go. "I told myself this was now a flying bomb and I just had to get out. I hooked up my static line above the navigator's hatch, stuck my feet out, and humped my butt out of there." He was just five hundred feet above the ground.

Never having jumped before, he was surprised by the impact as his chute opened. "The shock to my crotch felt as if it was going to cut my legs off." Then he looked down on the English countryside and saw he was drifting into an electricity pylon. For a moment he imagined himself frying on a power line. He pulled frantically on the cords, slipped to the left, missed the pylon by a few feet and then hit the ground. "A bunch of local farmers ran up and, as instructed, I told them I was an American airman and I had bailed out of my plane because it was on fire. I was under orders not to tell them the truth. At that moment we heard this huge explosion."

Pool thought it was his plane hitting the target on the other side of the Channel. It wasn't. The explosion was that of the other robot that had followed Pool up into the sky that day, piloted by Lieutenant John Fisher. His copilot had jumped in time at eighteen hundred feet, but Fisher stayed. The plane had gone into a climb rather than descending as planned and he had bravely gone back to the cockpit to try to correct this. Observers in an accompanying B-17 believe he just managed to wrest back control[30] when the plane stalled, fell back sideways, and then plunged to the ground in a wood just a mile or two inland from Aldeburgh Bay. The explosion blew a crater twenty-five feet wide and fifteen deep. Two acres of forestry were devastated. Of Fisher, no body part was ever found. Meanwhile, Pool's robot had continued on course, under mother's guidance. It was brought in over its target at Watten but then failed to respond to the remote instruction to dive. Enemy flak had probably damaged either the radio receiver or the control itself. All efforts to unstick whatever was jammed failed, and the pilotless—and now directionless—flying bomb just flew in circles at low level until a German antiaircraft battery scored a direct hit and it exploded in a fireball so huge it may even have wiped out the battery that shot it down.[31]

Two other robots went out from Fersfield that same day and both got to within sight of their targets. One had even managed to evade a barrage of flak from British coastal batteries as it passed Dover. But bringing them in surely and steadily to hit their targets proved impossible. Their attitudes were all wrong and one overshot by seven hundred feet while the other fell short by a quarter of a mile. There were spectacular explosions but no damage to the German rocket installations. However, all four crew had managed to bail out successfully, so the upshot of the first Aphrodite attack therefore was four robot bombers released, four failures, and one pilot killed. Back at base, Fain Pool was told that his mission had not been successful after all, and that Fisher was dead. He was unfazed. "I volunteered to go again but the colonel said no. He thought I must be mad. He said, 'I'm going to send you to the funny farm!' " Instead, Pool went back to his old bomber unit. "I had a forty-eight-hour pass and then I flew the rest of my tour as normal. But I couldn't tell anybody about Aphrodite. I was sworn to secrecy. I couldn't tell my crews where I had been for those six weeks or what I had been doing or anything. I didn't tell anybody for twenty-five years."

The project continued in his absence. Lessons were learned. "Mother" clearly needed more control over her infant, particularly on the run-in to the target. Relying on visual contact was hopeless, given the weather. Television cameras—more state-of-the-art technology—were installed in the cockpit and the nose cone of the robot to relay pictures of the control panel and the view ahead. They made little difference. Two more "babies" were sent out a few days later, but both crashed in the sea after the pilots had jumped. One ominously circled Ipswich before heading out across the coast and crashing in the water. The problem was traced to the radio equipment. It was just not sophisticated enough for the job it was being asked to do. A halt was called to operations. But not before the U.S. Navy had had a go. It had been conducting its own experiments into radio-controlled missiles and sent a unit to work alongside the Aphrodite team at Fersfield. This included a pilot named Joe Kennedy Jr., eldest son of Joseph Kennedy, the controversial U.S. ambassador to London before the war.

On 12 August, Kennedy took up a navy-converted bomber with U.S. Navy radio equipment on board and 24,000 pounds of explosives to aim them in the direction of the German submarine pens at the Heligoland naval base on the other side of the North Sea. At two thousand feet, just after the mother ship took control, there was either an electrical fault or something went wrong when Kennedy and his fellow crewman, Lieutenant Bud Willy, began arming the detonators. The plane exploded in midair over the Suffolk countryside. Both pilot and copilot died. Kennedy had been warned of the dangers: A fellow officer, an electronics expert, had told him earlier how unstable the load was and that almost anything—radio static or excessive turbulence—could set off the charges. With typical Kennedy bravado, he had ignored the risks. His death changed history. The next brother in line—John Fitzgerald Kennedy—became heir to the family's political ambitions and would be elected American president sixteen years later.

The precise cause of Joe Kennedy's death was obscured for years. It may have been that not even his powerful family was told the whole truth at the time. They knew he was on a highly secret project. He had written to his mother that "I am not allowed to say what it is" and then lied—as so many sons did to their mothers during the war—that "it isn't dangerous so don't worry." Two days before his death he wrote to his brother that he was not intending to risk "my fine neck in any crazy venture." He was on the verge of coming home. He had completed his tour as a navy pilot and had even sent most of his luggage to Southampton to begin the sea voyage back to the United States ahead of him. He just had this one last mission that he had volunteered for, and, as for so many young British and American men, it proved to be one mission too many.

To all intents and purposes, Aphrodite proved to be a military flop.[32] In all, nineteen missions were launched, four pilots were killed, and not a single target was hit. New technology had its limitations. Robots could not win this war. Only men willing to make the ultimate sacrifice could do that.

8

BACK TO THE CITIES

"We had been told the Luftwaffe was kaput. *It was not."*
—UNNAMED AIRMAN OF THE U.S. 445TH BOMB GROUP

THE AUTUMN OF 1944 ARRIVED WITH BOMBER COMMAND AND THE Eighth Air Force released from their commitments to the invasion of France. On the ground, the Allied armies had finally broken out of the Normandy box they had been held in for much longer than they ever planned. They swept east and north, liberating Paris and Brussels and then heading for the German frontier. In early September, Walter Hughes was stood down from combat duties and assigned to a new job—delivering supplies to the troops in France. The farmer's son from California did not take kindly to becoming a delivery boy, but the experience gave him a unique opportunity to see what the invasion had achieved. They first flew from Knettishall to an airfield on the south coast of England, a routine trip that nearly ended in disaster. "We flew in murky weather beneath an overcast sky. Passing near London, I picked up a peculiar warbling, siren sound in the earphones which grew rapidly louder." Here was something new and he had to quickly search his memory for a clue.

Suddenly, something we were told at training school popped into my mind—this was the warning that we were approaching a barrage balloon area. These were captive blimps in groups of dozens, deployed several thousand feet above sensitive targets. They were raised and lowered by cable and their purpose was to force enemy bombers to stay high, where their accuracy was much poorer. But they had other cables hanging hundreds of feet below them, any one of which could cut a wing off a B-24. In the murk, we couldn't actually see the balloons or cables, so I did a 180-degree turn and got the hell out of there, having learned another important survival lesson.[1]

They spent an uncomfortable night in makeshift accommodations on an empty airfield near the coast, deserted because virtually everyone had left for the battle over the Channel in France, and the next day supervised the loading of the Liberator's bomb bay with six thousand pounds of flour and field C rations. Everything had to be handed up through the tiny entrance hatch and then stashed around the racks in the bay. Once loaded they flew to Orly Airfield, southwest of Paris. This meant flying over areas where the post–D-Day fighting had been at its fiercest.

We flew low purposely in order to see. Caen was all devastation and, no doubt, misery. Many houses had no roofs or walls and streets were blocked by debris. The winding paths that passed for roads in Europe were inadequate for the invading army, so a great swathe had been cut through fence, hedgerow, and field, straight for Paris. It appeared as a raw scar on the earth, and the Red Ball Express, the army quartermaster's supply trucks, ran on it night and day. Scattered here and there were tanks and trucks, German and American, burned or blown up. Herds of German prisoners were in barbed-wire enclosures. On the beaches and just offshore were many boats, landing craft, and all manner of equipment, sunk, just sitting on the bottom—their job done. On the shore, scarcely any green showed. So fierce was the bombardment that the very earth looked as if it had been ploughed by a drunken farmer who, here and there, missed a spot.

Hughes and his crew returned to England, only to be sent out on another delivery run, and then another. They thought their war was going to peter out into routine supply work. "Patton was advancing through France almost without resistance. We began to think we had been shipped over too late to help with the war we were trained to fight. There seemed no more need for bombing planes." But they couldn't have been more wrong. This war was far from over, and they were soon back on frontline duties, more dangerous ones than ever before. Now began one of the most controversial episodes of the entire bomber war. Where were the bombers going to concentrate their efforts now? For the Eighth Air Force the preferred targets were oil installations. The argument for this was a persuasive one. Tanks could not roll or fighter planes strafe without fuel. Germany's access to oil fields in the east would soon be cut by the Soviet advance. Synthetic oil was keeping Germany at war. Destroy these operations and the war would be over.

But oil plants were particularly tough places to hit. The Germans did not need reminding that continuing the war depended on their ability to keep their planes and tanks topped up with fuel. They defended the sites where gasoline was refined, processed, and stored doggedly. Eddie Picardo recalled being on a mission to lay waste an oil refinery in northern Germany and

the flak was so thick it blotted out the sun. For a full ten seconds it was like a total eclipse. I thought it was all over for me and my buddies. Suddenly there was an enormous bang. A shell exploded directly underneath me and the concussion slammed me half out of the turret, then threw me forward against the gun handles and knocked the wind out of me. I thought we'd exploded and we would drop so fast there wouldn't be time to bail out. I covered my eyes with my arms. I was convinced I was going to die and I remember wondering what it would feel like. I didn't have time to be afraid of death, though. My big fear was seeing the ground coming up toward me.

He didn't die.

When I pulled my arms from my eyes, I looked around and saw that we were still in formation. What a great feeling that was! The intercom suddenly crackled on and I heard the pilot call back to one of the waist gunners, "Go and see what's left of Picardo." I shouted into the intercom: "What do you mean, what's left of Picardo? I'm fine." I was alive but I could just as easily be dead. Just earlier I had seen the plane next to us explode from a direct hit. You see a flash of fire for an instant, then it goes out and all that is left is smoke and pieces of debris. I saw no chutes open. Ten people dying in front of my eyes. It was almost impossible to come to terms with—alive one second, dead the next. How can you get your head round that? How can you explain it? When we landed I discovered a hole in the fuselage big enough to put a basketball through. It was on the right side of the turret, and there was another hole, just as big on the other side. My butt had been stuck out in the crosswind between the two holes and it was frostbitten. I had to soak my cheeks in warm water for a long time before I could feel it again. But at least we were back and alive, which was remarkable given the number of holes the flak had made in the fuselage.

Richard Timberlake, copilot in the 562nd squadron, seemed to get nothing but oil targets in that autumn of 1944. A refinery at Ludwigshaven came up on only his second mission. He was green enough not to recognize the black cloud in the distance as flak. As they got closer and began their run, it was then all too obvious that lying directly ahead was an inescapable curtain of shells and shrapnel. He remembered wondering, "How could any plane get through that? We soon found out, although in another sense we never found out."[2] All the men could do was ride it out. "In the clear August air, the gunners on the ground had a full view of us. As the flak came close, we could hear it exploding above the roar of the engines. But we sailed right through it and could see the oil plant ten miles ahead and five miles below us." Damage had been done, however. The cable controlling the elevators had been severed and the plane was in danger of going into a nosedive. Together Timberlake and the pilot hauled back on the stick with all their might to keep themselves level until the bombs had gone. They limped home, keeping a safe distance from the rest of the formation because of their lack of total control. Two days later they were off to another oil refinery in the far east of Germany and a few days later to another in Czechoslovakia. On this one he felt "a sharp feeling of insecurity. No longer was I watching all this action from a seat in a movie theater. I was right in the middle of it, jerking and cringing as the flak popped around us. We returned to our base with much battle damage, several wounded airmen, and everyone wondering how we could survive twenty or thirty more such episodes." But there was little time for reflection because they were back on the roster the very next day.

While the Americans concentrated their efforts on oil targets, the resolute Harris chose to send the men and machines of RAF Bomber Command, newly returned to his command, on the only mission he had ever had any faith in—destroying German cities and the factories, homes, and people in them. He felt he had done his duty well enough in supporting the invasion and its aftermath. A little vaingloriously, he claimed that it could never have been successful without the contribution of his bombers and those of the Eighth Air Force. In his memoirs he claimed all the credit for his bombers: They had battered down the Atlantic Wall to allow the troops to land, paralyzed the railways and thus delayed enemy reinforcements, and punched holes through the enemy defensive lines which the army had often been too slow to exploit. Without the intervention of Bomber Command, the invasion would have either failed outright or been "the bloodiest campaign in history," he declared. It was the truth—and one of which his men could be proud—but it was not the whole truth. Here was typical Harris hyperbole, the sort that made him enemies.

But he had been cooperative with others during this period—in his way. Charles Carrington attended morning conferences of the SHAEF air staff, a ragtag-and-bobtail meeting of up to thirty, chaired ineffectually by Sir Trafford Leigh-Mallory, the Allied air commander. Carrington found them "amusing," in sharp contrast to Harris's strict and sharply run sessions at Bomber Command.[3] Leigh-Mallory would be "hearty, genial, effusive," while Harris was

the strongest man in the room, always ready to prick bubbles or upset applecarts, growling out sardonic comments, often with shocking bravado. Jimmy Doolittle [head of the Eighth Air Force] often comes, and spars with Bert along the table. Jimmy admits ruefully that he has hit Strasbourg Cathedral; Bert [Harris] breaks in: "You've done better than me, Jimmy. I've been trying to hit Cologne Cathedral for years." Roderick [Hill, the air marshal in charge of the fighters defending Britain] exclaims with pride that the shooting down of doodlebugs improves daily. Harris grumbles: "That means you'll be hitting more of my bombers than ever."

The Great Ones discuss priorities in whispered asides. Has the time come to switch from rocket sites to German railways? Yes, they all agree. All but Bert. "Sorry to spoil the tune," he says. "My directive is to give first priority to Crossbow and I'll attack it for all I'm worth."[4]

Harris was cantankerous rather than defiant and in the end always followed orders if they were clearly and unambiguously given, while reserving the right to argue and discuss them ad infinitum (even ad nauseam). He admired Eisenhower—"a wise and immensely understanding man"—and was also generous in his praise for the general's second in command, the British air marshal Sir Arthur Tedder, whom he described as having "one of the most brilliant minds in any of the services." He thought the short period when he was under Eisenhower's control to be "the only time when I was able to proceed with a campaign without being harassed by confused and conflicting directives."[5] Included in the praise was a hefty sideswipe at the Air Ministry. He would soon be at loggerheads with his bosses there again.

Bomber Command was now a quickly growing organization, approaching for the first time the size and power that Harris had always wanted for it. More aircraft were coming off the production lines. More men were coming out of the training stations. New Lancaster squadrons were being formed. Navigation and bomb-aiming apparatus were improving all the time with the result that accurate all-weather bombing was now possible.[6] The first time he had put a thousand bombers in the air Harris had had to throw in virtually anything with wings to make the numbers up. Now he had men and machines to spare. But where should this immensely powerful force be directed? It could still be used to back up army operations on the European mainland and was indeed to be called in on occasions—to clear the approaches to Antwerp, for example, or provide diversions for Operation Market Garden, the Arnhem drop.[7] The generals in Eisenhower's command wanted it to concentrate on knocking out the German railway network. The strategists and scientists at the Air Ministry were persuaded by the argument that cutting off the enemy's oil supplies would bring the Luftwaffe and the Wehrmacht grinding to a halt.

To Harris, however, this was just another panacea target diverting him from his main task. There had been a lobby pressing for oil to be made a priority target as far back as 1940. The theory that Germany was on its last drop of fuel and needed one last push had been touted ever since. Why should it be any different now? Nonetheless, on 25 September he was instructed, along with the Eighth Air Force, to make the German petroleum industry his priority. Secondary targets would be transport—German railways, canals, and rivers—and those factories making tanks and motor vehicles. Harris made his opinion clear when the same message was reinforced a few months later. Instructed to bring "maximum effort" to bear on cutting off fuel supplies, he scrawled on the Air Ministry directive the derisive comment of a man who had seen and heard it all before: "Here we go round the mulberry bush . . ." How many more times did he have to argue his case that pounding Germany's cities would destroy her war industries and the morale of her people? Now, at just the moment when he had the means to carry out the job, he felt he was being spun off in the wrong direction again. He was being asked to hold back the hammer just when it might strike most effectively.

It has been fashionable—beginning with the RAF's own official account of the bombing campaign against Germany, published in 1961—to scorn Harris's judgment on this point. He had promised that he could end the war without the necessity of a land invasion of France. That had proved utterly wrong, but now he was still insisting that the war could be won by bombing alone. To understand his reasoning, we must look at it from the perspective of September and October 1944. The breakout from Normandy had led to Allied tanks and infantry racing through France and Belgium, only to become bogged down at the borders of Holland and Germany. Supply lines were overstretched while ahead lay stout German defenses. The failure of the July 1944 plot by dissidents in the German army to assassinate Hitler destroyed any hopes of an end to the war being negotiated with a replacement non-Nazi government in Berlin. The disastrous bridge-too-far paratroop drop behind enemy lines at Arnhem in September showed how intense and ruthless German resistance was going to be. The end seemed an awfully long way off—and would come only after every foot of the Third Reich had been taken in blood. As Harris himself put it, "The Boche would fight his damndest when driven back onto his own frontiers." The horrors of the Russian front would be repeated in the west with every town or village a corpse-filled Stalingrad.

Harris's aim now was to make that slow and bloody conquest of German soil unnecessary. While others disagreed, he believed that, at the very least, by shattering the cities still far away from the front line, he could bring the full horror of war to their inhabitants, weaken their resolve, encourage the mind-set that would bring surrender. As for the oil targets he was being asked to hit, to do so meant relying on intelligence about them—whether from the Ministry of Economic Warfare (MEW) or from British military intelligence—neither of which he had any faith in. He considered the MEW staffed by incompetent time wasters. As for what could be gleaned by spies, as one historian observed, "It was extremely difficult to find out what was going on in Germany. British spies in Germany were few and far between, and those available were not trained in industrial intelligence."[8] Harris had his own photographic intelligence of what was happening on the ground, compiled in his famous Blue Book, a growing scrapbook of aerial reconnaissance pictures showing the damage Bomber Command was doing to the German economy and which he proudly showed to distinguished guests at High Wycombe (and sent personal copies to the King and Stalin).

In that autumn of 1944, Harris stood out from all the other Allied commanders—Patton the only possible exception—in having a clear vision of what *he* needed to do. On the ground the generals were warring among themselves about how to take the fight across the German border.[9] American soldiers were reluctant to fight under British leadership. Churchill was in a twitch, worried about the V-2 rockets hitting London and the slow progress of the armies. He had even asked his chiefs of staff whether there was a case for using chemical and biological weapons against the Germans to break the deadlock and became impatient when they said the risk of retaliation in kind was too great.[10] In this climate, a man without doubts, who knew where the enemy was and was prepared to charge toward the guns, was invaluable and not to be held back.[11]

Fortunately for Harris, his orders had given him the loophole he needed. In what might be termed the small print of the Air Ministry directive was the concession that he could target German cities "when weather and tactical conditions are unsuitable for operations against primary objectives." Harris seized on it like a lawyer spotting an error in a contract. He did what he considered was his duty to the oil and transport targets, reassured that the Americans, more convinced about the importance of oil than he was, were pulling out more stops on this front. But then he took every opportunity to send his squadrons to cities, old and new. He resumed the battle of the Ruhr, revisited Brunswick and Nuremberg and others which had proved resistant to attacks in the past and spread the net to smaller communities such as Darmstadt, Bonn, and Freiburg. In between, he attacked oil sites more often than is generally acknowledged. His bombers made forty raids on oil targets in the five months from August to September. The performance of the Americans—against whom there was no complaint— was better, though not by such a large margin as Harris's critics suggest. The records show that the Eighth Air Force sent missions to oil targets on forty-eight days in this same period, just eight more than Harris did.[12] The comparison is not a precise one. Some of his raids involved relatively small forces of around a hundred aircraft, though others had more than double that number and to major targets such as Gelsenkirchen he sent more than seven hundred. But it indicates that the charge that he *neglected* oil targets is unfair.[13]

Should Harris have been firmly whipped into line and made to carry out his instructions to the letter and more closely to the spirit in which they were issued? In retrospect, some historians believe he should. At the time, however, there was no one willing to tell him he was wrong to be attacking the German cities. On the contrary, wherever he looked there was encouragement. Montgomery thanked Harris for what his bombers had achieved at Caen and added: "We know well that your main work lies further afield and we applaud your bombing of German war industries."[14] Eisenhower, in releasing Harris from his commitments to the Supreme Command, gave him leave to "return to the bombing of Germany. . . . If at any time you believe that we are neglecting opportunities for striking the German in his own country, do not hesitate to tell me about it."[15] Above all, he had the nod from Churchill. Harris sent a note to the prime minister on 30 September 1944 arguing that, since the Allies had air superiority, the combined might of Bomber Command and the Eighth Air Force should be used to "knock Germany flat" so as to make the ground invasion easier. Churchill's reply was positive. He agreed with "your good letter" and was "all for cracking everything in now on to Germany." He expressed some doubts— "I do not think you can do it *all*"—and to others he was explicit, saying, "I do not rate the contribution of the air force as high as he [Harris] does." But there was nothing to make Harris think that the prime minister was giving him anything other than a green light. As his biographer commented: "Here was the top-level encouragement Harris was hoping for."[16] He sent his men out to fight on all fronts, including the cities.

Harris also took up cudgels against his immediate superior, Portal, chief of the Air Staff. Over the next three months, more than thirty letters, some of them 4,000 words in length, went backward and forward between the two men. Portal argued for oil targets. Harris told him he was giving the plan his fullest support but refineries were not easy to hit and the weather was against him. Portal queried whether the Bomber Command chief's heart was really in it, or whether "the magnetism of the remaining German cities has not as much tended to deflect our bombers from their primary objectives as the tactical and weather difficulties which you described so fully." He asked for a reassurance that Harris was "wholeheartedly" attacking oil targets. And so it went on, backward and forward, Portal arguing that taking out the eleven synthetic plants in central Germany that were now (it was late December as he wrote) producing three-quarters of the enemy's aviation and motor fuel would bring the war to an end more quickly, Harris disputing the claim and declaring the job impossible. Portal was "profoundly disappointed" by his subordinate's attitude, Harris hurt by the suggestion that he was being disloyal or disobedient. It would get more bitter and more personal before it was over.

The war of words did not stop the war proper from continuing. In Harris's mind he was simply conducting a debate with Portal, arguing over the theory while still following his commander's instructions. Orders had been given and he was carrying them out to the best of his ability. "I am sorry you should doubt this. I am sorry that you also imagine my staff cannot be devoting its maximum thought and energy to the oil plan because of my views. I do not give my staff views, I give them orders. I have told them to miss no opportunity of prosecuting the oil plan and they have missed no worthwhile opportunity." *Worthwhile.* What a lot hung on this word. It was Harris's way of saying that he would target oil installations when he thought it was a productive thing to do. Otherwise there were cities to bomb.

The return to area bombing came just in time for Campbell Muirhead's final operation of his tour. "Brunswick—city flattening," he recorded in his diary, and cursed.[17]

> Twenty-nine ops, only four of them being over the Reich, and we end up with a bastard target like this. The seven of us [he and his crew] sit in the briefing room looking glum, not speaking, reflecting just our hellish luck

not to finish with a comparatively easy French effort. After the briefing, we all start snarling away—at the RAF, at Butch for being so dedicated to destroying German cities, at each other, our language worse than ever before. None of us exactly twitching, but not very far off it. Some frantic smoking on the way out to the bay and before we climb aboard. Plus more snarling and cursing.

Flak "like colored, twinkling confetti" and cones of searchlights awaited them as soon as they crossed the Dutch coast. They corkscrewed to escape and he felt "the sour taste of vomit" in his mouth, followed by a lurch in his stomach as he caught sight of a Messerschmitt fighter just below, the German crosses on its wings clearly visible. Night fighters about! They corkscrewed again. Leveling out, "I find my eyes drawn to the dreadful sight of two bombers, flames streaking aft, describing graceful curves earthward at a seemingly slow pace. Hope the crews managed to bail out."

Ahead, the flak over Brunswick looked solid, as if there was not one bit of sky that was safe from it. Muirhead was convinced that

this is the chop and on our very last one! Where has our effing luck gone? Can smell the cordite from the bursts all around us. There's also the rattle of the shrapnel hitting us, like being in a greenhouse during a hailstorm. We're on the bombing run now. This is what we came for and I must get it right. I have the aiming point sliding up smoothly. I press the button. Down go the bombs into what, even from 19,000 feet, seems a furnace of swirling, angry flame.

They sneaked home past German fighters focusing their attention on other Lancasters.

A bomber explodes in midair. Night fighters still after us and even follow us out to sea. Eventually, after what seems ages, the English coast. Suddenly everybody loves everybody. Jesus Christ! We've made it. We've done the thirty, although the last was a bastard. No thought of the number of people we must have killed. God, with the sky over Brunswick virtually crowded with bombers, the death toll must be massive. But Hitler should have thought about retaliation when he started the war.

As they landed, the wing commander was there to meet them with a crate of beer.

Never did beer taste as good as that bottle I had. Wingco [wing commander] then tells us that a special outfit of Lancasters called "Tiger Force" is to be formed to go to the Far East to bomb Japan and would we like, as a crew, to volunteer? He takes no offense at our rude, one-word reply, especially as "sir" is affixed to it. He grins and says, "The Japs cut *those* off, anyway."

It was over for Muirhead and his crew, the end of their frontline war. Only later did they discover how lucky they had been. Twenty-seven out of 379 bombers had been shot down that last night, a loss rate of 7 percent. A further twenty had been lost in another mission to the Opel factory at Russelsheim. Close on 250 men were dead. He could so easily have been any one of them. He was also lucky because his tour had been a short one of eleven weeks and at an opportune time—"sandwiched between the heavy losses of the earlier phase of the war and those which are certainly to come when the nasty stuff is resumed." Surrounded by empty beer mugs in the mess, his crew offered friends and onlookers advice on how to survive. It was simple, a rear gunner from a novice crew was told: "If you see *anything,* just yell 'Corkscrew' and get the hell out of there, even if the speck on your turret window turns out to be fly shit!"

Joining in the celebrations was Ken Newman, though his delight for Muirhead and his men finishing their tour—they were the first crew he could recall doing so—was tempered by the knowledge that he himself still had fourteen operations to go. He was not pleased at returning to "pointless city bashing—we felt we ought to be helping the army." It had also been a troubling mission. Brunswick had been lit up with a circle of static searchlights and German night fighters had been waiting in the dark to pick off any bombers that strayed into them. He survived crossing the ring of light but thought himself fortunate to have got away unscathed "yet again."

Newman disagreed with his commander in chief's battle plan: "The intention was to frighten the civilian population into overturning the Nazi regime. Some hopes! Brunswick and the casualties on both sides were totally unjustified."[18]

Whether the fight was justified or not, Bomber Command at least had new equipment with which to wage it. New Lancasters were pouring out of the factories, and one of them was handed over to Harry Yates. He and his men had only five operations under their belts, and it was a sign of the better times that the new plane was being entrusted to such an inexperienced crew. The seven of them stood and gazed at her, "our own beautiful, matt-black Lancaster B-1—ours!"[19] On board, "the cockpit was pristine. Not an inch of Perspex or a single dial harbored a scratch, smear, or speck of dust. There was a delicious scent of factory goodness about it. I settled into my seat and reached forward to the column, then down to the four throttles. It all felt right." The difference between a brand-new machine and the old warhorses they were used to was even more evident as soon as they were airborne. "She was taut and responsive. I couldn't ask for more—except that she should be lucky."

On that first trial run, he headed her westward from his base in Cambridgeshire to Buckinghamshire, where his parents lived. His mother, father, and sister were in the middle of lunch when he thundered over their house at little over rooftop height, rattling its foundations. They ran into the garden, waving the white cloth his father had torn off the table, sweeping aside the food and dishes. "We roared low overhead, with the cloth thrashing about wildly below, the dog barking and the women waving and blowing kisses and hopping up and down as if they were on hot coals. We climbed away, wings waggling." He discovered later that, as they watched the aircraft grow small in the distance, his father put his arm round his wife and daughter. "My sister kissed his face, which was wet with tears. Then they returned indoors and for a while could find no words to speak."

Back at base they were rostered for an operation to Bremen. This would be their first over Germany. "We were rookies," Yates remembered, "but at least we had a brand-new A1 kite that would give us every possible chance." The flak over the Dutch coast was light, but the good visibility ahead was worrying. It meant German fighters would be out hunting. And they were—in force. They were waiting at 25,000 feet, high above the bomber stream, and the first Yates knew of their presence was when bright orange flares, dropped on parachutes by the fighters, drifted past him, lighting up the cockpit so brightly he had to shield his eyes. "On the tail of the flares came the fighters. Colored tracers ripped across our path, aiming for another Lancaster, which heeled away in a corkscrew. This time it wouldn't be us."

Not from the fighters, perhaps, but they were now into the flak above Bremen as they began their bombing run. A searchlight caught them "and the gun batteries wasted not a second in pumping up heavy shells. I pushed the column forward to dive away but there was a huge explosion under the aircraft. We yawed and shuddered. Lumps of metal peppered the kite from nose to tail. I pushed her down into the dive but she felt soggy. We were still caught in the light and its intensity completely obliterated the instrument panel. I had no indication of attitude, altitude, or airspeed, nothing but aching light and the convulsions from the shellfire."

They fell 4,000 feet before Yates regained control and brought the plane level again. He checked round the crew. They were all OK despite the mauling. The aircraft was not. An engine was on fire and flames were licking over the wing. Over the intercom, Yates ordered everyone to stand by to bail out, "but for God's sake don't go until I tell you." He feathered the engine and switched on the extinguishers but with little expectation as the air stream fanned the flames. Lives were in his hands, waiting on his decision. "Should I give the order now and get everybody out, or try to blow out the fire in a vertical dive? This was a last throw of the dice but not guaranteed to succeed. Escape against the g-forces would not be possible. Equally, the wing could melt through and that would be that." The idea of bailing out through the top hatch terrified him—"an excellent opportunity to be chopped in two by a tail fin"—and so did the thought of capture. Nonetheless, they would have to jump, and he was just about to give the order when he glanced out and saw that the flames were dying down, "drawing back into the engine, reducing to a fizzle, then spluttering and dying away." He never knew what had done it, nor did he care. They were safe after all. "Excitement's over, boys," he called over the intercom. "We're going home." Everyone cheered.

Home, though, was still many miles away, and Yates's worry now became the real one of whether the undercarriage would work when he tried to drop it. The flak could well have severed the hydraulics or burst a tire. Coming in to RAF Mepal, they were given priority clearance. He tried the undercarriage. Nothing. Again—and the green light lit up. "The cart was down and locked." He eased the Lancaster onto the runway "like an elderly aunt feeling for her favorite armchair." There were congratulations all round, even a radio message from the CO in the control tower: "Good show, young Yates." But his brand-new plane was a sorry mess. "The wing was reduced to blackened and twisted sheet and fretwork. There were sixty-four holes, many as big as a football. Inside, debris littered the floor. How we all came through without injury I just couldn't imagine. There was no point in taking spanners and wrenches to this lot. She was a write-off—after one op!" The aircraft would not return to Germany, but there was no such respite for the crew. They went straight back on the roster as the offensive continued.

As the Allied invasion force pressed east, the Bomber Command planners could route more flights over occupied territory and now there were daytime operations to Germany as well as night trips. William Lovejoy had only ever seen Happy Valley in the dark, a brightly colored canvas below of "roaring red fires, strings of flaming onions, and the twinkling bursts of flak."[20] In the middle of October he saw it in the light. "It felt unreal to be over Germany in broad daylight, but it certainly made for more relaxed navigation. The Rhine was easily visible and pinpoints could be obtained, which made life easier. It was nine in the morning when we came over our target, Duisburg. Thousands of angry black puffs filled the sky and the going got a bit rough. By 9:15 the city was under a pall of smoke and looked like a burning wreck as we headed home."

Daylight had also given him the chance to *see* the might of Bomber Command for the first time, and on this particular day Harris had put on his greatest show ever. A total of 1,013 Lancasters, Halifaxes, and Mosquitoes, surrounded by an escort of hundreds of fighters, had set out that morning for Duisburg as part of Operation Hurricane, a deliberate exercise to intimidate the enemy. That same afternoon, the American Eighth Air Force sent 1,251 B-17s and B-24s (and more than 700 escort fighters) to other Rhineland targets. And it became a triple whammy that night when Bomber Command returned to Duisburg with the same 1,000-strong force to pulverize what was left after the morning run. Nearly 9,000 tons of bombs fell on the city in less than forty-eight hours. The stated intention of Hurricane was "to demonstrate to the enemy in Germany generally the overwhelming superiority of the Allied air forces in this theater." Here was shock and awe of a type not experienced since Hamburg in 1943. It was a warning to be heeded.

Lovejoy could hardly believe the sight of the skies over Germany packed with "Lancasters as far as one could see, with vapor trails behind them, over them, and around them and German fighters roaring in to the attack." Back in the air for the second raid less than eight hours after returning from the first, he could see the fires of Duisburg a hundred miles ahead. There was some resistance left on the ground and still flak to contend with. "The German gunners stuck to their task well," Lovejoy acknowledged. "But poor Duisburg received another huge battering and the immense smoking fires could again be seen all the way back to the Dutch coast. We all thought that perhaps it was a case of gilding the lily a bit, but, after all, Happy Valley had harassed, killed, and wounded us for years, so the feeling basically was that we had this day got some of our own back." Two incidents in those forty-eight hours would also make it clear that the enemy was still capable of fighting back. The morning briefing at RAF Mepal in Cambridgeshire had been interrupted by the sound of an explosion in the distance as another V-2 rocket hit East Anglia. And in German skies, Lovejoy caught sight of an enemy *jet* fighter. "It was utterly astonishing. The thing traveled like a bullet into one side of the bomber stream, firing cannons, and went out of the other side in a blur of movement. Its speed was simply unbelievable."

Daytime flying also meant Bomber Command crew catching sight of the enemy for the first time. Some encounters were bizarre. Bill Borrows of 433 Squadron recalled returning from a raid over France, relaxed, listening to Glenn Miller on the radio, the Channel in sight, when an enemy fighter came up alongside. "The pilot was apparently out of ammo because he flew along just out of range, grinning at us, giving the thumbs-up and pointing at the nude woman painted on the nose of our Halifax. As the gunners swivelled their turrets toward him, the German waved, flipped over, and dived away."[21] So this was the dreaded "Boche" they had been trying so hard to kill. Face-to-face, he looked just like them.

Those daylight skies so full of surprises for the Bomber Command crews generally, however, belonged to the Americans. This was still predominantly their territory. The Eighth had built up its strength, gone toe-to-toe with the German fighter force and was now carrying out the instructions to concentrate on transportation and oil targets. Spaatz and Doolittle still clung to their moral high ground. Their B-17s and B-24s operating in the day were precision bombers, they insisted, though the reality was that the terrible weather that autumn and winter forced them into more and more "blind bombing." The choice was simple—they could either attack through heavy cloud using unreliable radar devices to aim, or stay at home on foggy airfields in East Anglia and leave the tasks they had been set undone. The USAAF's official history would later admit that half the Eighth's blind-bombing missions ended in missed targets. And missed targets by a six-mile stream of aircraft meant bombs dropping—and killing—indiscriminately. This was particularly so since the marshaling yards and railway junctions that were often the Eighth's targets were invariably in built-up areas. Call it "blind" or "carpet," but the effect of the bombing was the same. When a thousand-strong force struck the Berlin rail yards, many thousands of people were killed.[22]

Bomber formations of that size—and more—were now leaving U.S. bases in England on a regular basis, though often splitting up on crossing the Channel and heading for different targets. They gave little thought to enemy fighters, knowing they had well-armed escorts around them, but they were still encountering a great deal of flak. Most Allied airmen had a healthy respect and even a sneaking regard for the German antiaircraft gunners, who showed no signs of giving up the battle. Ira Weinstein, a bombardier from Chicago, remembered being over Berlin "and you could have let the wheels down on the flak and just taxied over it. It was daylight but the sky was absolutely black. Planes were blowing up and going down, and parachutes coming out like popcorn."[23] Walter Hughes knew from experience that the Hamburg gunners were particularly good. They killed his best friend and very nearly broke his heart and his will.

Pete Scott was Hughes's copilot and, with similar quiet temperaments, they had been almost inseparable friends for nine months, ever since they had been teamed together in training. They had visited each other's homes in the United States, flown side by side across the North Atlantic, been in countless scrapes together ever since. On their first mission to Hamburg they had been almost driven off by the flak, it was so fierce and so accurate. When they were sent back, they knew they were in for a battle. When the target was revealed at briefing, Hughes immediately began to sweat, more so when they were warned: "You will be in range of 446 guns, each of which can fire three shells a minute, and you will be in flak nine minutes before 'bombs away' and three minutes afterward." But all emotions were concealed as they set out. "I learned later that Pete had told other members of the crew that he really didn't want to go on this one. But he didn't say it to me. I never discussed the possibility of death with any of them, not even as close a friend as him. That kind of discussion never entered my head."[24]

Nerves were not calmed by the weather, clear for once

with not a cloud in the sky to hide us from the gunners. Sure enough, over the target the flak was as heavy as any I'd seen, and it was accurate. The lead group ahead of us came under so much fire that they disappeared behind a curtain of smoke. Then we were in it. It was thick, bursting between me and the other ships. We bombed and wheeled away, and that was when there was the most terrific explosion I have ever heard. It wiped out all my senses—sight, hearing, awareness. It was completely overwhelming. I glanced at Pete and he looked at me, apparently unaware that he had been hit. I saw nothing in his eyes except surprise—no fear, no pain, nothing else. Then he slumped into the control wheel, forcing the plane into a dive. Even then I didn't think he was dead, just knocked out perhaps.

Hughes tried to pull his friend off the controls with one hand, at the same time attempting to level the plane with the other. He called for other crew to help him lift the copilot out of his seat and lay him on the flight deck. "That was when they told me he was dead. I think I knew. When I was holding him I had felt his heart flutter and give an extra strong beat. But I didn't want to accept it. I said, 'He'll be OK, just get an oxygen mask on him.' But he had gone. It was the worst moment of my life. And it continues to be. Not a day goes by that I don't think of that flight, or of Pete." Sixty years later, as he told this story, Hughes's voice trembled and tailed off into a sad silence.

They made it back to base. There, the medical officer climbed on board, "checked Pete over, just looked up at me and shook his head." A piece of shell an inch and a half long had killed him. It had hit him between the neck and the shoulder in a tiny spot not covered by his flak jacket. It clipped off the artery to his right arm before exiting through his back and lodging inside the cover of his parachute. The medic's view was that he would have bled to death in less than a minute. "I didn't break down and sob or anything like that. I was just empty. I think I could just function—nothing else." A few days later he accompanied his friend's body to the chapel of rest at the U.S. cemetery at Madingley near Cambridge.

The day was beautiful and the long ride in the ambulance was the first I had made through the English countryside. We turned off into a grove of trees and then to a chapel. As I got out of the ambulance and walked toward the chapel to complete my duty, I saw a group of German prisoners of war cleaning leaves from the path. Their leader called "Achtung!" and the men came to attention like bits of sprung steel. I was absolutely stunned. I could not bring myself to return the salute. If I could have found a club, my reaction would have been to start swinging. The chaplain jumped to my side and said I should ignore them. My hand shook so badly that I could scarcely sign my name when we reached the chapel. I worried the whole return trip about why in those few seconds I had felt such enormous rage.

He returned with his crew two days later for the funeral.

I watched the casket being lowered into the ground. I am not sure what it meant to me. It was almost unreal. There were no tears. I didn't really know how to express my grief. But this was the reality of death and the reality of war being brought home to me in the worst way. I think I now accepted that death was part of life and that I was no longer invincible. But I carried that fear with me when I got back in the air. I had twenty more missions to fly. Where could I find the courage? I suspect I wasn't as capable a pilot afterward, not technically but in terms of aggression. I felt such guilt over Pete's death. He was my friend and part of my crew and he was my responsibility and I led him and them into danger. I thought his family might blame me—because it was *my* responsibility . . .

The German antiaircraft gunners might still be keeping up a deadly fire from the ground but there was little comparable resistance in the air. Luftwaffe fighters were no longer posing any sort of threat. They seemed to have lost their appetite for battle. The bomber formations were surrounded by hundreds of Thunderbolt and Mustang fighters, whose introduction in large numbers earlier that year had tipped the balance in the Allies' favor. These days, the Messerschmitts and Focke-Wulfs seldom put up any resistance. American crews felt they ruled the skies. A degree of complacency had set in by the end of September 1944, when a routine mission set off to bomb the Henschel engine and vehicle factory at Kassel in the center of Germany.[25] It was another busy day for the Eighth. A little over 900 bombers were in the air, escorted by 640 fighters. Half this fleet were going to the city of Cologne, 214 to the oil installations at Ludwigshafen in the southeast, and 248 were on the run to Kassel, including 39 B-24s from the 445th Heavy Bombardment Group, based at Tibenham in Norfolk. Lieutenant Bill Dewey, setting out on his eighth mission, settled in his seat and felt life had rarely been better. He had always wanted to be a pilot— throughout training he had concealed the fact that he could type for fear of being sidelined into an office job. Now, just twenty-one, he had realized his dream. He was overseas and seeing things he could scarcely have dreamed about before. A few weeks earlier Glenn Miller and his orchestra had come to the base and thrilled everyone, and you didn't get opportunities like that back in Michigan.

"The 445th hadn't seen any German planes, any fighters, any opposition since February. We thought we had knocked Jerry out of the sky, that the war was practically over and everybody would be home by Christmas. So we weren't expecting anything untoward as we formed up in four squadrons as usual and took off."[26] As they neared the target, the American bomber force turned to the right to home in on Kassel, but, for some reason, the thirty-five planes of the 445th kept going straight. "We just followed our leader," said Dewey. "Nobody said anything." Ira Weinstein, bombardier in another aircraft in the group, remembered it differently. "I knew the minute we swerved off from where we were supposed to go. It was a navigation screwup. Everybody called in and told the guy who was leading us, 'We're making the wrong turn,' but he said, 'Stick with it.' It was a costly mistake."[27] Eddie Picardo saw them go. He was in the 44th Bomb Group at the tail of the main formation, and as his plane turned to began its run into Kassel, from his rear turret he could see the 445th still heading eastward, in the wrong direction. He couldn't stop himself yelling out: "Hey, what's the matter with you guys? The target is *this* way." But then flak started coming up at him "hot and heavy, and I forgot all about them."

The 445th bombed—hitting a field outside the town of Göttingen, twenty-five miles beyond Kassel—then turned round and headed for home.

They were now on their own—out of the bomber stream and without any fighter protection—and at a time when the Luftwaffe was experimenting with a new strategy to fight the bombers. Experience had shown that it took heavy cannon and rockets to bring down B-17s and B-24s, but any fighter carrying such a weapons load would be slowed down and become easy meat for the American escort fighters. The solution was *Sturmgruppen*—"assault groups"—of heavily armed Focke-Wulf 190s, which flew surrounded by more lightly armed fighters whose job was to ward off the Mustangs, like destroyers protecting a battleship. The German pilots of the assault groups were an elite. Picked for their dedication—their will and their motivation, in the words of one of them[28]—they pledged never to fire unless they were within two hundred yards of an enemy bomber and to ram it, at the cost of their own lives, if all else failed. And it was into just one such fired-up formation that the 445th strayed that day.

Dewey heard his tail gunner shout, "I see fighters!" and the first wave of FW-190s came at the American formation from behind and below in a line thirty abreast, wingtip to wingtip, like a cavalry charge, as some of the Americans recalled, or a football lineup. At first, some crews thought they were their P-47 escorts arriving to help them home—until they saw the swastikas painted on their sides. The line of German fighters peeled away and split up to concentrate their fire on individual planes. Dewey's was one. "The whole plane began to shake as their tracer bullets hit us. You could smell the cordite from the explosions. My copilot looked out and could see planes going down all over the sky. I began saying the Lord's Prayer to myself, praying like I never prayed before." Another pilot with a clear view of the entire formation saw "20-mm shell bursts like heavy flak, smoke, planes on fire, planes blowing up, parachutes cascading from damaged planes." He was mesmerized by the eerie sight of a line of four aircraft *engines* that had been blown from a plane flying forward in formation, and then slowly turning over and floating down like loose windmill blades.[29]

In his plane, radio operator John Cadden knew nothing until the fuselage was being raked with fire. "I could hear the bullets hitting. Then the whole airframe started to vibrate as our gunners opened up. There was yelling, almost screaming, on the intercom as the gunners reported that the fighters were everywhere, above, below, and all around us, like a swarm of flies. There seemed to be hundreds of them. The aircraft continued to shake as bullets poured into us. Strangely there wasn't any panic—just noise, lots of noise."[30] Cadden's rear gunner had been hit in the face and legs and knocked back out of his turret. Dewey's rear gunner was also out of action, his turret on fire. "He had to get out of it in a hurry. We had five fighters on us at one stage, pulled up underneath and all firing at once. But then it cut down to three and finally none. They had exhausted their ammunition on us. One of them waited below us. Our plane was just a Swiss cheese and I don't think he could believe that we could continue flying."

The bullets had stopped slamming into Cadden's plane, too. The German fighters had gone and for a moment there was calm. The skipper sent him to the bomb bay to open the doors for a possible bailout, and Cadden had them half open "when the second wave of fighters hit us and bullets started to ricochet around the bomb bay. And that's the last I remember. I was knocked out. When I woke up, my steel helmet was on the floor. It had been knocked off my head when I was hit and it had a big crease through it by the right ear. That was how lucky I was to still be in the land of the living!" But for how long? One engine was out, one was smoking, and the aircraft was riddled with holes. "We got the wounded up on the flight deck where they'd be warm. There was so much blood everywhere, it looked like a hospital emergency room up there. I'd never played nurse before but I gave the rear gunner a shot of morphine—right through his flying suit, heated suit and all, because at those altitudes it was too cold to pull his pants down. It quieted him down." A similar gory scene was being enacted on Dewey's plane. "Our gunners were wounded and another crewman's leg almost severed by shrapnel. The plane itself wasn't on fire, but it was shaking very badly. I sent my copilot to check on the damage, and when he reported back to me he looked pretty shaken up, too. All the control cables were ready to snap, and if that happened we were finished."

But at least Dewey's and Cadden's planes were still flying. Ira Weinstein's was one of the thirty-one that went down that day after that one encounter—the largest loss by a single USAAF group on any single mission in the entire war. Twenty-five of them were shot down within three to five minutes of each other in the initial battle, an unprecedented massacre. Three others crashed on French and Belgian soil on the way home and another three crash-landed in England. Only four returned to Tibenham that afternoon and they were badly damaged. And all because of a navigator's error in the lead plane.[31] Weinstein knew they were in trouble the moment the group missed the turn. He could never have imagined how much. "Suddenly everybody was on the radio, saying there were fighters. I got on the gun in the nose turret. I had never been to gunnery school, but I'd flown enough missions, so I knew what to do." Weinstein had, in fact, been on so many missions that this one was the last of his tour. He had volunteered and been assigned to a crew he had never flown with before. It was the Jewish festival of Yom Kippur and he had a three-day leave, but he had given it up to get in his final mission and then go back to his wife in Chicago. He shouldn't have been there, but he was.

I had never seen so many enemy fighters before. It was very frightening because they were flying in among us and I could see our aircraft being hit and then just exploding. Others were falling down from above us. There were too many to count. I didn't feel it when we were hit. I was busy firing away when somebody pushed me aside. It was the navigator and he was bailing out of the nose hatch. He saved my life. That was the first I knew our ship was on fire, and we were going down. So I bailed out. I went right out after him. But I didn't get very far. The straps of my parachute caught on the bombsight. The plane was now going down in a flat spin and I was dangling out about a foot below it. I managed with all my strength—I was young then—to haul myself back inside, unhooked my parachute and bailed out a second time. I suppose I must have been less than a couple of seconds from death.

Back in the air, Bill Dewey was steering his crippled plane westwards in the vague direction of home and trying to come to terms with what had happened.

In three minutes we had lost twenty-five planes. It was incredible. One minute we were a formation turning away from the target, then most were gone. Those of us left gathered as best we could into a group and headed home. But our ship had been so badly hit we couldn't keep up with the others. They went off into the distance leaving us, a lone B-24 in the skies over Germany. In the distance we saw a group of fighters coming toward us and our first thought was that the Germans were coming back to finish us off. But as they got closer we could identify them as P-38s, our own fighters coming to our rescue.

Dewey made it safely out of German air space into Belgium and was nearing the English coast. He knew he still faced the problem of getting his crippled plane down safely. He radioed ahead and was comforted by the American voice he heard at the other end:

a real joy to have him talking us in and looking after us. When I dropped down through the clouds and saw those beautiful white cliffs of Dover and that long runway [at Manston in Kent, an emergency landing point], boy, that was the most beautiful sight I had ever seen. The gear came down perfectly, so did the flaps and we landed like we were on feathers. As I climbed down from the flight deck to the ground, the medics were dragging the three injured gunners out through the waist window. They were covered with blood from head to toe. They looked like they were going to die, but they didn't. They survived, though even the rear gunner, who was the least badly wounded, never returned to flying. After what we had been through, he couldn't go on, and he was put on ground duties. As for the plane, the twin tails were shredded, as if a giant can opener had been taken to them. There were holes everywhere, bits missing, bits hanging off. A huge hole in the right wing, just behind the number three engine, was spilling gas. With the others in the crew, I just stood there looking at it, shaking my head and marveling that it had stayed in the air.

Back in Nazi Germany, Weinstein—a Jew—was on the run.

As I dropped down to earth, there were some little girls nearby having a picnic. When they saw me, they all ran away. I unbuckled my chute and I started to run, too, until I reached some trees I could hide in. When I looked up I could see parachutes and planes still falling. The sky was black with the smoke. I hid my chute and then down in a valley a couple of hundred yards away, I saw my pilot, Donald. I think his legs were broken because he couldn't get up. Then these farmers—four or five of them—walked up to him and stuck their pitchforks in him. He tried to fend them off but they stabbed him to death. It was horrific, unbelievable, happening before my eyes, and there was nothing I could do to stop it. Pure brutality. I knew they would do the same to me if they found me. No doubt about it. I hid until dark and then made my way down to Donald. I don't know why. I knew he was dead but I had to go and see. They had stripped him of everything and he was lying there in just his underwear, once a heroic pilot, now just a lump of bloody meat. I got his dogtags, and when I finally got to American hands a year later, I turned them in and reported the incident to the War Crimes Commission.

Weinstein hid himself in the forest, burying himself in its thick carpet of pine needles, and planned his next move. He fancied he could make his way to Switzerland, traveling only at night, but then he realized that would mean crossing rivers and lakes and he could not swim. He also heard shooting and the sounds of people searching. He stayed under cover for a few more days before he decided he had no option but to give himself up. But how was he going to manage it without ending up with a pitchfork in his stomach?

I was scared but then I came to a little town which had something like twenty churches in it. I thought, "If I'm ever going to get a fair shake, it'll be in a place like this." So I walked down into it. I must have looked terrifying. I was covered with soot from where the plane had been on fire and I hadn't shaved for maybe a week. Then a boy in his late teens sidled up and said, 'You're one of the American fliers they're looking for, aren't you?" I said, "Yeah—and how come you speak such good English?" He replied: "I went to high school in Milwaukee."

The youth took Weinstein to the town's mayor, who gave him some soup—'the best thing I ever ate"—and warned him that there was an SS battalion in the area. "If I turn you over to them, you're going to be dead," the German warned him. "So if you behave yourself, and don't try and run away, I'll call the Luftwaffe and they can come and get you. There you'll be safe." Two hours later he was handed over to the German air force. His ordeal was not over, as we will see, but he was alive and with the reasonable prospect of staying so. A prison camp might be hard, but it had to be preferable to being pitchforked to death by peasants.

In England, Dewey and his crew had returned from the emergency airfield in Kent where they had crash-landed to their home base of Tibenham. It was a mournful, empty place. That morning 304 Americans had flown to war. Two hundred and thirty-six were now posted as missing in action. Half of them were dead, the rest prisoners. "It was dark by the time we got there and there was nobody to meet us. A truck took us back to our hut." Still nobody. "I was empty inside, all my emotions were exhausted." Hours earlier, Paul Dickerson had been in the second plane that actually made it back to base after the mission. As he radioed for permission to land, the control tower asked where the rest of the group were. "We told them we *were* the group."[32] The enormity of the loss must have been sinking in among the senior officers because when Dickerson's plane touched down and came to a halt it was surrounded by military policemen.

We were told not to talk to anyone. They whisked us off to a debriefing room and locked us up. We were then asked question after question, as if they were trying to catch us in some kind of lie.[33] Finally we were told we could leave the debriefing and we went to the chow hall. Food had been prepared for several hundred but there were only about two dozen of us. Our meal was quiet and solemn in that big empty hall. No one was talking.

Dewey said: "The whole Group was shattered by the losses, right down to the military policemen and the cooks and bakers. There were a lot of empty bed spaces, empty lockers. The whole station felt empty. It was practically wiped out as far as flying personnel were concerned. The next day there were people and trucks going round clearing out the belongings of the guys who had been shot down." The shock was felt far beyond the 445th. Eddie Picardo, having watched from his rear turret as his comrades headed off in the wrong direction, was devastated when he heard the death toll. On his next mission he was doubly alert for enemy fighters, sweeping his turret from left to right, never daring to relax.

If it was any consolation, the Germans had taken casualties, too. Twenty-nine German fighters were brought down that day by cannon fire from the bombers and by the Mustang escort fighters that arrived when the battle was virtually over. Three groups of American fighters raced to the scene when they heard the news of the attack over their radios, engaged the last of the Focke-Wulfs, and claimed eighteen kills.[34] But the main battle had already been lost and won. And the message was clear. As the Eighth Air Force's preliminary report into the mission concluded: "Enemy continued to show capability to discover bomber formations and inflict serious damage." Or, as one unnamed American flier put it: "We had been told the Luftwaffe was *kaput*. But it was not."

Dewey, his duty done, made it back to the United States for the upcoming festive season. Weinstein, who had promised his wife he would be home for her birthday on Christmas Day, did not. And the war, for all the fervent hopes and prayers of millions, went relentlessly on.

9

THE LAST CHRISTMAS?

"I tried to forget about marshaling yards and antiaircraft batteries for one day at least."
—LANCASTER PILOT ON CHRISTMAS DAY, 1944

"IT WILL ALL BE OVER BY CHRISTMAS." THAT PROMISE, WITH ITS SEASONAL sentimentality, had been made often throughout the war. In 1944 there had been times when, to the overoptimistic or the misinformed, it had seemed a genuine possibility. But as the autumn turned to winter and the months rolled by, it proved a forlorn hope yet again. Peace and goodwill would have to go on hold for another year. This would be another Christmas of families parted, loved ones missing, reunions snatched between the fighting and the war work. The holiday season began early for Walter Hughes. A week into December, he and his crew were ordered to take seven days of rest and recreation at one of the Eighth Air Force's homes for war-weary American airmen, "flak houses" as the men called them. With the death of his copilot and best friend, whose lifeblood had flooded away in seconds when an artery was severed by a fragment from an antiaircraft shell, Hughes needed the respite and a change of scene. He had had to fight for it. A new squadron commander, fresh from flying a desk in Washington and ignorant of the realities of battle, was unsympathetic to the idea of stress. He had to be persuaded by the medical officer that the experience of bury-ing one of their own had been traumatic for Hughes and his crew. He pleaded with the major to give them a break. "Doc finally won the argu-ment," Hughes recalled, "and we took the train to London, transferred to the southern railway, and got off at a small station in the country. A station wagon met us and drove us to a castle on an estate. It was called Coombe House."[1] There to greet them were American Red Cross girls, "very genial and very lovely, one of whom we were all destined to fall in love with."

After a lazy afternoon to settle in, a wonderful dinner "and the quiet concern of the staff—they were very patient people," he began to feel himself coming down from the high anxiety he had been in. The next day there were beautiful grounds to explore. "A large formal lawn sloped down to a small lake. The only disappointment was that it was winter and all the trees were bare. But there was a greenhouse with a peach tree and grapes. We also found some small caves. One day we went horse riding and on another we drove to a golf course on the outskirts of Salisbury. Unfortunately it was closed. Because of the war, there was no one to look after the fairways and the greens and the grass was kept down by grazing sheep, which would have made putting impossible, anyway." And then, just as he felt his sanity returning, his week was up and it was time to go. But the break had done the trick. The shattered young man who had stood at his friend's graveside and thought he could not go on had been helped to find a reserve of courage and character to draw on. "It helped. It brought me back to the reality that there was still a life to be lived. My worries started to diminish and I realized I would be able to get into an airplane again and continue with the war."

In that first fortnight of December, U.S. airman Richard Timberlake, just managing to hold himself together after a crunching series of heavily defended raids on oil installations in the far east of Germany, was also taking time away from the war front. He and three other officers from his crew were at Aylesfield House, another of the half dozen rest-and-recuperation havens the Eighth hired for their exhausted crews. It was an hour's train ride from London and, as he wrote to his parents back home in the United States, "We get to sleep as long as we like in nice soft beds with real sheets on them. The house is the kind you read about in books, in the middle of a large estate and with beautiful grounds." An English butler in formal black attire woke them each morning with a tray of fruit juices, pulled back the curtains and announced that it was a beautiful day even if it was pouring with rain outside. And he was right. Every day there was beautiful. Timberlake went horse riding, something he had never tried before—"without flak in the offing, nothing seemed very risky." "Every evening we reverted to our dress uniforms—forest greens and pinks—and had supper served by the butler in the beautiful dining room. Of course, we talked shop to let off steam, although everyone was careful not to let off too much. Then there was after-dinner dancing and relaxation with the Red Cross girls who ran the place. The week was such an oasis in the desert of war that it could only pass too quickly."[2]

Meanwhile, at RAF Graveley near Huntingdon, Mosquito pilot Percy Brunt was eagerly counting the days away. "Just seventeen more to Christmas," he wrote to his fiancée, Ragland—"Rags," as he called her—scrawling one of his frequent letters to her while around him the other bods were boisterously playing the fool. He would definitely get back to London to see her over the holiday season, he told her, but whether it would be Christmas or the New Year he didn't yet know. "The CO is trying to fix it up for everyone to have one or the other but so far he has been unable to get his plan okayed."[3]

Brunt had been out partying, he confessed. He and his chums had been to a dance at the local WAAF station and then stayed drinking in the officers' mess until 2:00 A.M. They had then drunkenly driven the two miles back to their base. Perhaps he was nursing a bit of a hangover or maybe the antics of his crewmates were distracting him because this was one of his shorter letters to her, though it ended with his usual deep affection: "I miss you, my darling. You have *all* my love forever." She was rewarded with twenty-five kisses. He also sent his best wishes to her mother, who presumably therefore had finally come round to accepting their engagement after such a brief romance. They had known each other only four months when, back in the summer, he had proposed and she had accepted. It was the autumn, though, before he got the ring for her, the emerald she had said she wanted. She was now "branded" as his, he told her, writing the word in capitals and in red ink. He had her photograph to look at, but he yearned for the real her. "It is agony to be away from you so much when I love you so very, very greatly. Blast this ruddy war. If it was not for Adolph [sic] I should be with you instead of just having to look at your pictures. If I were without these now I believe that I would go stark staring mad!!"

Rags was a Wren working at the Admiralty, and much of their correspondence was about arranging simultaneous leave so that they could meet. She would come to Huntingdon or he would go to London, staying in hotels, passing themselves off as a married couple. Sometimes, if she arrived before him, she had to brazen it out with the hotel receptionist all on her own. "I have made the usual arrangement as regards registering if that's

OK," he told her in one letter. They knew the train timetable by heart, and elaborate schemes were constructed just to get an extra hour or two together.[4] There were times when they booked a hotel for two nights but one or the other of them could make it for only one. That was the nature of wartime romances. They lived their lives as if there were separate compartments, one marked "love" and the other "war." The dangers he faced were rarely alluded to. He wrote one Sunday, having just returned from bombing Germany, to confirm arrangements to meet in London on Tuesday, knowing that on the intervening day he would be making "another visit to our great friends in the Third Reich." He casually rattled off his plans with no mention of the very real possibility that they might be irrelevant, overtaken by disaster. "I should get down to Kings X at 1615 hrs, so seeing as you get off [from work] at 1600 I will go straight to the Hotel and dump my things. After that I can either collect you from home or you could come there, just as you would prefer." At the end he scribbled: "Roll on Tuesday."

Normally his letters were a simple refuge from the war: Could she help him find a birthday present for his godson? Would she get a tailor she knew to sew his officer's braid on correctly—"the new ring goes above the old one, leaving the width of a piece of braid between them." Or he would tell her about boyish fun in the mess—"one hell of a binge and singsong until about 2:00 A.M. Then went round pouring water on the fires of those who were in their beds. Great fun watching the steam and flames driving them out of their beds—and rooms!! Bad types aren't we, my sweetheart? But we were having great fun, so why worry?" Perhaps he opened up to her about his flying operations when they were together, but in his letters he only occasionally let her into his secret world. "Last night went off okay, though one navigator who bailed out is missing." But he spared her any real detail. "During the past few days we have had quite a number of interesting jobs but I cannot tell you about them yet. They will be interesting to relate in the near future." And that future was looking bright. He had had a job offer. He had been invited to apply for a test pilot's course starting early in the new year when his tour would be over. It would last nine months, and at the end he would be posted to an RAF experimental unit or to a civilian aircraft firm to work as a test pilot. "What do you think, my darling?"

Rags was due to get a long weekend off work just before Christmas, and they began planning for it a fortnight before. As the time got nearer, he confirmed that she should go to the hotel on the Friday evening—he enclosed a sketch map showing it 400 yards from the station and right opposite the war memorial—check into their room—"I expect it will be room 22"—and wait for him. He would be there, but not until nine P.M. at the earliest. On Thursday—14 December—he wrote a hurried note to catch the afternoon post, hoping it would get to her at home before she left for work in the morning: "Rags Darling, By this time tomorrow I shall be feeling a little more human because you will be just about leaving to come up here." He was no longer sure that he would be able to get away on Friday after all, but "I will come in at the very first chance." He had been celebrating in the mess the night before, he told her, two promotions, one of them *his!* "No time to tell you about it now so I will give you all of the gen when we meet. Goodnight, my dearest, All my love, Percy xxxx."

Did they have a wonderful weekend together, toasting his promotion and talking about his exciting job as a test pilot after the war? We will never know. That Sunday—17 December—he was back on duty in the afternoon and she was on the train back to London when at 4:35 P.M. he took off for Hanau, a town near Frankfurt. His Mosquito was one of forty-four on a spoof raid to draw enemy fighters away from the main force, which was heading on to Munich. On returning to base, for reasons no one knows, he overshot the runway at Graveley and crashed into trees. The plane burst into flame and Brunt and his navigator were killed.

Rags wrote nothing in her diary. In fact, the last entry had been for 13 October—"Got my engagement ring!!" She had been too busy living life to the full to fill in the day-to-day spaces after that. And then, with his death, there were no words to convey how she felt. Christmas must have been unspeakable for her, New Year's no better. It was not until 19 January that, in a brand-new diary, she confided: "I miss my darling so much. *Why does one have to go on?*" Eight lonely months later, the war long over, a star marked the date of 13 October, her engagement day, the only anniversary she had to remember him by.

The carols, the mistletoe, and the good cheer can have meant nothing to Percy Brunt's fiancée as she mourned the man she had wanted to marry. For all the elaborate planning, the separation of their lives into compartments, and their determination to pretend to themselves that the worst could not happen, it had. The "ruddy" war—as strong a swear word as the well-brought-up Brunt ever used to her—had won. She can have had little heart to spend the £50 he left her in his will with the instruction that she should pamper herself with some new clothes. Perhaps, however, she took up the offer to have whatever she wanted of his personal effects—she had only to ask his parents. As she heard his final words for her in his will—"You are my life. Cheerio for now and thanks for everything. My only regret is that this should have ever to be read to you"—the tears surely flowed. It must have seemed so senseless to her. *"Why does one have to go on?"* And the manner of his death cannot have eased her grief. To fly to Germany and back unscathed, with the end of his tour just round the corner and a bright future beckoning, and then to die just seconds from home—how could he have been so silly or careless or inconsiderate or any of the other things that those left behind accuse the dead of in their anguish?

That Christmas, the loved ones of the men who flew off in an Eighth Air Force B-17 named *Skipper an' the Kids* must surely have felt the same sorrow and frustration at lives lost unnecessarily. *Skipper* had the reputation of being a lucky ship.[5] Based at Knettishall in Suffolk, she survived more than sixty missions with the 388th Bomb Group, returning from heavily defended targets such as Berlin with plenty of flak in her side but still able to soldier on. She first came into service in May 1944, and it was one of her regular crews, captained by Tom Gothard, who named her. 'Skipper' was Gothard's pet name for his eldest son, and since other members of the crew had children, too, *Skipper an' the Kids* it was. But the signwriter who painted the name in twelve-inch-high letters on her nose misspelled "and" as "an'." *Skipper an' the Kids* she would be. She flew over Normandy on D-Day and demonstrated her extraordinary luck a fortnight later on a special "shuttle" mission, bombing Berlin and then continuing eastward to land, refuel, and rearm at an airfield in the Soviet Union. On the ground at Poltava in the Ukraine, the American fleet was caught unawares by German bombers; forty-seven out of seventy-three B-17s were destroyed and twenty-one badly damaged. *Skipper,* one of only five with slight damage, was able to complete the mission.

A month later, copilot Jim O'Connor flew in her on a hop across the Channel to pound the German defenses holding up the U.S. First Army at the strategic town of St. Lô. The flak was light but still put three holes in her fuselage. From that point on he and his crew considered her "our ship" and they would do another sixteen missions in her. He recorded: "She served us well, taking much battle damage while returning us safely through thick and thin. She was like a faithful old hound dog."[6] But there was always plenty of patching up for the ground crew to do, hammering out sheet metal panels and covering the holes, like the patches on a tramp's jeans, as O'Connor put it. Three times an engine was shot out over the target, and three times the tires were punctured by flak, making landing a risky roller-coaster. But *Skipper* made it home every time and by the middle of September, she was looking and sounding tired. Now, on each mission she would lag behind a little, straining to keep up with the pack. But she was still lucky. O'Connor reflected that she was still flying, whereas *Moonlight Serenade,* a shiny new B-17 personally christened by Glenn Miller during his orchestra's visit to Knettishall, was lost over Germany after just two weeks.[7] *Skipper* was clearly a stayer and a survivor, and any crew preferred that to fancy new equipment and a show business sponsor.

Then, at the end of September, with O'Connor and his crew on their twenty-eighth mission, *Skipper* took her worst battering. It was a mission deep into Germany to the Leuna synthetic oil installations near Merseburg, a thousand mile round trip. "We picked our way between islands of flak, and when we got there the target was eight-tenths cloud covered. The flak was extremely heavy and very accurate." *Skipper* came under fire, the number-two engine was shot out and at least seventy-five holes riddled the fuselage. They limped home, last of a bedraggled group, and touched down to discover the hydraulics had gone and all they could do was coast to a stop and hope not to run out of runway. "*Skipper*'s ground crew watched wide-eyed, mouths hanging open, amazed that the number-two engine hadn't fallen off the wing and the whole ship hadn't collapsed. It took a week to repair her. I don't think she was ever the same again.'

Nonetheless, he and his men were back in her soon afterward to take part in a record-breaking onslaught when the Eighth put 1,442 bombers in the air (with 900 fighters to escort them) to bomb oil sites. *Skipper* survived again, though it was a close call. The formation ahead of her over the oil plant at Böhlen was mauled by flak and fighters, and O'Connor could only watch as a dozen other bombers were shot down. But *Skipper* seemed invincible. Whenever she picked up some flak holes, "she just shuddered a bit and shook them off, like an old boxer."

And so it came to the thirty-fifth and last mission for the O'Connor crew, "fittingly in *Skipper,* with whom we shared so much blood, sweat, tears, and flak. She was faithful to the end." Though, again, it was a close call. This time, returning from bombing an arms factory in Hanover, the cockpit windows frosted over as they crossed the English coast, leaving them sitting in the middle of a formation, "like a hot dog in a bun," and flying blind just a few hundred feet off the ground. The engineer scraped a tiny hole the size of a dollar through the ice with a screwdriver and, squinting through this, the pilot was able to see enough to get them home and down safely. It was the end for the crew. They were on their way back to the United States, leaving "one old battle-scarred friend behind."

O'Connor and crew departed at the end of October. During the next month *Skipper* was taken up by different crews, collecting more damage. Her future was in doubt. Was she really fit for combat? As December began she was on the verge of being classified as "war-weary," and if that was made official, she might end up being cannibalized for spare parts. The best that could be hoped for her would be to be used for transport or as a training aircraft. But before any decision was made she would have to go on a proving flight to assess her potential. A cross-country trip to Prestwick in southern Scotland and back was suggested, with Corporal Joe Payne, an experienced flight engineer, and Master Sergeant Jimmy Brown, a ground crewman, on board to check her out. Brown grabbed at the opportunity—it would also be a chance to snatch some time with his Scottish girlfriend, Pat, perhaps even stay a few days and a hitch a lift back on another plane later. Other Knettishall airmen were also lining up to take a ride on *Skipper*. A rookie crew, recently arrived from the United States, needed to get some navigational practice in before going operational. Having trained on B-24s, they needed time in a B-17, and *Skipper,* if passed as fit for combat, might have been designated their plane.[8] Five of them—Second Lieutenants Jack Merkley (pilot), Robert Stoaks (co-pilot), William Frey (navigator), Leonard Bond (bombardier), and Corporal Albert Thomas (radio operator)—were ordered to make the trip, leaving their gunners and flight engineer behind. Two experienced instructors, a pilot (Captain John Littlejohn) and a navigator (Lieutenant Billy Rosebasky), would go with them. Then there was "Doc" Bell, flight surgeon of the 388th, who needed a lift to Prestwick, the large airfield in the southwest of Scotland used primarily for receiving aircraft crossing the Atlantic, where he had a special assignment to carry out on the orders of his commanding officer. The plane was a godsend for him—otherwise he would have had a long and tedious journey by rail and car.

But was there another, clandestine purpose for the flight, one not in the official records? Many former Knettishall airmen believe so. They say that, with a fortnight to Christmas, here was a chance to stock up the base with Scotland's specialty, whiskey. Such trips were not unusual. One 388th navigator recalled going on a secret mission to Scotland "and when we landed at Prestwick, there on the field was a supply of Scotch whiskey. We loaded it in the waist and brought it back."[9] He believed that every few months someone was assigned to get the whiskey for weekend parties. Another 388th officer recalled "great parties at the Officers' Club and, no matter how much we and our guests drank, we never ran out of Scotch, Irish whiskey or gin, though Bourbon was always in short supply."[10] He was sure that from time to time there were routine whiskey runs to stock up the various bars on the base and that the flight of *Skipper an' the Kids* on 10 December 1944 was one of these, a "booze cruise," no less.[11]

All in all, eleven men[12] were on board when the plane took off into high cloud that Sunday morning in mid-December. They had been warned of worsening weather conditions as they flew north and that Prestwick itself might be under low cloud and drizzle when they got there, though this was nothing unusual for the time of year. Captain Littlejohn, a hugely experienced pilot who had just returned to the 388th for his second tour of duty, had signed the flight acceptance form to take full responsibility for the flight, though there is no knowing whether he or the novice pilot Jack Merkley was at the controls when *Skipper* lifted off, an hour later than planned, as priority on the runway was given to bombers leaving on an operation to Koblenz. Even so, they would arrive at Prestwick between 12:30 and 1:00 P.M. and still have three hours to do what they had to do there before those returning to Knettishall were back in the air at 4:00 P.M. and home shortly after 5:00. The rookie crew, recently arrived by ship from the United States, was slowly settling into the strange ways of life in Britain and contemplating their first Christmases away from home. Albert Thomas had written to his parents, farmers in Ohio, with the Americans' perennial complaint about the weather in England—"I like to see the sun shine once in a while," he protested. "Forget about Xmas for the present time," he told them. "I may request something later." Leonard Bond had just received his first letters from his parents, farmers like the Thomases but in neighboring Michigan, and had written back to say he was fine though busy. There wasn't anything special he wanted for Christmas because there was so little room to keep anything in his quarters, he told them.

They cruised northward at ten thousand feet, the new crew presumably getting to know the idiosyncrasies of the veteran Fortress under Littlejohn's tutelage. Copilot Stoaks would have wanted a shot in the pilot's seat, too, and the three may well have been shuffling around. Below them, navigator

Billy Rosebasky from Montana may have been singing "Chattanooga Choo-Choo," his favorite song, at the top of his excellent voice, in between yelling out tips, drawn from the experience of his nine combat missions, to new-boy navigator Frey. Payne and Brown would have been doing their job of checking out *Skipper*'s worthiness to go back to war. As for Doc Bell, he would have had time to sit and ponder the temporary job he had been assigned to in Scotland and when he would get back south to Suffolk again. But all this is speculation. Because nothing more was ever heard from *Skipper* or the eleven men on board.

At Prestwick, the weather was much worse than the forecast had predicted and blustery snow showers added to the problems of low cloud. The control tower was listening on the bomber's radio frequency, waiting for a call. But there was nothing. For a moment, a blip on the radar indicated a plane on its initial approach to the airfield but then, once more, there was nothing. The minutes ticked away, turned into an hour, then an hour and a half, two hours. As darkness fell early on a gloomy December afternoon, there was still no sign. Telephone calls were made to alternative airfields but they had neither heard nor seen *Skipper*. At 7:00 P.M., when the eight hours' worth of fuel she had on board would have been exhausted, she was declared missing. Clues to her fate drifted in. A Royal Observer Corps post had plotted an unidentified aircraft some thirty miles from Prestwick, flying west off Arran, an island in the sea between the Kintyre peninsula and the Ayrshire coastline. Then a farmer on Arran reported seeing and hearing a plane low in the sky above him and heading down. The evidence suggested that *Skipper* had crashed into the rugged mountains on the island. Search planes were sent out over Arran but were forced to turn back in the worsening weather. When they resumed the search at first light next day, nothing could be seen from the air. On the ground, police and Home Guard units combed the less remote parts of Arran but found nothing. Then the snow set in and after a day or two any hope of finding *Skipper* and the eleven men on board was abandoned.

The last minutes of *Skipper,* survivor of so many dangerous bombing runs to enemy territory, will always be a mystery. The official accident report stated the obvious—"aircraft struck ground while in full flight"—and the cause a simple "unknown."[13] It is a fair guess that she had strayed off course, all too easy in the worsening weather, going miles farther north and west than intended and missing the direct approach across the sea and into Prestwick from the southwest. Perhaps whoever was in the pilot's seat at this stage had no alternative but to take her down through thick cloud with no certainty of what lay beneath. As they broke through the cloud base, instead of the sea and the sand dunes of Ayr and Troon they would have expected just ahead of them, they were twenty-five miles from the mainland and heading at more than 100 mph straight into the side of Benn Nuis, a 2,500-foot peak in the mountainous center of Arran. Perhaps they didn't even clear the cloud, but ploughed blindly into the mountain completely unaware of its presence. This was a mistake others had made—*Skipper* was just one of seventeen planes that crashed on Arran in the war, including brand-new bombers arriving in Britain after crossing the Atlantic.

Three months later, a local Arran climber responded to a bitterly cold but wonderfully sunny spring day by trekking up Benn Nuis. On the way down, his eye was drawn to metal glinting near the base of a cliff. There was a strange sound, too, breaking the silence of the hills—icicles, melting in the sun, were clattering down onto whatever was lying below. He peered over into a gorge and saw wreckage of what he thought was a light aircraft. He scrambled down and came across one body, "lying facedown, full flying kit with helmet, etc., one leg drawn up and the arms stretched out in front. It looked to me as if he had been alive when he landed there and was attempting to crawl away from the wreck."[14] He informed the police and a search party went out. At the wreck they found six more bodies, which indicated that this had been a sizable aircraft. A tail fin, the only recognizable piece of wreckage, pinpointed it as a B-17. Its number—H297286—was intact, identifying it as *Skipper an' the Kids*. As the search party spread out they found debris scattered over a quarter of a mile around—oxygen bottles, flak vests, parachutes, patches of steel armor plating. An American team came in from Prestwick and discovered the other four bodies. There was no evidence to settle who had been flying the plane at the time of the impact—the bodies of both Merkley, the trainee, and Littlejohn, the instructor, were found in the remains of the flight deck. But the official record would point the finger at Littlejohn, for no other reason than that he was the captain of the aircraft and he was the one in charge.

The bodies were brought back to England to be buried in the American military cemetery near Cambridge. Some were later returned to the United States after the war. Back home, the news shattered eleven families waiting to celebrate Christmas. Relations remembered Leonard Bond's mother breaking down in tears at the family's dinner table on Christmas Day. She told them she couldn't stand the thought of "Leonard lying dead some-

where in the snow." It was eerily perceptive of her—all she had been told
was that he was missing "in flight in European area." Only months later
would it be discovered that the bodies were indeed lying on a snowy Scottish mountainside. That was when the official telegrams and letters of condolence went out telling the next of kin that their men were confirmed dead
rather than just missing. Not that any of them could have held out any
hope. They had been spared the details of the flight in which their husbands
and sons died, but there had been no optimistic hint that perhaps they were
prisoners of war, as was usually the case when men were missing over enemy territory. Was it any greater a personal tragedy because these boys
were on a training exercise, checking out a plane on her last legs and shop-
ping for whiskey to drown their sorrows or toast Christmas and the New
Year? The answer has to be no. The tragedy was that the experienced men,
not to mention the plane they were in, *Skipper* herself, had survived so
much worse. As for the rookie crew, they died before their war had even begun. The waste of it all could scarcely be laid barer.

Peace and goodwill to all men? Hardly. As Britain prepared for its sixth
Christmas at war and the United States its fourth, there was little to raise
the spirits. Would it even be over by this time *next year?* On 16 December
Allied forces in Belgium were taken completely by surprise as German
tanks and infantry broke through in the wooded, snow-covered hills of the
Ardennes. A massive artillery bombardment was followed by twenty divisions pouring westward, overrunning American positions and splitting the
Allied front line. The Battle of the Bulge was underway as Hitler sent his
troops on a daring dash to try to recapture the port of Antwerp and its vital oil stores. Daring or desperate? The Americans rallied and stood their
ground, countering the counteroffensive, and in retrospect historians would
see this as the Führer's last throw of the dice, the final use of his favorite
blitzkrieg strategy to try and turn the tide. At the time, however, there was
no such certainty that it was doomed to failure. Even the normally optimistic press was predicting that months, at least, had been added to the
war. Ken Newman remembered those last two weeks of 1944 as a strange
time in which "we were constantly disappointed. We thought the end of the
war was not far away but we had been thinking that for some time and it
never seemed to get any closer. The next moment you thought, good God,
this is going to go on for another twelve months."

1. B-17s of the 388th Bomber Group cross the English coast on their way to attack a target in occupied Europe.

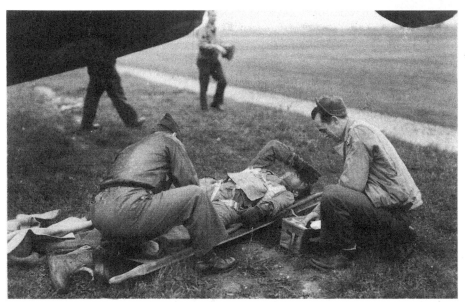

2. A U.S. crewman injured during an operation over Germany is tended by his colleagues.

3. Veterans of the 388th Bomber Group visit the site of their old base in England. A wreath has been laid to remember friends lost in action.

UNITED STATES ARMY AIR FORCES
388th BOMB GROUP (H)
RAF KNETTISHALL STATION 136
23 JUNE 1943 – 5 AUGUST 1945

FORTRESS FOR FREEDOM

306 MISSIONS   8051 SORTIES
191 AIRCRAFT LOST   524 KILLED
222 ENEMY AIRCRAFT   2 MISSING
    DESTROYED   801 PRISONERS

4. Bob Pierson back in the cramped Tail-End Charlie position for the first time in nearly sixty years. It is easy to see how difficult it would be to make an escape. The rear gunner's parachute can be seen on the left.

5. External view of the Lancaster rear turret with Bob Pierson manning the guns.

6. An RAF Lancaster attacks an oil refinery near Bremen in 1944.

7. View from the rear gun turret of the Lancaster up to the pilot's cockpit. The space is very confined.

WEDNESDAY, FEBRUARY 14, 1945

Evening Standard

FINAL NIGHT EXTRA•

THE BLASTING OF DRESDEN

1350 Forts and Liberators Over Germany To-day After Night Attack by 1400 'Planes of R.A.F. Bomber Command

KONIEV INSIDE BERLIN PROVINCE

Marshal Koniev, crossing river barriers, to-day continued his advance towards Dresden and the heart of Germany as the gap between his forces and those of Marshal Zhukov narrowed to about 15 miles.

A link-up between the two lines for an outflanking drive south of Berlin is expected soon, say Reuter.

Koniev's men are to-day storming the Queis River, half-way between Breslau and Dresden, now in turn the miles ahead.

FIRES SEEN BY KONIEV'S MEN

More than 1350 Liberators and Fortresses of the U.S. Eighth Air Force to-day attacked transportation and industrial targets in Dresden, Chemnitz, and Magdeburg, and a

MONTGOMERY ADVANCING ON THIRD SIEGFRIED BELT

Hochwald Line Is 10 Miles Ahead

This is How Part of the "West Wall" Looked to the British

Montgomery's British and Canadian tank columns are now fighting their way forward towards Rundstedt's third and final Siegfried defence belt—the Hochwald Line—guarding the west bank of the Rhine and about ten miles beyond present Allied positions, said war reports reaching Reuter to-day.

Since the offensive

The *Evening Standard* (London) of 14 February 1945 reports the U.S. and U.K. attacks on Dresden, stating that the operation was in support of the Russian advance. The paper also reports the continuing heavy ground fighting.

The tragic reality of the British and American bombing of Dresden.

10. A USAAF B-17 manages to return to safety after losing its nose—and tragically the bombardier—to flak over Cologne.

11. Two B-17 waist gunners stand guard in the cramped confines of a Flying Fortress. The aircraft floor is littered with spent shell casings.

12. An RAF Lancaster has its one hundredth bomb painted on the nose to signify one hundred completed operations. Hermann Goering's famous quote, "No enemy plane will fly over the Reich territory," is painted alongside.

13. WAAFS wave off a Lancaster as it departs for an operation over Germany. The well-wishers were always a welcome sight.

14. ACM Sir Arthur Harris became AOC-in-C, Bomber Command, on 22 February 1942 until September 1945. Known affectionately, if pragmatically, as 'Butch' to all bomber crews, Harris later became Marshal of the RAF and died on 5 April 1984, a few days before his ninety-second birthday.

15. An RAF crew enjoys a final cup of tea before departing for an operation.

16. Al Dexter's "Lucky Bastard" certificate presented after completing thirty missions.

17. A B-24 has its tail blown off by flak. The fate of the crew was unknown.

18. B-24 Liberators of the 8th Air Force drop their bombs.

9. Two USAAF B-17s collide on return to Thurleigh airfield in England. Twenty ien died in the air and a further three were killed on the ground by falling debris.

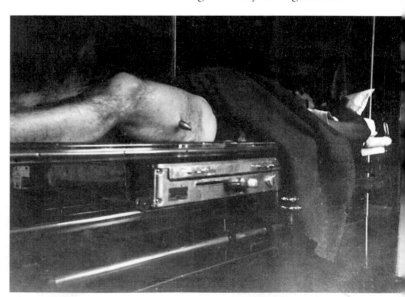

o. A lucky escape for
merican Staff Sergeant
lcarese, shot down in
B-17 in 1944. He is
en awaiting treatment
. a German hospital
ith a cannon shell
otruding from his
igh. The other nine
embers of his crew
re killed.

21. Campbell Muirhead (second from left) and his crew are debriefed after an operation to Bologna in June 1944 —the usual tea and cigarettes are much in evidence!

22. A Lancaster being loaded with weapons for an operation. The large cylindrical bomb in the background is the 4,000-pound "cookie."

23. A B-17 flies through a German flak barrage on its bombing run—the bomb-bay doors are clearly open and ready for the attack.

American pilot Walter Hughes was briefed every day to bomb the German positions, only to be grounded by the weather and have to sit helplessly back at base "while the situation became ever more desperate for the ground troops." The frustration got to everyone. Navigator Arthur White remembered days of mist, fog, snow, frost, and drizzle. "Ops were called and then canceled. We would be keyed up at briefing and then came the anticlimax—scrubbed. On some days we even got to the point of starting up the engines, keyed up for an op deep inside Germany, when the cancellation came through over the radio. It was a period of tension when it seemed that even nature was playing a cat-and-mouse game with us."[15]

A frustrated General Doolittle sat helpless, cursing the terrible weather. The U.S. forces on the ground were beleaguered and desperate to be relieved. German reinforcements and supplies were also being directed in to back up the offensive. They had to be stopped. With the wind howling outside and snow swirling across the runways in England, he talked to his closest aides. "I can't order men to fly in this weather," he told them. "You don't have to order them to fly, Jimmy," one said. "They insist on flying. They know the horrible spot the infantry is in and they're willing to risk whatever it takes to get those kids out of that predicament."[16] For ten days and nights the Eighth Air Force went up in what Doolittle's biographer claimed was weather that no air force had ever flown through before. "Through fog and sleet and rain, the bombers lumbered off runways dimly outlined by red flares. They felt their way into the sky, crept toward their targets, and dropped nearly a hundred thousand tons of bombs on the supply lines feeding the German front."[17]

With Bomber Command also doing everything it could in the atrocious weather to stop the German counterattack, large casualties were suffered in this period. In the week running up to Christmas, Bomber Command lost seventy-four aircraft in various missions over Germany. Flying Officer Henry Medrington, a navigator, was just one of more than three hundred RAF dead, fulfilling the prediction he had made to his family in a sad, fatalistic letter just a few weeks earlier.[18] In it, he asked his uncle to try and be at his mother's side at Curlews, her home in Hampshire, when the telegram arrived. She would be dreadfully shocked because Medrington had kept from her the fact that he was fully operational and had, at the time of writing, twenty-three sorties to his credit. He was on his twenty-sixth, four away from completing his number, when his Lancaster blew up and crashed in northern France on the way back from bombing Munich on 17 December. In that letter he had spilled out his heartfelt guilt at the contradictions of what he was doing. He hated the war—it offended "my humanitarian instincts and pacific convictions"—but he loved it, too. "In a multitude of ways, I have had rich experience and any amount of enjoyment out of this war and I am only faintly ashamed to admit it. I wouldn't have missed the experience for worlds." The comradeship he so delighted in lasted to the end. His entire crew perished in the crash.

He would have been horrified if he had known the torture his mother was subsequently put through. Having been told he was missing, she was then informed by his squadron commander that, since his body had not been found, there was a chance "that he was able to leave the aircraft by parachute and land safely." It was nine agonizing months before all hope was dashed. In October 1945 an Air Ministry official wrote to her that, "in the absence of evidence of his survival, it must be concluded that he has lost his life." Sympathy was expressed, for her bereavement, her suffering, her anxiety. But that was not how he wanted his death—and his life—to be remembered. He left a poem:

> If I should not return, well, there will be
> No opportunity for grief or sighing.
> For I aspired to the High Destiny,
> Wished to have died, yet feared the thought of dying.
>
> No more of that, no sweated lonely bouts
> With subtle, sly, insinuating dread,
> No strangling of my hope by unseen doubts.
> Be thankful, then, for I am better dead.
>
> Yes, I have loved to live, through the short years
> But I covet still the new-discovered sea.
> I will accept your envy, not your tears.
> Pity yourself but do not pity me.
>
> I'll have no weeping mourners, somber clad.
> The Lord gave, and the Lord reclaimed—Be glad![19]

A brief break in the weather gave Doolittle a chance. On Christmas Eve, he put up the biggest battle fleet of all against the Germans—2,056 bombers and 1,024 fighters. It did wonders for the morale of the Allied soldiers on the ground. Walter Hughes, one of those up in the air that day, later learned that "my brother Elmer was down there in General Patton's relief force, watching us go over. He said the footsloggers were treated to a fantastic sight that day. Everywhere, as far as the eye could see, were white condensation trails of the Eighth Air Force." It was more cheering to them than a stocking or a kiss under the mistletoe. It also brought the German offensive grinding to a halt. It had run out of fuel and ammunition thanks to the severing of supply lines by constant bombardment from the air.

It was difficult to get the right tone for Christmas that year. The crisis in the Ardennes meant that on many bases leave was canceled as the bombers waited on standby. Some crewmen managed to get away. The crew of Miles Tripp's Lancaster went on leave and were all invited to the wedding of George, the radio operator. The girlfriend whose brassiere he always carried with him on operations as a good luck charm was to be his wife. Tripp declined the invitation and headed straight for London and his WAAF, Audrey. "It seemed like crew disloyalty but I wanted to spend every available minute with her."[20] Their time together was rapturous. "The temporary reprieve from the threat of death sharpened my appetite for love. All senses were extended and magnified. Every waking hour was delightful, every trivial happening of universal significance." The days and nights raced by, and saying goodbye was an agony. At the station, "we couldn't bear the thought of final waves as my train pulled out, so we kissed and she walked away swiftly and I went up the platform in the opposite direction. By agreement neither of us looked back."

Those who remained on base enjoyed themselves. Flight Lieutenant Dennis Steiner's squadron, grounded for three weeks because of the weather, partied on a grand scale. On Christmas Day the sergeants were invited for drinks in the officers' mess and then they all trooped across to the airmen's mess to serve lunch to the lads. It was an opportunity for Steiner and his crew to say thank you to the ground crew who serviced their plane—"we singled them out and made sure they had plenty." Still in the festive spirit, he and his crew went into town, sat round a roaring fire in a pub, and he got into conversation with a WAAF from Scotland. It was a meeting that changed his life; after the war they married and were together for more than forty-five years.[21] Ken Newman snatched some time with his wife, Mollie, in between squadron duties. She had taken rooms for a few weeks in a house in a village just outside the camp, and though it was against regulations, he would spend nights with her there. He found it odd—"I would be lying in bed with my wife, knowing that a few hours earlier I had been on an operation and facing death." Unwittingly, he was also putting her in danger. A returning Lancaster, with its bombs still on board, skimmed the chimney pots of the house where she was staying, crashed, and exploded a hundred yards away. But there were compensations. They were invited for Christmas dinner to the house of a local farmer and gorged themselves on a double sirloin of illicitly reared beef followed by preserved fruit smothered in clandestine cream.

English schoolboy David Hastings was also gorging himself on the rarest of treats. The American crew who had adopted him as their mascot at their base just outside Norwich invited him in for "a super Christmas party—roast chicken, which we hadn't seen for years, ice cream and Coca-Cola, cookies, chocolate. All the things you couldn't get outside." Sergeant Ron Smith overindulged himself, too, but on something stronger than Coca-Cola. He staggered from the mess on Boxing Day, "well under the weather," as he recalled, and stood in the cold to clear his head. From inside, a clear tenor voice wafted into the night: "Gentlemen songsters all are we, doomed from here to eternity..." The sentiment crushed him. "Thoughts of home and Christmas past filled my mind, with a pang of remorse."[22] It had been a year since he had first met Tina at a WAAF Christmas party. Had he tried hard enough with the relationship? They had met up occasionally, though the arrangements always seemed so complicated, and they had written, but the correspondence petered out. The fear every time he sat in that rear gunner's seat had made him cynical. He preferred not to care, to live for the moment, drink too much, and crawl between his sheets to sleep. A real future with someone like Tina just seemed so far out of reach. When she had written to try and revive the affair, he had replied in an offhand way. That night he lay in his bunk and reflected on what sort of person he had become—"inward-looking, oblivious to normality and irritated by it." Everything that had once been important to him now seemed trivial. The war had changed him, and Christmas seemed to bring home to him precisely how much.

Reg Davey was also learning the utter rawness of war. He was an experienced navigator, veteran of high-risk operations such as the disastrous Nuremberg raid, but he had never faced such an ordeal as the one now in front of him. His tour completed, he was an instructor at RAF Feltwell, a training base in Norfolk. One night two Lancasters with pupil crews on board collided while doing circuits round the airfield. There was little left that could be identified after the explosion, but fourteen coffins were filled, mostly with sand to make up the weight. To make matters worse, he was delegated to represent the squadron at the burial of one of the dead men at his home on the outskirts of Birmingham and "and in my young life I had never attended a funeral of any sort before."[23] He accompanied the coffin by train.

It was a sad, lonely journey trying to get this dead bloke back to his parents—and at Christmastime too. I asked myself what I was doing here. I didn't know him and I wasn't very happy about meeting the parents. He was twenty-one years old and their only child as well. It must have been shattering for them. How should I react? What excuses could I make to them? I had seen so much death, so many empty bed spaces, friends killed, but meeting the parents of someone who had got the chop affected me more than anything.

Then, with their son at home at last, the parents decided on a candle-lit vigil beside the coffin on the night before the funeral. To Davey's horror, the mother asked for the lid to be removed so she could see her son for the last time. He made up excuses and finally one of the family grasped the truth, that there was little inside except sandbags. Quietly the mother was diverted from her wish.

The day of the funeral was bitterly cold. "It was snowing and the pall-bearer party was slipping around in the churchyard. The parents were completely cut up. I found it really upsetting to see them like that. It made me wonder what would have happened to me, to my mum and dad. Who would be standing next to my grave? It really brought home the realities of war to me and the pain and anguish caused by the deaths of so many fine young lads." He slipped away, back to base, as soon as he could, chastened by what he had seen, no stomach for the wake he was invited to. "Later there was a rumor that, after all the funerals were over, they found another body in a ditch miles away from the crash. Fourteen bodies—or rather bits of bodies in coffins—had been buried, and then they found another one, a complete one. It was quietly given a burial at Cambridge. They didn't say who it was. These things happen in wartime."

For those airmen who had turned their backs on the war, unable to stand its horrors any more, there was a childlike quality to Christmas. At "Hatter's Castle," the RAF psychiatric hospital in Derbyshire where men suffering mental breakdowns were lodged, there was a stocking to be placed at the foot of every bed. Penny Chapman, a nurse there, remembered sneaking through the rooms and dormitories in her Santa role. "The men were very good about it. Most lay awake but faked sleep."[24] The gaunt old Victorian house was covered with snow on the outside and decked with holly and laurel inside. A giant Christmas tree glowed at the bottom of the main staircase. It was her first Christmas away from home and, on her own, she blubbed at the thought "of Mum and home." But then other staff dragged her off to go carol singing and a rendition of "Silent Night" soon cheered her up. But she was not the only one who felt the sad, bitter edge of the festive season. Shortly afterward, one of the patients threw himself out of a window to his death, another casualty of the war that never seemed to be ending.

New Year's Eve was special for B-24 rear gunner Eddie Picardo. It was his last combat mission. Against all his expectations when he first landed in Britain, the end had come. "Doing it on New Year's Eve was nice. It meant that when 1945 arrived, we would be like the Baby New Year—ready to start our lives over again, free from the death cloud that hung over our heads."[25] He and his crew woke up in a state of excitement. Picardo could not stop himself telling everyone: "This is the one we've been looking for. Let's make it a good one." At the same time he was aware that plenty of airmen were killed on their final mission. "I was anxious to get out there and get it over with, but I didn't want to tempt fate by thinking too far ahead." He ate a hearty breakfast. The cook was in a generous mood. He put *five* freshly fried eggs on Picardo's plate, and when the gunner went back for more he got another *seven*. In wartime you never turned down such largesse. "I never ate a dozen fried eggs for breakfast," Picardo said. "I was stuffed but content." He would pay for his greed.

Their target for the day was not the heavily defended oil refinery he had feared but a munitions factory, an easier option. "So far, so good. When we arrived at our plane, everyone inspected it. The crew chief informed us they had done a good job on ours that day. 'This is the one you guys have dreamed about,' he said. 'Good luck.' It all seemed like a dream. Could this really be our very last?" He dreaded the thought of a last-minute cancellation and was relieved when a green flare went up and they were off.

"Our last takeoff. The engines looked good. We were on our way. We joined our formation heading over the English Channel, crossed the coast of Belgium . . . and suddenly, I started belching from all the eggs I had eaten. The gas was building up like crazy in my stomach. Then I started farting and I broke wind all the way to the target. It was awful."

They bombed through heavy flak but then soared away unharmed.

We were in formation and heading home. It was a great feeling. My stomach felt lighter and happier. I decided to serenade the crew with a ballad. Normally they hated my singing, but this time some of them even joined in, that's how happy everyone was. As we came in to land, I can remember the wheels hitting the ground. I kept saying to myself, "We've made it!" I was just elated. No more bombing missions. Never again would I have to get up in the morning not knowing if I'd be around by night. All those rosaries that I'd said had worked! Grandma must have been sitting up there in heaven watching over me. Everyone was cheering and slapping each other's backs, hugging. When we landed and parked our plane, the colonel was there to greet us. He handed each of us a big Havana cigar. I tried to smoke mine but it made me sick. Then it was our last debriefing, the best debriefing of all. We all had a shot of rye whisky and Pete, the top-turret gunner, made a toast—"Milwaukee, here I come!" That night we planned to have a big New Year's Eve party, but it didn't last long. We were so tired that by 10:30 P.M. we were all fast asleep. That was the end of it, my career as a tail gunner was complete. I could hardly believe it. Somehow I was going to walk away from the war in one piece.

There were celebrations too for Harry Yates and his crew. New Year's Eve was also the day of their thirtieth operation, the end of a tour that had begun back in the summer. They shared the same fears as Picardo. "We came to the door of the briefing room, seven men with one thought. Just this op and we've made it . . . just this last bloody one!"[26] There was a groan when the curtain was pulled back to reveal the target. Their last trip—one way or the other—would be to the Ruhr. They took off into thick cloud, emerged into sunlight over the Dutch coast, and were rocked by flak as they crossed into Germany. Discipline was not good in the formation that day; the stream began to break up under fire from the ground, and then the wind made accurate bombing impossible. As far as Yates could tell, their last run was a miss. "The bombs exploded beyond the sweep of the marshaling yard which was our target, indeed, beyond the town itself. It was a clear overshoot and would surely contribute nothing to the overall military objective." But success in bombers was measured not by hits on the target but by survival. "We came away with joy and relief bubbling up like champagne from a shaken bottle. We were alive! A party atmosphere swept through the aircraft. We crossed Holland at five thousand feet with the boys bawling a crass ditty into the intercom."

He offered his men a toast to be drunk in cold coffee: "To our future." It was a thought he had never dared to let cross his mind since they began. "N-Nan, you are clear to land," a WAAF's voice said over the radio. 'Her words brought a lump to my throat. I brought the aircraft down to a thousand feet. The undercarriage down and locked, I turned her with half flap down to make our *final* final approach. She settled on the tarmac to wild, triumphant cheering."

On the ground there were tears and smiles and photographs. In the mess, the drink flowed for hour on hour. At midnight, Norrie, the nineteen-year-old Tail-End Charlie, pulled Yates aside for a drunken confession. He wanted to talk about one of their very first missions, a trip to Kiel in north Germany when an enemy fighter had very nearly downed them. "I couldn't tell you before, Shhkip," he slurred. "Thought you might throw me off the crew. Well, it was my fault. The tail light was on. I forgot to switch the bugger off. That's why Jerry had a go at us. I'm sorry, Skipper." Everyone laughed. It was impossible to be angry with him. So, they might have died because of a silly mistake. It didn't matter now. The next day, Yates rose early, unable to sleep, and wandered the airfield. N-Nan was at dispersal, waiting for a new crew to take her over. He gave her one last inspection, then hurried away. That night she took off for the Ruhr again, to complete the job on the marshaling yards left unfinished the night before. She and her new crew never came back. A German fighter shot them down over Holland before they even made it to enemy territory.

They weren't even the first casualties of the new year; a dozen planes had already gone down before them. In the first seven days of 1945, Bomber Command lost a hundred aircraft. On New Year's Day, the Luftwaffe showed it still had teeth by mounting surprise fighter raids on Allied airfields in Belgium, France, and Holland. Thirty American and 162 British aircraft were destroyed on the ground. This followed a New Year's Eve on which twenty-seven bombers of the Eighth Air Force had failed to return and 250 men were missing in action. The old year had been rung out, but the tune played by the bells of the new one was the same sad funeral dirge as before.

BURNING DRESDEN

"One town on fire is very much the same as another—only the acreage was greater."
—BOMBER VETERAN ON DRESDEN

CHRISTMAS AND NEW YEAR PROVIDED NO TRUCE IN THAT OTHER BATTLE crucial to the bomber war—the one between Harris and the chief of the air staff, Portal, about where the efforts of Bomber Command were best directed. In deference to his commander's orders, Harris sent his Lancasters to oil and communications targets in Germany. In the first fortnight of January 1945 they hit eight railway yards, two canals, and six oil plants and depots, including Leuna, the Reich's star synthetic oil producer. Nearly six hundred aircraft made this trip, bombing in two waves several hours apart—a tactic now increasingly employed to cause maximum chaos—and it was later singled out by Albert Speer, Hitler's minister for production, as having been particularly damaging to the war effort. But in the same two weeks, Harris also raided Nuremberg, Hanover, and Munich, old favorites of his, smashing the city centers, industries, and housing—"the substance," as he put it to Portal, as opposed to "the shadow," which he considered the other targets to be. Harris's insistence on arguing the point continued to vex Portal. He refused to believe that Harris was really doing his best. "There is no doubt that you have so far done excellently," he wrote on 8 January 1945, "but this does not mean that you could not do still better. I can never feel entirely satisfied that the oil offensive is being conducted with maximum effectiveness by Bomber Command until I feel sure that you and your staff have really come to believe in it. Hence my continuing efforts to convince you."[1] Reading the correspondence sixty years later, it is hard to understand why Portal was so conciliatory. He clearly did not think Harris was acting "excellently," so why did he use that word? In his careful, courteous, diplomatic language were weakness and uncertainty of purpose that Harris could not fail to spot. Portal had known Harris long enough to have grasped that a man so sure of his own judgment was not to be swayed by debate. And yet debate is what the chief chose to engage him with.

Portal had solid arguments to make. Harris was *wrong*: Area bombing of cities had not brought Germany near to collapse, as he claimed it would. Harris was *wrong*: He had derided the policy of switching the attack to the German fighter force back in the spring of 1944 and yet the virtual wiping out of the Luftwaffe by the American air force had proved decisive. Shooting down Messerschmitts and smashing their production lines had been crucial to gaining superiority in the skies.[2] Harris was *wrong*: Oil was not another panacea but demonstrably Germany's Achilles' heel, as Ultra intercepts of top-secret enemy messages confirmed. At this point, Portal should have drawn a line and told his fractious subordinate that the correspondence was closed and he should either shut up or ship out. Instead he let his adversary play the wounded hero. Harris stood his ground on the uselessness of panacea targets, of which he remained convinced oil was just the latest. Then he challenged Portal to sack him. "You intimate," he wrote, "that I have been disloyal in not carrying out to the best of my ability policies which have been laid down. That I absolutely and flatly deny." Harris felt he was being placed in a no-win situation—when the policy he had never believed in did indeed fail, he would be blamed for supposedly not having tried hard enough to implement it. It was "heads I lose, tails you win, an intolerable situation. I therefore ask you to consider whether it is best for the prosecution of the war and success of our arms, which alone matters, that I should remain in this situation."

"Back me or sack me" was a dangerous strategy for Harris to play. But in this game of bluff, it was Portal who blinked. He denied charging Harris with disloyalty. On the substantive policy issue, he retreated into "agreeing to differ." He repeated his demand for more effort on oil targets, once again expressed his reservations about area bombing, but then let Harris off the hook. "I willingly accept your assurance that you will continue to do your utmost to ensure the successful execution of the policy laid down. I am very sorry that you do not believe in it, but it is no use my craving for what is evidently unattainable. We must wait until after the end of the war before we can know for certain who was right, and I sincerely hope that until then you will continue in command of the force which has done so much toward defeating the enemy and has brought such credit and renown to yourself and the Air Force."

It was a curious denouement. Three months of furious letters between two of Britain's top military leaders ended in a standoff, the senior man thwarted and yet unwilling to stamp his authority by the only means left to him—removing the thorn in his side. The conclusion has to be either that the thorn wasn't that hurtful to him—in which case, what was all the fuss about?—or that he shrank from removing it. After the war, Portal would come in for severe criticism from Harris's critics for not having sacked the man he so fundamentally disagreed with. Some said he was afraid, intimidated by the man himself and also by Harris's close personal relations with Churchill. An early draft of the official history of Bomber Command went so far as to accuse Portal of virtually abdicating his position as chief of the air staff.[3] He denied the charge, retorting that he had not taken Harris's resignation seriously because it had not been seriously offered. And anyway, "his good qualities as a commander far outweighed his defects and it would have been monstrously unjust to him and to his command to have tried to have him replaced on the grounds that, while assuring me of his intention to carry out his orders, he persisted in trying to convince me that different orders would have produced better results."[4]

The explanation does not wash. It makes the argument between them sound purely academic—two dons debating some obscure theory. In fact, the issues were real and present, and lives depended on them. The more likely explanation was that Portal was unnerved by Harris's utter conviction that he was right. If given a direct order to abandon area bombing of cities, Harris would have done so or had to resign. But in the continuing uncertainty of the early months of 1945, no such order was given. Nor should it have been. The Battle of the Bulge was only freshly won, new wonder weapons were raining down on Britain, and rumors were rife about the potential power of Germany's jet fighters. The borders of the Reich had not yet been breached, from the east or the west.[5] There was every indication that the Nazi grip on the German population was as strong as ever and that every village, town, and city would be a stronghold that had to be taken by force. Who knew for sure what it was going to take to force the surrender? Or how long it would take? In these circumstances, to remove a commander who still had not a single doubt that he had the key to ending the war in the shortest time and with the minimum of Allied casualties would have required immense strength of character and purpose. It would have taken a man more confident in his own opinions than Harris himself—and Portal was not that man.[6] It is clear, too, from what happened later, that Portal was keeping his options open. Perhaps area bombing could be useful after all.

So, yet again, Harris was given the green light for business as usual. As in the last quarter of 1944, he mixed his targets. On a given day he might send a third of his bombers to a city and split the rest between several different oil targets.[7] On another, it might be two city targets and one oil.[8] Sometimes, though less often than is generally assumed, it was cities only that were attacked.[9] Some crewmen were disturbed by these raids on civilian targets. Flying Officer Johnnie Jones of 467 Squadron, a rear gunner, looked down on Munich and wondered "how much of this once great city is left." In his diary for 7 January 1945 he wrote: "It must have been hell on earth for the poor devils down below. Mass murder, whole families wiped out, no doubt. I could not help but think when the bombs left the aircraft what a terrible thing I am doing. I am sure it must be wrong."[10] This was his second trip to Munich, and he thought the flak light and the opposition generally less than it had been. His impression was misleading because there were still many losses. Sixteen aircraft failed to return from this operation; 103 men were dead. It was the ninth major raid by Bomber Command on the city, and the losses were as high as they had ever been. The war was not losing any of its intensity or its risks, and feeling sorry for the enemy could be a premature sentiment. Johnnie Clark was navigator in a Mosquito going to Hanover and hardly needed his instruments to guide him there. It was still alight from the last raid and he could see the glow long before they arrived. "Seems as if we're only going to stoke up the blaze and turn over the rubble," he commented to his pilot as they steered through heavy flak and dropped their ton of bombs.[11] Both pondered the thought that they might be massacring innocent people. Two minutes later, heading home, an engine began to splutter and then cut out. Flak had cut the pipes feeding fuel from the wing tanks. They were running on reserve, and it was only a matter of time before they would have to bail out.

Once this would have inevitably meant falling into enemy territory— imprisonment or worse. But now, with the advance of the Allied armies on the ground, there was a chance of reaching their own lines first. They sat in the crippled plane and waited as long as they could, not an easy thing to do, Clark recalled, when every bone in your body is urging you to get out as quickly as possible.

I started to get ready to jump, clipping on my chest parachute. I realized I hadn't had it checked since I drew it from the stores several months previously. I hoped it would still open. Bloody hell, was this really happening to us? I bent down to lift the floorboard under my feet to get to the outer door. One press of the foot on a pedal and the whole door was supposed to jettison. I pressed down. Nothing happened. I pressed again. The door was jammed. At just that moment my parachute D-ring snagged on something and the canopy spilled out in front of me.

With an escape hatch that wouldn't open and a parachute that already had, Clark was in trouble, but he kept his nerve as they spiraled down through ten thousand feet. But when an engine caught fire, he decided not to wait any longer. He forced open the door, gripped the folds of his parachute tightly, "stuck my legs into the black void under me and slipped off the edge of the floor into the night."

He fell helplessly through the air, but then the wind caught the folds of silk and, with a jolt, slowed his fall to a gentle drift. "I sank into a layer of cloud. Snowflakes were whirling around me and it was freezing. Then I drifted out of the cloud and saw the ground white with snow below me. In no time I was dropping onto it, clattering down onto a frozen pond." He was in the middle of the countryside—but which country? Germany, Holland, or Belgium? He set a course by the stars and headed westward, staying off the roads and making his way furtively across fields. "Not a soul or house anywhere." He came to a canal, frozen over. Would it take his weight if he walked across? Or should he look for a bridge? Except a bridge would be guarded. But if the ice broke he would drown or freeze to death. He took the chance, and gingerly dragged himself over. Lying on the bank on the other side, catching his breath, he heard the crunch of boots in the snow and smelt cigarette smoke. As the steps came nearer, he wrapped himself in the white silk of his parachute as camouflage in the snow and waited nervously. Then he heard a voice—and it was English! He was behind his own lines after all. "I threw off my parachute shroud and scrambled up to see two soldiers. 'Thank God, you're British,' I cried. One of them barked: 'Get your effing hands up and keep them there!' I found myself looking at the wrong end of two rifles."

Clark blurted out his story—he was an RAF navigator and had bailed out from a Mosquito a couple of miles back—but the two squaddies were having none of it. "You couldn't have come from over there," one of them said, pointing in the direction Clark had indicated. "That's a minefield. You're a bloody saboteur, that's what you are! Now start walking." Bayonets prodded his back. He was taken to the field headquarters of a Guards battalion and ushered before an officer, who allowed him to put his hands down, listened to his story, and explained that the soldiers were right—he had indeed walked through a minefield. They could only presume the frozen topsoil had prevented the mines exploding and killing him. Clark was safe and would be back with his squadron a few days later. But he could reflect that here was an entirely new set of dangers for fliers to face. As if flak, fighters, SS troops, and angry German civilians were not enough to contend with, they now ran the risk of mines in no-man's-land and the bayonets of their own nervous frontline troops. And frostbite, too. Clark's pilot was injured, but survived. His flying boots fell off as he bailed out, and he then had to trudge for many hours through snow in his bare feet to reach Allied lines. He spent weeks in the hospital recovering.

For all Clark had endured, the thought that he might be massacring the innocent returned to haunt him in the next few weeks. Back in the air and bombing the central German town of Erfurt, he remembered the briefing officer's explanation that it was a center of light engineering but still wondered if that was sufficient explanation for it getting what he called "the heat treatment from us." Was it really contributing that much to the Nazi war effort? His doubts lasted until months later when he watched films of the Nazi extermination camps and was horrified to see the manufacturer's plates on the sides of the crematory ovens. They had been made in Erfurt.

In some ways, operations were becoming tougher rather than easier. Although more of the routes could now be flown over Allied-occupied territory, the targets were deeper into Germany, involving grueling flights of nine hours and more, and, with new navigation and bombing aids, were being attempted in weather that before would have been considered unflyable. Nor was there any letup from the hierarchy in its demands for maximum effort. The threat of being accused of LMF still hung over every single airman, and the final exhortations from squadron commanders at every briefing remained "No early returns" and "Press on regardless." The men generally responded with as much determination as ever to do the job properly. The skipper of Arthur White's Lancaster insisted they keep going even though the Gee and H2S navigation systems on board stopped working shortly after they got into the air. An engine was stuttering and the rear gunner's oxygen supply was blocked, but they carried on regardless. Over Munich, the aircraft was knocked off its bombing run when it had to corkscrew to avoid a head-on collision with a German fighter. They could have been forgiven for dropping their load anywhere and getting out of there, but the Canadian bombardier made them go round again. "What's the point in carting this lot all this way to drop them in a goddamn field?" he growled. "Let's put 'em where it hurts the bastards!"[12]

Turnover of crews was still high, partly because of continuing losses but also because more and more men were finishing their tours. The pre-Christmas weather had grounded many men waiting anxiously for their final missions. So many completed their quotas in the early weeks of 1945 that, after they had celebrated their good luck, they were left to cool their heels. There were not enough training or transport jobs to send them to. For all those finishing their flying duties, there was a steady stream of replacements, eager to fight. Some, like rear gunner Peter Twinn, were returning for a second tour, surprisingly eager to get back into the fray, given what they had already been through. Instructing was dull and disappointing and could not compete with the camaraderie and the adrenaline rush of live missions over Germany. "My old skipper rang me up in January 1945 and said he was going back for a second lot and asked if I would go with him. I didn't give it a second thought. It would have been safer staying on the ground instructing but I missed the excitement, and that you were actually doing the job you were trained for. I didn't think I was stretching my luck. As before, I told myself I was not going to be killed. You could not, you dare not, think in any other way."[13] He felt pretty sure the war would end that year—sometime. "But I still didn't plan for the future or talk to the rest of the crew about when it might end. It would be tempting fate to make plans before it was over."

As well as old-timers returning to the fray, there were also brand-new crews beginning their war, some of them anxious it might end before they had a chance to do their bit. Bob Pierson, the Lancaster Tail-End Charlie whose experiences began this book, was one such new arrival. Freddie Hulance was another among the January intake going operational for the first time. An expert pilot, he had spent the largest part of his war teaching recruits to fly. But the instructor itched for the real thing. "I felt we were winning the war and I had a growing feeling that it would be over in a matter of months rather than years. I didn't want to finish the war without some combat experience. I wanted to be able to say afterward that 'I was there.' At the same time, I wanted to survive, and I wasn't going to take any more risks than were strictly necessary."[14]

Hulance was typical of many of the men who went to war for the first time in those early months of 1945. He was caught in the tail-ender's dilemma—anxious to do his bit but also desperate not to die. The fatalism and resignation with which many men had flown into battle earlier were now replaced by a new and strangely unnerving sensation—hope. Ironically, it could increase the fear and make the job harder to do. As the end of the war began to be a serious possibility, climbing into the claustrophobic space of a Lancaster to fly against an increasingly desperate enemy and facing the prospect of never coming back called on ever deeper reserves of courage.

But Hulance's introduction to war was a gentle one. His first operation was the traditional familiarization flight for new pilots, as second pilot with an experienced crew. The green and red flares dropped by the Pathfinders and the explosions on the ground reminded him of childhood firework displays. There was no opposition. It was also a terrible fiasco. The target was Royan, a fortified town at the entrance of the Gironde estuary in southwest France. A German garrison was supposedly holed up there and the French Resistance and the Allied land forces wanted them blasted out. Intelligence said that all the French civilians had left. This was wrong. Three hundred and fifty Lancasters—again, coming in two waves, an hour apart—pulverized the center of the town with 1,500 tons of explosives, missing the garrison, which was outside the town, but killing a thousand locals.[15]

It was a controversial incident, over which the French and the Americans wrangled for years. But as a source of bitter debate and recrimination, it would be overshadowed by one of Hulance's next targets. On 13 February 1945 he flew his Lancaster to Dresden.

To many of the 8,500 British and American airmen who made the nine-hundred-mile round trip to the ancient capital city of Saxony, close to Germany's eastern borders, on the night of 13 February and the morning of the following day, it was a routine operation, if longer than they were used to. Flight engineer Freddie Cole of 619 Squadron thought it "uneventful, just another raid."[16] Flying Officer R. J. Elliott, navigator in a Lancaster of 227 Squadron, considered the raid "unexceptional."[17] It had gone "very smoothly." They arrived at the target exactly on time, were immediately called in by the Pathfinders directing the operation, and were among the first to bomb. He had no idea of the scale of the operation until much later. Flight Lieutenant E. G. White of 141 Squadron, circling the area in a Mosquito for the entire attack, recorded that "although the fires seemed to be bigger than when most cities burnt, it did not strike me at the time as being other than an ordinary attack."[18] By the time Peter Twinn's Lancaster got there, the area below was a mass of fires—"but it didn't stand out as something special. It was just another target. The fires were spread over a wide area and were very intense because of the large number of aircraft in the action." He was a veteran of Hamburg back in 1943 and had been unmoved by the firestorm then. "I didn't think about the people down below or the devastation we left behind. We were there to do a job. It was purely impersonal. We were spared the horror of fighting hand-to-hand or seeing the enemy in front of you. It was our job to get there, drop the bombs, and get home in one piece." Dresden was no different. "One town on fire is very much the same as another—only the acreage was greater." As for *why* Dresden was bombed, he had no doubts on that score either. "We were told before we took off that we were doing this operation at the request of the Russians, who were advancing from the east. Churchill agreed that we should bomb it. It was also a munitions town; they made armaments there."

Freddie Hulance remembered being told precisely the same at his briefing.

The target was nominated by the Russians, the first time I had ever known such a thing to happen. I know this was definitely said at the briefing because our squadron commander made no secret of his communist leanings and he was delighted that his squadron was going to help the Russians. And even though I didn't agree with his politics, I also thought it was good to help them because they had borne the brunt of the German attack. Dresden was a supply center for the Russian front. Afterward we learnt that it was also full of refugees, but we had no idea of that on the morning of the mission.

The raid itself hardly stood out in his memory.

The bomb load was a mixture of incendiaries and high explosives and we were the first wave in. Our bombardier had no difficulty finding the target. We were on our way home when my rear gunner got terribly excited about the fires we had left. He wanted me to turn the plane around and take a look back for myself but I said it would be too dangerous to maneuver across the stream of bombers. Anyway, I thought it would be a waste of time. When we landed back at base, a few people were talking about the fires, but we had seen worse. It was just another target and it faded into the memories. Only years later would it come back to haunt us.

The sight of the city ablaze stuck in Freddie Cole's mind. He could see the glow behind for an hour on the way home. But he was not perturbed. The briefing he and his crew had received was that Dresden was a staging post for enemy troops heading to and from the eastern front. Dave Francis of 460 Squadron had no qualms about Dresden: "It was just another target to be attacked, a multiple rail and road target between the eastern and western fronts. At that stage of the war our feeling was that the more damage and disruption we could inflict the sooner the war would end."[19] Johnnie Jones, who had agonized over the bombing of Munich a week earlier and felt he must be doing something morally wrong, put in his log that it had been "a good trip with only slight flak," though he thought the "damage done must have been colossal." He too recorded that the attack was "in support of Russian army."

Official reports also took this line. Each station logged its operations, and at one of the thirty-one from which bombers took off on the Dresden raid that night, RAF Hemswell in Lincolnshire, home of 150 and 170 Squadrons, the summary lodged in the station's files declared that "this attack was in direct support of the rapidly advancing Russian armies." The trip was arduous, "the longest yet undertaken by this station, some crews being airborne more than ten hours." But the operation was notched up as a great success, the report commenting that Dresden "has been knocked about a bit, like one of Cromwell's ruins."

Twenty miles from Hemswell, at RAF Kelstern, the weather had been so bad in the morning that the men of 625 Squadron had thought it unlikely they would be flying that night. Early in the morning sheets of rain had swept across the runway and the flatlands around, but the weather officer promised it would ease up in the afternoon. At 11:00 A.M. battle orders went up, and at 5:00 P.M. the men shuffled into the briefing room, checking their names with the security policemen at the door, then taking their seats on the benches facing the platform before springing to attention as the station commander strode in. The target was revealed as Dresden. Eric Thale recalled: "Agile minds worked out that we would be over enemy-occupied Europe for nearly eight hours. There was muttering from all and sundry."[20] The intelligence officer came to the platform and gave two reasons for the attack. First, it was part of Operation Thunderclap, a series of very heavy raids on east German cities aimed at causing such havoc that the enemy's war machine and civil administration would break down. It might even end the war. Dresden's built-up areas, industries, and railway were going to be the first to get clobbered. Second, since the city was just seventy miles from the Russian front, the attack would hamper German reinforcements "as Dresden is now a vital point in the communications and supply route to the eastern front."

The attack would be in two waves, the intelligence officer went on.

No. 5 Group will open the attack with 250 aircraft to get the fires going, with a time on target of 2215 hrs. Their marking point will be the sports stadium. There will be diversionary attacks on Böhlen, Magdeburg, Bonn, and Nuremberg to confuse the German fighter controllers as to the main target. One hour and forty-five minutes later, 1 Group will attack with 500 aircraft. The delay will ensure that all emergency services will probably have been called in from outside Dresden, so our attack will knock those out as well. Pathfinders will provide our master bomber, whose call sign will be "King Cole." The Main Force call sign will be "Strongman." The main threat from the enemy tonight will be flak. His fighter aircraft should be chasing the "window" feint force, which we hope will be indicating to the enemy that Frankfurt, Mainz, Darmstadt, or Mannheim are the main targets. By the time we get into the picture they will be running out of fuel and therefore landing. But just in case, our night-striking Mosquitoes will be patrolling the enemy's rendezvous beacons and airfields. Now, any questions?

There was silence. For anyone in doubt, the bombing leader then spelled out that the attack was "a fire raiser." Each aircraft would carry a 4,000-pound "cookie" and 8,000 pounds of incendiaries. Bombing would be on colored flares laid down by the Pathfinders, "but there should be no doubt of the real target as 5 Group will have the fires going jolly well by the time we get there. When the bomb doors are closed after bombing, would the bombardiers check the bomb bay for any hang-ups [bombs that had failed to release]. If there are, drop them live over Germany. We don't want them brought back. We've got plenty."

Thale remembered the flight out as trouble free. From the weather forecaster there had been a promise of large areas of cloud to conceal their approach but then a prediction of clear skies over the target itself. The route was complex, with many twists and turns to confuse the enemy. For the German controllers following their path on radar, Leipzig must have seemed the likely target, but fifty miles from it, the Lancaster turned toward Dresden.

As promised by the "met" man [weatherman], the cloud starts to break up and soon we notice a faint glow appearing in the sky ahead of us. We still have twenty minutes to run. Is that glow ahead coming from Dresden? We switch on the radio and hear the master bomber and his deputy. From their discussion we gather that visibility is excellent. The master bomber says that illumination flares are not needed and he orders the Pathfinders carrying them to go home. We are fifteen miles from the target and the whole area is just one sea of flames. Strangely there is no smoke. The fires are burning with such intensity that they are generating their own winds, which carry the smoke away and keep the target almost clear. These fires also quickly swallow up the marker flares. Realizing this, the master bomber issues an order to the main force—"King Cole to Strongman: no markers, bomb visually, bomb visually." Ahead of us the first wave of aircraft are dropping their loads and we see aircraft below us silhouetted against the fires. As the cookies explode, a shock-wave ring momentarily appears in the fire, to be swallowed up again in an instant. We commence our own bombing run at 0133 hrs, exactly on time. It is very turbulent now, either from the tremendous heat generated below us or from the slipstreams of aircraft ahead. There is a cold draught as our bomb doors open and the noise level increases. There are odd puffs of ack-ack but few and far between. Bombs away!

Heading home, Thale reflected on "a very successful attack with little or no opposition. At briefing, the intelligence officer wanted to know if we thought a return visit to the target would be necessary. Was he kidding?" But uppermost in Thale's mind was a different thought—"Seventeen trips completed, thirteen to go." That was what Dresden meant to him.

But Miles Tripp was horrified by his part in destroying the city. He had welcomed it as a target when he first saw it on the briefing-room map. It was a new destination for the bombers "and it was a safe bet that it would not be girdled by the black belt of defense worn by Ruhr cities or Berlin."[21] His misgivings began when he heard that it was full of refugees[22] and that what was being mounted was "a panic raid" to spread confusion and disrupt communications. "I remembered newsreels early in the war showing French refugees, their possessions piled on handcarts and prams, scattering as bombs fell from German dive-bombers. The memory disturbed me." For Robert Wannop, the flight to Dresden was so uneventful, peaceful even, that he could not help contrasting the tranquillity in the air with the panic that he realized would be spreading on the ground beneath them.

The air waves would be swamped with Berlin Radio warning the inhabitants of likely targets in our path to take cover. The air-raid sirens would be screeching. And above it all we sat somber and impassive, each man concentrating on the job in hand. I looked around the pitch-black sky and I couldn't detect a single one of the hundreds of other planes out there, not even a slight glow from a shielded exhaust. And yet I knew they would all be bearing down on the practically defenseless city which lay in our path.[23]

Wannop's engineer alerted him to the glow in the distance. "Must be from the first wave of Lancs, Skipper." He nodded.

They were two hours ahead of us. We've still fifty miles to go. It was 1:30 A.M. on February 14 when we finally dropped our load. St Valentine's Day. A day of love and affection, but we were not supposed to have such feelings for the poor devils below. Never mind that they were old men, old women, young people with their lives yet to live, babies, and babies unborn still in their mother's womb. . . . I had to pull the trigger, but who put the gun in my hand in the first place? Refuse and you're a coward. . . . Go, and you're a bloody hero! We stared with spine-chilling feelings into the holocaust below. The whole city was ablaze from end to end. It was like looking at a sea of liquid flames, inspiring in its intensity. It was so bright at bombing height that we could easily have read a newspaper.

In his Lancaster, at the back of the second wave, Tripp could barely take in the terrible sight below. This was worse than even his misgivings at briefing could have led him to imagine. "The streets of the city were a fantastic latticework of fire. It was as though one was looking down at the fiery outlines of a crossword puzzle; blazing streets stretched from east to west, from north to south, in a gigantic saturation of flame. I was completely awed by the spectacle." He could see no point in adding to the conflagration. As bombardier, he took charge of the aircraft, directing the pilot away from the heart of the inferno. "When we were just beyond the fringe of the fires I pressed the bomb release. I hoped the load would fall in open country." Back at base, he found it impossible to find the right words to describe what he had seen.

The crew spoke among themselves about the vast conflagration. Nobody had ever seen anything to compare with it and there simply weren't the adjectives available. Talk of "a fantastic glow in the sky" didn't describe acre upon acre of streets and buildings ravaged by fire typhoons and the enormous bowl of rosy light.

I am not sure which I found more distasteful—actually bombing refugees, or the idea that when the Allies were bombing refugees it was all right but when the Germans bombed refugees it was wrong. My quiver of outrage at the briefing and then dropping the bombs clear of the city in the hope that they would fall harmlessly in fields was a last gesture to an ideal of common humanity. It was at this point that I became something like a mercenary. I realized I was paid to do a job, and I had to do that job. If I was damned, I was damned.

He had already felt the war brutalizing him, choking off the better human emotions. Dresden pushed him over the edge. From then on, civilized ideals and cultural theories seemed to him "like so much hot air" in the face of man's terrible aggression. He was not alone in his disquiet. Squadron Leader Arthur Carter, a Pathfinder pilot who had switched to a staff job at the Air Ministry, called in on his old squadron the day after the Dresden raid and found his old comrades-in-arms shaken by what they had done. "There was a feeling in the mess that it was a horrible mistake. The firestorm had been horrendous and nobody knew why it had been done. They had been briefed that it was at Russian request but nobody wanted to help them anyway. Both we and the Americans hated their guts."[24] Robert Wannop cried. He went on leave, spending a precious seven days at home with his family, and "as I looked at my baby daughter, just a few weeks short of her first birthday, a lump came into my throat and my eyes filled with tears. Oh God, I had probably been responsible for killing or maiming such as her."

There are endless disputes about the Dresden bombing raid. Historians, propagandists, and polemicists argue over who chose the target and why, the numbers who died, its contribution to hastening the end of the war, whether it was a just cause or a war crime. But there is no dispute about one thing—the awful slaughter and destruction it wrought on a city of rare beauty. By all accounts, and by the Canaletto-style landscape paintings that remain, old Dresden was magnificent, a gem of the north European renaissance which blossomed into a baroque masterpiece in the eighteenth century. Its elegant palaces and churches inspired comparisons with Venice and Florence. But the idea that, because of this, it was somehow excused from the war was untrue. It had twice been hit by American bombers—in August 1944 and then again in October. An oil-processing plant was the target the first time and its railway yards in the second. But neither attack could have prepared the citizens for the savagery of 13 and 14 February. It was intended to be so. The instructions to the crews at briefing and the composition of the bomb loads they carried leave no doubt that "shock and awe"—a repeat of the Hamburg experience in 1943—was the intention. Nor would the fact that the city was crowded with refugees save it. Large numbers of civilians fleeing from the advancing Russians were passing through Dresden on their trek to find sanctuary in the German interior.

Their presence would simply add to the chaos and the breakdown of civil administration that was intended to be one of the results of the bombing. Germans would see that there was nowhere to escape to, that they were beaten, that the time had come for them to give up. The briefing notes of one intelligence officer at the time were explicit about this. "Administrative staffs and refugees are fleeing from Berlin toward Central Germany which they consider is the only safe area left, and the object of the attack is to so disrupt organization and transport as to create chaos and so bring about the collapse of the enemy's war machine."[25]

The first wave of Lancasters crossed the city in fifteen minutes, meeting token resistance.[26] Until a few months earlier, the city had been ringed by nine heavy antiaircraft batteries but, unknown to Bomber Command's planners, the guns had been dismantled and taken away for use in the land battle against the Russians. They were replaced by dummies made of wood and papier-mâché. A few light 20mm guns were all that remained to fire quarter-pound shells helplessly at the enemy fleet. In that first quarter of an hour, 880 tons of bombs fell, 500 tons of them high explosives, the rest shower after shower of four-pound incendiary sticks. The job of the "cookies"—4,000-pound bombs—was to tear down buildings but also to create high-pressure currents to fan the flames started by the incendiaries. Those Dresdeners who could find room in the woefully inadequate public shelters[27] or who fled to the cellars of their own houses cowered under the onslaught. One man recalled "a series of whistling sounds, then the building shook from a quick succession of steadily more powerful explosions, which drove us into the corner of the basement. The roaring crash of the bombs just didn't seem to stop. We hunkered down ever lower as one shudder succeeded another." When the shaking stopped and the drone of the bombers had gone, he ventured upstairs and looked out on a scene from hell. It was eleven o'clock at night but as bright as day from the flames. He went out into the street "and everywhere we turned, buildings were on fire. The spark-filled air was suffocating. Chunks of red-hot matter were flying at us. The more we moved into the network of streets, the stronger the storm became, hurling burning scraps and objects through the air."[28]

People were streaming down to the River Elbe or out of the city along roads lined with the rubble of fallen houses. Little Nora Lang held her five-year-old brother's hand as they tried to walk down the middle of the street "to avoid being hit by flying roof tiles or burned-out window frames or any other stuff flying around in that hurricane of fire."[29] The wind was getting stronger all the time, feeding the fires, which in turn fed the wind. A fifteen-year-old lad remembered "people wandering about helplessly. I saw my aunt, who called out to me to make for the river but the firestorm strangled her last words. A house wall collapsed, burying people in the debris. A thick cloud of dust arose and I could not see. A friend grabbed me and pulled me away across the rubble. Time and again, we stumbled over corpses. . . ."

As this scene was repeated all over the city, the second wave of RAF bombers came in, twice as many as before. Dresdeners thought the worst was over. It had hardly begun. Seeing the city center completely ablaze, the master bomber ordered the planes to widen the circle. They hit the suburbs, the parks where refugees were camped out in the open, the circus where the audience got out before the big top collapsed but the tigers burnt to death in their cage and the trick horse rider died with thirteen bomb splinters piercing her body. In the twenty-five minutes it took the second wave to cross Dresden, the city was struck by nearly a thousand tons of high explosives and eight hundred tons of incendiaries. A young German soldier, home on sick leave, was helping to clear debris at a hospital when the second strike came without warning. "We rushed back down into the shelter and stood shoulder to shoulder, it was so crowded. There came the deafening noise of the bomber formations and constant explosions, which shook the building. The lights went out. The ceiling, doors, and windows were blown in. Dust and smoke threatened to suffocate us. People were screaming, lashing out around themselves. A young mother threw herself over her pram in an attempt to protect her baby."

Nowhere was safe. Those who stayed underground risked being suffocated as the heat sucked the air out of their hiding places. Outside, the winds were now at tornado force, catching and hurling into the air not just debris but people, too. Twenty-four-year-old Margaret Freyer recalled seeing a woman carrying a baby in her arms—"She runs, she falls, and the child flies in an arc into the fire. The woman remains lying on the ground, completely still. My eyes take this in but I myself feel nothing. I just stumble on. The firestorm is incredible. There are calls for help and screams and all around is an inferno. I hold a wet handkerchief in front of my mouth, my hands and face are burning. It feels as if the skin is hanging down in strips."[30]

Survival depended on desperate measures. A group of men stood for six hours in a circle, each beating out the sparks constantly landing on the clothes of the man in front. Those who tried to flee found their feet trapped in hot, melting tar, like insects caught in molasses. As the dawn came up on what, ironically, was Ash Wednesday,[31] survivors looked around them to see charred corpses everywhere. Those who ventured down into the still-smouldering cellars to look for friends or relations retreated from the horror and the extent of the slaughter. Out on the road, one Dresdener recalled, "building after building was a burnt-out ruin. The dead were scattered across our path. The skull of one had been torn away; the top of the head was a dark red bowl. An arm lay with a pale, fine hand, like a model made of wax. Metal frames of destroyed vehicles, burnt-out sheds. Some people pushed handcarts with bedding and the like. Crowds streamed unceasingly past the corpses and smashed vehicles, a silent, agitated procession."[32]

And even then it wasn't over. At noon the same day, there was more roaring in the sky and 300 B-17s of the American Eighth Air Force arrived overhead to flatten anything and anyone left standing. They were a day late. They had been supposed to lead the raid on Dresden twenty-four hours earlier, ahead of the RAF, but had been grounded by the bad weather in England that morning. Quite by chance, Bomber Command had gone first, the destruction of Dresden laid at *its* door for that most British of reasons—the rain. When the Americans finally got into the air the next day, two thousand bombers and fighter planes headed for central Germany, launching full-scale city-busting attacks on Chemnitz and Magdeburg as well as Dresden. Heavy cloud covered the city as the Fortresses came in, and in thirteen minutes they dropped 1,900 five-hundred-pound high explosive bombs and 137,000 stick incendiaries. Though they bombed blind, on instruments, many hit the marshaling yards which were their target. But civilian casualties were inevitable. Dave Nagel, a B-17 crewman from New York whose father had fought the Germans in the First World War, had no qualms or illusions about what happened at Dresden or elsewhere. "We were supposed to be over a target when we let the bombs go, but we assumed it would be surrounded by civilians. I didn't know anyone who was remorseful. If you saw London like I saw it, you wouldn't have any remorse."[33] Another New Yorker, John Morris, a waist gunner with the 91st Bomb Group, agreed with the military necessity of the mission. "It was a sound strategy to prevent the Wehrmacht from falling back to regroup. So we bombed the hell out of the railroad yards and road hubs along their line of retreat. I don't rejoice at the tens of thousands of Germans killed there, but I doubt there were many Jews in that number. The good burghers of Dresden had shipped them all off to Auschwitz."[34] Nagel and Morris probably spoke for the majority of U.S. airmen that day, but theirs was not the only opinion. Radio operator Harold Hall of the 527th squadron thought at the time of their briefing that the raid smacked of indiscriminate bombing. "No mention was made of refugees in the city but the implication of foul play was strong. I have to say that I felt ashamed we had leveled ourselves to the Krauts."[35]

The Americans dropped their bombs on an area of Dresden untouched by the two night raids and to which many survivors had gone for shelter. Little Nora Lang, still clutching her brother's hand, had managed to get to safety here, only to be bombed again. No wonder the Dresdeners felt they had been singled out for special treatment. But the truth is that Dresden was not a special case, any more than any of the other German cities that had been bombed over the years. To the men of Bomber Command and of the Eighth Air Force, as we have seen from their diaries and logbooks, it was just another target. What made it a little bit special in their recollections was that it had been such a success, as they also noted when they got home. The official report of the operation, telexed from headquarters at High Wycombe to the Air Ministry and to all station commanders next day, confirmed this verdict. It praised the master bomber for his good and clear instructions and declared the attack highly successful. In fact, from the bombers' point of view, the Dresden operation was, if such a thing is possible, the *perfect* air raid.

By some fluke, all the factors that made for a successful bombing operation came together that night—"spoof" targeting kept the enemy guessing where the bombers were heading until it was too late; the total break in the cloud over the target; the absence of antiaircraft fire and fighter cover; the exceptional precision of the marking; the punctuality of the main force, dead on time at every point; the accuracy of the bomb drops, with none of the usual overshooting or creep-back; the twin-strike tactic catching fire and rescue services unawares. It could so easily have been otherwise. When the bomber squadrons visited other nearby German cities, the weather was against them. Chemnitz and Leipzig survived; Dresden did not. The severity on the ground was also due to freak factors, not least the absence of proper deep civilian shelters with firewalls, air filters, and sealed doors. Dresden's Nazi administrators had never got round to building them.

When the news of the raid broke, it was just another routine event for a war-weary world in which thousands of human beings were dying violently every day. The London *Evening Standard* of 14 February strung a headline across the top if its front page—"The Blasting of Dresden"—over a 250-word report:

Burning Dresden, pounded last night by 800 bombers of RAF Bomber Command, was again hit today by aircraft of the U.S. Eighth Air Force. The raids were in support of [Soviet] Marshal Koniev's troops, who are less than 70 miles away. The Germans may be using Dresden—almost as large as Manchester—as their base against Koniev's left flank. Telephone services and other means of communication are almost as essential to the German army as the railways and roads which meet in Dresden. Its buildings are needed for troops and administrative services evacuated from other towns. Dresden had large munitions workshops in the old arsenal. No major attack has been made before on the town.

The story shared a crowded front page with, among other stories, "Montgomery Advancing on Siegfried Defense Belt" and a report that Princess Elizabeth was suffering from mumps. A chilling story quoted a German Foreign Office spokesman as saying that "fanatical German men, women and children" were ready to "kill, murder, poison" any enemy soldiers who penetrated the frontiers of the Third Reich, while Moscow Radio was said to be reporting that Germany was preparing for a "last-ditch stand" in Bavaria.

Back in Dresden itself, the Reich authorities instituted a very quick cleanup. Thousands of troops and prisoners of war were drafted in to clear the streets of corpses and then dig through the rubble for more. Nazi efficiency helped—SS men who had previously worked at the Treblinka camp came to put to use their expertise at disposing of bodies. On their say-so, instead of one massive fire, funeral pyres were lit at staggered times to minimize the pall of fine ash that would otherwise have settled over the city. Bodies were meticulously logged, identified by the place where they were found, named if possible. They were counted—so that a month later it was possible for an official report to conclude that the known number of dead was 18,375 and to estimate that the final figure would be in the region of 25,000. Among the many wild casualty figures that would later be quoted, it remains the only one that has any official authority to it.[36] It is undoubtedly a minimum figure. Most responsible histories add between 10,000 and 15,000 more for the unknown number of refugees who died, bringing the consensus death toll to somewhere between 25,000 and 40,000. It was a staggering total, a terrible calamity by any standards. But, for one man, it was still not big enough.

The story of Dresden quickly moved beyond the world of hard facts when the Nazi propaganda minister, Dr. Joseph Goebbels, the original spin doctor, seized on it for his own purposes. At first, he had a problem: Was the fact that Allied warplanes could fly the skies of Germany with impunity one to be suppressed or broadcast? The decision was made for him by a blunder at Allied headquarters—"one of the great propaganda mistakes of the war," according to historian Frederick Taylor. An RAF spokesman gave a press conference in which he unwisely hinted that, among the other reasons for bombing Dresden, the evacuees massed there had been targeted to add to the panic behind the German front line. An American journalist interpreted this as an admission that the Allies had crossed the fine line between civilians as unforeseen casualties caught up in fighting and civilians as targets and that this had been deliberate terror bombing. The military censors failed to stop the story being transmitted, though they had every chance to do so, and Goebbels seized the opportunity for what was his final masterpiece of spin— one that still outlives him sixty years later. He did it by simply adding a zero to the casualties. In his hands, the number of dead in Dresden soared from tens of thousands to hundreds of thousands. The number of refugees said to have been in the city was inflated to a million. The true figure will never be known, but an estimate by a reliable Dresden historian puts it at only a fifth of that.[37] Goebbels fed the press in neutral Sweden with horror stories in which the death toll was given as at least 200,000. Dresden was described as a city without war industries, its factories turning out talcum powder and toothpaste, a peaceful center of culture which had been attacked out of a "desire to obliterate and annihilate the German people and all its remaining possessions." In a German newspaper, Goebbels—a man who despised the old German culture and values represented by Dresden—wrote that "a city skyline of perfected harmony has been wiped from the European heavens."

In the years after the war, the Goebbels version of what had happened at Dresden—the city's "innocence," the death toll, the motivation—took on all the characteristics of an urban myth. It has suited historians, commentators, and polemicists across the entire political spectrum to exaggerate and distort the truth about Dresden and to demonize those who attacked it. The extreme right claimed it was an Allied atrocity that stood comparison with the Nazi extermination of the Jews. The left took the line peddled by the new communist rulers of the city—after 1945 it was part of East Germany, a Soviet satellite state—and dubbed the air raid on Dresden a "crime against humanity" conducted by Anglo-American warmongers. It upped the death toll to 320,000, "murdered with bombs, phosphorus and sulfur." Any involvement by Moscow in the decision to bomb it was denied. This Cold War conspiracy theory went a step further and claimed the British and Americans had deliberately destroyed Dresden to ensure that all the Soviets inherited in the postwar settlement was rubble. Meanwhile, between the extremes, liberal consciences in the West, wracked by the horrors of war, found balm for their wounds in admitting that the Allies had been wrong. Throughout the war, a small bomb of pacifist campaigners had publicly opposed city bombing. Their protests, generally derided at the time, prevailed in the peace and became gospel in the sixties and seventies when the Campaign for Nuclear Disarmament held sway among liberals.[38]

The feeling became, as one historian of the bomber war writing in 1968 put it, that "Dresden was selected for no reason which anyone who fought in the strategic air offensive can justify. It was bombed without any regard to such trivial targets of military importance as it did possess."[39] Dresden became an emblem of man's inhumanity, and the men who bombed it pariahs. Harris was regularly denounced as a mass murderer and, though critics often distanced the aircrews from their leader, former bomber crews learned to keep quiet about what they had done in the war. The flak still flies. When a statue to Harris was unveiled in London in 1992, peace protesters daubed it with red paint. In that same year the Queen was booed in Germany for failing to make a formal apology for the bombing of Dresden. The feeling remains to this day. A German historian's book arguing that the Allied bombing of Germany was a war crime was a bestseller in Germany in 2002. The following year, when an exhibition of art from Dresden opened in London, the German novelist Günter Grass took the same line. He was a young soldier crossing through Dresden shortly after the raid and "saw the burned bodies, piled high for cremation. There was no military reason to bomb the city. It was a war crime." Interviewed at the same time, Kurt Vonnegut, the American writer who was a prisoner of war caught up in Dresden at the time, an experience he turned into his celebrated novel *Slaughterhouse-Five,* maintained Dresden was an open city. "It was untouched, the war was almost over, and it was a haven for refugees and for the wounded. It was as unwarlike as possible." He gave the death toll as around 135,000.[40]

For half a century the consensus was that Dresden was an innocent city far removed from the war which was needlessly attacked on the orders of a bully out of bloodlust and a mad desire for revenge. More recent research, however, has shown this to be totally untrue. Historian Frederick Taylor drew on archival material in Dresden denied to Western scholars until the Iron Curtain came down to show that its citizens may have thought themselves immune from the war, living in a *Kulturstadt,* an oasis which, by common consent, was inviolable, but they were deceiving themselves. Dresden may not have had the obvious heavy, smokestack industries of the Ruhr, but it did house the sort of precision engineering demanded by new weapons technology. The city's own description of itself proclaimed what was beneath the surface. Its yearbook for 1942 boasted: "Anyone who knows Dresden only as a cultural city, with its immortal architectural monuments and unique landscape, would be very surprised to be made aware of the extensive and versatile industrial activity that make Dresden *one of the foremost industrial locations of the Reich.*"[41] The city had 127 factories which purported to be turning out consumer goods and luxury items but which had secretly switched to war work. Zeiss, the biggest manufacturer, had long ceased making cameras for tourists in favor of bomb-aiming apparatus and time-delay fuses. A onetime manufacturer of typewriters and sewing machines was turning out armaments. Dresden china figures—for which the city was famous—were actually manufactured at Meissen, twelve miles down the River Elbe, and the workshops there had also been switched to war work and were turning out communications equipment for the army. A company which had once made waffle and marzipan machines was producing torpedo parts for the navy. Even an arts and crafts workshop was producing wooden tail assemblies for V-1 flying bombs. Machine guns, searchlights, aircraft parts, field telephones, two-way radios were just a few of the other war goods being made there. The city's chamber of trade admitted that "the work rhythm of Dresden is determined by the needs of our army."

But not only was Dresden pouring out materials for the war from its factories, it was also about to take a more active role in the fighting, whether its citizens wanted to or not. They may have thought it an "open city," to be left untouched because of its heritage, but their Führer thought otherwise. The German High Command had designated it a military strongpoint, part of the defensive line along the River Elbe at which the Soviet advance could be held. The order from Berlin was that it was to be defended at all costs. So peaceful Dresden was in reality a war factory and a fortress, and these factors alone made it a legitimate target for the bombers. But it was also a vital link in the German rail network, and it is this that probably sealed its fate. It was a crossroads for north–south and east–west traffic. Twenty-eight military transports a day came through Dresden with troops and tanks to fight off the advancing Soviet army. An Allied POW who was in a train shunted onto a siding on the night before the bombers came "saw with my own eyes that Dresden was an armed camp with thousands of German troops, tanks, and artillery and miles of freight cars transporting supply logistics toward the East to meet the Russians." The Soviets wanted those trains stopped.

The subject arose at the Yalta conference in early February 1945. Stalin, Roosevelt, and Churchill met to discuss the shape of a postwar Europe and lay down guidelines. But actually securing the victory was on the agenda, too, and in this Stalin—ever suspicious that Britain and America were dawdling, plotting, planning to negotiate a peace without him—sought help from his Western Allies. At the first plenary session, General Alexei Antonov made a specific request for "air action to hinder the enemy from carrying out the shifting of his troops to the east from the western front, from Norway and from Italy." Of Dresden as such, there was no mention, though it, along with Berlin, Leipzig, and Chemnitz, was an obvious target for such an action. But its name definitely came up at private sessions between the chiefs of staff, according to a British interpreter who was there. "Antonov very clearly said: 'Well, we want the Dresden railway junction bombed because we are afraid the Germans are putting up resistance, a last stand, as it were.' And we agreed to this. We agreed to pretty well everything."[42] The world-weariness of the interpreter's comment was suggestive of the mood in Yalta, at which concessions to the Soviets were commonplace. Britain surrendered a whole nation to communist rule—Poland, the country whose freedom she had gone to war to defend in 1939—so what mattered an air raid?

But such an attack suited Churchill anyway. For a while he had been pressing for Bomber Command to make a crushing raid on cities in eastern

Germany to try to break the German resistance. Operation Thunderclap had first been conceived back in August 1944 as a massive Anglo-American strike, preferably on Berlin, to shatter the morale of the German people. Some fifty thousand tons of bombs would be dropped on the capital in a couple of hours, and one estimate was that there would be in excess of a quarter of a million casualties. What is odd about this plan is that it originated from the Air Ministry. At its heart was the very idea that Harris had always promoted—that devastating air power could bomb Germany into submission—but which the ministry had so often challenged. Thunderclap was put on the back burner in the summer of 1944 because of American concerns that it was openly an attack on civilians with no pretence of targeting military or industrial sites. It was revived in January 1945, and seized on by Churchill. As a sign of good faith to the Soviets, he wanted to give the east German cities that stood in the way of their advance a good basting. When the Air Ministry demurred, preferring to concentrate efforts on its favored oil targets, he told them in no uncertain terms to get on with attacking the cities. Portal, who had been arguing this point with Harris for several months in their prolonged correspondence, found himself issuing an order to Bomber Command for "one big attack on Berlin and attacks on Dresden, Leipzig, Chemnitz, or other cities where a severe blitz will not only cause confusion in the evacuation from the east but will also hamper the movement of troops from the west."[43] By this time the Americans, in the aftermath of the Battle of the Bulge, seemed to have lost their earlier squeamishness about bombing whole cities, and they launched Thunderclap with a thousand-bomber raid on Berlin on 5 February which caused thousands of casualties. Dresden, a week later, was strike number two.

Harris, for whom the Thunderclap order was a vindication of everything he had been arguing, had his doubts about Dresden as a target. He declared it too far to go for too little gain and that not enough was known about its air defenses. Perhaps he was reluctant to put his men's lives at risk for the sake of the Russians. Or perhaps, perverse as ever, he just didn't like being told his target and so was being difficult.[44] But he carried out his orders. The irony from his point of view was that everyone else's fingerprints—Churchill's, Portal's, Stalin's—were on the operation except his. And yet afterward he had to shoulder the blame for it. In his memoirs he distanced himself slightly—"the attack on Dresden was at the time considered a military necessity *by much more important people* than myself."[45] But he leapt to the defense of the operation when others disowned it. How could he not? Dresden, with its factories and its strategic location close to the eastern battlefront, was no different in kind from other cities he had targeted. If he disowned Dresden because, in truth, it had not been his project, he would be disowning everything he believed in. Churchill had no such scruples. Having encouraged Harris, his friend, for years, having backed the bombing of Germany wholeheartedly, he suddenly came across his conscience.

Six weeks after Dresden, Churchill dumped—and dumped *on*—his old friend. Suddenly he was concerned. "The destruction of Dresden remains a serious query against the conduct of Allied bombing," he told the chiefs of staff in a minute. "It seems to me that the moment has come when the question of bombing German cities simply for the sake of increasing the terror should be reviewed. Otherwise we shall come into control of an utterly ruined land. I feel the need for more precise concentration upon military objectives rather than on mere acts of terror and wanton destruction, however impressive."[46] It was an astonishing volte-face. Six months earlier, the prime minister had been ready to launch chemical warfare against the Germans. Two months earlier, he had pressed for Operation Thunderclap to obliterate cities in the east. Now suddenly his conscience was stricken. In fairness to Churchill, there were new political realities to consider, the postwar future as well as the present fighting. It is significant that his change of heart came just three days after he had stood on the banks of the Rhine and pronounced that Germany was "whipped." It was the end of March, and in the six weeks since Dresden, the squeeze on Germany from east and west was such that for the first time he could be absolutely confident that victory was close. But Goebbels's propaganda had also clearly scored a success with him. There were questions in newspapers and in Parliament about bombing policy. The historian in Churchill must have alerted him to the damage the Dresden affair could do to his reputation. Dresden had been his baby, but he quickly disowned it when it threatened to become an embarrassment.

Harris picked up the orphan. More than that, he nurtured it and made it his own. People were just being silly and sentimental about Dresden, was his dismissive riposte to those who were troubled about the firing of such a fine city. "The feeling, such as there is, over Dresden could be easily explained by any psychiatrist. It is connected with German bands and Dresden shepherdesses. Actually Dresden was a mass of munitions works, an intact government center, and a key transportation point to the east. It is now none of these things."[47] The tone of callous disdain—*it is now none of these things*—did nothing for Harris's reputation. Tens of thousands of lives lost deserved more respect. But, as ever, Harris was his own worst enemy, and when the correspondence emerged ten years after the war, it further damaged his reputation. In fact, the "shepherdesses" remark was a throwaway line, a postscript to a letter in response to Churchill's accusations which in every other respect was rationally argued. The Air Ministry—which, to its credit, circled its wagons around him, as annoyed with Churchill as he was—asked for his comments. He replied: "To suggest that we have bombed German cities 'simply for the sake of increasing the terror though under other pretexts' and to speak of our offensive as including 'mere acts of terror and wanton destruction' is an insult. This sort of thing, if it deserves an answer, will certainly receive none from me, after three years of implementing official policy."

He defended his record.

I have always held, and still maintain, that "the progressive destruction and dislocation of the German military, industrial, and economic systems" could be carried out only by the elimination of German industrial cities, and not merely by attacks on individual factories, however important these might be in themselves. Overwhelming evidence is now available . . . that the destruction of those cities has weakened the German war effort and is now enabling Allied soldiers to advance into the heart of Germany with negligible casualties.

The policy of city bombing had always had a strategic basis and continued to do so because it would shorten the war and save Allied lives. "We have absolutely no right to give up these attacks unless it is certain that they will not have this effect. I do not personally regard the whole of the remaining war cities of Germany as worth the bones of one British Grenadier."

Dresden, Harris was saying, was a legitimate frontline target in a bombing campaign that was causing chaos in Germany and demonstrably reducing the enemy's ability to fight back against the invading Allied armies. The enemy was reeling from the onslaught. To choose that moment to stop would be folly. "The strategic bombing of German cities must go on." But if ordered to stand down his men, he would, and willingly. "I take little delight in the work, and none whatever in risking my crews." There was a caveat. "We should be careful of precedents. Japan remains. Are we going to bomb their cities flat—as in Germany—and give the armies a walkover, as in France and Germany? Or are we going to bomb only their outlying factories and subsequently invade at the cost of 3 to 6 million casualties?"[48] It was a good question.

None of the above is intended to deny the horror of Dresden. It is an explanation, not an excuse. Author Frederick Taylor, having established that Dresden was no "innocent" city but a legitimate target, added that no one should "minimize the appalling reality of such a vast number dead, so horribly snatched from this life within the space of a few hours, or to forget that most of them were women, children, and the elderly. It must count as one of the most terrible single actions of the Second World War." But had any moral line been crossed? The harsh reality of the time was that only total war would bring Hitler's Germany to its knees. The German people still had to learn there was no hiding place before they would surrender. Those who argue that the end was near do so with hindsight. That certainty was not apparent in those early weeks of 1945 when the Allied armies had still to cross the Rhine, and anyone bold enough to say the war was all but over would have received pretty short shrift from soldiers, airmen, and public alike.

Lancaster pilot Ken Newman's view was typical of those of fighting men at the time. He had flown the last sortie of his first tour shortly before Dresden, but his celebrations had been muted. "I was going on noncombat duties for six months, but then I was certain I would be back after that, back over the skies of Germany. I didn't think the war would be over by then."[49] There were those much higher up the military chain of command who would have agreed with him that the end was far from being nigh. Eisenhower had a besetting worry. There was no doubt that Germany was going to be defeated, but how precisely would the end be brought about? More to the point, how long would it take and how many men would have to die in the process? His biggest worry was of a shrinking Germany in which the diehards, led by Hitler, dug in. There were rumors of bands of "werewolves"—fanatical Nazis going underground to conduct a guerrilla war—and a Last Redoubt, a stronghold in the Bavarian Alps where an invader could be held at bay for months, perhaps even years. In the end, these demons were illusions, the result of clever SS propaganda. No such underground resistance had been properly organized, nor was there a Masada in the mountains to which Hitler would retreat and fight to the bitter end. But, in early 1945, there was much evidence pointing that way. And it seemed perfectly rational. Who could have foreseen that Hitler would kill himself? He had ordered his soldiers and his people to fight to the last drop of blood. Surely he would do the same? Indeed, of all the fates that were imagined for Hitler, killing himself in a bunker without firing a shot in his own defense was not one of them. In these circumstances, there was only one thing that could bring the German people to the brink of surrender—brute force. This was not a time to be merciful. If the war was to end quickly and cleanly, inflicting damage was just as necessary as ever. Dresden would be that shock. Since it also lay on the land route that the Führer and his entourage would have to take if he fled south from Berlin to his Berchtesgaden fortress, then that was another justification for destroying it.[50]

It should be remembered, too, that, for some people, the bombing of Dresden was a lifesaver. Professor Victor Klemperer was a Jew who had managed to remain in his own city throughout the Nazi period. But his freedom was about to end. He had been ordered to report for deportation— and everyone knew what that meant—on 15 February. As the air-raid sirens sounded on 13 February, one of his fellow Jews muttered: "If only they would smash everything up." The planes did precisely what she had asked for. Klemperer and his companions took advantage of the chaos to escape. They ripped the yellow stars off their clothes and mingled with all the other refugees leaving the city. They were not the only ones thankful for the Allied bombs. On the road out of Dresden, Klemperer met a young man clutching at his baggy trousers with his hand because his belt and suspenders had been taken from him. He was Dutch and had been a prisoner in a Dresden jail. The raid had given him the chance to escape and save his life. Robert Kee, a British prisoner of war in a camp south of Berlin, heard the sound "of a wholly unusual amount of bombing away in the distance." It was "cheered to the echo" by him and his fellow POWs.[51] Here was a sign that soon they might be going home. Jack Myers was locked in a cattle car with other British prisoners of war in a siding just outside Dresden. "We hadn't been fed for five days. A blast from the bombing loosened the doors sufficiently for us to get out and eventually to find potatoes to eat. We were marched through the still-burning city, and that is one of the happiest memories that I have of three years' captivity by one of the nastiest and most poisonous nations ever to seek to rule the world."[52]

Ben Halfgott, a fifteen-year-old inmate of a concentration camp at Schlieben near Dresden, saw the huge red glow from the city in the distance and "it was like heaven to us. We knew that the end of the war must be near and our salvation was at hand. When the Russians arrived [to liberate them] I weighed fifty kilos and you could see all my bones."[53] At the time of the raids, a Dutch woman, Elka Schrijver, was one of four thousand political prisoners in a jail near Chemnitz, southwest of Dresden. The male inmates were digging their own grave, a huge hole in the ground which they were told was for a water reservoir but which they would later discover had a more sinister purpose. "After our liberation, documents found by the Red Cross showed that this was meant to be a mass grave and that orders from Dresden had been received to shoot all of us. Subsequent to the Dresden raids, nobody had the courage to execute these orders. Those of us who were political prisoners in Saxony at the time directly owe our lives to those air raids."[54] The same went for a large group of German communists and resistance fighters from Czechoslovakia who were in a prison attached to the justice building and due for execution by guillotine. On February 15, the day after the main raids, the Eighth Air Force made its second visit to Dresden. Hampered by heavy cloud, the B-17s nevertheless managed a direct hit on the north wall of the prison building. Thirty prisoners were killed, but hundreds escaped through the gaping hole. The bomb also destroyed the scaffold and the electrically operated guillotine in the prison courtyard.

The moral balance on Dresden is hard to determine, and historians are sharply divided. "It is very difficult to justify the devastation that took place in the early months of 1945, when Germany's air defenses had almost collapsed and the destructive capability of Bomber Command reached its zenith," says Max Hastings. "By February 1945 it was plain that the war would be over within months. Attacks upon German cities had become largely irrelevant to the outcome. Area bombing should have been stopped in 1944."[55] Richard Kohn, a U.S. air force historian, on the other hand, urges us to think ourselves back in time:

Transport yourself backward into the United States and Great Britain of the Second World War. The Third Reich was resisting fiercely; even in its death throes it was still capable of altering the outcome, or at least extracting a meaningful price, as the Battle of the Bulge, the V-1s and V-2s,

and the jet planes demonstrated. Men were still dying, populations sacri-
ficing. The Russians were advancing. How would the war end? How
soon? Would the fanatics in control of the German state surrender? Thus
it is understandable that the West undertook massive blitz raids in early
1945, with all the forces available, and with diminishing numbers of targets in an effort to bludgeon Germany into surrender as quickly as possible. The wonder is that moral scruples entered as much into the calculus
as they did.[56]

The loss of life at Dresden can still wrench the heart six decades on, and
so it should. But it was undoubtedly a legitimate target even if its fate
seemed cruel, coming after years in which it had escaped any direct involvement in the fighting. And it can be argued that its destruction did hasten the end of the war. The collapse of the Third Reich came remarkably
quickly in the spring of 1945, sooner than Allied intelligence ever expected.
Dresden brought on a change of heart among the German people. German
historian Götz Bergander, a teenager in Dresden in 1945, acknowledged
that "the shock wave triggered by Dresden swept away what was left of the
will to resist, as the Germans now feared that such a catastrophe could be
repeated daily. Awareness of the inevitable defeat increased and the belief in
miracles disappeared. Above all, there was a growing realization that it
would be better if the end came soon."[57] The diehards might be prepared to
fight to the bitter end, but Dresden was a warning of how bitter that end
could be. The slaughter during that terrible twenty-four hours in February
1945 was a clear sign that it was time the killing stopped altogether.

FACE TO FACE WITH THE ENEMY

"I saw a beam with ten nooses dangling from it. . . . They were going to hang us."
—RAF AIRMAN CAPTURED BY GERMAN CIVILIANS

THE MISSION SEEMED JINXED FROM THE VERY START. AS HE LINED UP HIS B-17 on the runaway at Knettishall Air Base, U.S. pilot Lieutenant Norman Kempton noticed one of the tires seemed low. He pulled aside to have it checked and lost his place in the formation. He had been rostered in the safest position—high element number three—but now when he came to take off he was back in low number two—"coffin corner." It was a short haul down the French coast to Bordeaux, but enemy fighters were in the air waiting for them as they arrived over the target. The flak was heavy, too, and Kempton immediately lost an engine to it. The waist gunner was hit by a bullet, and flak took out the tail. With fuel pouring from the wing tanks, bailing out was the only course of action. He ordered the crew out at eight thousand feet, and having satisfied himself they were all safely gone, he left the pilot's seat, dashed for the bomb bay, and somehow managed to find his way out. "The roar of the aircraft was suddenly gone. I seemed to be floating, spinning on my back in absolute quiet. Then the chute filled and I looked around to see the aircraft above me. It stalled and began spiraling down toward me. For one terrible instant I thought it was going to run me down, but it turned away and hit the ground a quarter of a mile away."[1] He landed in the middle of a swamp about five miles from the coast. He knew he was in a part of France occupied by the Germans and they would be hunting him. Quickly he splashed his way through the shallow water to the only piece of cover he could see, a small island half a mile away. "When I got there I picked a small patch of high grass and covered myself with reeds. Soon I heard voices and footsteps. They came within twenty feet of me and I caught a glimpse of two German soldiers. They had an American between them, who I think was my copilot. The three of them went off and I felt very lucky. Scared but lucky. I was determined they would not catch me."

And they didn't. Under darkness, Kempton headed south, navigating by the stars, following standing Eighth Air Force instructions to aim for neutral Spain. As dawn broke, he ran into a French farmer who recognized he was a downed airman and motioned to him with signs and gestures to hide himself. The Frenchman went away and returned an hour later with coffee and bread. "Nothing ever tasted so good!" Kempton recalled. The farmer took the American to his home and hid him for a day. He swapped his battledress for an ill-fitting suit, striped shirt, and a black beret. Then the farmer took him to a main road and left him at a bus stop. Kempton took the bus into Bordeaux, paying for his ticket with French currency from the escape and evasion kit all fliers were issued with before setting out on a mission. Alone in the middle of the city, unable to speak the language, the American pilot began walking south again. "I brushed shoulders with many German soldiers and sailors but they paid no attention to me because they thought I was French. I gave a wide berth to a large building with Nazi flags, military vehicles and automobiles and many German uniforms outside, which I assumed was the German headquarters." Eventually he found himself out in the countryside again. "So far, so good. I had been very lucky. I guess I must have really looked like a Frenchman with my black beret and black, worn, baggy coat. I began to think that maybe I really could make it into Spain, but I was still at least a hundred miles from the border and still in the densely occupied zone of France, within ten miles of the coast." As night fell, he knew he would have to find shelter. He chose a house at random and knocked on the door. The old woman who answered it slammed it in his face and he ran off. "I couldn't blame her for being afraid. If she was seen helping me, she could have been shot by the Germans. The worst that could happen to me was that I would be taken a prisoner of war, or so I thought. I hadn't realized that if I was caught in civilian clothes I could be shot as a spy." He took a chance at another house and this time was taken in, fed, and allowed to sleep. And so his journey continued, helped by friendly French farmers, dodging police and army patrols, until eventually he was passed into the hands of the Resistance.

A short stocky man in a leather coat came to pick me up in a car and drove me to a town called Montauban and I stayed in a farmhouse on the outskirts with a family by the name of LaPlace for four or five weeks. I could not speak a word of French, and they could not speak English, but somehow with sign language and a few common Latin-related words we communicated and got along. There was a little girl aged five who was studying English in school and would sometimes help her mother with a few basic words. Day after day I spent in an upstairs attic bedroom, always out of sight of the neighbors or anyone who might come to visit. Only at night, after dark, could I go outside and walk through the vineyards to get a little exercise. The LaPlace family treated me royally, even though they had so little for themselves. Food was hard to get. Most meals consisted of potatoes or onion soup with wine and, of course, dark, coarse bread, which was very tasty.

Finally, he left and was taken to another farm, where he was introduced to two other American airmen also on the run. The three of them were then taken by car south in the direction of the Spanish border. They traveled by train to the towns of Pau and Lourdes at the foot of the Pyrenees. Basque guides took them over the mountains, walking in single file through the night along narrow tracks, avoiding the German border patrols.

The last day before crossing into Spain, we walked during the day. We were high above the tree line near the top of the mountain walking in three feet of snow. Visibility was zero. We reached a clifflike ridge overlooking a deep valley. The guides pointed down the valley and said, "There is Spain." They could go no farther. "Good Luck! You're on your own." We worked our way down the ridge, spent the night in a shepherd's hut, and then followed a river valley downstream until we came to a road and a village. There we turned ourselves in to the Spanish police, who contacted the U.S. consul. That night we slept in a bed for the first time in about ten days. The next day we were taken by bus to Pamplona, where a man from the U.S. embassy took charge of us. Ten days later we were back with our units.

Kempton was luckier than he ever imagined. He was one of the very few downed Allied airmen to make it home during the war. Significantly, his experience had been in early 1944 and he had been shot down over France, where there was at least the chance of a friendly reception from some locals on the ground. As the year progressed and more and more missions were over Germany itself, the chances of a lost airman finding friends down below were remote. On the contrary, when they came face to face with the enemy, many found themselves in the middle of their greatest nightmare, among a hostile population wanting revenge for the attacks on their homeland. It was certainly so for Flight Sergeant Roy Shirley.[2] His Lancaster was hit over Cologne, but, amazingly, he was too caught up in a gun battle with German fighter planes to respond to the call to bail out. In the mid-upper turret, a Messerschmitt 109 had come so close it filled the space in front of his eyes as it raked the port wing. Then he swung his turret to get in a burst of gunfire at a Focke-Wulf 190 which was arrowing in from the other side. The skipper yelled for the crew to jump, but in the deafening noise inside the fuselage, Shirley didn't hear the order. It was only when a bullet from an enemy fighter shattered his gunsight and he dropped down from the turret that he realized what was happening. The inside of the plane was alight, smoke was swirling around the twisted spars and shredded wires. He saw the wireless operator, Pip Parratt, struggling toward him, yelling "Get out, get out. Everyone else has gone!" As the plane pitched crazily in its death throes, Parratt clawed at the door in the side of the fuselage, trying to wrench it open. Shirley grabbed the escape axe from the wall and just as he was aiming a blow, the door sprang open. The axe went spinning out into space and Parratt was just about to follow it when the plane went into a spin and the centrifugal force slammed the door shut again. They were trapped, flung to the floor and held there by the pressure of the twisting, turning aircraft as it headed for the ground. Shirley would recall a sensation of being detached from his body—of looking at himself and his comrade as if from a distance. "I could see two men lying in that stricken Lancaster and knew they weren't going to get out; they weren't going to make it." Then he blacked out.

The Lancaster spun down toward the railway marshaling yards that had been the target of the raid. Another crewman was drifting downward on his parachute and saw it strike the end of an ammunition train. The rear section of the plane sheared off, and the ensuing explosion blew it away. No one on board could possibly have survived, the parachutist thought. But he was wrong. Shirley came to, aware that he was lying on his back with heaps of railway debris hovering above his head—"like Hornby train models," as he described it. He was covered in blood and could not move. He found it hard to take in that he had fallen from eighteen thousand feet and survived. But for what? A ring of angry faces was staring down at him. He had heard the stories of kangaroo courts and lynchings of downed Allied airmen. Then, to his relief, he saw German soldiers stepping in to hold back the civilians, though how long they would be able to protect him and his fellow *Terrorflieger* from the mob, he did not know. To his surprise, a man stepped forward from the crowd, knelt down beside him, and said, in English, that he was a doctor. He had been a prisoner of the British on the western front in the First World War. He had been treated well. He was about to make sure that this English prisoner was dealt with properly, too. The doctor jammed a needle in Shirley's chest and he lapsed into nothingness. He awoke in hospital. Parratt was in another bed, and another patient whispered to him that he had been extremely lucky. One airman from the raid had been hanged from a lamp post. Germany was a risk-filled place for Allied bomber crews to be on the run.

The last items airmen were issued with before heading to the stands to board their planes were their escape and evasion kits. In the Eighth, it was the copilot who signed for them and hoped to return them afterward unused. Each was a masterpiece of miniaturization and ingenuity. The packet was small enough to be slipped into the pocket of a flying suit but contained, Walter Hughes recalled,

money, German or some other currency that was usable in the occupied areas, some high-density, nonperishable food cubes, morphine for pain control if wounded and Dexadrine, an antisleep stimulant which some crewmen who actually took it said stopped them sleeping for three days. There were also "escape pictures," photographs of each of us taken in a shirt and jacket of European design and manufacture. If we came down in France or other occupied countries, these would help the Resistance to fake documents for us. The kit, which was wrapped in watertight cloth and sealed, contained maps showing railroads, canals, and forests (for hiding). It did not show areas for crossing frontiers, but intelligence told us orally where they were. A simple compass was made in the form of two buttons. I sewed mine into the fly of the trousers I wore on every mission. Cut them off and place one on the other and you had your compass. In northern Germany, we were to go to a seaport and look for a non-German ship and try to stow away. In southern Germany, we were to try to get to a thin sliver of Switzerland sticking into Germany.

Despite the obvious dangers of being lost behind enemy lines, not all the men of Bomber Command and the Eighth Air Force fully grasped the need to prepare themselves to deal with the situation of finding themselves on the ground in enemy territory with nothing but the meager contents of those escape packs and their own resourcefulness to get them through. Nicky Knilans, an American pilot serving with the RAF, was a man who took war very seriously. He refused to have a seminaked woman painted on the side of his Lancaster bomber, U.S. style, because, as he explained to his crew, "flying into combat is not funny—it is a cold-blooded battle to kill or be killed."[3] Yet he gave scant attention to how he and his men would survive in enemy territory if they had to bail out. This was the fate of tens of thousands of airmen, but, surprisingly, most seemed to give it little thought in their preparation. When Knilans's commanding officer sent him and his crew out on an escape and evasion exercise in remote East Anglian countryside, they headed surreptitiously for the pub instead. It had begun seriously enough. "Our caps and money were taken away and we were put in a bus that had the windows papered over. After a long ride we were dropped off in groups of three. We were on the bank of a small canal and the flat countryside around us had no houses or buildings. I asked my navigator where we were, and he said that without his maps he was as lost as I was." They found a road, a car came along and the driver, a fellow pilot, gave them a lift to the White Horse, a pub they often frequented and where Knilans's credit was good enough for them to drink the day away and borrow their bus fare back to base from the barmaid. It was hardly a realistic lesson in staying alive when lost in a foreign country where you didn't speak the language and where steel-helmeted soldiers (or, worse still, SS troops) and angry civilians were hunting you down and not caring whether they brought you in dead or alive.

The attitude many men took to being shot down was exemplified by the crew at a briefing navigator Arthur White once attended. It had been a particularly somber occasion. The intelligence officer described the importance of the target and its heavy flak defenses. Crews were warned of fighter airfields close to their route, which took them near more heavily defended cities. The weather officer warned of severe icing conditions and ten-tenths cloud cover up to twenty thousand feet. There was a danger of fog closing down base before the crews returned. The CO ended the briefing by reemphasizing the dangers and warned of the risk of collisions in the air. Finally: "Any questions?" There was deadly silence, and then a little sergeant air gunner stood up. "About our escape kits, sir?" "Yes, sergeant." "Is there enough foreign currency in them for us to have a bloody good piss-up if we get shot down?'[4] To be fair, some took the training and lectures seriously, and Frank Haslam, a wireless operator, put the lessons to good use when his Lancaster was shot down. He remembered the tips about observing any farm or house from a hiding place before making any contact, and he eventually managed to make it back to Allied lines. He was debriefed by an intelligence officer who turned out to be the very man who had given him an escape and evasion lecture months before at his base at RAF Spilsby: "I told him that I had done just what he said and calmed myself down by performing a bodily function!"[5]

But too many airmen shrugged off the lectures from the intelligence staff about what to do if they were shot down. To take the matter too seriously felt like tempting fate. It was like when you were told that your identity tag—which was the only personal item an airman was supposed to take on an operation—was made out of asbestos so that if you burned to death you could still be identified. The thought was too awful to take in. Like so many others, Campbell Muirhead dismissed the very idea. "It couldn't happen to me," he told himself, "and if it did I'd be beyond caring anyway."[6] But he kept half an ear open as an instructor told them what was likely to happen if captured. What he heard was not tips on how to survive what would undoubtedly be a difficult and dangerous experience but a warning about conduct when in the hands of the enemy. Don't let the side down, was the message, or else. It was the LMF story all over again, as if they couldn't be trusted not to reveal all their secrets to the enemy.

We were told exactly how long we'd be kept in the Luftwaffe reception center before being transferred to a POW camp and what would happen there. They harped on and on about giving only name, rank, and number; absolutely nothing else. We were told that the first Luftwaffe officer to interrogate us would in all probability be a hectoring bully full of threats about what would happen if you refused to tell him anything more. He would be followed by a charming, polished Luftwaffe officer who, in apologizing for his colleague's loutish behavior, would offer cigarettes (Capstan usually—the Germans picked up tens of thousands of them at Dunkirk) and murmur that this really wasn't an interrogation or anything like that, just a personal chat between two operational flying men. He was, by far, the more dangerous of the two. He might suggest that, as an officer and a gentleman, if you'd give him your parole, he'd take you out for a drink. He'd maybe even add that he knew a couple of rather gorgeous girls who, their boyfriends or husbands being away at the front, were feeling rather frustrated. At this stage all humor departed from the intelligence officer's face, and his pace of delivery slowed to accentuate the gravity of his words. "If he does this," he intoned, "it's because you've told him *more* than just your name, rank, and number. You've told him enough to make him feel you're worth working on. And, be in no doubt about it, we back here will know about it. If you're at that center more than two weeks before being despatched to your POW camp, a little mark will go against your name and we'll want a word with you after the war."

Someone asked the inevitable question: "What if we're tortured?" The lecturer was emphatic that the Luftwaffe did not resort to such methods. But, he added, "if you get picked up by the Gestapo or the SS, well, that's a different matter." I felt like saying one would probably have little choice in the matter, that one could hardly say to the Gestapo or the SS, thanks all the same but I'd rather hold on until the Luftwaffe turn up.

In fact, the picture painted bore little relation to what was actually happening to some aircrew who dropped reluctantly into enemy hands, particularly in these closing months of the war. As the screw tightened on Germany, a retreating enemy was prepared to throw all conventions—Geneva included—to one side to stave off defeat or wreak revenge. The crews became aware of this increased threat to their lives by word of mouth. Ken Newman had been issued a revolver around the time of D-Day, a precaution in case things went wrong with the invasion and there was a counterattack on Britain. He should have turned it in when the danger was past, but he kept hold of his and always flew with it. He explained: "Aircrew shot down over Germany had been lynched by civilians before the German armed forces had been able to take them prisoner. I thought it was a good idea to have a revolver with me so that I would be able to defend myself."[7] Robert Wannop was over Cologne in what would turn out to be one of the last Bomber Command raids on that much put upon city. Its guns were still spitting defiance, and he found himself in flak as dense as he could ever remember. As they dropped their bombs and pulled away, shells raked the fuselage, and an engine caught fire.

> A knot of fear hit my guts. I heard myself muttering prayers that we wouldn't have to bail out near the target, for we had only recently been warned about the fate of shot-down aircrew. The Germans had received such a mauling from the air that civilians were taking matters into their own hands. Captured aircrew were being unceremoniously lynched from the nearest lamppost or tree. We were advised, if possible, to surrender to the army or police. They, at least, were reported to be honoring the conditions of the Geneva Convention.[8]

To Wannop's relief, the fire blew itself out and he limped back home, calling in Mustang escorts to protect his back from any marauding German fighters. Others, though, took their chances as fugitives in a hostile land. U.S. navigator Jack Edwards was one such unfortunate. He had survived twenty-five missions when his luck deserted him. It was late September 1944 and he was in a B-17 leading a raid on the notorious oil plant at Merseburg when flak caught them twice in the nose, then in the wings, waist, and tail. But that wasn't what downed them. The ship powered away after they had unloaded their bombs, only for a B-17 on their wing to take a direct hit and veer out of control into them.

> We immediately went into a spin. I was thrown from the navigator's desk clear into the Plexiglas nose where I was pinned by the centrifugal force of the spin and unable to move. The skipper brought us out of the spin, but he could do nothing about the dive. I scrambled to the escape hatch,

helped the engineer kick out the door, which was difficult to do against the slipstream, and then tumbled headfirst out. My chest parachute was held on with only one strap and I struggled to fasten the other one to the harness. It took me three goes before I managed it, and I was at 3,000 feet, having free-fallen 17,000 feet before I pulled the rip cord. Then a strong wind pulled at the chute and eventually dumped me in the side of a large coal pile in the yard of our target, the oil plant. I looked up and could see our own bombs falling on me! I lay flat on the ground and just hoped they would miss. When there was a lull I dived underneath a coal truck as the next wave of B-17s came in and dropped their loads. When the raid was over, the Germans emerged from their shelters and began to clear up. By now I had teamed up with another American airman who had come down in the same spot, and we both lay hidden. We wondered whether we had any chance of getting away. We looked at our escape maps and realized we were more than two hundred miles from the nearest neutral country or Allied lines. The only escape for us would be to walk back to France.

That night we crawled away from the plant on our hands and knees. We slipped past gun emplacements unnoticed and made our way out into the countryside. We finally found a haystack, crawled under it, and went to sleep. It was pretty cold, and I woke up shivering. We lay up during the day and walked at night. We tried the roads, but there were too many Germans about, so we stuck to fields. For food we took grapes from vineyards we found. We drank water from a river. Then we hid under bushes in what we thought was a little forest but turned out, when we woke, to be the park of a little town. Some soldiers out walking with their fräuleins spotted us and we were captured and sent to a POW camp.[9]

Falling into the hands of the German military was always preferable. When Al Arenowitz bailed out on the wrong side of the Rhine in March 1945, he fell straight into trouble. "I landed in the middle of a clump of trees in a meadow. As I hit the ground the wind pulled my chute back and knocked me over. Then I heard a sound behind me: 'Hände hoch!' I turned around and saw a man in a Home Guard uniform pointing a rifle at me."[10] Arenowitz was not tempted to resist. As he had floated down he had sensed the danger below and decided to get rid of the pistol he was carrying in his holster. "Somehow my gut feeling was that I might be better off without that .45. I was afraid having it might encourage somebody to take more drastic action than if I didn't. It's not an accurate gun anyway, unless you are real close to a person." He put his hands up and surrendered. "Then two young fellows from the Luftwaffe arrived on motorcycles, put me in a sidecar, and drove me off. They stopped at one point and one asked the other: 'Is this the place?' This scared the hell out of me. I thought they had brought me to this spot to execute me. But they were just lost and were wondering which way to go. Eventually they got me to their antiaircraft battery, boasting that they had shot me down from here, which may well have been the case. I was interrogated but stuck religiously to my name, rank, and serial number. I refused to tell them anything more, and they didn't force the issue. I was then taken to a Luftwaffe base near Dortmund and eventually to a prison camp."

Edwards and Arenowitz suffered the fate of tens of thousands of American and British airmen, a spell behind barbed wire and days of anxiety and uncertainty before they were free. But at least they had managed to avoid any nasty confrontations with the locals. Others were not so lucky.

On the night of 14 March 1945, a force of just over 250 Lancasters and Mosquitoes left for an attack on what, surprisingly at this stage of the war, was a new target for Bomber Command. The Americans had made regular runs to the synthetic oil refinery at Lutzkendorf near Leipzig in the far east of the now rapidly diminishing Third Reich, but the RAF had not had it on its list of targets until now. To an experienced pilot like John Wynne, it did not seem an operation much out of the ordinary, though it was a long way—nine hours there and back—"and most of it over enemy territory, and the longer you were over their territory, the longer they had to have a poke at you."[11] With a full tour behind him, carried out in the Middle East, and a period as an instructor, he had come back to frontline duties with 214 Squadron. To his disappointment, it was not frontline enough. "We weren't a bomber squadron. We flew B-17 Fortresses loaded with jamming equipment to disrupt the enemy's radio and radar. Generally it was a very safe job. We accompanied the main force, and while they attacked we flew up and down high over the target, corkscrewing the whole way if we wanted to, and that was it." He would have preferred to be bombing, had begged his station commander for the chance, but had been refused. So here he was, as he saw it, in a milk-run job. It was soon to go sour on him.

Operating the extrapowerful radio transmitters in Wynne's B-17 was Tom Tate, an experienced radio operator. He was another airman with a full tour and a period of instructing behind him. He had volunteered for this work after two years away from the front line because he thought he might otherwise find himself being sent to the Far East. "I didn't want to be operating against the Japanese in the Pacific. I knew terrible things had been happening to the prisoners of war there. When I heard that John Wynne was putting together a crew, I volunteered my services. I thought it would be the lesser of two evils."[12] He had last flown regular combat operations during the terrible raids of 1942, when a man counted himself lucky if his number of sorties got into double figures. He had never expected to get through the war alive; he had even told his wife not to expect him to return. But he had made it through that earlier tour by some miracle, and his new job, while not completely out of the firing line, felt safe enough.

I was now twenty-six, an old man compared with most of the youngsters, more experienced, more confident. There were still dreadful losses, but I wasn't really thinking in terms of being shot down as I had been back in 1942. Now we were daring ourselves to think about the end of the war. The squadron was having little talks, politics were being discussed, what sort of world we wanted when the war was over, that sort of thing. I wasn't a political person, but I discovered a lot of my friends were taking the socialist line. We talked about how things were going to be better for everyone when it was all over. But I had my doubts that the war was going to end that quickly. The German army was definitely weakening, but I believed the civilians would never capitulate. The elderly men and the young boys were still under the commanding influence of Hitler, and they were putting up the fiercest resistance.

Wynne flew the Fortress in circles above the main force as they came in on their runs to bomb the Lutzkendorf refinery. After hearing reports on the radio of enemy fighters in the area, he slipped down low, braving the light flak that was coming up from the ground. He could see the fuel tanks of the refinery on fire and was content to stay around as long as he could to help the bombers inflict even more damage. "We knew that the quicker we could demolish the enemy's oil production, the quicker the war was going to come to an end." But the damage was both ways that night. Eighteen Lancasters were lost, a casualty rate that compared with some of Bomber Command's worst nights. Wynne saw two aircraft go down as he headed home, one of the last aircraft to leave the target area.

I was sure I had got past the danger zone when suddenly the aircraft was hit by a single shell. There was a metallic bang, followed a second later by a flash. I couldn't work out what had happened. The sequence was wrong—normally there would be a flash and then a bang or a flash and a bang together. I came to the conclusion that I'd been shot at by a fighter underneath us and my immediate reaction was to fly the bastard into the ground. So I took her round in a series of low-level corkscrews, expecting to see an explosion as the enemy fighter hit the ground. But there was nothing, and so I decided it couldn't have been a fighter after all.[13] We then did a battle damage check and discovered holes in the bomb bay from shell fragments. That was no problem, nothing to stop us getting home. We flew along merrily homeward, across the middle of Germany and then, when we were about fifty miles east of the Rhine, east of the Allied lines, the number two engine caught fire and we couldn't put it out.

And so began one of the most extraordinary individual incidents of the bomber war, one that encapsulated all the dangers that aircrews faced at this confused tail-end period of the fighting, when the finish of it all at last seemed a tempting possibility but when there was clearly so much more to endure before it really was over. Here was an experienced crew who had been at war for years, now looking out and seeing the engine going up in flames and with it their hopes of surviving intact. The fate they had lived with for so long and pushed out of their minds on operation after operation had finally caught up with them. Wynne said nothing to the crew. The gunners and the engineer could all see the flames and make their own assessment. If an enemy night fighter was in the area and making a beeline for this vulnerable light in the sky, they would not need telling that it was their job to get him before he got them. As pilot, he simply flew on, hoping to reach Allied territory before ordering everyone to bail out. But where was safety? Where was the Rhine, along whose western banks the Allied armies were lining up for the assault on the German heartland? "We're crossing it now, Skipper," the navigator, Dudley Heal, told Wynne.

Wynne ordered the crew to don parachutes, open all hatches and prepare to jump. Down in the belly of the aircraft with his radio transmitters, Tom Tate had heard the flak rattling the plane but, with no window to look through, had no idea there was a serious problem. "I was blissfully unaware, thinking that we were happily on our way home. Then I heard the words I had always dreaded, that had always sat fearfully at the back of my mind—'The engine's on fire. Prepare to bail out.' I stood by ready to put on my parachute and go straight through the hatch." Wynne hung on, waiting until the last possible moment to give the order to abandon ship. He decided to keep flying for another five minutes if he could, getting as much Allied-held land under them as possible. It was a risk. He knew that every minute the fire was eating its way through the protective wall behind the engine cowling, edging toward the fuel lines in the wing and into the wheel bay. He was gambling, literally playing with fire against their very lives. "Then the whole aircraft began shaking so that I couldn't read my instruments. Small fittings were breaking off and falling. There was no point in keeping nine men on board when we were only fifteen hundred feet aboveground and the wings were about to explode. I ordered the crew to jump. It was an orderly abandonment. They went out one at a time. There was no panic."

Here the story takes two directions. For now we will leave the other nine men in the crew slipping out of their burning Fortress as it flew low over the European countryside and stay with John Wynne. He did not jump.

I was still responsible for the airplane. We were on a heading for an emergency airfield at Rheims in eastern France and I thought I might try and get there. I was on my own and so I tried to think like the pilot of a single-seater aircraft. Surely a Spitfire pilot wouldn't bail out just because of engine trouble. The crew had to go because their safety was my first concern. But now they were gone and I was on my own, I could still try and get the aircraft back—and if things did go wrong I still had time to get myself out. I flew on quite happily for the next forty minutes, sticking at fifteen hundred feet because I couldn't get the aircraft to climb. I was on the course the navigator had given me for Rheims and I was sure I would get there eventually. I tried radioing to ask them to light the runway but I couldn't raise anybody.

Wynne was a vastly experienced pilot, a man who studied flying skills when other pilots preferred to party. He was at the peak of his performance and, having survived as an airman since the very beginning of the war, he was not going to give in easily with the end so near. Yet what he was now attempting would test his skills and his nerve to the limit.

The engine was still on fire and I considered what would happen if the propeller fell off. Would it come winging in through the fuselage and take my legs off? And what if the engine mounting broke loose and the whole bloody lot fell off? I was well aware that if and when I bailed out I would have to go fast, because this aeroplane wasn't going to fly in a straight line for very long. I was still getting no response on the radio. I assumed everyone at the other end had buggered off to bed, leaving me out there on my own. Typical bloody incompetence! Eventually I told myself this was all plain silly and the best thing I could do was jump like the others had done and walk home. And that's what I set about doing.

He set the trim of the aircraft as best as he could, leaving it to fly itself on a level course, jumped down from the pilot's seat, and headed down the narrow steps toward the escape hatch. Something jolted him to a halt. The tube of his oxygen mask was trapped under the straps of his parachute and tying him to the seat. He was stuck. In the dark he couldn't even see to turn round to unhitch himself. In those vital seconds, the aircraft had lost its trim and begun to nose downward. As it picked up speed and went into a full dive, he realized he would have to take off his parachute, unhook himself from the oxygen supply, then put his parachute back on again. It would all take too long, fumbling helplessly in the dark as the plane angled downward at terminal speed. There was no way he was going to get out in time.

"Now I was scared. I'd been really scared once before, lost over the Mediterranean after being struck by lightning at night in total blackness. But not scared witless, not frozen with fear. You know you have a problem and you have to get a grip of it quickly. Your sense of self-preservation tells you that this is going wrong but I can still do something about it." That something was to regain control of the plummeting plane. He forced his way back up the steps into the cockpit and, still standing, grabbed the controls and righted the aeroplane. Now what to do? His first thought was to try and gain enough height to give himself another chance to bail out. Squirming in that tight, dark space, he took off his shoes and undid his clothing so he could unhook himself from the tangle of his oxygen tube. Once he was free he chose not to sit down:

I didn't get back in my seat. I reckoned that, if the wing caught fire, I could get out much more quickly if I was standing. So there I was standing in the middle of the cockpit, with a hand on either control, and I flew like that for thirty minutes. Was I mad? Only an idiot would try to fly an airplane at night, standing up and on three engines with the fourth effectively in reverse!

The aircraft was still vibrating, but at some point the connecting rod from the propeller finally disintegrated and the shaking stopped. The fire also went out. Suddenly I was in a plane that was running on three engines but was safe. That's when I made the decision not to bail out after all. I still couldn't raise Rheims on the radio, so I thought I had better head for somewhere I knew there would be help—and England was the only place I could think of. But to do that I would need to plot a new course and that meant I needed maps. I trimmed the aircraft and left her to fly on her own as I dashed down the steps from the flight deck, across the still-open escape hatch to the navigator's compartment up in the Fortress's nose. I grabbed whatever was on the table and rushed back to my seat. I went pretty fast, nervous about leaving the controls, but, in my haste, I missed some of the things I needed and I had to make that desperate journey three times before I had the log and the right charts. At one point I was clutching this heap of papers to my chest as I ran and my parachute snagged on something. The bloody thing opened in front of me and fell in a heap. I just undid the harness and threw it off. I told myself I didn't need a parachute any more. I'd made my decision. I was going to land this plane in England and that was it.

I jumped back in my seat, put all this stuff on the engineer's seat and went though it, working out the route home. At one point the engine caught fire again for about ten minutes but it was just some oil getting onto a bit of hot metal somewhere. It didn't come to much, only a flickering of flame, and then it went out. I was relieved. I had no parachute and there was no way I would be able to get out if the flames had spread.

Wynne continued with his solo odyssey, coaxing along the plane that usually had a ten-man crew. He was his own copilot, peering ahead for landmarks, his own navigator as he struggled with the maps, his own wireless operator as he tried to contact airfields in his path.

At one moment I seemed to be flying over the sea and then over the land and then over the sea again. It was all very mysterious. Then I realized it was fog forming below me, which was a good thing, because that meant there was virtually no wind, so I wasn't drifting, I was on course. Then eventually we went over the gray of the sea and there was no more land and then quite a time later I could see a shoreline with waves breaking along it. It was the south coast of England. There was Beachy Head sticking out, glowing a dull gray in the night. It was a tremendous feeling. I could see a little red beacon winking away, which indicated an airfield within five to ten miles. I flew there and fired off flares with the colors of the day but there was no response. So I just kept going on my heading to home. Somewhere up along that line I knew I was going to come to a whole heap of airfields. And then, to one side of me, a searchlight came on and I flew to it and through the beam, showing them who and what I was. The searchlight pointed the direction for me, waved me in the direction of safety. It guided me over London, and then I headed due north, picked up RAF Oakington in Cambridgeshire on the radio and asked for permission to land. In fact I came down at Bassingbourn, which was an American base ten miles from Oakington, but I didn't realize this straightaway. Just as I came to a halt on the runway, the propeller fell off and cartwheeled through the navigator's compartment of the airplane, making a handsome hole.

At the end of his ordeal, after so calmly and efficiently handling problem after problem, Wynne suddenly lost his composure. He called the tower to say he was stuck on the runway and could not move but there was no reply. His mind went into overdrive. Where was he?

For some reason I thought I must have landed in Germany after all. A truck came out with a couple of chaps with tin hats on and I thought they were bloody Krauts! And that meant there was only one thing I could do.

We had a little demolition bomb to blow up the aircraft so that it would not fall into enemy hands, and I was holding this in one hand and my loaded pistol in the other hand as I jumped out, walked over to the vehicle, stuck the gun in the driver's face, and demanded to know where I was. "Bassingbourn," he replied. The penny dropped when I saw the white star painted on the front of his jeep. I really had made it. They took me to the mess and I had the best breakfast of my life. This American chap said, "How do you like your eggs, sir, sunny side up or easy over?" and he had to explain what he meant. Anyway, I had it all—bacon, muffins, pancakes, syrup, out of this bloody world.

Back at his squadron the next day, Wynne reported that his crew had bailed out over Allied territory and that he had brought the aircraft back on his own. He presumed his men were safe.

I was sent on leave while I waited for my crew to turn up. I was at my parents' home when I got a telephone call. They had back-plotted the navigator's log and realized that the crew had not jumped out into France as we thought. They were in Germany. It was a real shock. There I was thinking the buggers were running around somewhere in France, probably enjoying themselves in a farmhouse, when they were in enemy territory after all. I couldn't believe it.

The navigator of Wynne's Fortress had been wrong, though it was hardly surprising. Two hundred miles of low flying and constant corkscrewing back from Lutzkendorf in a crippled plane and in a wind of unknown force had thrown off his calculations. They had not passed the Rhine as he thought. As the crew bailed out, thinking they were about to drift down to safety behind their own lines, they were in fact still east of the river. They were about to land in very dangerous country.[14] Tom Tate, sitting in the belly of the B-17, remembered the order to jump.

I looked at Gordon Hall, my fellow wireless operator, and saw the state of despair on his face. But a sense of self-survival takes over and you do whatever is necessary to save your life. There was no time to think shall I or shan't I, or do I have to? The gunners had taken the escape hatch off the side of the aircraft and I just had to dive through. I shook Gordon's hand and off he went. I wished I had said something to him as he jumped. I could have said, "Good luck, all the best, see you in prison camp," something cheering like that. But I just shook his hand, didn't really look at him. I wish I had said something because he didn't survive. I moved to the escape hatch and just toppled out. I had my hand on the parachute D-ring but I don't remember those few moments of free fall. It was oblivion as far as I was concerned. I just felt the tug when the canopy opened and then I was floating down in dead silence. It was a dark night, no moon. I looked up and saw the aircraft disappearing. Naturally I thought everyone had got out. I had no idea that John Wynne was still up there, flying it home.

Tate hit the ground with a rush but picked himself up and waited in the darkness, considering his position. He was pretty confident he had fallen on the right side of the Rhine, that he was in friendly territory, a feeling that was endorsed when he heard an English voice nearby. But it was just one of his own gunners. Together they hid their parachutes under a bridge and then started walking in what they believed to be a westerly direction. Then "we came to a cemetery, and I flicked on my cigarette lighter to look at the names on the gravestones—and they were all German. We were not in France after all. But we just had to accept it. We could do nothing about it. But it was a huge disappointment." They trudged on and, in the dark, stumbled into a village. Perhaps they should have skirted it but Tate told his companion: "Let's go through the middle. It's past midnight, the place is in complete darkness, everybody is in bed sound asleep." It was a mistake.

We started creeping through and then we were surrounded by lots of men. We were captured, taken to the village hall. It was dimly lit and there were many people in there. I thought it best to try and establish friendly relations and I asked for a glass of water, in German, "*Eine glasse wasser, bitte.*" And they brought me one. After an hour or so, some official-looking people came by and asked me questions. I replied with just my name and number, the usual routine. Then I was taken outside, leaving Bradley, one of our gunners, behind, and I was taken to a town called Bühl. We traveled through the night by horse and cart, and on the way I saw the deplorable state of the German defenses. They had nothing but horses and carts to supply the front line, nothing more than that. I didn't feel scared. I had survived the trauma of bailing out, and all I could now do was submit to whatever was going to happen to me. I suppose I thought they might kill me, but there was nothing I could do about it. I remembered being scared back in 1942 when I was a new recruit, but here was my worst nightmare coming true and all I could do was go along with it. I don't think bravery came into it at all. I was just there and I had to accept the inevitable.

At Bühl, I was taken to a headquarters building where I was interrogated by civilians over several days. When I was being questioned, Dudley Heal, our navigator, was brought in. We had been briefed never to acknowledge fellow crew members. Poor old Dudley. He looked shocked, in a terrible state. I said I didn't know him and they took him away. Finally they took me to the prison in the town. My escorts knocked on the front door and it was opened by a woman jailer who grabbed my hair and began pulling it out. I was terrified. She was vicious, shouting at me that I was the enemy. I thought she was going to kill me. I presumed that at sometime or other she must have been bombed and had suffered and was now getting her own back. Eventually I was put into a cellar and there were six others from my crew there. But this was no jolly reunion. We were all tired and depressed and probably in shock. Eventually a conversation got going. The wife of one of the crew was about to have a baby back in England and he was worried for her, so we talked a lot about that. It was strange talking about the birth of a baby in those circumstances. I suppose we were concentrating on something other than our own dreadful predicament. The cellar was foul. There were no facilities and we had to use one corner as a toilet. The smell was awful.

The next afternoon five armed guards arrived and they took us out on the road at gunpoint and they thumbed a lift for the twelve of us. Things were so bad in Germany it was their only means of getting around. It was comical, all of us waiting by the side of a road. Finally a lorry stopped and we got in. Some were inside the cabin, the rest of us sitting on the back with a couple of guards. Driving along, everything seemed fine, so normal, as if life was just carrying on as usual. There was no sense of being in danger, nothing to concern us. We passed through a few villages. And then, after twenty miles or so we came to Pforzheim. . . .

What the seven airmen did not know was that four weeks earlier, this medieval town on the edge of the Black Forest had been hit hard in one of the most punishing Bomber Command air raids of the entire war. It had been a repeat of Dresden. Just as Dresden had stood in the way of the advancing Soviet Red Army in the east, so Pforzheim was ahead of the American ground forces poised to strike into Germany from the west. It had railway connections and industries that had once been geared to luxuries—it was known for its jewelery—but now turned out precision war instruments and materials. More than 360 Lancasters had pounded it one Friday night ten days after Dresden, dropping close on two thousand tons of bombs in twenty-two minutes, setting off a firestorm and killing between 17,000 and 20,000 people, a quarter of the population. Barely a fifth of the town's buildings were still standing after the Lancasters left. The rest was a wreck, as Tate and the others who had bailed out from John Wynne's B-17 could see only too well when the lorry dropped them on the city's outskirts the following month. Pforzheim lay in a valley with hills an either side, and Tate recalled standing on the crest and looking down and seeing nothing but a great void.

I had never seen anything like this. I had seen the damage in London where the docks had been destroyed, and in Sheffield, too, but never a whole city in ruins. The shock was tremendous. Our escorts walked us down a hill toward what had been the center. The main roads had been cleared and there were narrow paths between the rubble on each side. There was no traffic whatsoever, but lots of people about, and when they recognized our blue RAF uniforms they started bombarding us with anything they could lay their hands on. I didn't blame them. The utter devastation was awful to see. Afterward, I still thought that there was a good reason for what Bomber Command had done, and Pforzheim was a legitimate target. But there is a difference between talking about targets and then seeing the reality of what it was like on the ground. This was complete desolation. This was the awesome power of the Lancaster bomber.

Strangely, I didn't think those people in the middle of Pforzheim were going to kill us. They were beaten as people, and when they threw rocks and stones at us it was more an act of defiance. But the guards did well to shelter us. They spread out with their rifles ready and we finally got to the far side of the city. Then we climbed the hills out of the city until we came to a village called Huchenfeld.

This was where they had been heading. Just outside the village was a small Luftwaffe airfield which was where all Allied airmen captured in this area of Germany were initially brought to be registered and interrogated before being taken on to a main camp for prisoners of war on the outskirts of Stuttgart. But that night, 17 March 1945, the village was thronging with people who had been bombed out of Pforzheim, and their feelings were being inflamed by members of the Hitler Youth under the direction of the local Nazi Party leader.

The seven prisoners were locked in the basement of the village school with one of the five men who had brought them from Bühl as sentry. Tate recalled:

We were brought pails of water and I took my flying boots off, washed my socks, and hung them up to dry and lay down on my coat and within moments I was sound asleep. The other fellows did the same. We didn't talk; there was nothing to say. The next thing I remember was being hauled off that coat and dragged up the iron staircase out of the cellar. I didn't even have time to put my boots back on. The sentry had been pushed to one side and held back behind the door so he couldn't interfere. Lots of people were milling around and there were more of them when we got out onto the street. Three men were holding me. Were they men or were they boys? I don't really know. All I remember clearly is being forced down the road with the others. I was half asleep and I thought to myself, "What an earth is going on now?" and then someone hit me across the head and cut it open. And that was when the truth dawned— this was a lynching. They assumed we had taken part in the destruction of Pforzheim, though in fact we had had nothing to do with that operation. They seemed determined to get every one of us.

A few yards down the road, we turned off the main street and I found myself facing the church. To the left of it was a big barn. Its main doors were shut but there was a small door in the middle that had been left open, and through it I could see inside. A single bulb was burning, and from its light I saw a massive beam with ten ropes and nooses dangling from it. I realized instantly that they were going to hang us. That glimpse saved my life. I would have gone passively into that barn if I had not been forewarned what they had in store for me. Knowing that this was my only chance, I burst away and ran like mad, even though I was in bare feet. One of my crew saw me go, and he put his head down like a rugby player and ran, too. Someone fired a shot. For a moment I hesitated. Perhaps I had better give myself up. But then I remembered the ropes and the nooses. I darted right, between houses and across fields until I came to the forest. I dug myself into the mounds of dead oak leaves on the ground and waited. In the distance I heard a long burst of automatic gunfire. I could hear people searching for me but they didn't come very close. Finally I fell asleep. When I woke in the morning, I just kept walking to get as far away from Huchenfeld as I could.

Later that day, Tate, having put as much distance as he could between himself and the village, came upon a group of German soldiers. He decided to surrender. At least he would be in military hands and could expect to be treated correctly. His gamble paid off. "I was taken down into an underground bunker where an elderly officer was sitting at a table. He invited me to sit down and listened to my story. He was a friendly man who had been to Oxford. He had my feet attended to, gave me some bread and water and told me to fall in with his troops. I was then marched to their barracks, about half an hour's walk away." While he was being held there a woman brought some shoes for him. They had belonged to her husband, a soldier who had been killed in the fighting. Tate could only wonder at the different sides of human nature he was encountering. One group of Germans wanted to murder him; now here was one who went out of her way to help even though she had as much reason to hate him as the others had. He saw these Janus faces again when he was taken from the barracks to the railway station.

Escorts sat on each side of me. One was a senior NCO, armed with a pistol, the other man had a rifle. We had been waiting about an hour when a dozen men came in and began talking among themselves. I realized they had come for me. My life was being threatened again. The senior NCO took off his cap and put it on my head, either to try and disguise me or to make it clear I was one of them. Then an army officer arrived and he confronted the crowd. He stood up in front of them and told them I was a prisoner of war and that I was protected by the Geneva Convention. Just then the train came in and I was hustled on board. My escort stood at the windows with their guns in their hands until we had left the platform behind and were on our way. The NCO gave me some schnapps and some bread. I asked him what had happened to my friends and he said: "Your comrades are safe." Eventually I arrived unharmed at a POW camp.

Later he would discover that the German NCO had lied, perhaps too ashamed to tell his prisoners the truth. The mob who had arrived at the station had come with blood on their hands and were thirsting for more. Tate was one of three who ran from Huchenfeld when they realized they were about to be lynched. One of the others, Jimmy Vinall, the flight engineer, had been recaptured the next day in another village. He was held in the police station, but then a mob of Hitler Youth came for him, dragged him outside, and beat him up. Then a fifteen-year-old boy, half crazy with grief and anger, was given a gun. Just weeks ago he had dug through the rubble of Pforzheim and found his mother's crushed body and those of five brothers and sisters. Egged on by the others, the distraught boy shot Vinall in the head. Hearing of Tate's capture, the mob had then made their way to where he was being held and would have murdered him at the station if his guards had not stood their ground. The other four who had failed to get away at Huchenfeld were dead, too. In the chaos after Tate's escape, the plan to hang them had been abandoned. They were gunned down in the churchyard. That was the firing Tate had heard as he hid out in the forest. The bodies were left lying there overnight, their eyes still open, as one witness recalled. The congregation stepped round them as they arrived for Sunday service the next day.

Back in England, all these events passed John Wynne by. A pilot without a crew, he spent some time instructing, then went back into action with a new team. As soon as the war was over, he geared up to join the Tiger Force to go to the Far East and fight the Japanese. "I was too busy to find out what had happened to my lost crew. I assumed they were POWs and would come back when the war was over." He would not learn the truth—as we will see later—for nigh on half a century.

Allied airmen men continued to fall into enemy hands until the very last days of the war, their survival on the ground as much a matter of pure chance as it was in the air. Radio operator Paul Krup of the 398th Bomb Group was on his way to bomb an airfield and army base near Berlin on 10 April 1945 when they were attacked by a German jet fighter.

His cannon shells opened a hole big enough to drive a truck through. Our waist gunner's left leg and arm were blown off. The ship went into a dive. The walls caved in, the floor gave. I thought "This is it" and started to pray. Then the plane leveled off and I got up and found my chute and put it on. I tried to find a spare chute for our wounded waist gunner, who was lying there unable to move. He saw me and waved me away to bail out, which I did, and none too soon, because the ship exploded about a moment later.[15]

Krup's luck held when he hit the ground, too, because a German army patrol got to him before a crowd of angry civilians. "This Wehrmacht lieutenant chased them away. He took me to a first-aid station where my face was bandaged." He was taken away to a POW camp, where his stay proved to be very short. The end really was in sight now.

FINISHING THE JOB

"We would be famous. We would be the men who killed Adolf Hitler."
—WIRELESS OPERATOR ON THE BERCHTESGADEN RAID

AS BRITISH AND AMERICAN TROOPS POURED ACROSS THE RHINE IN THE last week of March 1945, Germany's defeat was only a matter of time. But how much time? No one could tell how stiff the resistance would be, though American pilot Walter Hughes had an inkling. He flew his B-24 low over the Rhine to parachute-drop supplies to Allied soldiers in the front line and had been cheered by the sight of the massive flotilla of landing craft ferrying tanks, trucks, and troops across the river. But on the other side, he saw how hard the Germans were fighting for their homeland. "We saw parachutists caught in the trees, hanging dead in their harnesses, gliders, C-47 transport planes, and even a B-24 crashed and burning. Individuals were shooting up at us from the ground. When we got home, the ship had holes from pistols and rifles."[1] If these really were the final days, they were not going to be easy.

Hitler promised a "slash and burn" defense of the Reich, town by town, street by street. His mechanism of state control—fear, engendered by the Gestapo, the SS, and the Nazi Party—was still intact, and the people would be made to fight whether they wanted to or not. On the Allied side there was a determination not to show mercy. In 1918, the German people had been left feeling cheated rather than defeated, and out of that resentment had come a new and even more virulent militarism. This time they had to be crushed so they would never countenance being a threat to world peace again. The stage was set for a bloody end to the war.

There was still no certainty of when that end would come. General Eisenhower, the Allied military commander, dreaded Hitler retreating into a Last Redoubt, an issue that began to dominate Allied thinking more and more in the spring of 1945. Intelligence experts dismissed the idea—they could find no evidence of a stronghold being built in the mountains in Bavaria or of Nazi forces and arms being directed there. But the SHAEF leader and his two most influential generals, Omar Bradley and Bedell Smith, sensed danger. Bradley spoke of as many as twenty SS divisions holing up there, supplied by underground factories and defended by aircraft in hidden hangars. The diehards could hold out for a year, was his pessimistic forecast, and the war might not be over until 1946. This, then, was clearly no time to pull off the troops and ground the bombers. As Sir Archibald Sinclair, the secretary of state for air, told the House of Commons, "We shall not make the mistake of supposing that Germany is defeated before the cease-fire sounds."[2] On the contrary, this was the moment to go in for the kill and finish off a still-dangerous enemy once and for all.

How dangerous had been demonstrated to the Allied airmen one terrible night in early March. From numerous airfields in eastern England, more than 750 Lancasters, Halifaxes, and Mosquitoes had taken off in the evening for a whole variety of different operations typical of this late stage of the war. A large group went to bomb a synthetic oil refinery at Kamen near Dortmund and another to demolish an aqueduct on a vital canal link in the Ruhr. A posse of fast-flying Mosquitoes raided Berlin, a regular occurrence now, while a small force of Lancasters laid mines around Germany's North Sea coastline. Close on a hundred training aircraft were sent out on a diversionary sweep across Germany to pull enemy fighters away from the main targets. But the Luftwaffe night fighters were playing a deadly game of their own that night. Around two hundred Junkers-88 fighter-bombers deliberately abandoned their homeland to the British bombers and flew low over the North Sea, underneath the radar, to England. There they lurked in the dark skies between the Thames estuary and the North Yorkshire moors, crept into the returning streams of bombers as they prepared to land at their airfields and caused havoc. Between 12:20 A.M. and 2:20 A.M., twenty-four Bomber Command aircraft were shot down and ninety-seven men killed.

Experienced bomber pilots were always aware of their vulnerability when circling to land and "in the funnel," on the final glide path in. But some crews would still have been relaxing after their uneventful flights to Germany, the navigators stowing away their maps, the gunners, weary after hours without moving, stretching their arms and legs, perhaps even standing down and leaving their turrets, anxious to get to the door and breathe in some good clean air after hours in the fetid fuselage. The German fighter pilots could not believe their luck as the British bombers, their navigation lights on, presented themselves as the easiest of targets. The bomber crews were taken completely by surprise. Oberleutnant Walter Brieglib recalled stalking a Lancaster from beneath, then pulling the trigger on his upward-pointing *Schräge Musik* guns to fire into the plane's belly. Twice they jammed, but he still had time to pull back, come up directly behind his still-unsuspecting quarry, and shoot her down with his nose cannons.[3]

Bob Nelson of 207 Squadron was dropping into RAF Spilsby in Lincolnshire when his rear gunner reported a mysterious aircraft behind. Nelson had already been given permission to land, but he decided not to take the risk, piled on the power, and overshot. The Junkers on his tail showered the runway with small antipersonnel bombs. Nelson was appalled by how long the airfield lights stayed on after this, illuminating more potential targets, before someone on the ground grasped that they were under attack and switched them off. The alert went out on the radio and incoming planes hurriedly diverted. The now blacked-out airfields flashed the Morse letter R for "raiders" into the skies. "We made ourselves scarce," Nelson said. "We went out over the Wash, where we were immediately fired on by our own antiaircraft guns—and hit! Eventually we were diverted to an airfield in Leicestershire."[4] Running out of aircraft to attack, one German pilot recalled machine-gunning a car, a train, and then firing the last of his ammunition into a warehouse in the seaside town of Scarborough before buzzing a convoy of merchant ships in the North Sea and heading home.[5]

Saddest of all that night was the number of novice crews wiped out. Pilot Officer Arthur Thomas and Flying Officer Nicholas Ansdell had arrived at RAF Wickenby with their crews just three days before, straight from training. They were returning from a night-flying exercise when the enemy fighters caught them. Freda Barty, a Land Army girl, heard gunfire and looked out of the window of the farmhouse where she was staying. "This plane was a mass of flames as it flew past. Then we heard an explosion as it hit the ground. We all ran up the hill to see if there was anything we could do, but the wreckage was ablaze and ammunition was going off and we couldn't get near. Then the German plane came back and flew low over us with machine guns blazing. We all dived for cover in a strawstack." Eight of the aircraft shot down that night were on training flights; forty-four men died before they had even gone on operations.

But the Germans paid a price for their daring. Twenty-five of the four-man Ju-88s failed to return home. A handful were shot down on English soil, the last such German casualties of the war, and the rest ran out of fuel or crash-landed. The raid was without any tactical or strategic benefit. Bomber Command was not deflected from its task. Its airfields reverted to the highest state of alert, and incoming airmen remembered an important lesson; that they were never safe was the underlying message in what had occurred. The Germans were indeed going to fight to a standstill. The raid had taken place on the two thousandth day of the war. How many more days of fighting would there be? It was a foolhardy airman who, that March 1945, told himself his future was guaranteed.

Miles Tripp was increasingly nervous as his war neared its close. Since Dresden there had been another long-distance raid, to Chemnitz, some shorter ops, battering German defenses in the Rhineland to assist the Allied armies on the ground, and then back to that old and dangerous stamping ground, Happy Valley, the Ruhr. A madness seemed to have come over his skipper, an Australian named "Dig" Klenner. Whenever they got back to England he would skim the Lancaster so low over the countryside that the crew were more worried than when they were in flak over Germany. He zoomed in on a bus on a country lane, head to head at hedge height before pulling up and away at the last minute. He dived down over a football field and they could see the faces of the players. He threaded the Lancaster between trees on a hilltop as if he thought himself invincible. Tripp took his captain to one side and asked him to stop. "My nerves won't stand any more."[6] The Australian agreed—his aerobatics were a curious expression of relief at having survived another operation, a blowing off of steam, but on the last occasion he had even managed to frighten himself. Yes, he wanted to live, he reassured his bombardier. He would be more careful.

Tripp's crew must have thought their job would never end. A full tour, once twenty-five operations, had been extended little by little until it was now forty. Sometimes it seemed as if the RAF authorities didn't want them to survive. But they got there and Tripp spent the night before their fortieth and final operation with his WAAF girlfriend, Audrey. "This time tomorrow, it'll all be over," he told her. She rested her head on his shoulder and said, "I'm scared." Back at base, everyone seemed to know it was the crew's last operation and, over breakfast, there were many calls of "All the best." The cheeriness evaporated when, at briefing, they saw the ribbon on the map ended at Essen. The Ruhr again. "Could be worse," said one of the crew, but Dig Klenner just grimaced. It was noticeable that his eyes were bloodshot, as if he had had a sleepless night.

More than one thousand Lancasters and Halifaxes would be on the daytime raid, the biggest ever by Bomber Command to a single target. Tripp and Co. would certainly be going out with the loudest of bangs. The aim of the operation, they were told, was to wipe out the damaged Krupp factories and completely dislocate the transport system, though Essen had been hit so often since 1940 that it was amazing anything was left to destroy. There was one more announcement: Tripp's crew would lead the squadron into battle, an honor, the wing commander declared, "because they achieve the distinction of being the first crew in the Group ever to complete forty trips on a first tour.[7] I'm sure we all wish them the best of luck." At dispersal, Klenner, the skipper, called the ground crew together and promised them "a piss-up" that night "and if any of you are standing by closing time, I'll want to know why." But as they took off, Klenner was fighting hard to conceal his fear that it was all going to go wrong on this very last trip. His nerves were calmed only when one of the crew told everyone he was getting his hair cut *tomorrow*. Yes, there would be a tomorrow; yes, it would all be over; yes, they would have survived.

Tripp felt surprisingly comfortable and calm, even when flak began to rake the sky as they crossed into Germany. He lined up his sights and pressed the bomb release button for the last time. Six tons of explosives dropped away, the bomb doors closed, and they were on their way home for the final time, the rest of the squadron flying in a V-shaped formation behind them and the congratulations ringing down the radio. Tripp heard the familiar calls from the cockpit—"Wheels down, half flap, into the funnels, full flap"—and then they were down. On the bus to debriefing they sat in silence. "The Skipper's hat was tipped back on his head and I have never seen a man look so happy. He gazed at each of us in turn as though fixing this moment forever in his memory. He didn't speak, but he grinned until his cheeks must have ached." In the pub that night, as the rounds of drinks were polished away and common sense departed with them, they talked about sticking together and going to fight the Japanese. "And we all swore that, come what may, we would all keep in touch with each other for the rest of our lives."

For Miles Tripp, the war had ended. For wireless operator Peter Marshall, it was just beginning. The day after Tripp's final flight to Germany, Marshall made his first. He was glad to be going into battle. "The army was making inroads on the ground, and there was a sense that the war was coming to a close. I had spent two years being highly trained and it would have been a waste to miss out. I wanted to prove that I could do it. But people were still being shot down. It wasn't a safe environment we were entering, as we would soon find out."[8] On that first operation, hemmed in over Dortmund with Lancasters all around, a four-thousand-pound bomb from above missed his plane by a whisker, taking out the aircraft in front instead. "Seven people had just disappeared in front of me. It could have been us if we had been a little bit farther forward—the gap between life and death measured in a few yards. I thanked God it was them and not us. That may sound callous but it was the only way to be. I was nineteen, a month away from my twentieth birthday. The two gunners were three months younger than me. We were naïve young men, almost too young to fully understand what was happening."

Three days after that first blooding, Marshall flew to Würzburg on an operation that would be ranked alongside Dresden and Pforzheim in this end period of the war for its ferocity. It was a smallish force, just over two hundred Lancasters, but their devastating accuracy smashed the old cathedral city and killed five thousand people in little more than a quarter of an hour. Würzburg was a middle-sized city in middle Germany which had escaped the war, unlike Schweinfurt, just twenty miles away, whose ball-bearing factories had been regularly attacked by Allied bombers. Before 1945, a lost Lancaster had dropped its payload there one night, and a handful of B-17s had once let loose their bombs, but, that apart, Würzburg was intact, so much so that its citizens thought it blessed in some mysterious way. A rumor went round that Winston Churchill had once studied at the sixteenth-century university there and had ordered it to be spared. It was the same sort of nonsense that had been spoken about Dresden. The city had many hospitals, and others argued that it had been declared an open city for casualties. More nonsense.

The fact is that Würzburg had always been on Bomber Command's list of potential targets, if low down. It had light industries, some of them military in nature, railway and river links, a large military barracks, and a Luftwaffe repair field which serviced experimental jet fighters. It was also an administrative center for the area. The problem for the people of Würzburg was simply that, as Germany was invaded from west and east, the war was coming closer every day until finally it engulfed them. There were a number of raids in February and early March. Hermann Knell, a schoolboy at the time, was fully aware that his hometown was increasingly in the firing line of Allied forces. He sat in the shelter at his school studying Shakespeare, memorizing Mark Antony's famous speech from *Julius Caesar*. He was puzzled. "Nazi propaganda told us day in and day out how base anything English was—their culture, their political system, and their values. As if to confirm this, their aircraft were bombing and strafing us. And yet here we were studying their literary achievements. It did not add up."[9]

The big raid came on the night of 16 March 1945, by which time Knell and his family had fled to a village outside the city in anticipation of what might happen.

There was a roaring noise of aircraft engines and we could see through the closed shutters that the sky was red. We knew at once that the hour had come. The sky was full of markers, Christmas trees as we called them, and soon the explosions started. Obviously this was a major attack and I was scared. The stream of aircraft seemed endless. When they had gone, my father and I climbed on our bicycles and pedaled toward the city to see what had happened to our home there. Rubble, wires, glass, craters, and uprooted trees barred our way. The inner core of Würzburg had become a cauldron of fire. The roar was deafening and the smoke suffocating. When we tried to get to our flat we were driven back by a wall of flames, heat, and smoke. We met neighbors who told us that our building was completely in flames. Many people were hit by falling debris, or worse, never escaped their shelters and were killed by the heat or carbon monoxide. No words can describe the suffocating and pungent smells of a burning city and the stench of decomposing and seared human flesh.[10]

Peter Marshall knew none of this until years later. At the time, Würzburg stuck in his mind for the death of one person rather than thousands. "What I remember the operation for was that the crew we shared accommodation with—including a particular mate of mine I'd been with for two years—didn't turn up at debriefing. By the time we had been for breakfast, it was obvious they weren't coming back. We went back to our billet, and down their side it was empty. That's when I first realized that, even at this stage, war wasn't quite the game I thought it might be."

In the German armed forces, there were those who still thought the country could be saved. All they needed, they argued, was time—time for the Führer's secret weapons to come onstream, time to build up the force of jet fighters which might even now turn back the tide of British and American bombers devastating the country, factory by factory, refinery by refinery, city by city. Given time, too, the Western Allies would surely realize that their real enemy was not Germany but the communist Soviet Union and join with the Luftwaffe and the Wehrmacht—though probably *minus* Hitler—to push the Red Army back where it came from. A senior air force officer had a plan to buy some of that vital breathing space.

Oberst [Colonel] Hajo Herrmann was a Luftwaffe ace who had flown the new Me-262 jet fighter and was convinced it could still swing the outcome of the war, at least to the point where Germany could survive more or less intact rather than be dismembered or destroyed. Herrmann's belief in the power of the jets was shared by Allied airmen who had seen them in action. Eighth Air Force pilot Walter Hughes recalled an attack by six of them while he was attempting to bomb an oil refinery near Hamburg in late March. "In a single pass we lost three B-24s in less than ten seconds. These were the fastest and most dangerous fighters we had ever seen or could imagine. We saw one knocked down, but it took thirteen P-47s to do it, and it may have been out of fuel. If Hitler had enough of those planes and pilots there would have been fewer B-24s in the sky, and then who knows what might have happened?"[11] After the war, Hermann Goering, the head of the Luftwaffe, told his Allied interrogators he believed that, given four or five months more, Germany would indeed have had enough jet aircraft not only to stop the defeat but to win the war. "Our underground factory at Kahla had a capacity of 1,000 to 1,200 jet airplanes a month. With 5,000 to 6,000 jets, the outcome would have been quite different."[12]

But in March 1945 there just weren't enough of the jets to make a real difference—and never would be, Colonel Herrmann reasoned, unless the American bombing formations could be stopped from systematically wrecking the factories producing the jet planes and the airfields where pilots were learning to fly them. His do-or-die plan was to throw as many conventional planes as possible into one big assault on the American Fortresses and Liberators and down so many of them that they would have to stop the air raids on Germany for long enough to give the German jet force a chance to develop in numbers and in operational strength. And the striking edge to that force of conventional planes to be thrown at the Americans would be special squadrons of kamikaze fighters.

Aging Junkers fighter-bombers would be packed with explosives and flown into the middle of the American formations, where a very short fuse would be triggered by the pilot just before he parachuted to safety. It was the same concept as the Americans' Aphrodite programme,[13] though without the advanced remote-control technology the Americans used and with even less of a safety margin.

Herrmann put his plan to Goering, who authorized him to issue an appeal for volunteers. The top-secret message went out to all Luftwaffe units on 8 March 1945. It was couched in typically apocalyptic but this time totally appropriate language. "The fateful battle for the Reich, our people and our homeland has reached a critical stage," it began. "Almost the whole world has sworn to destroy us in battle and, in their blind hate, to wipe us out. As never before in the history of the Fatherland we are facing a final destruction from which there can be no rebirth. I turn to you, therefore, in these deciding moments and ask you to rescue the life of your nation from a final downfall. A place of honor in the glorious history of the Luftwaffe will be yours. You will give the German people a hope of victory, and you will be an example for all time."[14] It was signed by Goering.

More than two thousand pilots volunteered. Some were old hands but most were new recruits with only the minimum of training and experience. In some cases, entire units put themselves forward as one. As Adrian Weir, the historian of this incident, records, "They were not coerced into volunteering and none appears to have been driven by any fervent Nazi fanaticism. They had all experienced the bitter consequences of warfare and as soldiers they intended to do what they considered their duty."[15]

Their leaders let them down. Herrmann thought he had an agreement for 1,500 fighters to be put at his disposal, a force that might indeed have made a difference. In the event, fuel—the Reich's desperately diminishing resource—slashed the number of aircraft allocated to the operation to 350. The mission that might save the Fatherland—shrinking by the day as the Soviets began their drive to Berlin from the east and in the west as Field Marshal Model's 350,000-strong army was surrounded in the Ruhr—was whittled away.

In the last week of March, the volunteers arrived at an airfield at Stendal in northern Germany. They were indulged with cognac, cigarettes, and chocolate before at last being told the precise nature of their mission: Their job was to ram American bombers in midair. They would fly standard Messerschmitt Bf-109 fighter planes stripped of all unnecessary weight— armor plating, for example—to give them an extra burst of speed. They would be escorted to the American formations by jet fighters, whose job would be to use their phenomenal acceleration to lure the U.S. escort planes away. Then the volunteers would have a free run to dive at their targets. On impact, their propellers would bore holes in the American bombers while the pilots would hurl themselves out of their cockpits.

As Easter 1945 came and went, the pressing urgency of the mission was evident. General Eisenhower broadcast a message to German troops calling on them to surrender, while in southeast Europe Soviet troops took the oilfields in Hungary, which had been the last German hope for maintaining fuel supplies. No more time could be spared. April 7 was designated for the attack. On that day, American airmen were assembling for their battle orders at airfields up and down eastern England. They had been pounding German railways, oil refineries, and troop concentrations for weeks virtually unopposed. They had not seen a conventional German fighter for a month, though small bands of jets had been in evidence. To all intents, it seemed the enemy had surrendered the skies. Thirteen hundred bombers set off that day, with 900 fighters to protect them. So little opposition was expected, the pilots were told they could bomb from 15,000 feet, which meant the gloves and heavy jackets essential on higher, colder flights could come off.

As the armada assembled and headed across the North Sea and over the Dutch coast toward Bremen and Hamburg, Colonel Herrmann scrambled his force, now depleted to just seventy stripped-down planes. The pilots lifted off with military music in their headsets, interspersed with the voice of a woman reminding them of what the Allied bombers like the ones they were now about to face had done to the people of Dresden.

The first "suicide" Messerschmitt to try and speed past the screen of escorts protecting the flank of the American formation was shot down by a Mustang. But more came arrowing in after it, their stripped-down frames giving them an extra 20 to 25 mph in the air. Suddenly the Americans realized they had a fight on their hands for the first time in a long time. Me-262 jets arrived on the scene, drawing some of the Mustangs away, as planned, into high-speed chases and dogfights. But not enough. Some U.S. fighter pilots realized that it was the propeller-driven Messerschmitts, flying directly at the bombers and making no attempt to avoid contact, that were the real threat. The first successful ramming caught the left wing of a B-24, removing two feet of its tip and damaging the outer engine. But the bomber kept flying. It turned for home on three engines and limped off the battlefield, wounded but not downed. It would make it back to base, exposing another mistake by the Germans—they had seriously underestimated the robustness of the Fortresses and Liberators.

They had also failed to grasp how much flying skill would be needed for the suicide planes to get past the protective screen of Mustangs. Inexperienced pilots had been chosen over the experienced, for what seemed obvious reasons. But the raw, barely trained German airmen were no match in air combat for the American escort pilots. One of the few to get anywhere near his target was Unteroffizier Heinrich Rosner, who lined himself up behind a B-24 and then ripped into it with his propeller. The bomber veered off course and straight into another B-24. Both fell away before breaking up in midair. Rosner jumped clear, released his parachute, and then blacked out. He woke up on the ground, concussed and with a broken collarbone but alive. But his was a rare triumph. Even when they got through the fighter screen, success was elusive. One Messerschmitt dived on the tail fin of a bomber, shearing it off, but the Fortress kept going. The German fighter's wing was torn off by the impact and sailed through the sky to crash into another B-17. But both American bombers survived these impacts and flew home. Another managed to get to friendly territory in eastern France and make an emergency landing despite a six-foot gash in the fuselage, a smashed-up ball turret, and two engines out.

Lewis Smith of the 385th Bomb Group, a pilot from Wichita, Kansas, appeared to have had no idea that he had faced a new and dangerous enemy tactic that day. His diary recorded events on what was his thirty-fifth mission and the final one of his tour. It was among the worst he had ever been on in his year and a half in Europe.

There were dogfights going on all over. And there were lots of jet trails. Five Me-109s came in on our tail. The gunners opened up on them, but they kept right on coming and four of them went right through the formation. The one right behind us broke into flames at about 200 yards and dived into our number-four man flying right beneath us. Both blew up. After that, two or three planes would come in from different angles every two or three minutes. We were pretty busy for about forty-five minutes. When we were about halfway down the bomb run, three jets directly above us dived straight through the formation, knocking one guy out. He got the ship under control and seven or eight chutes were seen before the plane hit the ground. It hit in a wooded area and covered about a mile with flame and bombs.[16]

But apart from giving Smith and many other Eighth Air Force men a scare that day, for the Germans the suicide operation was a failure. They failed to hinder the day's mission. They also got nowhere near to shocking the Eighth Air Force into canceling its aerial assault on Germany, which had been Colonel Herrmann's ultimate intention and ambition. The Eighth lost seventeen bombers that day, of which thirteen could be attributed to the suicide force; 117 men were missing in action. It was an unwelcome number of casualties but nothing to cause great alarm. Indeed, far from making a dramatic impact on the Americans, the new assault plan went virtually unnoticed and officially unremarked by them. Intelligence reports at the end of the day spoke of "signs of desperation" among the German pilots and "fanatical attacks through a murderous hail of fire" but went on to suggest that "evidence of suicidal ramming" could not be substantiated.

Perhaps, though, the attack had jolted the Americans more than they were willing to admit. It is possible that Eighth Air Force leaders knew precisely what had happened but did not wish to give any credence to the idea of German suicide squads. The Americans had been battling with kamikaze pilots in the Pacific since October 1944, and huge damage and loss of life were being inflicted by them as the Japanese fought to keep the Allied invaders from their homeland. There was no wish for the idea to take hold in Europe. The official view was that any ramming in the skies over Germany on 7 April had been accidental and all rumors to the contrary were quashed.

Fortunately for the Allies, the operation had been too little too late. But who can say what might have been the outcome if Herrmann had been allowed to put the 1,500 fighters initially promised in the air, twenty times the number he actually was able to deploy? And what if casualties had been inflicted in the same ratio and instead of seventeen Fortresses and Liberators, his men had downed between 250 and 350? At the very least, such a blow to the Eighth Air Force might have bought some time, and time might still have changed events significantly.

Much of Bomber Command's and the Eighth's last month of operations was spent on targets in the coastal regions of the Baltic and the North Sea and the approaches to Denmark, where it was thought the Germans might set up last-ditch northern defenses. These were no milk runs. They often took place during breaks in otherwise dreadful weather and were always races against time. Twenty-one Liberators of the 491st Bomb Group hit the submarine pens at Wilhelmshaven, encountering unexpectedly accurate flak as they flew in. Most of the aircraft were hit, and one called *Heavenly Body* dropped out of the returning formation with an engine out. Over the North Sea it continued to lose height—the trouble had spread to the other engine on the same side, making her virtually uncontrollable—and it was clear that she was not going to make it home intact. Ditching in those freezing, still wintery waters to the east of the British mainland could not be avoided. The air-sea rescue service was alerted by radio, and a Catalina flying boat was quickly on the scene, and in fact followed the B-24 down as she hit the water. What followed next was a chilling example of just why airmen feared those waters. The sea was rough, and as the plane was about to touch the surface, a large wave caught a wingtip and flipped her over. She broke up with such speed that the rescuers in the flying boat, though there in an instant, could pull just two of the ten crew from the sea in time. Staff

Sergeant William Brigham, one of those rescued, saw engineer Darrence Siebert swim to a piece of wing and cling to it, only to have the wing with his friend on it sink beneath the waves. He then found the pilot, Lieutenant Robert Siek, floating face down. He turned him over but the skipper was dead. Brigham himself, numb from exposure and exhaustion, was about to lose consciousness when a pole was thrust at him from the Catalina. He found the strength to grab it and hang on as he was dragged from the water. It took three men on the rescue plane to haul him in because of the weight of his sodden flying suit. Even then the drama was not over. The sea was too rough for the flying boat to take off. They were also just twenty miles from the Danish coast, still occupied by hostile Germans. An SOS was sent out and the Catalina—with rescuers and rescued inside—tossed backward and forward on the waves for four and a half hours before a British ship arrived on the scene. In heavy and dangerous seas, the men were taken on board, and then the flying boat was sunk with shell shot to prevent it falling into enemy hands.[17] Those deaths, at the very end of March, turned out to be the 491st's final combat losses. However, April 1945—when conventional wisdom says the war was virtually over—claimed five hundred more RAF lives on operations in the same region. Bombardier Dickie Parfitt recalled the dangers of sweeping in low over Kiel.

> Harbors with battleships anchored in them were not healthy places and we were going in at 10,000 feet, which was not good for survival chances. The flak was very hot, and we got the full treatment. It was a long run up with the wind coming straight at us, and I was having to make lots of course corrections. The lads were breathing heavily until I called, "Bombs gone." The next day Mosquitoes went in to photograph the target and we were rewarded with a picture of the pocket battleship *Admiral Scheer* upside down in the harbor. Everybody was chuffed [very pleased].

A few days later, from the east, Marshal Zhukov launched the final assault on Berlin, pouring two and a half million Red Army soldiers into the fight to break the Nazi resistance and kill off the Third Reich. Hitler, in his bunker under the chancellery, had a fortnight to live.

Parfitt took some leave, went home to the mining town in Kent where he had grown up, and felt strangely alone.

Most of my mates who had joined the RAF had either been killed or taken prisoner. Frank Hawkins, who had lived next door to me, was dead. So was a very good friend of mine who had been a navigator early on in the war; he'd been shot down, but got back to England. He crewed up again, went back into combat, and eventually was killed over Germany. He had been through so much, managed to survive, and then put himself in danger again. I suppose he must have been keen. I must have been incredibly lucky.

His luck was holding for the time being, but a risky adventure still awaited him. They were done with the north of Germany and pocket battle-ships. A different target needed attention in the south. They had not flown for three days when "we were woken unexpectedly at three A.M. Nobody was pleased, and a few rude words were uttered. Briefing was at 4:00 A.M. and it was there, to our excitement, that we discovered the target on the blackboard was Berchtesgaden, Hitler's hideaway home."

Berchtesgaden was a village high in the mountains above Salzburg where the Führer had long had his Alpine retreat, the Berghof. Its panoramic view of the peaks from high terraces and rooms with large expanses of glass in-spired him, or so he told the streams of visitors who came there. The Führer was less keen on the Eagle's Nest, a pavilion perched above the house on the top of the mountain and reached by a steep winding road. He thought the air up there too thin and not good for his blood pressure. Berchestgaden had become a court, like Louis XIV's Versailles, and Nazi leaders such as Goe-ring and Martin Bormann bought or built their own houses in the village to be on hand for the Führer when he was in residence. The village grew into a town with hotels for the many visitors and was swollen in size, too, by the battalion of SS troops there to mount a guard and the antiaircraft gunners manning air defenses set in the cliffs. Here was a fortress that would be the focal point of any southern Last Redoubt.

This continued to concern the Allies. Although it was now accepted that a major last-ditch defense led by Hitler himself was unlikely, Allied intelligence still believed that fanatical Nazis planned to launch guerrilla warfare from there. Eisenhower directed his Third Army under General Patton south toward Bavaria and Austria as Ultra intercepts confirmed more and more talk of "the Alpine Fortress" in German communications.

On 24 April 1945 an intercept revealed a message from Hitler ordering one of his generals south from Berlin to prepare "a last bulwark of fanatical resistance."[18] The next day Bomber Command was alerted to bomb Berchtesgaden.

"THE ARCHCRIMINAL'S HIDEOUT" was how one RAF intelligence officer wrote up his advance notes for the briefing he was to give to the crews for this mission, "the target we've been waiting for, for five and a half years."[19] Here was a description to inspire them for the job. He made a note to himself to "stress importance of accurate bombing as it is desired to finish the job in one blow." He required more capital letters for his final message—"MAKE A NEAT JOB." Parfitt recalled hearing the news at RAF Fiskerton:

> We were very excited. Our target was to be the SS barracks. We were told some of the Nazi top brass were hiding there, perhaps even Hitler himself. We really didn't know. We also had the feeling that this had to be our very last operation. But it would be a tricky one. The bombing leader warned us about the height of the mountains. We would be flying in a group gaggle like geese with the flight commander leading the way. If any of us saw a German fighter, we were to fire a Very pistol and then all close in for cover and greater firepower. Mustangs from Fighter Command would escort us.

Navigator Bill Kiley of 150 Squadron considered the dangers. "It was a long flight and there were bound to be heavy defenses. I genuinely thought this might be an operation too far. But I didn't want to miss it. Here was a chance to get Hitler for yourself."[20]

At RAF Strubby, Peter Marshall's was one of six crews from 619 Squadron put on standby the day before and then summoned to a briefing in the early hours of the morning.

> We had our eggs and bacon, the perk that still went with the job, filled our Thermos flasks with coffee and collected a packet of sandwiches, flying rations of chocolate bars, sweets, chewing gum, and our escape kits. I had my lucky mascot, a little Hawaiian dancer-type doll that a girlfriend had given me. The war might be drawing to a close, but the dangers were far from over, and I needed all the help I could get. This was going to be

my sixth op. We went into the main briefing room, speculating on what would be revealed as our target on the map. We sat in hushed anticipation as the squadron commander grasped the cord and pulled open the curtains, saying dramatically as he did so, "Gentlemen, your target is . . . Berchtesgaden, where it is believed Hitler has set up his 'headquarters' to fight to the bitter end." The red ribbon ran south from Strubby over London, then on into France (where we were told we would link up with long-range fighter aircraft, mainly American Mustangs and Thunderbolts, who would protect us from enemy air attack along the way), then east toward Lake Constance and onward over the Bavarian mountains to a pin locating Berchtesgaden.

Excitement spread through the briefing room as crews burst into noisy chatter. Everyone knew the war in Europe was drawing to a close but to be going after Adolf Hitler, with him and his henchmen as the target, made this operation different. Targets usually didn't have identifiable faces attached to them, but this time we knew names and what they looked like. This time it was personal. But we knew it was going to be heavily defended and we would have to be on our toes if we weren't going to get the chop.

For Freddie Hulance, a pilot with 227 Squadron, the operation was unwelcome. He had genuinely thought his war was over, that he had flown his last raid over enemy territory.

Then I heard the Tannoy [public address] announcement, "There's a war on," the code for an operation. It was a shock to be going on another mission when I was sure it was all over and we were safe. I had also just heard that my wife was pregnant, and I had more reason than ever to want to survive. The squadron was buzzing with rumors that this was a *big* one. And I reasoned that it had to be a long one as there wasn't much of Germany that was unoccupied by that time. I had a premonition that it was Berchtesgaden before the briefing, and when the target was revealed, I remember being pleased with myself for being right. But I was scared. I really didn't want to go. It would be too awful to be shot down on what was obviously the last raid of the war. I was more fearful on this mission than on any other, more aware of the need to get back and be safe. Only six planes were going from each squadron, and when the target was known, those who weren't going were saying they wished they were. I was thinking precisely the opposite. I wished I wasn't on the Battle Order.[21]

Unlike Hulance and most others, Peter Marshall did not think this was going to be the final operation of the war.

I saw no reason why we shouldn't still be fighting at Christmas if Adolf and his gang had got to Berchtesgaden. It was a fortress and impregnable, with connecting tunnels and crack German SS troops there. The war could have gone on for a long time trying to winkle them out. No, to me this was just another trip—before the next one and the one after that.[22]

The briefing revealed three separate targets for the operation—the Berghof itself, the SS barracks behind it, and the Eagle's Nest above. The raid was to be in daylight, and good visibility was expected.

The six Lancasters of my squadron were given a dual role. We were to lead the bomber stream on the approach to Berchtesgaden, dropping Window [chaff] to disorientate the radar-directed antiaircraft guns. These were positioned high up on the surrounding mountainsides and could set up a deadly accurate cross fire on the bomb run. Then we were to circle round and come in with the last wave of aircraft to hit the SS barracks.

Dickie Parfitt's bomber took off from Fiskerton in Lincolnshire to link up with the force of 360 Lancasters heading for southern Germany. "American Mustangs joined us, shepherding the loose aircraft into line. We crossed into the zone where German fighters were still active. I noticed a Lancaster out to port on its own, possibly with engine trouble, and saw two enemy jet fighters approach and take it out. It spiraled down and its bomb load exploded. That made everybody nervous. The gaggle leader ordered us to tighten up."[23] Peter Marshall had seen a fast-moving blip on his radar screen that he took to be an enemy jet fighter stalking them. As it overhauled them, the Lancaster corkscrewed away and the gunners blazed at the retreating fighter, which went down in flames. "We flew on and into the most wonderful scenery. I stood most of the time on the step with my head in the astrodome. You could see snow-capped mountains for miles, right across Switzerland into Italy. It seemed such a paradox to be enjoying this view while we were on our way to deliver death and destruction."

The lovely scenery was also producing problems. The mountain ranges interfered badly with the navigation equipment on the Mosquitoes, there to mark the target. In other planes, too, crews found it impossible to identify the right mountain among so many similar snow-capped peaks. But not Marshall's, and as they got closer to Hitler's home, he found himself mulling over what they were about to do.

It seemed so odd to be on our way to attack Berchtesgaden. As a boy, back home in Henley-on-Thames before the war, I saw newsreels in the local cinema of the German Führer standing on the terrace and looking out over a panoramic view from Lake Königsee to Salzburg. I certainly never dreamed that one day I would be flying along Lake Constance, heading toward that same Eagle's Nest, intent upon destroying the home of that man in the newsreel—and hopefully him as well. I wanted to get Hitler. If he and his men were there, we would be famous. We would be the men who killed Adolf Hitler.

His thoughts of glory were interrupted by the call to action. Over the radio, the squadron leader ordered them to follow him into the first run.

We went along the shore of Lake Constance, above the Bavarian mountains, over Lake Walchensee, and ahead we could see the 2,522-meter high summit of our target poking through the patchy cloud. We began filling the air with our strips of "silver paper" and encountered no opposition as we ran over the target at just before 9:00 A.M. It seemed as if the Germans had not woken up to what was happening. We skipped across the target and then wheeled away in a wide turn as the rest of the force came in behind us. Our rear gunner looked back and reported that flak bursts were now appearing in the sky behind us. Visibility was fairly good and the antiaircraft gunners had plenty of aircraft to aim at.

Parfitt was in the main pack as the flak started flying.

We were right in the mountains, just clearing the tops and the sides, and there was fierce gunfire coming at us from fortified positions on both sides and from the valley below. It was hot. There would only be chance for one bombing run. We wouldn't want to go round again. The master bomber was on the air giving me instructions. Our bomb doors were open and suddenly we were there and not far off track. I called for a few corrections and then it was "Bombs gone." We climbed away and headed for home.

Meanwhile, Marshall was coming back round for his bombing run. "We had to go and join on the end of the stream. It was always a dangerous thing to do. Nobody liked going over a target more than once. By now the flak was fully developed, heavy and accurate, and Berchtesgaden had become a not very pleasant place to be. The target was by now obscured by smoke, and the planes in front of us were surrounded by bursting flak, the worst I had ever seen." It was proving difficult to get a fix on the SS barracks, a long line of buildings heavily camouflaged to merge in with the rest of the village of Berchtesgaden. As they slowed in their search of the ground, a Lancaster ahead suddenly burst into flames.

The pilot was a man by the name of De Marco. I think he had done about twenty or so trips, but this was going to be the end for him. It started to peel away, flames pouring from the wing, and then disappeared. We thought they had all bought it. But all we could do was keep going on our bombing run. We were all silently willing the bombardier to hurry up. Eventually he was satisfied with his aiming point and pressed the button. We dived away from the target before climbing to port to miss the mountains. It was time to go! Below us, smoke was pouring from the burning buildings. We headed home, aware that one of our squadron was no longer with us.

We landed back at Strubby at 12:48 p.m. after being in the air for eight and a half hours. And that was it. It turned out to be the last major bombing operation carried out by our squadron and one of the very last Bomber Command attacks of the war. Headquarters must have thought Hitler was there, otherwise they wouldn't have sent us in the first place, would they? Of course, Hitler and his henchmen were not there after all. But they might have been. It was worth the risk.

Dickie Parfitt disagreed. He could see no point in jeopardizing men's lives at that stage of the war, particularly when he later learned that Hitler had been in Berlin. "Maybe the powers that be thought so, but I didn't. But there was an air of celebration in the aircraft on the way back because we realized this really was our last trip. As we came over the English coast and I saw the white cliffs of Dover, I thought, 'I've made it. I'm through this. I'm safe.' That evening we all went into Lincoln and had a few beers. It felt a bit of an anticlimax after having been over Adolf Hitler's house that very morning!" But nothing could dent one flier's happiness at what he had done. In his logbook at the end of the operation he wrote that it was "a pleasure to bomb today as I believe Hitler was at home when we called and, as far as I could see, when we left, there was very little of his joint left."[24]

As ever, there were casualties to be logged. Two Lancasters had gone down and their crews were missing. One of them was Freddie Cole, flight engineer in the plane piloted by Canadian Flying Officer Wilf De Marco, which Peter Marshall had seen hit in front of him. They had just released their bombs and were in that most nervous of moments waiting for the automatic camera to record their performance on the target when they were hit by cross fire. Arthur Shannon, the bombardier, recalled: "I had watched the bombs fall and was pleased to see one hit the SS barracks. The photoflash had just gone off when there was a big explosion. It was clear we only had a short time to get the hell out of it."[25] He clipped on his parachute and was first out of the escape hatch. Navigator Norman Johnston was dead. He had, for once, left his safe cubby hole. Curiosity got the better of him. This target he had to see. He was standing beside the pilot when gunfire hit a propeller and sent a sliver of metal shrapnel smashing through the windscreen and into his face. As he fell, he flung his hand out and caught the D-ring of Cole's parachute, lying on a seat. The silk spilled out into the cockpit. Flames were shooting from the back of the Lancaster, and there was a yell for everyone to get out. Cole gathered up the folds of his parachute into a big, untidy bundle and headed for the escape hatch. Wireless operator Jackie Speers, another Canadian, was supposed to exit from the rear, but the flames forced him forward. He reckoned the gunners behind him must be dead. He saw the navigator's body, then hit the pilot's knee hard, the usual drill as you evacuated to alert him to follow. "There was no response," Speers recalled. "The front of the cockpit had been blown away. He could not have survived."[26] Speers found Cole sitting on the edge of the hatch wrestling with his parachute. He made sure the harness was clipped on and then gave his friend a mighty shove in the back and out of the falling plane. Speers followed immediately.

As the silk billowed out and held him, Cole saw the blazing Lancaster he had just left fly into the side of a mountain and explode. "That was a truly horrendous sight. I knew some of my mates were still on board. As I floated down I was hit hard by the realization that they were dead. But there wasn't time for tears. They came later. For now I had to think about my own survival. I came down in a meadow and was immediately captured by SS soldiers. They were really hostile, but then an officer came along and calmed them down. He stopped them from shooting me."[27] Cole was taken by truck to Salzburg and imprisoned in the police station. Meanwhile Shannon had landed in a fir tree and slid to the ground, breaking a leg. 'I was lying on the ground in agony, with no chance of getting away, when the Germans arrived. They kicked me down the mountainside. Once they leveled their guns at me and I thought I was going to be shot." Speers was picked up by German civilians. At first they treated him well. He had shrapnel in his left leg and could not walk, and they carried him on a ladder to a farmyard. Then he was put in a hay cart to be taken to the village and handed over to the police. On the way, Allied fighter planes roared into the valley and began shooting up the area with rockets. The people escorting him scattered, but when they came back they were angry, and women shrieked at him and threatened him with pitchforks. Fortunately for him, soldiers came to his rescue.

> I was taken to a building where Freddie [Cole] and Art [Shannon] were being held, though I was not allowed to see them. Then I was taken to a different town and held captive for two weeks with other wounded prisoners, most of whom seemed to be amputees who had lost hands, feet, ears, noses, legs, or arms, from frostbite, I think. I was interrogated many

times by the SS, who did not believe we could fly all the way to Berchtesgaden from England. They insisted that we must have taken off from one
of the Allied airfields in Italy. By this time my leg was badly infected and
I thought I might end up like those other poor sods. But then the Americans arrived and everyone was running around saying "Hitler kaput."

The Führer had shot himself in Berlin on 30 April.

All the prisoners, including the entire seven-man crew of the other Lancaster
shot down over Berchtesgaden, were eventually returned home. The assault
on Hitler's mountain home had cost four lives just a fortnight before the war
ended. They were not the last casualties by any means. That same day, close
to five hundred Lancasters and Halifaxes had gone north to knock out gun
batteries on the Frisian island of Wangeroog, which controlled the entrance
to the remaining key German harbors. Seven planes crashed, six as a result
of inexplicable midair collisions over the target or over the sea in perfect visibility and weather conditions. Forty-eight men were dead. The enemy guns,
which were concreted into bunkers, were largely undamaged. Stray bombs
hit a camp for forced workers and prisoners of war, more than one hundred
of whom died. On the same day, the Eighth Air Force put up its final missions in anger. Five hundred and ninety B-17s and B-24s headed for an airfield and a munitions factory in Pilsen in Czechoslovakia and for marshaling
yards in Bavaria. Six Fortresses were shot down by antiaircraft fire and a
further 180 damaged by flak. Forty-two men were missing in action. One
who came home from Pilsen, however, was a twenty-seven-year-old lieutenant colonel named "Manny" Klette, the son of a Lutheran minister who
had emigrated from Germany to the Midwest. He had been flying missions
solidly for two years and one month, refusing to bring his tour to an end.
Pilsen had been his ninety-first sortie. He had logged combat flying time of
689 hours 25 minutes. But it was over at last for him, too. At the end of the
day, the Eighth, its job done, was officially stood down from duties.

For Bomber Command, there was still work to do on the north German
coast. There had been no offensive operations for almost a week, and most
airmen believed their war days were over. It came as a shock on 2 May
when 8 Group, the Pathfinders, and 100 Group, which provided bomber
support, were put on battle orders. A last operation was needed to Kiel. Ad-

miral Karl Dönitz, Hitler's successor, had set up his headquarters in the vicinity. Shipping was thought to be massing for an evacuation of soldiers to Denmark or Norway, from where resistance would be continued. That night a small force of Mosquitoes—some armed with hundred-gallon barrels of napalm, a highly flammable liquid the Americans had recently developed—made low-level attacks on four Luftwaffe airfields. They ran into heavy flak, and one of the Mosquitoes exploded in midair close to the town of Schleswig. Its two-man crew were killed. Then a main force of Mosquitoes attacked Kiel itself in two raids, an hour apart. They were covered by two dozen Halifaxes carrying radio equipment to jam the enemy's early-warning radar. Two of these support aircraft collided just south of the city and crashed, the remains of one coming to rest, appropriately, against the wall of a cemetery. Three men survived but thirteen were killed, all men on their second tours. They were the last RAF casualties of the bomber war.

But Bomber Command and the Eighth Air Force were still active, their crews now turning their hands to mercy missions. In western Holland, the Germans were cut off but refusing to surrender, clinging on to power until the very end. The local population were starving in their millions after the Nazi commissioner cut civilian rations. People had left the cities to forage in the countryside and were said to be living on tulip bulbs. Thousands were dying. A deal was struck with the Germans for food to be dropped, and for a week at the end of April and the beginning of May, more than 3,000 sorties were made across the North Sea to deliver close on 7,000 tons of food from the air.

The aptly named Operation Manna was heaven for the crews—they were flying but not killing or being killed. As one of them put it, "Whereas our former missions dealt in death, now we were bringing life."[28] Dickie Parfitt was happy to help the Dutch.

They had risked everything to help Allied airmen downed at Arnhem. Now it was our turn to help them. But at the beginning it was not risk-free. The drop zones were surrounded by German artillery, checking that it was food that was being dropped and not weapons! We carried 5,000 pounds of food in sacks crammed into panniers in the bomb bay. On our first operation we were briefed to go in at one hundred feet, *very* low for a four-engined aircraft. If shot at, we were not to return fire. Soon after we crossed the Dutch coast, the Hun opened up on us with a short burst, but we ignored it and kept going. I could see markers ahead and, most amazingly of all, "Thank you, boys," written in tulips. I let the food go. Down below people cheered and waved flags. Many crews donated their sweet rations, throwing them out attached to small homemade parachutes with notes that said, "Voor het kind—for the children." There were some problems. Margarine was dropped as packets but converted to flat pats on impact!

Robert Wannop became tearful as he dropped food parcels and could see

children running out of school waving excitedly. The roads were dotted with hundreds of people waving, their faces wreathed in smiles of happiness. One hell of a lump came into my throat. Nobody spoke in the aircraft. It wasn't a time for words. My vision grew a little misty. Perhaps it was the rain on the windscreen . . . ! Union Jacks were spread out on the tops of buildings, and Dutch flags flapped from nearly every window. On one building a sign painted in huge white letters said: "Thank you, RAF." These brave people, who so often risked their own lives to save an airman and return him safely to England, were thanking us! I felt very humble.

Bob Slockett, a USAAF tail gunner in the 561st squadron, recalled looking down from the rear of his B-17 at just three hundred feet above the ground as crates of food spilled out of the bomb bay and seeing hundreds of Dutch people on bicycles racing from all corners of Amsterdam to the drop area. It was an "awesome sight,"[29] he recalled, though he kept his fingers coiled round the trigger of his guns just in case the Germans broke their agreement not to fire their flak guns at the mercy planes. And for some of his countrymen, there was still a price to pay. An Eighth Air Force Fortress was damaged by German gunfire on 7 May and another ditched in the sea after an engine caught fire. Only two were rescued from the water; eight died, the Eighth's last casualties. The next day the war was officially over.

There was one more humanitarian task for the aircrews to perform.

They were sent to pick up the tens of thousands of British and American prisoners of war now in transit camps all over Europe or waiting patiently at far-flung airfields to be flown home. Ron Smith flew happily in his usual Tail-End Charlie slot to Lübeck on the Baltic coast, unaware of what he was about to encounter. He was shocked to the core by the sight of his passengers as they got down from lorries and queued for a place on the planes.

Here were men who had endured years of torment in captivity, some since as long ago as Dunkirk, shuffling along with their pitiful little parcels of meager belongings, gazing in awe at the might of a hundred four-engined bombers, for them something from another world. The clowning and laughter of the impatient aircrews ceased abruptly. All my efforts to encourage conversation were of no avail. They responded neither to us nor to each other, following any instruction with a numb obedience. I wanted to say to each one, "It's all right now, I can only try and understand what you have been through, but we are proud to be here to take you home." Instead, it was only by smile and gesture that I could endeavor to show my feelings. I seated them all as comfortably as possible, along each side of the sparse interior of the fuselage, devoid of any proper seating, though a distribution of blankets helped. As the English coast appeared below, the sight of his homeland was all too much for one man. Tears ran down his cheeks, and I put my arm around his shoulders as he sobbed.[30]

Among those prisoners of war eager to get home was Corporal Albie Thompson from Worcester. He had been captured back in May 1940, overrun in Belgium as the Germans raced through into France in the early months of the war, forcing the British Expeditionary Force back to Dunkirk. He had been a pioneer of the prison camps, sent to Stalag XXA at Thorn, one of the farthest-flung outposts on the eastern edge of the Third Reich, in land that had been stripped from conquered Poland. There he had been put to hard physical labor, digging ditches and laying cables as the months of imprisonment turned into long years of deprivation and depression. All that kept him going were the letters from his mother and his childhood sweetheart, Mary Crampton, and the company of his pal, Ron Harrison. They had been friends from boyhood, joined up together in 1940, lost each other in Belgium, and been reunited as prisoners at Thorn in the summer of 1941. As the war ended they had been part of that terrible exodus on foot and by train from the east through the winter of 1945, ahead of the advancing Soviet army, eventually ending up in southern Germany, where they were liberated by the Americans. From there they had been flown to Paris, where they celebrated VE Day, and were now in the queue at Juvincourt for the very last leg home. They were issued blankets and cushions to make themselves comfortable in the rather primitive interiors of the Lancasters, not designed for passengers. They had English newspapers to read to bring them up to date on events. The past five years of captivity were slipping out of their minds. A bright future beckoned with the girls they had not seen since they were teenagers.

They filed toward the planes lined up on the apron to receive their passengers, two dozen at a time. Harrison went ahead, but the hand of an official came down and stopped Thompson. The one his pal was getting on was full. He would have to take the next one. After four years together, they waved their goodbyes. They would see one another in England. Eventually it was Thompson's turn and at around midday he climbed into a Lancaster from 514 Squadron for the final leg of his five-year odyssey. The passengers were a mixed crowd of Irish, English, South Africans, and an American, officers and enlisted men together. One came on board at the last minute. He was twenty-fifth in the line and should have waited for another plane but he persuaded the skipper of the Lancaster to let him aboard. Now, with the door closed, they moved along the perimeter to the runway, gathered speed and took off, climbing unsteadily. The pilot radioed to the tower that he was having problems with the controls. The passengers were grouped unevenly in the back and his trim was affected. He requested permission to come around and make an emergency landing. As he turned back towards the runway, the Lancaster went into a spin and crashed into the ground. The crew and passengers were all killed.

Back in Worcester, Mary Crampton was waiting for Thompson, the man she had not seen for five years. Ron Harrison, his friend, had arrived at her house with his girlfriend Betty to tell her that Albie was on the plane after him. They put up a "welcome home" banner. The telegram from the Air Ministry saying he was dead arrived the next day. Mary was shattered. They should have been man and wife. They had planned to marry on his last leave before his unit was posted to France all those years ago. The license had been issued and the ceremony arranged, but his leave had been canceled at the last minute. Now, once more, with the war ended and their life together apparently about to begin all over again, he had been taken from her, and this time forever. She had once written to him: "I've often pictured what our first meeting might be like, wondering whether it might be springtime or your favorite season, autumn, when you come home. When it is, it will be summer to me."[31] Now all she had was a winter of grief and regret. It had been a hard war. For some—and Mary Crampton was not alone—the aftermath would bring horrors, too.

13

VICTORY?

"It brought home to me that war was such a terrible thing."
—BOMBER COMMAND VETERAN ON SEEING THE DEVASTATION
IN GERMANY

AMERICAN NAVIGATOR BILL RELLSTAB AND HIS CREW WERE PROVIDING A
cross-Channel taxi service in their stripped-down Fortress, flying Eighth
Air Force ground crew back to England from a three-day spree of letting
their hair down in Paris. With the war winding down, the generals had decided to let the base staff get a taste of European glamour before everyone
was shipped home. The date was May 8, 1945, and after taking off from
the Villacoublay airfield, they passed over Paris, swooping down to circle
the Eiffel Tower. Skipper Lou Tilley dipped a wing in a parting salute as
Rellstab plotted the course for their base in East Anglia, an hour's flying
time away. Rellstab recalled:

> I set the usual course back to base—Paris to the coast, across the Channel
> to Eastbourne, then a wide swing west around London before turning
> back east to the Third Division bomber bases in East Anglia. This sweep-
> ing arc around London was a matter of life or death. For six years, it was
> one of the most heavily defended cities in the world, and the air space
> above it was a forbidden zone, not only to German planes, but to our
> own. I was tuning in to the Armed Forces Network radio for some dance
> music and what I heard was the announcement of the German surrender.

I switched to intercom and told the skipper the good news. He asked for a course to London. We were going to buzz Piccadilly Circus, he told me. This did not seem a good idea to me. I didn't want us to be the one plane shot down over London after the war had ended because some antiaircraft gun crew didn't get the word in time, or did get the word, but after six years of ironclad defense of London, didn't believe it.

But I had my orders and so I plotted the course, and when the Thames came in view, we dropped to a lower altitude and flew up it toward the city. As the huge, four-engined B-17 thundered over the city, just clearing the building tops at what seemed like mast height, I was in the Plexiglas nose viewing the scene of a lifetime. There were hundreds of thousands of people in the streets, swarming over the statues in Trafalgar Square and Piccadilly Circus. It was as if you had kicked off the top of a huge anthill. I could see their faces. They were all turned up toward us and they were shouting and laughing and waving their arms wildly at us, and I was smiling and waving back. What a way to end the war! Nothing could ever beat the joy of being alive on May 8, 1945.[1]

RAF wireless operator Peter Marshall had also been airborne when he heard the news. He was just twiddling the dials to pass the time as his Lancaster was flying back and forth across the airfield at Strubby dropping sandbags on the grass, practicing in case they were assigned to food runs to Holland for Operation Manna. Bored, the pilot had just decided to head for the Nottinghamshire town of Mansfield, fifty miles away, where the bombardier's family lived, and scare the locals with some noisy, low-level passes. There wasn't anything for the radio man to do, so Marshall was tuning into the BBC Home Service. Suddenly the music broke off for a special announcement. The war in Europe was over. "I connected myself back into the aircraft intercom system and told everyone what I had just heard. None of us could believe it. The war was over! There was this incredible feeling, a sense that we had survived, that we were live heroes instead of dead heroes."[2] The skipper spared the ears and the nerves of the people of Mansfield. "Bloody good show!" he announced. "We'll land immediately. It's time for some leave."

Down on the ground, the partying began. "We just opened the bar and everybody was boozing it up. The Canadians and the Australians were excited they were going home. But we were also wondering what we were going to do now. Were we going to be unemployed? It slipped my mind that there was the Far East and the Japanese were still unbeaten. We were a newish crew and we were probably going to be sent there."[3] Others saw instantly that the end of the war in Europe contained the seeds of unwelcome change. Nobody was going to need tens of thousands of aircrew any more. Reg Davey was worried "about going back to a normal life. The war had occupied most of my adult life. I feared for my future."[4] Ken Newman shared his anxieties. "I and many thousands of the younger people in the services felt apprehensive. The older ones had jobs, homes, and families to return to, but we had barely started our adult lives before they were interrupted. We had got used to life in uniform and were comfortable with it, despite the darker side. We had difficulty in imagining what was about to follow."[5]

But the future could wait for now. First there was some serious celebrating to do. Bob Slockett and his crew got to fly over hysterical crowds in Paris. The B-17 from Knettishall took a spin round the thousand-foot-high Eiffel Tower at a few hundred feet below its summit. "The tens of thousands of people were so close we could almost see the whites of their eyes. The sight of them brought tears of happiness and pride to my eyes. After several tight and low turns around the tower and an even lower pass over the people in the streets below, we headed back to base, flying low over small French towns, whose grateful residents waved at us as we flew overhead."[6] Back in England, for Eric Banks and his mates, the timing of VE Day was a problem. It was *before* payday. He withdrew his entire savings of two pounds from the Post Office and pooled it with his friends. It was a night to remember—proceeding unsteadily from pub to pub, loud choruses of "Rose of Tralee"—though, not surprisingly, there were just blanks the next day where some of the details should have been. "At one point I may have addressed my companions on the evils of drink," he recalled tentatively.[7] It was enough that the evil of war was over. Dennis Steiner and his crew borrowed a builder's wheelbarrow, loaded it with WAAFs and paraded them round the town of Gainsborough in Lincolnshire.

We made a thorough nuisance of ourselves, climbing lampposts and drainpipes to take down the bunting and flags that had decorated the streets. Returning to base in an Austin Ruby car, our bombing leader drove it between the undercarriage and fuselage of the lined-up Lancasters. There was not a lot of room to spare! Next day, the mess was decorated with our purloined bunting until the mayor arrived in high dudgeon to reclaim it. He was well and truly entertained and had to be driven home, having lost all interest in his bunting.[8]

At his station, Reg Davey remembered all the aircraft being grounded to prevent inebriated crews from celebrating the end of the war with impromptu aerobatic displays and thereby adding to the final casualty list. A few days later he stood in a crowd in the square at Peterborough and listened to a loudspeaker relaying Churchill's victory speech. He cheered it along with everyone else, not noticing the prime minister's failure to mention Bomber Command in his list of credits. That wounding omission would become apparent soon enough. Dickie Parfitt took instant leave and went to Kent to celebrate the end of the war with his mother. What stuck in his mind about this period was people "going about their business *without fear*. We went to the pictures, a dance, attended a fête and a flower show."[9] It was a time to think of the future—he found himself buying some furniture. Freddie Hulance, his fears that he was going to die on that last raid to Berchtesgaden having proved unfounded, spent VE night in a pub in Chester with an old RAF friend he had not seen or heard from for years. He discovered that the friend had just returned from fifteen months in a POW camp in Germany. There was much to talk about, not least the fortunes and misfortunes of war. Hulance knew he had been the luckier one.

For some, though, VE Day was a somber and sober time. WAAF Pip Beck recalled a bonfire on the parade ground and a dance in the NAAFI [canteen]. "I didn't drink much. It was a curiously muted celebration, as if everyone was putting on an act. Perhaps we were. Too much had happened. So many people had died—so many known personally."[10] American pilot Walter Hughes had no sense of celebration at all. "There were guys at the base who went out and got roaring drunk. It wasn't for me. I was too affected by the war and the deaths I had seen. On that day I thought about Pete, my best friend, who had died by my side. I had nothing to celebrate. I thought about him every day. I still do."[11] Unlike many of his countrymen, Hughes had never felt comfortable in England, and his journey back across the Atlantic shortly after the end of hostilities—sleeping on a bunk in the squash court of a crowded liner full of German refugees who seemed to him to be getting better treatment than servicemen like him—left him even less enamored of the country and the continent he was leaving. He slept fully clothed the whole way, convinced the ship was going to sink in the terrible midocean storms or be torpedoed by rogue Nazi submarines.

It was not until he got all the way home to California that he really felt his war was over and he could get on with his life. Within weeks he had married the girl who had written him a letter every week he had been away, and he never piloted a plane again. On his discharge from the air force he was entitled to a private pilot's licence but at his last station they didn't have the forms. "At the time it was not so critical because I thought I was afraid of flying. It took almost a year before I found out I wasn't afraid of flying, *I was afraid of being shot at.* I had learned a skill at great expense to the government, one at which I was damn good, and which I never used again. It was all wasted." But Hughes was probably unusual in the sense of letdown he felt on getting home. Most men were just glad to be there. Earl Beitler of the 466th Bomb Group recalled "yelling and hollering as we crossed the border from Canada into Maine. End of war! End of mission! Back on U.S.A. soil! HOME! Thank you, God."[12] His return had been far from easy. All those Fortresses and Liberators—well, those that were not too damaged and become "hangar queens"—had to be flown back across the Atlantic to be prepared for shipping to the continuing war in the Far East. The trip back across the northern polar route turned out to be every bit as hazardous as coming out had been. *Dolores Jean,* Beitler's ship, only just made it. The first leg from Valley in Wales to Iceland was fine, but it was on the next leg to Goose Bay in Labrador that the weather closed in and he had mechanical problems.

We were at 10,000 feet and close to the southern tip of Greenland. We could see great ice fields below us, stretching far to the north. We were on automatic pilot when, without any warning, the wheel slammed back into my chest and the plane surged into a vertical climb that, within minutes, would fall off into an irreversible spin and dive. I disengaged the autopilot, pushed the wheel to the wall, and the nose came down in time. Some of the men I was carrying in the back—mainly ground crew who had never actually flown before—were thrown around and injured. Then ice began forming on the leading edges of the wings and the plane began to feel sluggish. Below we could see nothing but cloud—and no sign of Labrador. I had no wish to let down through the cloud not knowing if there was sea below us or mountains. Then, through my window, I saw a break in the cloud and waves breaking on a shoreline. I put her down in a spiral and we broke through the cloud at five hundred feet over Goose Bay. The gas supply by now was showing zero.

And then it was a hop and a skip home to Massachusetts.

Back in England, the hole left by the departing Americans was a shock. One minute there was a bustling, busy base, then next just a windswept and empty airfield. Schoolboy David Hastings had befriended the airmen since their arrival, and they had taken him to their hearts. To one crew and its skipper, Lieutenant Al Dexter, he was the mascot that kept them safe. School exams kept him away from his favorite base on the outskirts of Norwich for three weeks in May 1945, and when they were over he cycled out there again.

> And when I got there they were all gone. There wasn't a single airplane there—nothing. A friend and I cycled through the main gate. Nobody there, no guards, nothing to stop us. The whole place was completely un-guarded and empty. We cycled up to Al's hut—nobody there—and we went into the mess. It was like a place of ghosts. It was weird to go into the accommodation huts which the last time we had been there had been full of American airmen and full of trucks and noise and people moving about and then to suddenly find that it was utterly deserted. We cycled out to the tower and that was really like the *Marie Celeste*. In fact the two of us ended up cycling down the whole length of the runway as fast as we could. It was something that we'd never done. Now we did it as a tribute to the crews. We wanted to see what it was like to thunder up that run-way where we had watched the B-24s take off and land so many times.[13] And that was my war over.

The war was over but suffering was not. Back from a POW camp and safely home in Wembley Park, Middlesex, wireless operator Charlie Green forced himself to write a letter he dreaded—to the mother of his skipper, who had stayed at the controls of their Halifax bomber to give his crew a chance to escape. Officially, her son, Pilot Officer John Bunn, was still listed as missing in action. Green's sad task was to tell her he was definitely dead:

We had just dropped our bombs [on Hanau on the night of 6 January 1945], and I heard Johnny say, "Wizzo [splendid], now for home" when we were hit by flak. It set our wings and one engine on fire, which then spread to the fuselage. Johnny told us to bail out. The navigator and bomb aimer bailed out safely, as did the mid-upper gunner, but the engineer lost his head and with it his life, because he simply couldn't find his way out in the panic. Poor chap, it was only his second trip. I unfastened Johnny's safety straps and clipped on his chute. Just as we were both going to leave, we heard Roy's voice over the intercom telling us he was trapped in the rear turret. Johnny told me to get out. I told him he should come, too, because we could do nothing to help Roy.

By this time we were falling like a stone. I pleaded with Johnny, but he just smiled one of his old smiles and said he would hold on a few seconds longer so that Roy would have a little longer to free himself. I bailed out, and as my chute opened the aircraft hit the ground and blew up. I and the three others who escaped owe our lives to your son's bravery and absolute disregard for his own personal safety. Believe me, it has upset me to have to write this letter to you. But I thought it would be better if you knew just exactly what did happen that night. Your boy gave his life to save others. To me he will always remain in my memory as one of the bravest men who ever lived and died for their country. I owe my life to him and shall never forget it. This has been a poor letter, I'm afraid, and will be a blow to your hopes [that her son might after all have survived]. Please God, He will comfort you in your distress.[14]

The human suffering was not one-sided; far from it. In the months after the end of the war, the Air Ministry decided that ground crew should get the chance to go on flying trips to Germany to see the indirect results of their skills and hard work. Robert Wannop took one such group,

flying at only a few thousand feet to give our passengers the best possible view. They gazed in astonishment and sometimes horror at the scene below. We, too, were viewing the devastation at close range for the first time. The amount of damage caused by the combined efforts of the RAF and USAAF had to be seen to be believed. Town after town lay in complete havoc and ruin as though a giant bulldozer had run amok. Here were chaos, death, and destruction. The very heart of industrial Germany had been gouged out beyond repair. The homes of millions of people had gone as whole towns stood derelict. We could see a trickle of shabbily dressed people trudging along the battered streets. What they were doing or where they were going God alone knew. Where did they sleep? What did they eat?[15]

American airman Bob Slockett took Eighth Air Force ground crew on a similar tour but seemed less troubled by what he saw than his British counterparts were. He acknowledged the extent of the damage. "Essen, Hanover, and Frankfurt were a shambles. Any structures still standing were just shells with debris in the center. But in defense of the near total destruction of Nazi Germany from the air by the Allied air forces, we must remember that Hitler and his cohorts started it. Early in the war they attacked England with bombers and then followed later with buzz bombs and V-2 rockets." This was a common view among U.S. airmen. Author Gerald Astor interviewed scores of Eighth Air Force veterans for his book *The Mighty Eighth* and concluded that "few express regrets for what they did and most believe the German people of that time should recognize that their failure to resist the Nazi leaders justifies the devastation that befell their country." As the Americans headed home, happy that the job that they came to do was done, there were few recriminations. Nor would there be sixty years later. They were proud of their achievement, wanting only to be remembered, as Augustus Bolino put it, as "gallant warriors." Postconflict America, untouched by the physical devastation of war, welcomed back its fighting men as heroes and quickly returned to business as usual.

Defeat was terrible to see in Germany, but back in Britain victory after five and a half years at war was bittersweet. After that initial euphoria of VE Day, there were darker sentiments in the air. The country the men returned to was wrecked and impoverished after six years of fighting. The future looked precarious and frightening, while the past could not just be put away and forgotten. What they had seen and done still crowded the minds of fighting men. The world moved on, but not everyone moved with it. For some men, survival was all they had ever wanted. They got on with their lives, married the girls they had been courting through the war, or, if they were married already, returned to pick up on a family life that probably had never really had a proper chance to flourish.

Bob Pierson and Joyce, prevented by her father from getting married at the start of the war and having lived through it only by suppressing the constant fear of the danger Bob was in every time he flew, finally made it down the aisle. "We had always talked about the future and what we would do," Joyce recalled, "how we would have a nice house one day and a family. That's what we were looking forward to." The dream sustained them—and came true. "It all worked out beautifully in the end. I was so jubilant on VE Day. It was like a weight being lifted off. We had come through it. There was nothing to hold us back. I was lucky because so many people I knew lost their loved ones. But Bob came back, and I was just grateful that he was all right. We had three children and seven grandchildren."[16]

But wartime romances were often frantic, ill-judged affairs, and Tom Tate, for one, had married a woman he barely knew.

My mother had died when I was young and when I was twenty I got to know this lady who was eight years older than me. It was a friendship. She took care of me. When the war broke out and I joined up, I suggested to her that it might be a good idea to get married. I didn't expect to survive the war and if I died she would at least get a pension. So we married. I was twenty-one and Alice was twenty-nine. When I was away on duty, I wrote to her telling her not to be upset if I was killed and just to get on with her life. But, to my surprise, I did survive. When I came home in 1946 she said: "I won't hold you to this marriage if you don't wish to stay with me." But I did stay. I took out a mortgage, we bought a house, and we were married for fifty-one years and nine months until her death in 1991. It could not have been a happier marriage and friendship. I have no regrets. I was just grateful to have survived. I was one of the lucky ones.[17]

Not all men found the contentment that Tate had. Many felt disappointed at the peacetime world they returned to. It seemed cruel and uncaring after the comradeship of war. Tail gunner Ron Smith was one who knew, with great sadness, that his life would never be the same. He felt a tug at his heart when he left his squadron for the last time.

It came to me forcibly that I did not want to leave. I needed the consolation that I was still part of the squadron, of the aircrew whose reminiscences I could share. I needed the oily, distinctive smell of that rear turret, the half-fearful anticipation of being called to briefing, and, above all, the moments of sheer ecstasy when leaving the enemy coast behind after surviving yet another raid. What experience in my now certain future was going to compare with all that? It was like being reprieved, set free and hesitating at the gates, bewildered at the normality of everyday life.[18]

The intense experience of war marked him. What he had seen, the years of what he called Russian roulette, left him alone and rootless. Despite job and marriage and family, for the rest of his life he would feel an outsider.

As well as cruel and uncaring, the world these men returned to seemed harshly ungrateful, too. What they had done did not seem to matter. Dennis Steiner, with twenty-four operations as a bombardier behind him, holding his nerve as well as the lives of his crew in his hands over a dozen German cities, went back to his prewar employers to be told that, since he had been a lad when he left the company to go to war, he was entitled to only a lad's job and a lad's wage on his return. He was offered less than a third of the pay he had been getting as a flight lieutenant.[19] Others were unhappy to discover that their skills were redundant. Now the fighting was over, who needed a fully trained bombardier, or even a pilot for that matter? Arthur White had expected to return to his family's textile business, but it closed down just before the end of the war when his father died. "I then discovered that a navigator's wing and a tour of ops were no qualifications for anything in Civvy Street."[20] Nor did years of brushing with death give a man immunity from it in peacetime—a polio epidemic killed his wife, leaving him with their three-year-old son to bring up on his own.

Some men had physical and mental problems to deal with. American pilot Nicky Knilans, as disciplined and controlled a skipper as it was possible to find, discovered that, with the war over and the adrenaline no longer pumping, he was in an acute state of nervous exhaustion. He had physical ailments, too. "My unwinding nervous system left me with a heavy accumulation of water in my sinuses and behind my eyes, causing me great headaches and great difficulty in reading. But I did not believe I needed a psychiatrist. All I needed was rest."[21] However, he suffered depression for two years before he hauled himself round. Johnnie Clark's problem would not be solved for two decades. He had parachuted from his burning plane, the straps hastily and untidily clipped in place, and suffered a serious jolt in his pelvic region when the parachute opened. An examination by a doctor at a family planning center twenty years later revealed that this had given him a crude vasectomy, which was why he had been unable to have children. An operation made him whole—and fertile—again.[22]

Not all war damage was as easily reversed. Dennis Wiltshire had had a nervous breakdown after collapsing with fear and stress on a flight back from raiding Germany. He was eventually discharged as unfit for duty. He would have problems of acute anxiety for years afterward, spending time in hospitals and psychiatric institutions. It was the 1950s before he got his life together again, but then, twenty years later, he had another breakdown, related to the first. "I never really got back to normal," he said, "and all because of those experiences in the war."[23]

Bill Low had fractured his spine in five places when hitting the ground hard after being shot down, but the damage was as much to his morale as to his body.

When I came back after being a POW, I was miffed by how everybody else had got on and I was left with nothing. A lot of my contemporaries in Leeds had gone to work in the arms and aircraft factories to get out of going into the services. When I came back, they had all married, bought houses, and had a car in the garage waiting for petrol rationing to come off. I didn't feel it was fair. They had had a good time, no danger, no bombs, few air raids. I had severe back pains, no job, and most of the girls I knew were now married. I did wonder if what I had done had been worth it. I became very cynical. I hated going back to Civvy Street and the thought of a boring nine-to-five job. I missed the comradeship and the way of life. I found it terribly hard to get back to normal life.[24]

How quickly the gratitude to Bomber Command evaporated. In early March 1945, the House of Commons heard the secretary of state for air deliver a eulogy. "The effect of the strategic bomber offensive is felt on every front," Sir Archibald Sinclair said, "hampering and enfeebling the power of Germany in every element. Allied bombing is on such a colossal scale that Dr. Goebbels has had to admit that 'it can hardly be borne.' The swelling crescendo of destruction is engulfing oil plants, tank factories, and the communications of the German armies on every front as the Allied armies surge forward into Germany."[25] That same day, one MP singled out the bomber crews for carrying out "one of the most difficult moral performances that anybody has had to face in this war, sitting for hours in a narrow, uncomfortable cockpit or rear-gun turret and then bombing in cold blood. We owe a great *debt* to these men."[26] In that same debate, Richard Stokes, the member for Ipswich, was a lone voice protesting about area bombing, one of the few who had done so throughout the war. With renewed vigor, he asked: "At this period of the war, is the indiscriminate bombing of large centers of population, full of refugees, wise?" With Dresden as an example, he then asked: "Is terror bombing now part of our policy? If it is, I think we shall live to rue the day we have done this. It will stand for all time as a blot upon our escutcheon." A little more than two months later, with the war over, Germany defeated and the danger past, more and more people were drawn toward this form of questioning, led, of course, by the prime minister, Winston Churchill. The "debt" spoken about in the House of Commons was, it seemed, about to be welshed on.

Harris was quick to pay his own dues. Standing down his crews, he told them:

Your task in the German war is now completed. Famously have you fought. Well have you deserved of your country and her Allies. To you who survive, I say this: Content yourselves and take credit with those who perished that, now the cease-fire has sounded, countless homes will welcome back a father, husband, or son whose life, but for your endeavors and your sacrifices, would surely have been expended during long further years of agony to achieve victory. No Allied nation is clear of this debt to you.[27]

Three days later came the shattering blow in Churchill's victory broadcast to the nation. Harris and his former American counterpart, General Ira Eaker, listened to it on the radio together "with mounting incredulity," according to Harris's biographer, Henry Probert, as the prime minister listed what he considered the crucial moments of the war and the key contributors. "Of the strategic bombing campaign there was not one word. Harris always retained his admiration and affection for his old friend, Churchill, but he never forgot the slight on his men."[28]

The prime minister tried to make amends in private. He wrote to Harris expressing the nation's gratitude for Bomber Command's glorious part in the victory, speaking of "duty nobly done" and describing its contribution as decisive. Harris immediately copied it to his men, along with his own reply thanking Churchill for his unflagging support and personal understanding of the Command's needs. But the harm had been done. Churchill, his eyes now on the threat from Moscow, may have had good reason to play down the role of those who had devastated Germany at his behest. But Harris felt betrayed. In private, he was bitter, and more so when the prime minister took a part in turning down his request for a special Bomber Command campaign medal. Campaign medals were traditionally struck for those who had fought in foreign theaters of war, no matter what their job. As Harris put it, "Every clerk, butcher, or baker in the rear of the armies overseas had a 'campaign' medal,"[29] and he thought his ground crew, who had done a marvelous and thankless job, deserved nothing less. He pressed for a decoration that could be presented to Bomber Command aircrew and ground crew alike to recognize their unique combined achievement.[30] The idea was shot down in flames, for reasons still unclear.[31] The decision from above was that the ground crew would be entitled only to the ubiquitous and nonspecific Defense Medal.

What further rankled with the aircrews of Bomber Command then, and still does to this day, was the withdrawal of their unique and distinctive Aircrew Europe Star. After the D-Day landings it was replaced by the more general France and Germany Star awarded to all members of the three services who operated in northwest Europe after 6 June 1944. The result was that a man who had flown thirty operations in the last year of the war, dodging the flak and the fighters, would now be wearing the same medal as a clerk who had served in the rear echelons of the invasion forces.

Harris fought back in typical fashion—loudly and personally, with harsh words and threats. The fact that peacetime politics demanded soft words and subtlety escaped him. To his superiors at the RAF—the wrong target, in any case, since the matter was out of their hands and they were as miffed by the decision as he was—he thundered that he too would have the Defense Medal *and nothing more!* He would not be the recipient of honors "while my people—who have given for so long such devoted service—are denied any recognition beyond the gesture so far made. I will be proud to wear the Defense Medal and that alone—and [I will be] as bitter as the rest of my personnel. I will not stand by and see [them] let down in so grossly unjust a manner without resorting to every protest which is open to me." He added a sting in the tail. "I shall now leave the Service as soon as I can and return to my country—South Africa."[32]

Harris was now a square peg in a round hole. He didn't fit a peacetime RAF. Words like "affront" and "injustice" peppered his thoughts and his correspondence. Everything had become dust and ashes to him. The Air Ministry spoke of his "violent and intolerant personality"[33] and suggested a quick departure. He announced his retirement in the autumn of 1945 and went, grumbling that he had been a few months short of qualifying for the full pension of an air chief marshal and that the Treasury insisted on sticking by the rules. He was the loser by sixty pounds a year, a not inconsiderable sum, as a result of the sort of pettifogging bureaucracy which had been the bane of his working life during the war and which was making many of those lower down the Bomber Command scale than him equally disenchanted with postwar Britain and their place in it. Nor would there be the handy retirement job of a colonial governorship or some other public post for Harris. He had few friends in the Labour government that ousted Churchill in the general election in the summer of 1945. His personality and his politics were against him.

He left the country with his family to work for a shipping line in South Africa, a willing exile who returned for the occasional official function and reunion, though he turned down the vast majority of invitations simply because there were too many. To his Bomber Command crews, he was as distant and as elusive now as he had been when he directed them from High Wycombe, but they seemed to respect and admire him as much as they always had, perhaps more. After all, he had stood up for them, made common cause with them, and been badly treated in return. Some believed—wrongly, in fact—he had been sacked, that out of spite he had been denied the honor of a seat in the House of Lords due to a commander of his eminence and achievement, and that he had been forced to leave the country in disgrace. The treatment of him was a slight on them all.

Harris may have grown in the affections of his men, but to the rest of the world he was increasingly the symbol of a war whose horrors people wanted to forget. His own memoirs, written quickly and published in 1947 before any other Second World War commander of significance had had time to get into print,[34] did nothing to rescue him. He wrote with candor of the campaign to devastate cities, offered no apologies or caveats, and was entirely unsentimental about civilian casualties except to proclaim the truth that they were an inevitable consequence of war and always had been. The book was shocking in its bluntness: "The idea was to keep on at small targets for their strategic importance but, to put it crudely, not to mind when we missed." Its matter-of-fact tone could easily become offensive, as when he almost casually admitted to starting the "fire tornadoes" of Hamburg and Dresden and at one point spoke of "uselessly devastating two perfectly good French towns." These hasty words concealed his true moral position. He thought war shameful and that mankind would only avoid its own self-destruction by adopting some form of world government. But if wars had to be fought, then men like him were there to fight them to the best of their ability. He damned the politicians who had failed to tell the public the truth about the bombing he had carried out on their behalf. "There was nothing to be ashamed of, except in the sense that everybody might be ashamed of the sort of thing that has to be done in every war, *as of war itself*."

But such humanitarian asides could not soften the overall tenor of the book. Churchill had warned Harris to be careful in what he owned up to, cautioning him "not to admit anything not justified by the circumstances and the actions of the enemy in the measures we took to bomb Germany."[35] The wily diplomat and statesman, fully aware of how history is made, was advising his old friend to argue his case thoroughly. He should, for example, make it clear that "we gave the Germans full notice to clear out of their munition-making cities." Harris ignored the advice, preferring to state what he saw as the truth in all its uncompromising brutality rather than cavil and cajole. He got the mood wrong and paid the price with his reputation.

The publication of a spate of wartime memoirs and histories in the mid-1950s and early 1960s left him exposed to more vilification. It began with Clement Attlee, deputy to Churchill during the war and then postwar Labour prime minister, who wrote of his worries about area bombing in general and Harris in particular. Harris demanded a public retraction. "I am weary of the repeated attempts since the war to saddle me, and me alone, with the bombing policies ordered and approved by HM Government, *of which you were a leading member*."[36] Then came the official history of the bombing war, with whose academic authors Harris had, in his curmudgeonly way, refused to cooperate. He could not, therefore, complain when it failed to reflect his views—though complain he did, accusing the authors of having come to the project with preconceived unfavorable ideas about Bomber Command. The man who had been so expert at putting his case to those whose support he needed during the war let his pomposity get in the way of promoting his version of events for posterity.

When the rigorously researched and immensely detailed four-volume official history—*The Strategic Air Offensive Against Germany 1935–1945*—was published in 1961, Harris dismissed it without even reading it in full (or possibly at all). It "exaggerates our errors and decries our victories,"[37] he declared. In fact the volumes were very fair to Harris, judging that the bombing offensive had been vital to the victory and that Harris had been a great commander, though one who had made mistakes, his claim that bombing alone could defeat the enemy being one of them and the failed battle of Berlin in 1943 another. It also concluded that his policy of returning Bomber Command to the devastating of German cities after the summer of 1944 instead of concentrating all, instead of only some, of his efforts on oil and transportation links, could be seriously faulted.

Inevitably it was the brickbats rather than the blessings that made the headlines. The view that prevailed was that the *Official History* condemned the whole of the bombing offensive as a costly failure. A review by the left-wing Labour MP Richard Crossman used the book to lay into Harris for his fanatical belief in terror bombing and for having been utterly wrong in almost every major decision he made. Crossman relished the fact that the legend of Bomber Command's contribution to the war had at last been comprehensively rubbished. The tone was set in the press and in popular opinion, and it fitted the times. The Berlin Wall had gone up that same year, 1961. It was as if a generation struggling with the concept of nuclear annihilation—a concept that became all too real in the Cuban missile crisis of the following year—had backdated its fears and found a safe villain from the past to vilify.

It was an odd attitude to adopt in the circumstances. The one thing that was certain in an uncertain nuclear age was that war would be total and civilians would be the targets. There would be no pretence of hitting military installations. Whole cities and their populations would be wiped out, and everyone knew it. There could be no rules of engagement, no chivalry, no Geneva Convention, in an exchange of intercontinental ballistic missiles. The confusing gray area in which Harris and Bomber Command had operated no longer existed. Perhaps the blame fell on him because what he had done had blurred the moral picture in the first place. The route from Hamburg to Dresden to Hiroshima and then to a world that saw itself on the edge of self-administered extinction was undeniable. Books on Dresden quoting huge and inaccurate casualty figures further added to the shame heaped on Harris and his men. Economic and military analysts of the war also began to question whether the bombing of Germany had achieved anything at all apart from terrorizing its inhabitants. Had it done anything to slow down the Third Reich's military production? To some historians, it seemed not. As the years went by, Harris's standing plummeted even further, until there were those who argued he was guilty of war crimes.

In the United States, there were none of these recriminations. America had moved on. A military that had once worried in case it was seen to be targeting civilians in Germany had changed gear in the Pacific. Even before the end of the war in Europe, B-29 Superfortresses had firebombed Tokyo, dropping 1,700 tons of bombs and turning sixteen square miles of the city with its flimsy wood-and-plaster buildings into an inferno. Eighty thousand people died. That attack, on 10 March 1945, was the start of a relentless five-month bombing campaign that destroyed half the habitable area of sixty-six Japanese cities, made a quarter of the population homeless, and killed at least 300,000 civilians and perhaps as many as 900,000.[38] The expressed intention was the one that Harris had always intoned (and for which he had been ridiculed)—that destruction on this scale would induce the enemy to surrender and make a costly invasion and city-by-city (or in Japan's case, island-by-island) conquest unnecessary. U.S. analysts put the potential American casualties of such an invasion at a million or more soldiers, sailors, and airmen, a powerful argument not only to continue the bombing but to go a stage farther when the Japanese continued to resist. In August 1945, the world's first atomic bomb fell on Hiroshima, killing a hundred thousand men, women, and children. One bomb was not enough. Japan surrendered only after a second bomb three days later flattened the port of Nagasaki. An immediate effect of the surrender was that the RAF's Okinawa-bound Tiger Force of a thousand bombers, promised to the Americans as reinforcements for their conventional war on Japan, was stood down. Men like Ken Newman and Peter Marshall, who had been rostered for duties in the Pacific, were mightily relieved, and their families even more so.

The United States was in the vanguard of a new world order with new weapons that outdated anything Bomber Command or the Eighth Air Force had carried. Two-ton cookies were pinpricks now. The Hiroshima bomb was ten thousand times more powerful. And it needed only one aircraft to deliver that deadly firepower instead of an armada. In the atomic age that began in the summer of 1945, what had happened to Hamburg, Dresden, Pforzheim, and Würzburg was already history. And it was a history largely unclouded by controversy and doubt on that side of the Atlantic. The tone was set by USAAF general Curtis LeMay—who had been an Eighth Air Force pioneer in England before transferring to the Pacific theater, where he commanded the B-29 squadrons that devastated Japan. "As to worrying about the morality of what we were doing—," he said, "nuts! I was a soldier, soldiers fight. If we made it through the day without exterminating too many of our own people, we thought we'd had a pretty good day."[39] It was an attitude that might appal the increasingly vocal British critics of the conduct of the bomber war, but many an airman who had been in the front line would nod his head in agreement.

The Americans were happy to draw a line under the European war. A Washington intelligence briefing document of July 1945 was straightforward in describing what the bombers—both American and British—had achieved and unashamedly triumphalist in its language. "A broken Reich states the case for strategic bombing" it was headlined, and went on:

In past wars it has always been necessary to dispose of an enemy army before being able to destroy, occupy, or dictate terms to the enemy nation (which, in the last analysis, is the real foe). The recent European war was unlike all others in that this time the enemy nation was destroyed almost ahead of the army which was supposed to defend it. . . . Her bridges are down, her canals ruptured, her harbors clogged, her rail yards pitted, many of her factories blasted and silent, her cities gutted. Wherever Germans gathered to build things or even to live together in large numbers may now be found scenes of desolation like those on the face of the moon. It is safe to say that at no time since the locustlike days of the Tartars has the physical property of a nation been ground into such small and useless fragments.[40]

Not surprisingly, it declared that the most important factors in the final victory had been the USAAF-led campaigns to knock out the Luftwaffe and the German aircraft industry, destroy transportation links, and, finally, deprive the German military of fuel by attacking oil production. But it also acknowledged the long-term benefit—"a somber undertone to this symphony of aircraft-rail-oil destruction"—of the RAF's "continuing campaign against German manufacturing in general, sapping the energies of factories and machine shops of all kinds in the cities they were methodically erasing." The result was that Germany's armies had found

the country at their backs had become an industrial graveyard. They retreated across the Rhine, falling back through one ghost city after another. They were out of food, out of gas, out of ammunition, out of transport. They surrendered in droves—a wrecked army in a wrecked nation. Nobody who was not there when the roof fell in to see it for himself can grasp the scope of the destruction which was meted out to the Germans. Of their fifty largest cities, all were from 30 percent to 80 percent destroyed. Dazed citizens wandered through crooked little paths between mountains of rubbish. The patched and repatched factories were silent, their twisted metal guts slowly rusting in the sun. Children played on the tracks of otherwise motionless rail yards. Sheep grazed on airfields. Of the complex and wonderful edifice on which countless Germans had labored for generations, little remained but the bare bones.

The authors of this intelligence assessment had had access to the post-surrender interrogation reports on leading Nazi generals and industrialists, and it quoted the reason they gave for their country's defeat. Generaloberst Georg Lindemann declared unequivocally that "the reason Germany lost the war was Allied air power." Generalmajor Kolb said that Allied day and night strategic bombing "forced Germany on the defensive from the middle of 1940." Another general, Georg Thomas, thought that "without bombing the war would have lasted for years longer" and Feldmarschall Albert Kesselring that "Allied air power was the greatest single reason for the German defeat." Alfred Krupp, the arms manufacturer, said air attacks left his works operating at only 40 percent of capacity, though he thought the Allies would have caused him more problems if they had concentrated their attacks on transportation links. "They made a mistake in failing to bomb rail lines and canals much earlier. Transport was the greatest bottleneck in production." Another industrialist said: "The virtual flattening of the steel city of Düsseldorf contributed at least half of the collapse of the German effort." A tank manufacturer, Oscar Henschel, said he was able to produce only forty-two Tiger tanks a month in the latter stages of the war instead of 120. He reckoned there had not been enough attacks—"If the bombers had kept up their attacks on my plants for two or three successive days, they would have been put out of commission for months."

And so the reports went on. Some of the beaten Germans picked out the attacks on transportation as the vital ones in their defeat—"The army could not bring up its reserves as the railways were cut" (General Karl Bodenschatz). Others saw the blitzing of oil plants as the crucial factor—"It was the Allied bombing of our oil industries that had the greatest effect. We had plenty of planes and pilots but lack of petrol didn't permit the expansion of training" (Luftwaffe General Adolf Galland). The Washington report listed the views of twenty-nine German leaders and ended with a photograph of a thirtieth—Adolf Hitler. "Not available for comment" was the tongue-in-check caption.

That, then, was the American verdict on the bombing war over Germany. It contained no criticism of the British. On the contrary, it celebrated the Combined Bomber Offensive as a brilliant transatlantic partnership. Ironically, however, that Washington assessment contained the seeds of Harris's and Bomber Command's later discomfort. Those comments from German leaders were precisely the points that critics would pick over in the postwar postmortems. Oil and transport were targets Harris had been reluctant to concentrate on and yet these were the ones his enemies saw as the cause of their defeat. He had done more against those targets than is generally assumed but less than he might have. Harris had misjudged the situation. The important thing to remember in assessing him, however, is that he had his reasons, which, at the time and on the information available to him, seemed sound. In his memoirs he explained himself: "In the event, the offensive against oil was a complete success, but I still do not think it was reasonable, *at that time,* to expect that the campaign would succeed. What the Allied strategists did was to bet an outsider, and it happened to win the race."[41] He had thought it wiser to stick with the favorite and continue with "a method of attack which was indisputably doing the enemy enormous harm." But, he added, he had targeted oil as directed, and the success on this front would have been impossible without Bomber Command's contribution. And he also had a debriefed Nazi whose evidence he could call in his support. He had Albert Speer's word to his interrogators at Nuremberg that there had been a shortage of manpower for the armaments factories because so many workers had to be diverted to building air-raid shelters and clearing up the damage after attacks. He had Speer's opinion, too, that, had the Hamburg blitz of 1943 been quickly followed up with attacks on another six German cities—as Harris had wanted to do but did not have the resources at that time—it would have crippled "the will to sustain armament manufacture and war production, and brought about a rapid end to the war."[42]

The truth is, of course, that, like every other military commander, Harris had made mistakes, some (if not all) of which he owned up to. The question is whether those mistakes warranted the wholesale rejection of everything he did by postwar critics and the demeaning of the men under his command. Here the observations of two military historians are useful guides. To Richard Holmes, professor of military studies at Cranfield University and the Royal Military College of Science,

like the firestorms that were its most dreadful expression, condemnation of the bombing campaign has fed upon itself until the flames of cant and the smoke of hypocrisy have obscured its many accomplishments. Not least was the saving of countless Allied soldiers' lives. But the primary aim of the campaign was always to make life for the average German more burdensome and less productive. Area bombing substantially reduced German productivity, not least by driving the working population into air-raid shelters night after night, and the proportion of the German war effort diverted to air defense was considerable, including 75 percent of the dual-purpose 88mm guns that were the bane of the Allied armor.[43]

As for Harris, Denis Richards, biographer of Portal and of Bomber Command itself, concluded: "The public perception of him simply as a wrecker of German cities obscures his general qualities as a commander—his intelligence, courage, decisiveness, technical competence, and dominant but not unfriendly personality. Through his clarity, firmness, and obvious determination to give the enemy a hard time, he enjoyed the awed respect and obedience of his entire Command."[44]

As the attacks on Harris and Bomber Command gained momentum, the

men who fought the bomber war became increasingly dismayed. Some historians attacked him but exonerated them, extolling their courage, claiming
even that they were victims themselves, sent by a man who was either evil
or mad to risk their lives over Germany, and all for nothing. It was a return
to the old First World War slogan—lions led by donkeys. But the men—
Harris's "old lags," as they were proud to be known—stood by him. Having returned to England from South Africa in the mid-1950s, from then
until his death in 1984 at the age of ninety-two he was a hero guest at reunions. He would tell the veterans they had never been given the recognition they deserved, and they would stand and cheer him to the echo.

To outsiders, the veterans kept quiet about their war. Harris himself
rarely spoke in public. But among themselves, they clung to their achievements and lionized their commander in chief. The alternative was unaccept-
able, unfair, and undeserved. If they were to accept the criticisms, at best
they would have to acknowledge that their wartime efforts, and, more important, the sacrifice of over 55,000 dead comrades, had been to no purpose. At worst they would have to view themselves as accomplices in
atrocities.

And, just as it had been back in the war, it was them against the world.
Bomber Command's esprit de corps, always high even at the worst of times
in the war, became, if possible, even greater as they came under attack in
peacetime. At a reunion for the whole command in 1977, Harris told the
men: "You inflicted on the Germans the greatest of all their lost battles. But
in all the war histories, you have been subjected to the sneers and smears of
so-called leading military historians."[45] Tail-End Charlies would not stop
applauding him at a dinner of the Air Gunners' Association. Responding to
the emotion of the occasion, Harris asked them: "Will you go back to
Dresden or Nuremberg or Berlin tonight?" and according to one of those
present, "Every man there would have stepped forward and said: 'Yes, sir,
we will go.' "[46] And no one could be in any doubt that they meant it.

14

FORGOTTEN HEROES

"Those were sad days indeed for us all."
—SIR ARTHUR HARRIS TO ALBERT SPEER, 1972

A FEW YEARS AFTER THE WAR, EIGHTH AIR FORCE WAIST GUNNER WALTER Mayberry returned to Knettishall, his station in Suffolk. He had last seen it from the air, looking out of his turret as his B-17 Flying Fortress took off for a mission to Nuremberg. The plane was shot down and he saw out his war at Stalag VIIA at Moosburg until it was liberated by General George Patton's forward troops at the end of April 1945. Knettishall was left a ghost town when the Eighth went home in the summer of 1945, and ghosts were all Mayberry could find when he returned several years later. His mind was flooded with memories as "before me, distorted shapes in the gathering darkness, stands a row of barracks, quiet and deserted; shelters that once knew the voices of many men, walls that knew their dark and lonely hours and shared their happiness and their sorrows; walls that once listened to tales of home, of war. Once friendly places now empty, deathly still and stark." He walked along "paths that once felt the step of GI shoes and heavy flying boots, paths now overgrown and reclaimed by the creeping grass."

He saw the runways stretching out into the distance, "long ribbons of white that once felt the weight of a thousand warplanes, heavily laden with men—and death for those who trembled below." It was deserted and deathly quiet, but he heard in his mind the noise of a hundred giant engines thundering in the morning air. I hear the quiet voices of men talking, soon to go off into the dawn, and I see a thousand khaki-clad warriors in endless rows, marching to the heart-stirring strains of martial music, their colors whipping in the cold wind. For a fleeting instant, I see again those silver giants taking to the air. I hear the low murmur of last-minute "good lucks," and the thunderous roll call of men long gone. I feel a great sorrow, the sting of tears—and lift a heavy hand in final salute.[1]

His pride, emotion, and nostalgia were very different from what the men of RAF Bomber Command were—and are—feeling. Their hurt at the postwar savaging of their reputation along with that of their commander in chief has not lessened with time. After the fortieth anniversary of VE Day in 1985, former aircrew were incandescent at what they saw as snubs to them in the media coverage. One old crewman wrote of his "disgust and dismay" at reading in newspapers.

groveling and sanctimonious apologia for the bombing of German targets. By all means let us forgive but not forget. It was very sad to see so little mention of the mighty effort of Bomber Command in winning the war. The great exploits and victories were relegated to fifth-rate skirmishes and wasted efforts directed by misguided warlords. Let the critics with their carping tongues and biased pens, the agitators, and the detractors visit any military cemetery in Europe and see the profusion of headstones marked "Bomber Command."[2]

Today—two decades on from that anniversary—the eyes of a smaller band of men, now in their eighties, still sparkle with anger. Voices are raised. "People talk as though we slaughtered women and children because we wanted to, because we enjoyed it," said Bill Kiley. "I get very bitter about the criticism. They don't understand. Britain was fighting for its life."[3] "We took the fight to the enemy, but as soon as the war was over, there was a nasty smell about Bomber Command. Even Churchill didn't want to know us—which was pretty sad considering the losses and the sacrifices that were made," Ken Newman concluded. He felt let down at the time and still burns with resentment at the slight to their honor.[4]

"We are classified as the next best thing to murderers," said engineer Jack Watson, a veteran of seventy-seven operations, a man who had returned from Nuremberg to see the names of a quarter of his squadron wiped from the operations board, twenty-eight friends dead.

When the war finished, the country kicked out Churchill, and Labour came in and they suddenly realized that they had bombed Germany to hell and flattened it and now they would have to help build it up again. Then they started talking about the terrible civilian losses. None of the politicians wanted to take responsibility for that. They were so worried about the public reaction. So we took the blame. I feel bitter. It's sickening to think that all those men died to keep this country free and their memory is being tarnished. I am proud of what we did.[5]

If nothing else, he argued, the bombing war diverted German arms from the front line to protecting the cities.

If the bombing campaign hadn't have been carried out, D-Day would have been a complete fiasco, because the stacks of 88mm guns that were around the cities, especially Berlin, would all have been on the Atlantic wall and killing our troops as they came ashore. Our bombing campaign also forced the Germans into building fighter planes instead of bombers. If they had been able to produce just bombers, imagine what they could have done to this country.

Pilot Freddie Hulance, whose operations included Dresden, had no time for critics of Bomber Command, delivering their judgments with all the benefits of hindsight.

After Dresden I think there were 400 Bomber Command aircraft lost with their crews. The war was far from over. I saw my role as saving lives rather than taking them. What I did was help shorten the war rather than allowing it to continue for a longer period. I once heard someone describe the bombing of Dresden as a "holocaust." Well, that was a word I first heard at the end of the war when we were shown what the Germans had done to the Jews. Knowing the real meaning of "holocaust," I am even more proud to have been in Bomber Command. I don't think we need to justify our actions—perhaps explain them but not to make excuses. There was a war on and we had to win it.[6]

Like many veterans he was baffled by people who seemed to think it could be won without casualties. The reality was different, according to Arthur White, and those discrediting Bomber Command needed to remember that. "When I saw a target I was awestruck at the devastation we had helped to create, but I consoled myself with the thought that this was war. It was us or them."[7]

Reg Davey, a navigator who also lost friends at Nuremberg—"the cream of our youth"—and knew it could just as easily have been him, believed that, unfashionable as it might sound today, they were being patriots.

We were fighting for our country. We knew that Hitler was a tyrant and we hated him and the other leaders like Goebbels and Goering. But I felt no personal hate against the German people. I just knew we had to win the war to stop them taking over the whole of Europe. We went through it so that we are all free today. But it was a near thing. When I look back on those days, I think of them as very thrilling. I am very grateful that I was allowed to take part, grateful that I survived, grateful that I was in the company of some very brave people. A lot of people who were in Bomber Command in the war don't talk about it. They have pushed it out of their mind. But I am happy to hold my head up and say I did my bit for my country. I try to tell people, to spread the word, to let them know what happened and what we went through.[8]

It upset Dickie Parfitt that, over the years, so much attention and adulation went to Fighter Command and the Spitfire and Hurricane pilots, as if the Battle of Britain ended the war rather than began it.

People forget that fighter pilots were in the air for two hours at the most and if they were shot down it was usually over their home ground. We in bombers were over Germany, sometimes for eight hours, and if we went down there was a good chance of being shot or lynched. I am asked, "Did you kill people?" and the answer is "Yes, I obviously did." We were fighting an all-out war. People don't understand what we went through. Flying took its toll on us physically but also, more than we realized, mentally. The losses were terrible—55,000 men killed. I think the government refused to give Bomber Command a separate medal because they were frightened of upsetting the Germans in the period after the war. So many friends sacrificed their lives, and their efforts weren't recognized or appreciated by people living in freedom because of what they and Bomber Command had done. As for Harris, the fondness for him came when the criticism of him started. We weren't just protecting Butch, we were protecting our own reputations.[9]

It was hard to forget what had been the greatest, most influential experience of your life, to put it behind you and never revisit it. Alongside the awfulness of war and death and destruction, as most veterans recognized, had gone excitement and comradeship the like of which they would never see again.

Boris Bressloff never lost his guilt at not saving his friend, Jimmy, trapped in a burning Lancaster from which Bressloff escaped. As an old man, the memories would flood back and with them the tears. He could never stop himself from thinking that "if I hadn't been so selfish, there was just the slightest chance I might have saved him. I shall die feeling guilty about that."[10] He recalled his Bomber Command years as "a time of horror, fear, happiness, excitement. All the normal human emotions were there but exaggerated. There was the joy of realizing you're young and you're fit and you're with people that you loved. I really did. I loved my lot. Wonderful guys." Peter Twinn, a Tail-End Charlie who fought his war from the rear gun turret, said:

It was a wonderful experience which I wouldn't have missed, despite all the dangers, the fears, seeing friends not come home, seeing aircraft shot down. It was something that not many people have had the chance to experience. It was something unique to us and the time. We were damned lucky to have the opportunity to do it and to get through it. We did things we'd never dreamt of. We had friendship we had never imagined possible. Seven blokes in a crew as close as a family. In fact, they *were* family.[11]

But, as families often are, they were not always very good at keeping in touch. Miles Tripp's crew had dispersed in March 1945 with heartfelt (if drink-fueled) pledges to stay in contact "for the rest of our lives." They lost each other immediately, and stayed lost for more than twenty years, when Tripp, his conscience pricked and his curiosity aroused about the men he had lived and fought with and been prepared to die alongside, set out to track them all down. It took him two years, but he finally got all seven of the crew together (albeit one on the end of a telephone in Australia) in 1969. Reunions flourished as the men got older—and could throw up huge and happy surprises. Peter Marshall was visiting RAF Coningsby in Lincolnshire in 1997 on a squadron reunion when he saw three men he was sure were dead. To the best of his knowledge they had died on the raid to Berchtesgaden fifty-two years earlier. "I was walking across the car park with my friend Ralph and he said: 'Look! There are three ghosts.' It was De Marco's crew. We thought they had all bought it when his Lancaster crashed in the mountains, but it turned out they had escaped. It was amazing that they appeared after all that time."

It was not just old comrades who met up again after an interval of many years. David Hastings, the schoolboy who had hung around U.S. bases near Norwich, could never forget the remarkable times he had as a boy with his American friends, and as he got older he looked for ways to recreate them. The crew that had adopted him—under their skipper Al Dexter—had completed their tour in November 1944 and gone home.

At the end of his last mission, I gave Al a model of his B-24—she was called *Pugnacious Princess Pat* after his wife—I had carved out of wood. I remember they were absolutely wild with joy that day, and, at one level, so was I. I had spent so much time hoping and praying and willing them through each mission. I had shared their tension when they got to their twenty-eighth mission and thought they had only two more to go and then they suddenly found they had to go up to thirty-five. I didn't see them leave for their thirty-fifth but I know they were anxious that they might not make it. But I was there for their return, and they were the happiest I ever saw them. Al was an old-school pilot, so he just did a normal landing—he didn't do anything stupid—the low-level buzzing of the base that some of the others did in their excitement. He just landed and taxied back in and they were all waving like mad out of the windows. There was so much hand shaking and laughter and I walked round the airplane for the last time to check for bullet holes. There weren't any. It was sad for me, I suppose. I was an adopted member of the crew and they were great friends with the whole of my family. They had become very much part of our life, and the thought of losing them was horrific. But, at the same time, I realized what it meant to them that they were going home. They had been in a foreign country a long way from home for a long time. I knew Al's wife would be longing to have him back. When I gave him the model of his plane, he was really moved by it and emotional. I didn't realize at the time how much our friendship had meant to him and the crew. What apparently kept them going was having me and my family as friends. It meant a lot to them to fly missions but then to have these English people they could come and see, visit in their home, and spend a normal life with.[12]

On Dexter's way back to Minnesota, the model of *Pugnacious Princess Pat* was damaged, and it may have been his embarrassment at this that led to Dexter failing to keep in touch with his young friend back on the other side of the Atlantic. Perhaps he was also busy getting to know his own family again and throwing himself back into making a living as a civilian. But the sad fact is that the two lost touch. The boy, though, did not forget. He grew up, became a successful businessman, learned to fly, and always hankered after the chance to see his wartime buddy again. "I tried everything. Every time there was a reunion or convention involving former U.S. airmen I would phone all the hotels asking if they had a Dexter staying there. And I lost count of the appeals I made in the newsletters of ex-servicemen's organizations. Then one day the phone rang at home, I picked it up and a voice said: 'Hi, I'm Al Dexter.' " The wartime friendship of an American pilot and the English boy who hero-worshipped him was renewed, as strong as ever.

But memories were inevitably tinged with sadness. Bill Carman was just one of countless airmen troubled by the death of comrades, and forced to address the question that seemed to hang in the air constantly but to which he could never find an answer "Why them and not me?" He had bailed out of a burning Lancaster on his twenty-eighth operation in August 1944. Only two of the crew survived. "I don't know how I got away and the others didn't. It must have been fate. And why me? I'm not particularly religious. The mid-upper gunner survived, too, but he was Salvation Army and I could understand him being saved. But not me. When I went to see the graves of the others I felt so bad. They were good pals . . ."[13] The parents of his dead comrades had also come to see him and he could see in their eyes the same question—why was he alive when their son was dead? "I couldn't explain it. You can't, can you?" And as he told his story sixty years later, his voice trailed off into tears. He recovered himself and added: "It was all so long ago now but the guilt doesn't diminish with time." He too had buried his past to begin with. "I had no time for reminiscing. I just got on with life. Other people didn't want to know. If you talked about your wartime service, you thought to yourself that you were shooting a line and so you shut up." He carried his survivor's guilt alone until, thirty years after the end of the war, he was drawn to aircrew reunions and discovered he was by no means the only one with those feelings. "That experience was happening everywhere."

As well as guilt at having survived, many former aircrew also felt hate. They despised the Germans for starting the war, pursuing it with such cruelty, and then costing even more lives by refusing to surrender even though all was lost. There were individual reasons to hate as well. Lieutenant Ira Weinstein had seen his pilot pitchforked to death after surrendering and run the gauntlet of Germans desperate to lynch him. Safely back in the United States, he went on a sad mission of condolence. He was determined to fulfil his pledge to himself to tell the parents of his crew how their sons had died.

When I got back to the States I said to my wife, "All those parents get is a killed-in-action notice, nothing else, no explanation from the government. They must wonder what happened." I found out where they lived from the War Department and then I telephoned and told them who I was and that I had been on the same mission as their boy. I offered to visit them and, of course, they all wanted me to. It was very difficult for me. I was twenty-four years old, hardly an adult yet. There were lots of tears. What could I say? Was I really going to tell them the truth—that their kid was burned to a crisp and died in agony? I held back on the gory details, just told them that we were in a terrible battle and that they were probably shot during that battle, and that I buried their bodies. But it was a horrible experience, not something you forget. Every now and then I wake up at night thinking about those meetings.[14]

Ira swore to himself he would never go back. He kept to his word for forty years of a profitable peace, in which time he built a successful business in Chicago and raised a family. Well off, he traveled the world but avoided Germany. Nor were there any BMWs or Mercedes in the Weinstein driveway. When fellow veterans tried to persuade him to go on a reunion trip to Germany, he refused. But he did enter into a correspondence with a local historian from the area in which he had been captured. For his children and grandchildren, Weinstein was also reconstructing his past, putting together the history of his war.

With the old century gone and a new one beginning, in 2000 he relented for reasons he still could not totally explain. But it was time to put away the past. Aged eighty-one, he went back. "One can never get rid of the memories, but one can overcome the feelings," he told a German newspaper that reported his visit. There were strange reunions. He met the boy— now a man in his sixties—who had found him when he was on the run after bailing out and saved his life by turning him in to the local burgomaster and not the SS. In the village in central Germany where it had all happened— where Weinstein had been the enemy, the *Terrorflieger,* and a small lad's kindness was all that stood between him and a bullet in the neck—the two of them walked down the street and, as the American recalled, "I'm not ashamed to admit that the tears were flowing." The return had become a reconciliation, fifty-six years to the day since his plane had been shot down.

For wireless operator Tom Tate, there was an important reconciliation, too. He had escaped a lynching in Huchenfeld, a village outside the German city of Pforzheim, in 1945 but discovered after the war that five of his fellow crew had been murdered by local youths. He returned with war crimes investigators, picked out the perpetrators, gave evidence at their trial, and left Germany with the satisfaction of knowing that death sentences and jail terms had been handed out to those responsible. Like Weinstein, he swore he was done with Germany. He would never return. But those five deaths continued to trouble him deeply. He could not forget. "Why was it important to remember those five out of the millions? Because they were my friends and I was with them until the last moment and I almost suffered the same fate. Therefore my life will always be wrapped up with them in some way."[15]

For fifty years he kept up his hatred of the Germans until, in retirement, he picked up a magazine by chance and saw an article about a village in Germany that had asked for forgiveness. It was Huchenfeld. With increasing astonishment he read of how a new pastor had come to the village and been told of the killing of the British fliers. He was determined to make amends and to put up a memorial to the dead men. His idea met strong resistance. There was still resentment in the area about the Allied bombing, particularly the devastation of Pforzheim. Older inhabitants saw themselves as the victims of an atrocity, not accomplices in a murder. But the pastor persisted, and, in the face of much opposition, he had a plaque mounted on the church wall listing the names of the five British airmen above a simple statement— "Father, forgive." It was the first step in a remarkable journey that would bring sworn enemies together and bring closure to a troubled past.

The village's angst was reported in an English newspaper, which was seen by a niece of Flying Officer Harold Frost, one of the murdered men. She brought it to the attention of his widow, Marjorie. For forty-seven years she had never known what had happened to her husband, only that he had gone missing in action over Germany. Now she learned of his fate—killed out of revenge by German villagers. Though frail and in her seventies, she decided to visit Huchenfeld to see where her husband died and to be at the official unveiling of the plaque in his memory. In the church, she asked to meet any of the men in the village involved in her husband's death, of which there were several still living there. At first they were too ashamed to confront her, afraid of a hostile reaction. "Bring them to me and I will tell them I forgive them," she said. The healing process had begun and would soon sweep more of the original characters into it.

John Wynne was the pilot of the badly damaged RAF bomber from which the crew that ended up as prisoners at Huchenfeld had jumped and fallen into the arms of a lynch mob. Having managed to fly the plane home single-handed, he assumed his crew had been captured and been POWs for the duration of the war. In 1992, now a hill farmer in North Wales with the war long forgotten, he heard about the reconciliation village in Germany. For the first time he discovered what had happened to his crew, that five of them had died. His first reaction was anger and shock at their murder in cold blood. Then he spoke to Marjorie Frost and anger turned to understanding. He and his wife joined in the reconciliation process, symbolizing his own forgiveness for what had happened by presenting the village nursery with a splendid wooden rocking horse carved by a Welsh craftsman. It was then that Tom Tate read of the Huchenfeld events and contacted John Wynne. They spoke on the telephone. For the first time since Wynne had ordered him and the rest of the crew out of the plane, Tate heard his old skipper's voice. When their emotional greetings were over, Wynne suggested that Tate join him on his next visit to Huchenfeld. The villagers would be thrilled to meet one of those who had escaped. Tate, who had sworn never to return to Germany, went back, and has been back every year since. He feels it is his duty.

For Sir Arthur Harris, there was also a form of reconciliation with his old enemy. He had, as the result of his experience in the First World War, always held that the only good German was a dead German, a view not untypical of his generation and one that must have made his Second World War job easier to perform. But, in the aftermath, he mellowed, and he had a surprisingly warm correspondence with Albert Speer, Hitler's armaments minister. Leaving prison after serving the full twenty years of the sentence handed down at the Nuremberg war crimes trial, Speer published his memoirs and sent a signed copy to Harris. The inscription was to the man "who caused me so many sleepless nights of despair—now, but only now, best wishes for many times of good luck and of satisfaction." Harris replied with his thanks, adding "Those were sad days indeed for us all and one can but hope that the nations will show more sense in the future."[16]

Bob Pierson, a Tail-End Charlie whose story we have followed closely in this book, found sixty years later that his conscience was both troubled and clear at the same time. He knew what he had done and why. His regret was for man's eternal recourse to violence, not for the deeds he had been called on to carry out.

The results of what I did still prey on my mind. Anybody who fought in a war has got to have some regrets about having had a part in it. When I think about those bombing missions I went on, I wonder why it had to be like that, why there couldn't be another way, one that didn't involve killing and destruction. It can never be right to kill and maim. The world needs to find other solutions to its differences. And then I remember what would have happened to Britain and to all those countries that Germany had conquered if I had not done what I did. I look on what I did—helping to bomb Germany—as no different from the job of a soldier holding a rifle. Nor was it different in one sense from what people who stayed behind making munitions were doing. We all had a job to do once the country went to war. It was just that mine happened to be at the sharp end.[17]

Rear gunner Eddie Picardo summed up the thoughts of many veterans as he recalled his experiences from the comfort of his Seattle home. "When I look back now I remember saying that if I ever got through the war alive I would enjoy every day of my life. I've done a pretty good job of that. I never thought of myself as a hero. A survivor, yes, not a hero. And lucky—oh, damn lucky."[18] American pilot Walter Hughes, enjoying his retirement amid the beauty of Hawai, found the memories of the wasted life of his best friend, killed in action, were still powerful. He found little consolation in the passing of time. "Was it all worth it? I struggle with that question frequently. It is one I have never been able to answer. I look back on it all as an episode in my life that is never black and white but always shades of gray. In the end all I see is the utter folly and utter stupidity of human beings trying to kill each other. Such is the waste of war."[19]

Sir Robert Saundby, deputy commander in chief of Bomber Command, Harris's right-hand man, wrote movingly in the same vein after the end of the war. "It is not so much this or the other means of making war that is immoral or inhumane. What is immoral is war itself. Once full-scale war has broken out it can never be humanized or civilized. So long as we resort to war to settle differences between nations, so long will we have to endure the horrors, barbarities, and excesses that war brings it. That, to me, is the lesson."[20]

Perhaps the final word on the subject of the bomber war should be left to one of those most greatly affected by it, not an airman, a military leader, or a politician, just a civilian. Mrs. Joan Lamberts, a Dutch woman, lived for five years under the heel of a cruel conqueror. When the war was over, she wrote from her home in Arnhem to the RAF: "During the occupation, the throb of your bombers overhead at night sounded like music in our ears. *It was an anchor to which we clung in the dark days.*"[21] Here was an epitaph that all the Tail-End Charlies, British and American, the forgotten heroes of the Second World War, could be proud of.

NOTES

WHERE A REFERENCE IS GIVEN FOR AN INTERVIEW, BOOK, OR DOCUMENT, that reference will hold good for the remainder of the chapter. For instance, all quotations from and references to Bob Pierson in chapter 1 are from his interview at the Imperial War Museum, Leeds, and his interview with John Nichol as stated in chapter 1, note 2 below. Similarly, all quotes from Campbell Muirhead come from his *Diary of a Bomb Aimer* as in chapter 1, note 15 below. All other references are attributed as stated.

PREFACE: SHOULDER TO SHOULDER

1. Excerpt from "For the Fallen" by Laurence Binyon, 1914. These words are traditionally spoken at all remembrance services in the United Kingdom.
2. Information from an Eighth Air Force press release, reproduced in 388th BG Newsletter.
3. Taken from Eddy Coward (ed.), *The Poems We Wrote: An Anthology of Air Force Poems* (Eddy Coward, 1997).
4. Members of the Women's Auxiliary Air Force.
5. Jörg Friedrich, *Der Brand* (Propyläen Verlag, 2002).
6. Harry Yates, *Luck and a Lancaster* (Airlife, 2001).

7. Arthur Harris, quoted in Air Commodore Henry Probert, *Bomber Harris* (Greenhill, 2001).

Chapter 1: In the Firing Line

1. Jim O'Connor, "The Year I Can't Forget," private diary (Iowa, 1999).
2. Incident recounted in Gerald Astor, *The Mighty Eighth* (Dell, 1997).
3. Bob Pierson, interviewed at Second World War Experience, Imperial War Museum, Leeds, November 2002, and by JN, May 2003.
4. Peter Twinn, interview with JN, June 2003.
5. "It was well known that isolation prompted combat refusal and in German bombers all the crew, including the gunners, were concentrated together for that reason, enjoying physical and psychological comfort in a heated cabin and in close proximity one to the other." Richard Holmes, *Battlefields of the Second World War* (BBC Books, 2001).
6. Miles Tripp, *The Eighth Passenger* (Wordsworth Editions, 2002).
7. Peter Twinn, interview with JN, June 2003.
8. Chan Chandler, *Tail Gunner* (Airlife Publishing, 2001).
9. Bob Pierson, interview with JN, May 2003.
10. Of these, 15,000 were heavy guns with a range of 25–35,000 feet. The rest were light guns, which did not have the same reach but were still a threat.
11. Ron Smith, *Rear Gunner, Pathfinder* (Goodall, 1987).
12. Eddie Picardo, *Tales of a Tail Gunner* (Hara Publishing, 1996) and interview with JN, September 2003.
13. Roger Freeman, *Mighty Eighth War Diary* (Jane's, 1981).
14. Story related in Gerald Astor, *The Mighty Eighth* (Dell, 1997).
15. Campbell Muirhead, *Diary of a Bomb Aimer* (Ditto Publishing, 2002).
16. Richard Holmes, *Battlefields of the Second World War* (BBC Publications, 2001).
17. All figures from Robin Neillands, *The Bomber War* (John Murray, 2001).
18. The death toll of British airmen in the Battle of Britain (10 July to 31 October 1940) was 544. On the night of 30 March 1940, 670 men of Bomber Command died during a raid on Nuremberg. See chapter 3.
19. This is demonstrated by an analysis of the fatalities in just one month. In January 1944, Bomber Command flew in excess of five thousand missions over Germany, a large number of them to Berlin. A total of 366 Lancasters and Halifaxes failed to return; 1,840 men died; a further 500

bailed out and became prisoners of war. If we narrow our analysis down to the Lancasters, of the 241 that were shot down, blew up, or crashed, in more than half (124) the entire crew died. Of the 108 aircraft crashing on enemy soil but with survivors, on only ten occasions did the entire crew survive to go into captivity. In two-thirds of cases more than half the crew died. In a third, there was only one survivor.

20. This is the archive at the Air Historical Branch at RAF Bentley Priory.
21. Air Ministry Directive 23, 5 May 1942. Quoted in the official history by Charles Webster and Noble Frankland, *The Strategic Air Offensive Against Germany 1939–1945* (HMSO, 1961).
22. Ibid. Combined Chiefs of Staff Report, 31 December 1942.
23. Arthur White, *Bread and Butter Bomber Boys* (Square One, 1995).
24. Churchill to Chiefs of Staff, 28 March 1945. Quoted in the official history by Charles Webster and Noble Frankland. *The Strategic Air Offensive Against Germany 1939–1945* (HMSO, 1961).
25. George Patton, quoted in Carlo D'Este, *Eisenhower* (Weidenfeld & Nicolson, 2002).

CHAPTER 2: FLYING FORTRESS BRITAIN

1. *A Short Guide to Great Britain* (U.S. Government Printing Office, 1942).
2. Curtis LeMay, *Mission LeMay* (Doubleday, 1965).
3. Eddie Picardo, *Tales of a Tail Gunner* (Hara Publishing, 1996) and interview with JN, September 2003.
4. Billy Southworth, quoted in Gerald Astor, *The Mighty Eighth* (Dell, 1997).
5. Report by D. M. Butt to Lord Cherwell (scientific adviser to the War Cabinet) 18 August 1941. Butt analyzed 4,065 photographs taken by RAF bombers in 100 raids in June–July 1941.
6. Which some advisers in the Air Ministry recommended, arguing that the RAF's bombers would be better employed fighting German submarines in the North Atlantic. The lobby for continuing to bomb Germany prevailed; Churchill concluded it was vital to maintain morale at home to be seen to be taking the war to Hitler.
7. From Stephen Budiansky, *Air Power* (Viking, 2003).
8. It is hard to see how else it could have been arrived at since, as the United States had not yet gone to war, there can hardly have been any empirical evidence to call on.

9. Arthur White, *Bread and Butter Bomber Boys* (Square One, 1995).

10. Anthony Verrier, *The Bomber Offensive* (Macmillan, 1968).

11. Harris, quoted in Air Commodore Henry Probert, *Bomber Harris* (Greenhill, 2001).

12. The American commanders had more problems than Harris. Whereas the RAF was entirely independent of the other services, the USAAF—the United States *Army* Air Force—was still part of the army set-up and would not be granted full independence until after the war.

13. "Impact—Strategic Air Victory in Europe," produced by the Office of the Assistant Chief of Air Staff, Intelligence, for distribution to squadrons, July 1945.

14. There has been much criticism of Harris for going his own way and not tying in his efforts more closely with the USAAF. But the Pointblank Directive of June 1943, which ordered the two air forces to combine their bomber offensives, was careful to stress complementarity and cooperation rather than integration of effort. "Fortunately the capabilities of the two forces are entirely complementary," article 4(a) declared. It continued:

> The striking power of the RAF bombing is designed to so destroy German material facilities as to undermine the willingness and ability of the German worker to continue the war . . . The United States bombing effort is directed toward the destruction of specific essential industrial targets. It is considered that the most effective results from strategic bombing will be obtained by directing the combined day and night effort of the United States and British bomber forces to all-out attacks against targets which are mutually complementary in undermining a limited number of selected objective systems. All-out attacks imply precision bombing of related targets by day and area bombing by night against the cities associated with these targets. The timing of the related day and night attacks will be determined by tactical considerations. This plan does not attempt to prescribe the major effect of the RAF Bomber Command. It simply recognizes the fact that when precision targets are bombed by the Eighth Air Force in daylight, the efforts should be complemented and completed by RAF bombing attacks against the surrounding industrial area at night. *Fortunately the industrial areas to be attacked are in most cases identical with the industrial areas which the British Bomber Command has selected for mass destruction anyway.* [Emphasis added.]
>
> See also note 24 below.

15. Probert, *Bomber Harris*.

16. Sir Arthur Harris, *Bomber Offensive* (Greenhill, 1998).

17. Maximum bomb load of a standard Lancaster was 14,000 pounds—just over six tons. A B-17's capacity was 7,600 pounds—just over three tons.

18. From Budiansky, *Air Power*.

19. Bert Stiles, *Serenade to the Big Bird* (Lindsey Drummond, 1947)

20. From Robin Neillands, *The Bomber War* (John Murray, 2001).

21. Southworth and Regan, quoted in Astor, *The Mighty Eighth*.

22. The incident apparently took place on a bombing run to St. Nazaire. The story was related by Staff Sergeant Bill Fleming, waist gunner on the plane that day and quoted in Astor, ibid.

23. Spaatz to General Eaker, quoted in ibid.

24. The 5,000-word directive was complex, ambiguous, and appeared to be trying to be all things to all men. Harris was aided in his interpretation by a preamble which declared that the overall objective of the bombing mission was "to accomplish the progressive destruction and dislocation of the German military, industrial and economic system and the undermining of morale of the German people to a point where their capacity for armed resistance is fatally weakened."

25. Bill Fleming, quoted in Astor, *The Mighty Eighth*.

26. Beirne Lay, quoted in *Impact—Strategic Air Victory in Europe* (U.S. Government Printing Office, July 1945).

27. See Verrier, *The Bomber Offensive*.

28. Ira Weinstein, from Aaron Elson's Web site www.kasselmission.com and interview with JN, September 2003.

29. Ibid.

30. Figures for Big Week losses vary in different publications. These figures are day-by-day sums from Eric Hammel, *Air War Europa: A Chronology* (Pacifica Press, 1994).

31. Annual report to Congress by commander in chief of USAAF, February 1944. Quoted in *Hansard, House of Commons,* 6 March 1945.

32. Jim O'Connor, "The Year I Can't Forget," private diary (Iowa, 1999).

33. F. H. Hinsley, *British Intelligence in the Second World War,* vol. 3, part 1 (HMSO, 1984).

34. Walter Hughes, "A Bomber Pilot in World War II," private account, and interview with JN, September 2003.

35. James Parton, *Air Force Spoken Here* (Adler & Adler, 1986).

36. Eddie Picardo, quoted in Gerald Astor, *The Mighty Eighth*.

37. Billy Southworth, interview with JN, June 2003.

38. David Grant, quoted in Mark Wells, *Courage and Air Warfare* (Frank Cass, 1995).

39. Reg Davey, "Hitler Had Nothing to Worry About," private account; and interview with JN, June 2003.

40. Boris Bressloff, interview with JN, June 2003.

41. Ralph Golubock, quoted in Astor, *the Mighty Eighth*.

42. Stiles, *Serenade to the Big Bird*.

CHAPTER 3: BOYS INTO MEN

1. The letter was received by Bill Kiley, signed by Archibald Sinclair, secretary of state for war, and dated 4 May 1942.

2. Medical officer, quoted in Mark K. Wells, *Courage and Air Warfare* (Frank Cass, 1995).

3. Dickie Parfitt, *Bombs Gone* (privately published), and interview with JN, May 2003.

4. Bill Kiley, interview with JN, May 2003.

5. Bill Carman, "Three Times Lucky," private account; and interview with JN, May 2003.

6. Bill Low, interview with JN, May 2003.

7. Campbell Muirhead, *Diary of a Bomb Aimer* (Ditto Publishing, 2002).

8. Harris, quoted in Air Commodore Henry Probert, *Bomber Harris* (Greenhill, 2001). The authors are grateful to Air Commander Probert for allowing them to quote his excellent biography of Harris.

9. Ken Newman, "Left, Left, Steady," private account; and interview with JN, July 2003.

10. Reg Davey, interview with JN, January 2003.

11. Boris Bressloff, interview with JN, June 2003.

12. Bruce Wyllie, interview with TR, November 2003.

13. Miles Tripp, *The Eighth Passenger* (Wordsworth Editions, 2002).

14. Robert Wannop, *Chocks Away* (Imperial War Museum 980/30/1, and Square One, 1989).

15. Tom Tabe, interview with JN, April 2003.

16. John Wynne, interview with JN, April 2003.

17. Flight Lieutenant D, Steiner Papers, Imperial War Museum, 92/29/1.

18. Martin Middlebrook, *The Nuremberg Raid* (Penguin 1973 and Cassell 2000). The authors are indebted to Mr. Middlebrook for the details of the raid in his invaluable book. Unless specified otherwise, the quotations from air crew on the raid are also taken from this source.

19. Ibid.

20. Charles Webster and Wable Frankland, *The Strategic Air Offensive Against Germany 1939–1945* (HMSO, 1961).

21. Harris, quoted in Norman Longmate, *The Bombers*.

22. Details from Jonathan Falconer, *The Bomber Command Handbook* (Sutton, 2003).

23. Muirhead, *Diary of a Bomb Aimer*.

24. Eric Banks Papers, RAF Museum, Hendon, archive X003-1521.

25. This compared with 17*s*. a day for a flight sergeant and 14*s*. 6*d*. for a sergeant.

26. Roy Day, diaries, held privately.

27. See chapter 6, "Orders from on High."

28. Harry Yates, *Luck and a Lancaster* (Airlife Publishing, 2001).

29. Johnnie Clark, *One Man's War* (Peacock Press, 1994).

30. Peter Marshall, interview with JN, May 2003.

31. Eric Thale Papers, RAF Museum Hendon, archive, AC 95/87.

32. Personal memoir: contributed by Mrs. Brooks's husband, Thomas, after her death in 2001.

33. Pip Beck, *A WAAF in Bomber Command* (Goodall, 1989).

34. They did marry, and when JN interviewed them in May 2003, they had celebrated their fifty-seventh anniversary. "He was a handsome lad then," Pat said. "Still is."

35. Published in Eddy Coward (ed.), *The Poems We Wrote: An Anthology of Air Force Poems* (1997), and reproduced here in an abridged form with grateful acknowledgment to the compiler.

CHAPTER 4: FLYING IN THE FACE OF FEAR

1. Miles Tripp, *The Eighth Passenger* (Wordsworth Editions, 2002).

2. Campbell Muirhead, *Diary of a Bomb Aimer* (Ditto Publishing, 2002).

3. Squadron Leader David Stafford-Clark, quoted in Mark Wells, *Courage and Air Warfare* (Frank Cass, 1995).

4. Tony Iverson, interview with JN, June 2003.

5. Air Vice Marshal Alexander Annan Adams, *Passing Experiences: An Autobiography* (privately published, 1980).

6. Bill Carman, "Three Times Lucky," private account; and interview with JN, May 2003.

7. Reg Davey, "Hitler Had Nothing to Worry About," private account; and interview with JN, June 2003.

8. From Mel Rolfe, *Flying into Hell* (Grub Street, 2001), and Freddie Cole, interview with JN, July 2003.

9. Arthur Prager, quoted in Gerald Astor, *The Mighty Eighth* (Dell, 1997).

10. Boris Bressloff, interview with JN, June 2003.

11. The fresh eggs set aside for operational crew were a source of much debate. At Campbell Muirhead's squadron, a truculent airman questioned the mess president about the eggs of men who did not return from a mission. Since sometimes nearly half the planes did not return, that meant an awful lot of eggs were going spare. So what happened to them? Were they being misappropriated? The result was a mess president outraged at this attack on his honor—plus a decision that eggs and bacon would henceforth be served before an operation and after. Muirhead himself was embarrassed by the eggs. He would be eating a fresh one reserved for fliers while a ground crewman next to him would be struggling to digest "that dreadful powdered egg, which I wouldn't give to the cat—and which the cat wouldn't eat anyway!" (*Diary of a Bomb Aimer*)

12. Eddie Picardo, *Tales of a Tail Gunner* (Hara Publishing, 1996), interview with JN, September 2003.

13. Chuck Halper, in Astor, *The Mighty Eighth*.

14. Tom Tate, interview with JN, April 2003.

15. Woodbridge, according to pilot Ken Newman, had one huge runway 250 yards wide and 3,000 yards long, divided into three landing strips with extended undershoot and overshoot areas. "The two landing strips on the right were for those who were able to make radio contact and were expected to be able to land on their undercarriage; if the brakes failed the aircraft would be brought to a halt by the soft surface in the overshoot area. The left-hand runaway was reserved for those so badly damaged that they only just made it to the U.K. and would probably have to belly-flop; no prior radio announcement of their presence was necessary, although it was obviously desirable. Such aircraft were usually unceremoniously swept aside by a bulldozer to make way for the next one, after the crew had been extricated. There was a story going around of a

badly shot-up aircraft that landed there and when the crash crew reached it they found all the aircrew were dead—the pilot had lived just long enough to get the aircraft on the ground." The Woodbridge runway was marked by a searchlight pointing directly upward. Newman said: "I was always glad the facility existed but hoped I would never need to make use of it."

16. Boris Bressloff, interview with JN, June 2003.

17. From the archives at the Lincolnshire Aviation Heritage Center, East Kirby airfield, and the Medrington family.

18. With all respect to FO Medrington, his figures sound more like rumor than "incontrovertible fact." The authors are unaware of any analysis (at the time or since) that would back his claim about what forms of action caused most casualties. His figures for percentage of crew surviving a crash and for those bailing out evading capture seem wildly optimistic. But they illustrate what airman believed at the time.

19. "How sweet and noble it is to die for one's country."

20. Bob Pierson, interview with JN, May 2003.

21. Eric Banks Papers, RAF Museum, Hendon, archive X003–1521.

22. Bert Stiles, *Serenade to the Big Bird* (Lindsey Drummond, 1947).

23. See chapter 2, "Flying Fortress Britain."

24. Peter Marshall, private memoir; and interview with JN, May 2003.

25. Ron Smith, *Rear Gunner, Pathfinder* (Goodall, 1987).

26. Ken Newman, "Left, Left, Steady," private account; and interview with JN, July 2003.

27. All personal effects went to the central depository at RAF Colnbrook, Slough, before being distributed to next of kin.

28. Taken from the *Bomber Command Association Newsletter,* April 2003.

29. Of the 55,500 men of Bomber Command killed in the war, 8,195 died in accidents, according to Air Ministry figures. Bomber Command records for the two full years of 1943 and 1944 logged 2,681 such accidents in which 6,000 airmen were killed and 4,400 injured. As for the Eighth Air Force, its record showed 1,660 accidents in the seventeen months from the beginning of 1944 until the end of the war. Figures from the Bomber Command War Diaries and Wells, *Courage and Air Warfare.*

30. Eric Thale Papers, RAF Museum, Hendon, archive, AC95/87.

31. Bill Dewey, interview with JN, October 2003, and www.kasselmission.com.

32. Jack Watson, interview with JN, May 2003.

33. Jim O'Connor, "The Year I Can't Forget," private diary (Iowa, 1999).

34. O'Connor completed his tour three weeks later. "How sweet it was to be alive and going home," he wrote in his dairy.

35. John Wynne, interview with JN, April 2003.

36. Bill Kiley, interview with JN, May 2003.

37. Chan Chandler, *Tail Gunner* (Airlight Publishing, 2002).

38. Wells, *Courage and Air Warfare*.

39. Bruce Wyllie, interview with TR, November 2003.

40. Related in Chaz Bowyer, *Guns in the Sky* (Corgi, 1981).

41. December 1942, PRO, AIR 20/2859. Quoted in Wells, *Courage and Air Warfare*.

42. Dickie Parfitt, *Bombs Gone* (privately published), and interview with JN, May 2003.

43. Major Hubert ("Nicky") Knilans, "A Yank in the RCAF," RAF Museum, Hendon, archive B2445.

CHAPTER 5: NO EARLY RETURNS

1. Eddie Picardo, *Tales of a Tail Gunner* (Hara Publishing, 1996); and interview with JN, September 2003.

2. Walter Hughes, "A Bomber Pilot in World War II," private account; and interview with JN, September 2003.

3. From www.kasselmission.com and interview with JN, October 2003.

4. Campbell Muirhead, *Diary of a Bomb Aimer* (Ditto Publishing, 2002).

5. Air Vice Marshal Alexander Annan Adams, *Passing Experiences: An Autobiography* (privately published, 1980).

6. *The Lancet*, 28 September 1918. Quoted in Barry Price, "The Recognition and Acceptance of War Neurosis in British Military Aviation 1912–1945," M.A. dissertation, University of Hertfordshire, January 2002. The authors would like to thank Mr. Price for his assistance.

7. Air Vice Marshal Sir John Salmond, evidence to the War Office Committee of Enquiry into Shell Shock, 1922, quoted, ibid.

8. David Stafford-Clark, *Psychiatry Today* (Pelican, 1952).

9. Quoted by Mark Wells, *Courage and Air Warfare* (Frank Cass, 1995), to whom the authors are deeply grateful. His book, brilliantly researched and full of insights, was an invaluable source for this chapter.

10. Harris to Portal, January 1943. PRO, AIR 20/2860, quoted in Wells, *Courage and Air Warfare*.

11. Wells, *Courage and Air Warfare*.

12. Harris, quoted in Air Commodore Henry Probert, *Bomber Harris* (Greenhill, 2001).

13. Wells, *Courage and Air Warfare*.

14. Miles Tripp, *The Eighth Passenger* (Wordsworth Editions, 2002).

15. Jack Harris, interview with JN, May 2003.

16. Peter Marshall, private memoir; and interview with JN, May 2003.

17. Ken Newman, "Left, Left, Steady," private account; and interview with JN, July 2003

18. Arthur White, *Bread and Butter Bomber Boys* (Square One, 1995).

19. Roy Day, private diary.

20. Few were as skilled as David Stafford-Clark, who had made a detailed study of thousands of men at his squadron. See "The stages of stress," Appendix 1 in his *Psychiatry Today*.

21. Medical officer, quoted in Wells, *Courage and Air Warfare*.

22. Aviation expert Mark Wells believes that as many as two-thirds of all flyers in Bomber Command might have had this sort of temporary treatment at squadron level at one time or another. But, if so, it is strange that instances do not appear regularly in the memories and memoirs of the men themselves. One would expect medical officers to figure prominently as people the men could turn to. They do not, perhaps because men were wary of being marked down as potentially problematic.

23. An anonymous friend of Miles Tripp, quoted in *The Eighth Passenger*.

24. Dickie Parfitt, *Bombs Gone* (privately published); and interview with JN, May 2003.

25. Tony Iverson, interview with JN, June 2003.

26. Robert Wannop, *Chocks Away* (Square One, 1989).

27. Dennis Wiltshire, private memoir, and interview with JN, June 2003.

28. From an article in *Air Mail*, the RAFA magazine, April–June 2001.

Chapter 6: Orders from On High

1. This account is largely (but not wholly) based on an article by Flight Lieutenant J. Phillips of the Air Ministry public relations department. It followed a day spent with Alexander Adams, who endorsed it to the extent of including it in his private memoir. He thought it "a fair picture of the work on the ground of a squadron commander preparing his aircraft for

action." Air Vice Marshal Alexander Annan Adams, *Passing Experiences: An Autobiography* (privately published, 1980).

2. Group Captain James Pelly-Fry, *Heavenly Days* (Crecy Books, 1994).

3. Ibid.

4. Charles Carrington, *A Soldier at Bomber Command* (Leo Cooper, 1987).

5. Ibid.

6. Air Vice Marshal Robert Saundby.

7. Group Captain John Searby, quoted in Air Commodore Henry Probert, *Bomber Harris* (Greenhill, 2001).

8. James Parton, *Air Force Spoken Here* (Adler & Adler, 1986).

9. Harris to Portal, Chief of Air Staff, when the war was over (May 1945); Harris Papers, RAF Museum, Hendon.

10. Sir Arthur Harris, *Bomber Offensive* (Greenhill, 1998).

11. Probert, *Bomber Harris*.

12. Harris to Portal, May 1945.

13. His early RAF career path meant that he and Barbara, his first wife, spent much time apart, and he was involved—though to what extent is unknown—with another woman. Barbara told his biographer that she would never have divorced him over the other woman but that the very rude way in which he spoke to her finished the marriage (Probert, *Bomber Harris*).

14. Ibid.

16. Diana Collins, *Partners in Protest* (Gollancz, 1992).

16. Jacqueline Assheton in the preface to a reprint of her father's *Bomber Offensive*, in 1990.

17. Dudley Saward, one of his former staff officers. Saward, *Bomber Harris* (Buchanan and Enright, 1984).

18. "We were expected to get on with our job with ever-increasing success, at ever-increasing tempo, regardless of the weather, [yet] if we ever suffered losses in any way comparable with those of the enemy, there was immediate indignation and surprise. I found these two attitudes incompatible and incomprehensible but they were nevertheless to be found in the minds of the highest and the lowest in the land." (Harris, *Bomber Offensive*)

19. Ibid.

20. Ibid.

21. Ibid.

22. Details courtesy of *After the Battle* quarterly magazine, no. 87 (published by Battle of Britain International Ltd of London E15).

23. James Parton, *Air Force Spoken Here.*

24. There are many different versions of this story and the exact words Harris used.

25. Quoted in Carlo D'Este, *Eisenhower* (Weidenfeld & Nicolson, 2002).

26. Wing Commander W. E. McCrea, quoted in Probert, *Bomber Harris.*

27. Norman Ashton, quoted in ibid.

28. Campbell Muirhead, *Diary of a Bomb Aimer* (Ditto Publishing, 2002).

29. Harris was far from unique in protecting his patch during the interminable turf wars between the services. For example, the disastrous Dieppe raid was scaled down because the navy refused to back it up with the battleships the army thought necessary.

30. Message from Eisenhower, quoted in Quentin Reynolds, *The Amazing Mr. Doolittle* (Panther, 1956).

31. Ibid.

32. Chan Chandler, *Tail Gunner* (Airlife Publishing, 2002).

33. Bill Low, interview with JN, May 2003.

34. Curiously, the postwar generation accepted without question that civilians would be wiped out by warfare. In the age of nuclear missiles, everyone would. As Harris, a civilian himself after 1945, laconically remarked, "My part in the next war will be to be destroyed by it, [along with] a very great part of the civilized world."

35. Nickname for William Joyce, who broadcast propaganda from Berlin to Britain every night.

36. Boris Bressloff, interview with JN, June 2003.

37. Robert Wannop, *Chocks Away* (Square One, 1989).

38. See chapter 10, "Burning Dresden."

39. Harris, *Bomber Offensive.*

CHAPTER 7: D-DAY AND BEYOND

1. Janet Pack, *The 388th Anthology*, vol. 2 (Writers Club Press, 2001).

2. Martin Garren, quoted in Gerald Astor, *The Mighty Eighth.*

3. Major Hubert ("Nicky") Knilans, "A Yank in the RCAF," RAF Museum, Hendon, archive B2445.

4. Campbell Muirhead, *Diary of a Bomb Aimer* (Ditto Publishing, 2002).

5. Ibid.

6. Bill Low, interview with JN, May 2003.

7. William Lovejoy, *Better Born Lucky Than Rich* (Merlin, 1986).

8. Ken Newman, "Left, Left, Steady," private account; and interview with JN, July 2003.

9. The two missions ended with 277 men dead, 55 captured, and 10 landing in enemy territory but evading capture.

10. Jim O'Connor, "The Year I Can't Forget," private diary (Iowa, 1999).

11. Lovejoy, *Better Born Lucky Than Rich*.

12. Sir Arthur Harris, *Bomber Offensive* (Greenhill, 1998).

13. Freddie de Guignand, quoted in Alistair Horne, *Monty: The Lonely Leader* (Macmillan, 1994).

14. Charles Carrington, *A Soldier at Bomber Command* (Leo Cooper, 1987).

15. Bomber Command, in fact, was sent on four more operations to bomb the German front lines, on one of which the marking plans went awry and thirteen Canadian soldiers were killed when their trenches were hit.

16. Jim Hill, quoted in Gerald Astor, *The Mighty Eighth*.

17. Buzz bombs, bumble bombs, and robot bombs were other commonly used names, according to Philip Ziegler in his book *London at War, 1939–1945* (Sinclair-Stevenson, 1995), from which much of the information on the V-1 assault has been taken.

18. Evelyn Waugh, quoted in ibid.

19. *388th Anthology*, vol. 1.

20. *Gielgud's Letters* (Weidenfeld & Nicolson, 2004).

21. There would be attacks of various intensity from September 1944 and on into 1945. A total of 1,200 flying bombs would be fired toward London, but only sixty-six of them reached anywhere near the capital.

22. F. H. Hinsley, *British Intelligence in the Second World War*, vol. 3, part 2 (HMSO, 1984).

23. In his memoirs Harris claimed a huge success for Bomber Command in countering the V-1s. His argument was that the Germans had originally intended to launch flying bombs at the rate of six thousand a day, which would have reduced London to ruins, laid waste the whole of southern England, and made the D-Day invasion impossible. However, his men's success in obliterating launching sites in late 1943 and early 1944 meant that when the barrage came in the summer of 1944 there were never more than ninety-five in a day—a "sore trial" to Londoners but not the disaster it could have been. This seems a pretty far-fetched claim. Could V-1 production ever have reached the levels that Harris claimed he had saved Britain from? It seems unlikely. A more plausible argument in his favor,

however, is that the attacks on the Peenemünde site disrupted the development program enough to delay the use of V-1s and V-2s by three months—thus ensuring that Operation Overlord was not affected by flying bombs or rockets landing in southern England.

24. Fain Pool, interview with JN, September 2003.

25. This detail—and much more—is taken from an article by Stewart P. Evans in *FlyPast* in October 1983 and an article by Roger Freeman in *FlyPast*, December 1998.

26. Some thousand-pound bombs had been fitted with vanes that could be steered by radio from the aircraft that dropped them. But the whole project—though it was in effect the start of the United States' guided missile program—was rudimentary.

27. The AP man was Franklin Banker, and he did not break the silence he had agreed to until six months after the war. Even then the details he revealed were very sketchy.

28. It would emerge later, after the area fell to the Allies, that the bunkers had resisted even the biggest and most sophisticated of bombs dropped on them, but other bombs had devastated the area around and made access to the bunkers virtually impossible. Instead of sending their flying bombs and rockets from these sites, as they intended, the Germans took to moving the weapons round the countryside to be launched from other pads and from mobile launchers.

29. Pool reckoned that, even stripped of everything internally except the pilots' seat, the B-17, with all the explosives on board, was more than two tons overloaded. See Pool, "Project Aphrodite," *Daedalus Flyer*, Summer 2000.

30. Ian McLachlan, *Final Flights* (Patrick Stephens, 1999).

31. Suggested by Pool himself in *Project Aphrodite*.

32. Work continued on the Aphrodite project with improved radio receivers and television transmitters. In September, another robot was aimed at the German naval base on Heligoland, but it crashed into the sea. One Aphrodite pilot died when his parachute failed to open. One aircraft, embarrassingly, came down in a field in Sweden. Research continued with a new code name, Castor, an altogether more apt classical reference since Castor was one of the twin sons of Zeus. Its backers pressed for more chances to try out their brainchild against the retreating German forces. Then the technology was switched to the Pacific theater for possible use against the Japanese, but the atom bomb project was given priority over it.

CHAPTER 8: BACK TO THE CITIES

1. Walter Hughes, "A Bomber Pilot in World War II," private account.
2. Janet Pack, *The 388th Anthology*, vol. 1 (Writers Club Press, 2001).
3. See chapter 6, "Orders from on High."
4. Charles Carrington, *A Soldier at Bomber Command* (Leo Cooper, 1987).
5. These quotes are taken from Harris's autobiography *Bomber Offensive* (Greenhill, 1998).
6. Within geographical limits. Oboe—the most important new radar aid— was limited by the curvature of the earth. At heights of less than 30,000 feet it could not operate successfully much farther into Germany than the Ruhr.
7. William Lovejoy was sent on this mission and at the time thought it "the daftest operation of the entire war." They were ordered to fly up and down near the German-Dutch border, make as much noise as they could, and switch their lights on and off. He recalled: "Up to now, our whole object on night raids had been to remain as anonymous as possible, and here we were being asked to draw attention to ourselves. Well, we did it— flying low, making lots of noise, and flashing lights—but it didn't make much sense." Not until after the war did he discover they had been creating a diversion for Operation Market Garden, the unsuccessful Allied paratroop drop to seize the Lower Rhine bridges. The intention had been to lure German fighters away, but it did not work. (Interview with JN.)
8. Anthony Verrier, *The Bomber Offensive* (Macmillan, 1968).
9. The extent of the bickering is brilliantly captured in Carlo D'Este's biography *Eisenhower* (Weidenfeld & Nicolson, 2002). "Eisenhower was beset on all sides by unhappy commanders scrapping for an equal share of the logistical pie. Montgomery's seemingly endless demands for priority were mirrored by Bradley and Patton, who conspired to milk the supply system for all it was worth. Caught in the middle was Eisenhower, whose authority was challenged repeatedly."
10. Churchill's opinion was that it was "absurd to consider morality on this topic when everybody used [gas] in the last war without a word of complaint from the moralists or the Church." In accepting the advice of the chiefs of staff, he commented: "Clearly I cannot make headway against the parsons and the warriors at the same time." Quoted in F. H. Hinsley, *British Intelligence in the Second World War*, vol. 3 (HMSO, 1984).
11. According to historian Anthony Verrier in *The Bomber Offensive*, "In Sep-

tember 1944, the Allied ground offensive simply ran out of steam, out of ideas, out of its more effective units and formations, and even to some extent out of material. There was disagreement between Roosevelt and Churchill, let alone their subordinates, not only on how the ground campaign should be fought but what its overall objective should be. . . . They were not of one mind and it follows therefore that airmen who knew what they wanted to do were allowed to go ahead and do it, and in their own way."

12. Eric Hammel, *Air War Europa: A Chronology* (Pacifica Press, 1994).

13. Could he have done more? Yes. How much more? That is a moot point. His critics give the impression that the vast tonnage of bombs he dropped on cities in this period could—should—have been diverted to refineries and synthetic oil plants. The equation is too simplistic. Every target was different and needed different treatment. Some oil sites, particularly the major ones in the east, were too distant for routine missions and certainly beyond the range at which precision bombing was possible. Harris also underreported how many oil targets he had attacked—when his Lancasters area-bombed cities they inevitably hit oil installations, but these were not recorded as such.

14. Air Commodore Henry Probert, *Bomber Harris* (Greenhill, 2001).

15. Ibid.

16. Ibid.

17. Campbell Muirhead, *Diary of a Bomb Aimer* (Ditto Publishing, 2002).

18. Ken Newman, "Left, Left, Steady," private account; and interview with JN, July 2003.

19. Harry Yates, *Luck and a Lancaster* (Airlife Publishing, 2001).

20. William Lovejoy, *Better Born Lucky Than Rich* (Merlin, 1986).

21. Bill Borrows, quoted in Robin Neillands, *The Bomber War* (John Murray, 2001).

22. The Americans claimed a death toll of 25,000, but this was never verified and some historians dispute that the figure was anywhere near as high as this.

23. From Aaron Elson's Web site www.kasselmission.com and interview with JN, October 2003.

24. Walter Hughes, "A Bomber Pilot in World War II," private account; and interview with JN, September 2003.

25. Major Howard Davis, a ground officer of the 445th, wrote in his diary for 29 September, the next day, that "our group [had grown] complacent and confident because of the apparent lulling wings of the Luft-

waffe." *Kassel Mission Chronicles Newsletter*, Summer 1999. The authors are grateful to Kassel survivor Bill Dewey for his help on this subject.

26. Taken from www.kasselmission.com and interview with JN, October 2003. The authors are grateful to Aaron Elson for his help researching this subject.

27. Others back up Weinstein's version that the failure to turn was queried. Frank Bertam, quoted in Aaron Elson, *Nine Lives* (Chi Chi Press, 1999), said: "I think almost every plane in the formation that had a halfway good navigator saw what was going on and called immediately."

28. Captain Werner Vorbeg, writing in the Kassel Mission Reports.

29. Jack Mercer, Kassel Mission Memorial Association.

30. John Cadden, interview with JN, October 2003, and www.kasselmission .com.

31. The reason for the error remains a mystery and is still argued over by Kassel mission survivors. The route was set by Major Don McCoy, the commander of the wing, in the lead plane, and he was killed. Was he lost? Did his navigator read the radar wrongly? Having been warned that he had missed the turn, did he decide not to rejoin the main force but bomb their secondary target, Göttingen (in which case, why did he not radio for escort fighters to follow him)? Or did he believe he was still on course for Kassel? The questions are all unanswered.

32. The Kassel Mission Reports, supplied by Bill Dewey.

33. One of those asking the questions was a senior officer from Eighth Air Force headquarters, Colonel James Stewart, the film actor.

34. To add to the American casualties on that day, one Mustang pilot was lost. He collided with a German fighter in midair. Both pilots died.

CHAPTER 9: THE LAST CHRISTMAS?

1. Private account, Walter Hughes, "A Bomber Pilot in World War II."

2. Janet Pack, *The 388th Anthology,* vol. 2 (Writers Club Press, 2001).

3. Flight Lieutenant S. P. Brunt Papers, Imperial War Museum 01/1/1.

4. For example: "If you came Friday evening I could get into Hunts as soon as we finished our 'visit' and then we should have until Sunday morning together. On the other hand if you caught the 10:35 on Saturday I could probably meet you in Hunts and then we should have until Sunday as in

the first plan. I'm taking it that you will have to go back Sunday because you said you were on duty early Monday morning—correct?" (Ibid.)

5. Much of this information comes from Graham Herbertson's research into the aircraft and its final flight. The authors are grateful to him for his expertise on the subject.

6. Jim O'Connor, "The Year I Can't Forget," private diary (Iowa, 1999).

7. Miller himself went missing on 16 December 1944. The plane he was in disappeared in foul weather over the Channel on his way to prepare a concert in Paris.

8. Jack Merkley's sister told researcher Graham Herbertson that her brother mentioned in a letter that *Skipper* was going to be assigned to them.

9. August Bolino, "A Navigator's Story," in Janet Pack (ed.), *The 388th Anthology* (Writers Club Press, 2001).

10. Lieutenant Edison Jeffus was a weather officer at Knettishall and had reason to know about any unusual flights because he (or those working for him) would have been required to provide a weather forecast for them (from Graham Herbertson's research, see n. 5).

11. Others serving on the base at the time confirm that the rumor was that *Skipper* was on a whiskey run.

12. The eleventh was Staff Sergeant Wade Kriner, a twenty-year-old gunner. No reason has emerged for his being on the flight.

13. The USAAF report, dated 25 March 1945, also described the flight as "nonoperational cross-country flight" and the pilot's mission as "navigational training."

14. Verner Small, interview by researcher Graham Herbertson, 2001.

15. Arthur White, *Bread and Butter Bomber Boys* (Square One, 1995).

16. Quentin Reynolds, *The Amazing Mr. Doolittle* (Panther, 1956).

17. Ibid.

18. See chapter 4, "Flying in the Face of Fear," pages 111–12.

19. Published with the permission of the Medrington family.

20. Miles Tripp, *The Eighth Passenger* (Wordsworth Editions, 2002).

21. Imperial War Museum 92/29/1.

22. Ron Smith, *Rear Gunner, Pathfinder* (Goodall, 1987).

23. Reg Davey, "Hitler Had Nothing to Worry About," private account; and interview with JN, June 2003.

24. Article in *Air Mail,* magazine of the Royal Air Force Association, April–June 2001.

25. Eddie Picardo, *Tales of a Tail Gunner* (Hara Publishing, 1996); and interview with JN, September 2003.
26. Harry Yates, *Luck and a Lancaster* (Airlife Publishing, 2001).

CHAPTER 10: BURNING DRESDEN

1. Quotes taken from correspondence between Portal and Harris contained in PRO, AIR 8/1020.
2. Portal wrote: "Had the American air force joined with Bomber Command in bombing cities instead of fighter production, there is every possibility that the whole combined offensive might have been brought to a standstill. It was only by a narrow margin that they gained the ascendancy which virtually cleared the skies for Overlord [the D-Day invasion], the prerequisite for its launching."
3. Sir Charles Webster and Noble Frankland, *The Strategic Air Offensive Against Germany* (HMSO, 1961).
4. Taken from Denis Richards, *Portal of Hungerford* (Heinemann, 1997).
5. The Soviet Red Army did not cross onto German soil from the east until 31 January 1945. The Western Allies finally penetrated the Siegfried Line a little over a week later.
6. Even Anthony Verrier, no great fan of Harris, thought him "the one man sure of his objectives among the many who were divided. Above all, he did not much mind what people thought or said about him, Churchill excepted. Portal appears to have been extremely concerned with preserving amity among his colleagues. It was doubtless desirable, indeed a necessary, aim but it made him impotent when dealing with his subordinate" (*The Bomber Offensive*, Macmillan, 1968).
7. As on 16–17 January when he sent 370 bombers to the city of Magdeburg; 328 to a synthetic oil plant at Zeitz near Leipzig; 240 to an oil plant at Brux in western Czechoslovakia; and 138 to a benzol plant at Wanne-Eickel in the Ruhr.
8. For example, 2–3 February—500 bombers to Wiesbaden; 250 to Karlsruhe; 320 to the Wanne-Eickel refinery.
9. For example, 1–2 February—400 bombers to Ludwigshafen; 340 to Mainz; 280 to Siegen. Ludwigshafen and Siegen included raids on railways.
10. Private diary, Imperial War Museum 98/30/1.
11. Johnnie Clark, *One Man's War* (Peacock Press, 1994).

12. Arthur White, *Bread and Butter Bomber Boys* (Square One, 1995).

13. Peter Twinn, interview with JN, June 2003.

14. Freddie Hulance, interview with JN, June 2003.

15. The Royan attack was a SHAEF operation, and the U.S. officer in charge was held to blame. Bomber Command was completely exonerated. It had followed orders.

16. Taken from Mel Rolfe, *Flying into Hell* (Grub Street, 2001), and Freddie Cole, interview with JN, July 2003.

17. "The Wartime History of No 227 Squadron," provided by Freddie Cole.

18. E. G. White, private memoir, Imperial War Museum 90/11/1.

19. Dave Francis, quoted in Robin Neillands, *The Bomber War* (John Murray, 2001).

20. Eric Thale, "Dresden, I Was There," private account; RAF Museum AC95/87. Much of the detail of the Dresden briefing is taken from Thale's account.

21. Miles Tripp, *The Eighth Passenger* (Wordsworth Editions, 2002).

22. Curiously, when, after the war, he tracked down the other members of his old crew, he and one other were the only ones to recall the mention of refugees at the briefing. Five of them had no recollection of this at all.

23. Robert Wannop, *Chocks Away* (Square One, 1989).

24. Memoirs of Squadron Leader Arthur Charles Carter, RAF Museum, Hendon, archive X001–3554.

25. Flying Officer John Noel. His note to himself was actually in reference to the attack on Chemnitz, forty miles from Dresden, the day after, but the situation he was describing was exactly the same. RAF Museum, Hendon, archive X002–5699.

26. Losses were small. Eight Lancasters crashed, two after colliding with each other over East Anglia.

27. It was not just Dresden that suffered in this way. Virtually all building of underground bunkers for civilians had ceased in 1943. Supplies of concrete were limited and priority went instead to extending fortifications in the east and west and building underground factories. Civilians were last in line, according to German historian Olaf Groehler, quoted in Frederick Taylor, *Dresden* (Bloomsbury, 2004).

28. Otto Griebel, *Ich War ein Mann der Strasse* (Altenburg, 1995). Quoted in Taylor, *Dresden*.

29. Much of the information in this section is taken from Frederick Taylor's excellent *Dresden;* unless otherwise stated, all quotes are taken from this

source. The authors are grateful to Mr. Taylor for allowing them to quote from his work.

30. Margaret Freyer, quoted in Alexander McKee, *Dresden, 1945* (Granada, 1983).

31. In Christian tradition, the first day of Lent, the day after Shrove Tuesday.

32. Victor Klemperer, *To the Bitter End* (Phoenix, 2000).

33. Dave Nagel, quoted in Gerald Astor, *The Mighty Eighth* (Dell, 1997).

34. John Morris, quoted in ibid.

35. Harold Hall, quoted in Frederick Taylor, *Dresden*.

36. The controversial historian David Irving in *The Destruction of Dresden* put the death toll as high as 200,000, based on reports he had from East German sources. In 1966, three years after publication, he wrote a letter to *The Times* admitting that he had been misled. He had subsequently seen and accepted the official report from a civil defense chief in the city of 18,375 confirmed dead and a total death toll estimated at 25,000.

37. Götz Bergander, quoted in Taylor, *Dresden*.

38. Campaign for Nuclear Disarmament was a U.K. political pressure group.

39. Verrier, *The Bomber Offensive*.

40. Grass and Vonnegut interviews in the *Royal Academy Magazine*, Spring 2003, for the "Masterpieces from Dresden" exhibition.

41. Dresden yearbook, quoted in Taylor, *Dresden* (italics added).

42. Hugh Lunghi, quoted in ibid.

43. Portal, quoted in Neillands, *The Bomber War*.

44. Were Harris's doubts genuine? Dresden was a long way, but not really that much farther (fifty miles) than Leipzig, Chemnitz, or Berlin.

45. Sir Arthur Harris, *Bomber Offensive* (Greenhill, 1998).

46. Quoted in Air Commodore Henry Probert, *Bomber Harris* (Greenhill, 2001).

47. Harris, *Bomber Offensive*.

48. PRO, AIR 20/3218.

49. Ken Newman, "Left, Left, Steady," private account; and interview with JN, July 2003.

50. This is more than just fanciful. According to Henry Probert's biography, Harris once implied that the main impetus for the attack on Dresden came from SHAEF, "which was eager to close the route along which Hitler's government might try to move south to the National Redoubt" (Probert, *Bomber Harris*).

51. Robert Kee to *Sunday Telegraph*, 18 February 2002.

52. Jack Myers to the *Sunday Express*, 22 January 1967.

53. Bon Halfgott, quoted in Neillands, *The Bomber War*.

54. Elka Schrijver, to *The Times*, 20 October 1967.

55. Max Hastings, *Royal Academy Magazine*, Spring 2003.

56. Former chief of the Office of Air Force History and president of the American Military Institute. Speaking at a symposium in Germany in 1988 on the conduct of the air war.

57. Götz Berlander, quoted in Probert, *Bomber Harris*.

CHAPTER 11: FACE TO FACE WITH THE ENEMY

1. Janet Pack, *The 338th Anthology*, vol. 1 (Writers Club Press, 2001).

2. Personal account in the *Observer*, 23 December 1973 by Roy Shirley. Reproduced in "By Oboe Victor to Cologne," written by Bill Manning and provided by the Little Staughton Pathfinder Association.

3. Major Hubert ("Nicky") Knilans, "A Yank in the RCAF," private memoir, RAF Museum, Hendon, archive B2455.

4. Arthur White, *Bread and Butter Bomber Boys* (Square One, 1995).

5. Story related by Frank Haslam's son (also Frank) to the authors, May 2004.

6. Campbell Muirhead, *Diary of a Bomb Aimer* (Ditto Publishing, 2002).

7. Ken Newman, "Left, Left, Steady," private account.

8. Robert Wannop, *Chocks Away* (Square One, 1989).

9. Pack, *388th Anthology*, vol. 1.

10. Ibid.

11. John Wynne, interview with JN, April 2003.

12. Tom Tate, interview with JN, April 2003.

13. Only later would Wynne solve the mystery of the sounds: A flak shell had hit a tire on the port wheel and then ricocheted and exploded, "which explains why there was a thump and then a flash."

14. Sixty years later, Wynne would hear no criticism of his navigator for this mistake. "He was doing a bloody good job in the circumstances."

15. Paul Krup, quoted in Gerald Astor, *The Mighty Eighth* (Dell, 1997).

CHAPTER 12: FINISHING THE JOB

1. Walter Hughes, "A Bomber Pilot in World War II," private account; and interview with JN, September 2003.
2. *Hansard,* 6 March 1945.
3. Walter Brieglib, quoted in Ivor Haythorne, "The Gisela Tragedy" (unpublished account). Unless otherwise attributed, quotes about this incident are from Haythorne's work.
4. Ibid.
5. Leutnant Arnold Doring, quoted in W.R. Chorley, *Bomber Command Losses,* 1945 (Midland, 1998).
6. Miles Tripp, *The Eighth Passenger* (Wordsworth Editions, 2002).
7. Ironically, shortly after the Tripp crew's final operation, the forty order was rescinded and a first tour went back to being thirty operations. This meant they were probably the only crew in the Group to complete a forty-op first tour.
8. Peter Marshall, "But He Might Have Been," private memoir; and interview with JN, May 2003.
9. Hermann Knell, *To Destroy a City* (DaCapo Press, 2003).
10. Ibid.
11. To be fair, not all Allied pilots agreed with this assessment. Squadron Leader Arthur Carter, a bomber pilot of vast experience with 178 operations in Coastal Command and then in Pathfinders, thought the German jets flawed. He wrote in his memoirs: "The Me-262 was about 80 mph faster than us and I was caught by them a couple of times. But they were a lousy gun platform at that speed. They juddered and vibrated all over the place and could not shoot straight. They fired off a wide spray of tracer and then vanished. I was never even touched." RAF Museum, Hendon archive, X001–3554.
12. Hermann Goering, quoted in "Impact—Strategic Air Victory in Europe," from the Office of Air Staff Intelligence, Washington, July 1945.
13. See chapter 7, "D-Day and Beyond."
14. Quoted in Adrian Weir, *The Last Flight of the Luftwaffe* (Cassell & Co., 1997), an excellent full account of this entire incident.
15. Ibid.
16. Herrmann appeal, quoted in Gerald Astor, *The Mighty Eighth* (Dell, 1997).
17. From *Second Air Division* magazine (Turner Publishing, Kentucky, 1998).

18. F. H. Hinsley, *British Intelligence in the Second World War*, vol. 3, part 2 (HMSO, 1984).

19. Flying Officer John Noel Papers, RAF Museum, Hendon, archive X002–5699.

20. Bill Kiley, interview with JN, May 2003.

21. Freddie Hulance, interview with JN, May 2003.

22. Peter Marshall, interview with JN.

23. Dickie Parfitt, interview with JN.

24. Flight Sergeant F. Whitfield Papers, RAF Museum, Hendon, archive A1497.

24. Much of this account is taken from Mel Rolfe, *Flying into Hell* (Grub Street, 2001). The authors are grateful for the use of his work.

26. Ibid.

27. Freddie Cole, interview with JN, July 2003.

28. Flight Lieutenant Dennis Steiner Papers, Imperial War Museum 92/29/1.

29. Janet Pack, *The 388th Anthology*, vol. 1 (Writers Club Press, 2001).

30. Ron Smith, *Rear Gunner*, Pathfinder (Goodall, 1987).

31. From Kathleen Lawrence-Smith, *Operation Exodus* (Anchored Magazine Publications, 2003).

CHAPTER 13: VICTORY?

1. Janet Pack, *The 388th Anthology*, vol. 1 (Writers Club Press, 2001).

2. Peter Marshall, "But He Might Have Been," private memoir; and interview with JN, May 2003.

3. On return from leave, Marshall and his crew were ordered to Okinawa in the Pacific Ocean to carry out long-range bombing attacks against the Japanese mainland as members of the new Tiger Force. But, as Marshall himself concluded, "That is another story."

4. Reg Davey, "Hitler Had Nothing to Worry About," private account; and interview with JN, June 2003.

5. Ken Newman, "Left, Left, Steady," private account; and interview with JN, July 2003.

6. Ibid.

7. Eric Banks Papers, RAF Museum Hendon, archive X003–1521.

8. Dennis Steiner Papers, Imperial War Museum 92/29/1.

9. Dickie Parfitt, *Bombs Gone* (privately published); and interview with JN, May 2003.

10. Pip Beck, *A WAAF in Bomber Command* (Goodall, 1989).

11. Walter Hughes, "A Bomber Pilot in World War II," private account; and interview with JN, September 2003.

12. *Second Air Division* magazine (Turner Publishing, Kentucky, 1998).

13. David Hastings, interview with JN, June 2003.

14. Charlie Green to Mrs. Bunn, RAF Museum, Hendon, archive X002–5787.

15. Robert Wannop, *Chocks Away* (Square One, 1989).

16. Bob Pierson, interview with JN, May 2003.

17. Tom Tate, interview with JN, April 2003.

18. Ron Smith, *Rear Gunner, Pathfinder* (Goodall, 1987).

19. Dennis Steiner Papers, Imperial War Museum 92/29/1.

20. Arthur White, *Bread and Butter Bomber Boys* (Square One, 1995).

21. Major Hubert ("Nicky") Knilans, "A Yank in the RCAF," RAF Museum, Hendon, archive B2455.

22. Johnnie Clark, *One Man's War* (Peacock Press, 1994).

23. Dennis Wiltshire, interview with JN, June 2003.

24. Bill Low, interview with JN, May 2003.

25. *Hansard,* 6 March 1945.

26. Major York, MP for Ripon, ibid.

27. Special Order of the Day, 10 May 1945. Harris Papers, RAF Museum, Hendon.

28. Air Commodore Henry Probert, *Bomber Harris* (Greenhill, 2001).

29. Sir Arthur Harris, *Bomber Offensive* (Greenhill, 1998).

30. The British were notoriously stingy when it came to handing out any sort of medal, unlike the Americans. The U.S. military authorities believed in routinely recognizing service as well as acts of bravery and doing so often. It was good for morale. The Eighth Air Force awarded 500,000 medals to its men during its time in England. The vast majority of these—440,000—were the Air Medal, which was given to crew after six combat missions and added to with leaves and clusters. The class-conscious RAF differentiated between officers and other ranks. Officers completing thirty missions were awarded the DFC, NCOs the DFM. Twenty thousand DFCs were awarded and 6,600 DFMs (Mark Wells, *Courage and Air Warfare,* Frank Cass, 1995).

31. Explanations are still being sought by Bomber Command veterans—and still being turned down. Mrs. E. Hayward, wife of a veteran in Peterborough, wrote to the prime minister, John Major, in the 1990s and received this reply from Michael Portillo, the defense secretary:

The creation of medals is the prerogative of the Sovereign. In this, the Sovereign takes advice from the Government of the day who, in turn, are advised by an Inter-Departmental Committee of officials on which the Services are represented. The case for a Bomber Command medal (amongst many others) has been considered by the Committee. In 1945 they concluded that there was insufficient justification to recommend the creation of a separate award in addition to those for which the majority of Bomber Command personnel already qualified. After the War, the Committee recommended that no further awards be instituted for World War Two. Both recommendations were endorsed by the Government of the day and approved by His Majesty King George VI. We have no plans to review these recommendations. I am sorry to have to send a disappointing reply. (*Bomber Command Association Newsletter,* April 1997.)

32. Harris Papers, RAF Museum, Hendon.
33. Sir John Slessor, quoted in Probert, *Bomber Harris.*
34. Harris, *Bomber Offensive.* The £10,000 fee he got would have been welcome to Harris, given his postwar finances, and may have been the reason he chose to write his memoirs so soon.
35. Churchill to John Lawrence, Harris's private secretary. Quoted in Probert, *Bomber Harris.*
36. Harris, quoted in ibid.
37. Ibid.
38. Figures from Robin Neillands, *The Bomber War* (John Murray, 2001).
39. LeMay, quoted in Richard Holmes, *Battlefields of the Second World War* (BBC Books, 2001).
40. "Impact—Strategic Air Victory in Europe," from the Office of Air Staff Intelligence, Washington, July 1945.
41. Harris, *Bomber Offensive.*
42. Speer, quoted in ibid.
43. Holmes, *Battlefields of the Second World War.*
44. Dennis Richards, *The Hardest Victory* (Hodder & Stoughton, 1994).
45. Harris, quoted in Norman Longmate, *The Bombers* (Arrow, 1983).
46. Ibid.

CHAPTER 14: FORGOTTEN HEROES

1. Walter Mayberry, "Return to Knettishall," private account.
2. J. B. Hughes DFM, writing in *The Marker* and reproduced in the *Bomber Command Newsletter*, 1986.
3. Bill Kiley, interview with JN, June 2003.
4. Ken Newman, interview with JN, July 2003.
5. Jack Watson, interview with JN, May 2003.
6. Freddie Hulance, interview with JN, June 2003.
7. Arthur White, *Bread and Butter Bomber Boys* (Square One, 1995).
8. Reg Davey, interview with JN, June 2003.
9. Dickie Parfitt, interview with JN, May 2003.
10. Boris Bressloff, interview with JN, June 2003.
11. Peter Twinn, interview with JN, June 2003.
12. David Hastings, interview with JN, June 2003.
13. Bill Carman, "Three Times Lucky," private account; and interview with JN, May 2003.
14. Ira Weinstein, interview with JN, September 2003.
15. Tom Tate, interview with JN, April 2003.
16. Air Commodore Henry Probert, *Bomber Harris* (Greenhill, 2001).
17. Bob Pierson, interview with JN, May 2003.
18. Eddie Picardo, interview with JN, September 2003.
19. Walter Hughes, interview with JN, September 2003.
20. Foreword by Air Marshal Sir Robert Saundby to David Irving, *The Destruction of Dresden* (Papermac, 1985).
21. Joan Lamberts to Lord Tedder, RAF Museum, Hendon, archive DC74/31/1 (italics added).

REFERENCES

PUBLISHED SOURCES

Adams, Air Vice-Marshal Alexander Annan, *Passing Experiences: An Autobiography* (privately published, 1980).

Astor, Gerald, *The Mighty Eighth* (Dell, 1997).

Bailey, Ronald, *The Air War in Europe* (Time Life, 1998).

Beck, Pip, *A WAAF in Bomber Command* (Goodall, 1989).

Beevor, Antony, *Berlin* (Viking, 2002).

Bekker, Cajus, *The Luftwaffe War Diaries* (Corgi, 1969).

Birtles, Philip, *World War II Airfields* (Ian Allen, 1999).

Boog, Horst, *The Conduct of the Air War in World War II* (St. Martin's Press, 1990).

Bowman, Martin, *The Eighth Air Force in Camera* (Sutton, 1998).

———, *USAAF Handbook* (Sutton, 2003).

Bowyer, Chaz, *For Valour: The Air VCs* (Grub Street, 1992).

———, *Guns in the Sky* (Corgi, 1981).

Bryant, Chris, *Stafford Cripps* (Hodder & Stoughton, 1997).

Budiansky, Stephen, *Air Power* (Viking, 2003).

Camden History Society, *Hampstead at War* (Carlisle House Press, 1977).

Carrington, Charles, *A Soldier at Bomber Command* (Leo Cooper, 1987).

Cawdron, Hugh, *Based at Burn Mk II* (Hugh Cawdron, 2001).

Chandler, Chan, *Tail Gunner* (Airlife Publishing, 2002).

Chorley, W. R., *Bomber Command Losses, 1944* (Midland, 1997).

——, *Bomber Command Losses, 1945* (Midland, 1998).

Clark, Johnnie, *One Man's War* (Peacock Press, 1994).

Clayton, Anthony, and Russell, Alan, *Dresden: A City Reborn* (Berg, 1999).

Collins, Diana, *Partners in Protest* (Gollancz, 1992).

Collins, Canon John, *Faith Under Fire* (Leslie Frewin, 1966).

Cooper Alan, *Beyond the Dams to the Tirpitz* (Goodall, 1991).

——, *Target Dresden* (Independent Books, 1995).

Coward, Eddy (ed.), *The Poems We Wrote: An Anthology of Air Force Poems* (Eddy Coward, 1997).

Delve, Ken and Jacobs, Peter, *The Six-Year Offensive* (Arms & Armour, 1992).

D'Este, Carlo, *Eisenhower* (Weidenfeld & Nicolson, 2002).

Elson, Aaron, *Nine Lives* (Chi Chi Press, 1999).

Falconer, Jonathan, *The Bomber Command Handbook* (Sutton, 2003).

Freeman, Roger, *Mighty Eighth War Diary* (Jane's, 1981).

——, *Mighty Eighth War Manual* (Jane's, 1984).

Friedrich, Jörg, *Der Brand* (Propyläen Verlag, 2002).

Hammel, Eric, *Air War Europa: A Chronology* (Pacifica Press, 1994).

Harris, Sir Arthur, *Despatch on War Operations* (Frank Cass, 1995).

——, *Bomber Offensive* (Greenhill, 1998).

Hastings, Max, *Bomber Command* (Pan, 1999).

Hinchcliffe, Peter, *The Other Battle* (Airlife Publishing, 1996).

Hinsley, F. H., *British Intelligence in the Second World War*, vol. 3 (HMSO, 1984).

Holmes, Richard, *Battlefields of the Second World War* (BBC Books, 2001).

Horne, Alistair, *Monty: The Lonely Leader* (Macmillan, 1994).

Hoseason, James, *The 1000 Day Battle* (Gillingham Publications, 1979).

Howell, Eric, *The Other Ranks Story* (NPG, 1998).

Irving, David, *The Destruction of Dresden* (Papermac, 1985).

Jasper, Ronald, *George Bell, Bishop of Chichester* (Oxford University Press, 1967).

Keegan, John, *Who's Who in World War Two* (Routledge, 1995).

Kenny, Mary, *Germany Calling* (New Island, 2003).

Klemperer, Victor, *I Shall Bear Witness* (Weidenfield & Nicolson, 1998).

——, *To the Bitter End* (Phoenix, 2000).

Knell, Hermann, *To Destroy a City* (DaCapo Press, 2003).

Lacey Johnson, Lionel, *Point-Blank and Beyond* (Airlife Publishing, 1991).

Lawrence-Smith, Kathleen, *Operation Exodus* (Anchored Magazine Publications, 2003).

LeMay, Curtis, *Mission LeMay* (Doubleday, 1965).

Lewis, Bruce, *Aircrew* (Cassell & Co., 2000).

Longmate, Norman, *The Bombers* (Arrow, 1983).

Lovejoy, William, *Better Born Lucky Than Rich* (Merlin, 1986).

McKee, Alexander, *The Devil's Tinderbox* (Souvenir Press, 2000).

———, *Dresden, 1945* (Granada, 1983).

McLachlan, Ian, *Final Flights* (Patrick Stephens, 1999).

Middlebrook, Martin, *The Berlin Raids* (Penguin, 1990).

———, *The Nuremberg Raid* (Cassell & Co, 2000).

———, and Everitt, Chris, *The Bomber Command War Diaries: An Operational Reference* (Midland, 2000).

Muirhead, Campbell, *Diary of a Bomb Aimer* (Ditto Publishing, 2002).

Natkiel, Richard, *Atlas of World War II* (Bison Books, 1985).

Neillands, Robin, *The Bomber War* (John Murray, 2001).

Nichol, John, and Rennell, Tony, *The Last Escape* (Penguin, 2002).

Olsen, Jack, *Aphrodite: Desperate Mission* (G. P. Putnam, 1970).

Overy, Richard, *Bomber Command, 1939–45* (HarperCollins, 1997).

Pack, Janet, *The 388th Anthology* (2 vols.) (Writers Club Press, 2001).

Parfitt, Dickie, *Bombs Gone* (privately published, n.d.).

Parton, James, *Air Force Spoken Here* (Adler & Adler, 1986).

Pelly-Fry, James, *Heavenly Days* (Crecy Books, 1994).

Picardo, Eddie, *Tales of a Tail Gunner* (Hara Publishing, 1996).

Pickering, Sylvia, *Tales of a Bomber Command WAAF* (Woodfield, 2002).

Price, Dr. Alfred, *The Luftwaffe Data Book* (Greenhill, 1997).

Probert, Air Commodore Henry, *Bomber Harris: His Life and Times* (Greenhill, 2001).

Reynolds, David, *Rich Relations* (Random House, 1995).

Richards, Denis, *The Hardest Victory* (Hodder & Stoughton, 1994).

———, *Portal of Hungerford* (Heinemann, 1997).

Rolfe, Mel, *Flying into Hell* (Grub Street, 2001).

Saward, Dudley, *Bomber Harris* (Buchanan and Enright, 1984).

———, *The Bomber's Eye* (Cassell & Co., 1959).

Scott Robert L., *God Is My Copilot* (Ballantine, 1984).

Sebald, W. G., *On the Natural History of Destruction* (Hamish Hamilton, 2003).

Smith, Ron, *Rear Gunner, Pathfinder* (Goodall, 1987).

Stafford-Clark, David, *Psychiatry Today* (Pelican, 1952).

Stiles, Bert, *Serenade to the Big Bird* (Lindsey Drummond, 1947).

Sweetman, John, *The Dambusters* (Time Warner, 2003).

Taylor, Fredrick, *Dresden* (Bloomsbury, 2004).

Terraine, John, *The Right of the Line* (Wordsworth Editions, 1997).

Thorne, Alex, *Lancaster at War* (Ian Allan, 1990).

Tripp, Miles, *The Eighth Passenger* (Wordsworth Editions, 2002).

Verrier, Anthony, *The Bomber Offensive* (Macmillan, 1968).

Von Below, Nicolaus, *At Hitler's Side* (Greenhill, 2001).

Vonnegut, Kurt, *Slaughterhouse-Five* (Jonathan Cape, 1970).

Wannop, Robert, *Chocks Away* (Square One, 1989).

Ward, Chris, *Dambusters* (Red Kite, 2003).

Weir, Adrian, *The Last Flight of the Luftwaffe* (Cassell & Co., 1997).

Webster, Sir Charles and Frankland, Noble, *The Strategic Air Offensive Against Germany* (HMSO, 1961).

Wells, Mark K., *Courage and Air Warfare* (Frank Cass, 1995).

White, Arthur, *Bread and Butter Bomber Boys* (Square One, 1995).

Wistrich, Robert, *Who's Who in Nazi Germany* (Routledge, 2002).

Yates, Harry, *Luck and a Lancaster* (Airlife Publishing, 2001).

Ziegler, Philip, *London at War, 1939–1945* (Sinclair-Stevenson, 1995).

LETTERS, DIARIES, AND ACCOUNTS

Adams, Alexander

Anderson, John

Armstrong, George

Banks, Eric

Bartlett, Les

Blunt, Barry

Bolino, August

Bosomworth, Jack

Bressloff, Boris

Brotherhood, Ken

Burke, Bill

Cadden, John

Carman, Bill

Allward, James

Anthony, D.

Bairstow, Larry

Barlett, Alan

Blanchard, Eric

Blyth, J.

Bormann, J.

Bramley, Ron

Brooks, Morfydd

Brunt, Percy

Burnside, Dudley

Cannon, Paul

Carman, Marie

Carrow, Ray
Catesby, Ron
Chew, Alan
Cole, Freddie
Cook, Byron
Davey, Reg
Day, Roy
Elliott, Ralph
Finkbeiner, Chuck
Flexman, Alfred
Fribush, Mervin
Goss, Chris
Guy, John
Hart, Katherine
Hawkins, R.
Heal, Dudley
Hinxman, G.
Holland, Bill
Hughes, Walter
Hus, D.
James, Ken
Jones, Fred
Jones, Jim
Kiley, Bill
King, Geoff
Knilans, Hubert "Nicky"
Lawrence-Smith, Kathleen
Leonard, Norman
Lovejoy, William
Lowther, Nancy
Marcusson, Floyd
Mason, Norman
McCauley, Bob
Medrington, Stan
Moseley, Dick
Newman, Kenneth
Noel, John
Parfitt, Dickie

Carter, Arthur
Charnley, Mark
Clegg, Max
Commin, Beryl
Coward, Eddy
Davies, Jim
Dewey, Bill
Fernyhough, George
Fish, Freddie
Ford-Jones, Martin
Godwin, James
Grierson, Bill
Hamilton, Ken
Hastings, David
Haythorne, Ivor
Herbertson, Graham
Hoare, Peter
Holmes, John
Hulance, Freddie
Iverson, Tony
Jones, Ernest
Jones, J. A. T.
Kempen, J. V.
Kiley, Pat
Kitching, Vera
Lamberts, Joan
Lee, Ken
Leto, Oreste
Low, Bill
Mahoney, Florence
Marshall, Peter
Matthews, John
Medrington, Henry
Mercer, Jack
Newbery, Ron
Nisbet, Patricia
O'Connor, Jim
Parfitt, Gerry

Payton, Dale

Peet, Clyde

Pierson, Joyce

Pool, Fain

Reed, Richard

Reid, Joan

Robinson, John

Rodda, Foss

Sautherley, Doug

Scott, Donald

Skeet, Michael

Steiner, Dennis

Stewart, Ken

Taylor, A. R.

Thorpe, George

Twinn, Peter

Watson, Jack

Weinstein, Ira

White, E. G.

Whitley, John

Wilson, Tom

Wingham, Tom

Wooldridge, Louis

Wynne, John

Yoder, Arden

Pearl, John

Pierson, Bob

Plassman, Raymond

Rackliff, Peter

Rees, William

Reid, John

Robinson, Kelso

Rolfe, John

Scandrett, Chaz

Simpson, Alan

Smith, Joyce

Stevenson, Bill

Tate, Tom

Thale, Eric

Tritton, Doug

Tyrell, Ralph

Watts, Sylvia

White, Arthur

Whitfield, Frank

Wilcox, Bert

Wiltshire, Dennis

Wolfson, Frank

Wyllie, Bruce

Yeomans, Marjorie

ACKNOWLEDGMENTS

THERE ARE MANY PEOPLE WHO WILLINGLY GAVE US THEIR EXPERTISE AND time while we wrote this book. We have tried to acknowledge them all but we apologize to any one we neglect to mention. Our heartfelt thanks go to:

Jan Pack from the 388th Bomb Group Association, who provided many accounts and pictures from her archives and also invited us to spend time with the group during their visit to the UK.

David and Deborah Sarsons at the 388th Museum for their help in tracking down many veterans.

David Hastings, chairman of the 2nd Air Division Memorial Trust, who not only proofread the draft but provided pictures and assisted in contacting many veterans.

Doug Radcliffe and Marion Brame at the Bomber Command Association for helping with countless books and pictures and providing many of the contacts to the veterans.

Peter Elliott and his staff at the Department of Research in the Royal Air Force Museum, and Stephen Walton at the Imperial War Museum, for their advice and their time in searching the archives for stories and accounts.

Nigel Parker, editor of the *Bomber Command Association Newsletter,* Andrew Wise, editor of the *RAF News,* and Collin Pullen, editor of the *RAF Association* magazine.

Frank Haslam and Cal Younger for reading the draft and offering expert and much-appreciated comment.

Ian Cundall at BBC Leeds and Barry Price for their research and knowledge of LMF.

Sebastion Cox, head of the Air Historical Branch, for being a sounding board for our ideas.

Fred and Harold Panton and everyone at the Lincolnshire Aviation Heritage Centre, East Kirkby Airfield, for their assistance during our visit.

Graham Herbertson for his excellent research into the "Skipper and the Kids" incident.

Martin Middlebrook, Chris Everitt, and Bill Chorley for their indispensable reference books on Bomber Command.

To Sean Desmond and everyone at St. Martin's Press and our agents Mark and George Lucas for their continuing advice and support.

To our wives, Suzannah and Sarah, we extend our love and gratitude. We thank them for their comments, advice, and fortitude.

Finally, to the veterans themselves and their families. They wrote to us, sent us their private letters and diaries, and allowed us to delve into events sometimes best forgotten. We thank and salute them.

INDEX